QUESTIONS & ANSWERS:
Trademark &
Unfair Competition

LexisNexis
Law School Publishing
Advisory Board

QUESTIONS & ANSWERS:
Trademark & Unfair Competition

By

VINCENT F. CHIAPPETTA

Professor of Law
Willamette University College of Law

 LexisNexis

ISBN#: 0-8205-6880-5

NOTE TO USERS
To ensure that you are using the latest materials available in this area, please be sure to periodically check the LexisNexis Law School web site for downloadable updates and supplements at www.lexisnexis.com /lawschool

Editorial Offices
744 Broad Street, Newark, NJ 07102 (973) 820-2000
201 Mission St., San Francisco, CA 94105-1831 (415) 908-3200
701 East Water Street, Charlottesville, VA 22902-7587 (434) 972-7600
www.lexis.com

(Pub.3229)

DEDICATION

TO VALRI

ABOUT THE AUTHOR

Vincent Chiappetta joined the Willamette University College of Law faculty in 1997 where he teaches intellectual property; property; business and commercial law; and science, technology and law. He has received the Jerry E. Hudson Award for Excellence in Teaching and has been named College of Law Teacher of the Year.

Prior to teaching Professor Chiappetta served as vice president and general counsel for Tektronix, Inc. (1993-1997), as associate general counsel (trademarks) for Levi Strauss & Co. (1992-1993) and as associate general counsel (Europe, Africa, Middle East) for Apple Computer, Inc. (1987-1991) (located in Paris, France). He also practiced law with the firm of Meyer, Hendricks, Victor, Osborn & Maledon in Phoenix, Arizona from 1977 to 1987 and from 1991 to 1992. He received his law degree from the University of Michigan and his B.S.E.E. (Computer Science) from the Massachusetts Institute of Technology.

This is unabashedly a study aid, meaning it is specifically intended to help prepare for class, to clarify what happened in class and to provide a means for review/self testing as you move through the course or prepare for the final exam. As explained below, it is structured both to permit incremental learning and confirmation of knowledge as well as to serve as a doctrinal reference.

The material has been divided into separate Topics which together cover the full range of doctrinal issues in trademark law plus the related fields of false advertising and rights of publicity. The first 19 trademark Topics are further arranged to address the "big picture" considerations in trademark law in the following sequence: WHERE does the applicable law come from and WHY does it exist; WHAT qualifies for trademark protection; HOW is that protection obtained and, finally, what does the owner of a valid trademark GET (what rights, against whom, subject to what limitations, with what remedies and for how long). Those considerations, in the order they are presented, are the core of all trademark analysis. Working through the Topics sequentially will provide both a complete understanding of trademark law and a structure and methodology for answering any related questions, both on an exam and in real life.

Each individual Topic is also structured to incrementally develop the covered issue and related rules. If the Questions are answered in the sequence in which they appear they will flesh out the particular Topic's doctrine (and quirks) in a gradually unfolding, increasingly detailed, fashion. In particular, watch for series of related Questions building off of a single fact pattern — they indicate important refinements to a basic rule. This progressive development within each Topic also means that if time presses, when the Answers are read in sequence they provide a reasonably orderly and coherent description of the Topic's related doctrine — allowing this to also serve as a form of "inverted hornbook."

Even though no one ever reads the manual (myself included), I nonetheless offer the following "usage tips" which will help maximize value to those deciding to invest a few minutes before diving into the materials. First, many of the Questions are "multiple choice." Some of them are straight-forward "driver's exam"-type questions which confirm an objectively correct answer. Many, however, delve into the law's many ambiguities and, consequently, you may vehemently disagree with my view of the "best" answer. Don't let that hang you up. If you can articulate a clear and correct basis for why your response is better than mine, you understand the material. Feel free to justifiably vent a bit regarding my obtuseness (or worse) and move on. If, however, you don't see a logical path explaining my choice, it is well worth a few minutes clarifying the point in your mind. Second, to keep the Answers clear many are followed by (relatively) brief "Notes" which elaborate on non-core but related doctrinal or practical details. So the Notes do merit attention as a supplemental post-script. Third, as you work through the Topics keep an eye on the big picture — remembering that trademark law is an integrated subject — and confirm you understand where each Topic fits into and affects the larger analytical structure (Where/Why; What, How, Get). To help make those connections many Answers contain explicit cross-references to other Topics; you should confirm you understand the indicated relationship. Fourth, many Topics contain slightly longer "short answer" Questions designed to tie the related doctrinal pieces together. They are worth additional time both in answering and in considering how your answer matches the substance *and* structure of the "model" Answer. Finally, the Final Exam tracks and reflects the big picture structure of trademark law. It is designed to confirm you can identify and apply the full range of factual and doctrinal considerations. You may find Questions 432 and 435 particularly useful as a last step in your preparation for the real final — they are mini-traditional essays which cover a wide-range of trademark law issues in a single go. The Answers to the Final Exam Questions provide basic summary confirmation, not detailed doctrinal discussion or citations to the law. That information can, however, be easily accessed, as at the end of each Final Exam Answer is a cross-reference to the relevant Topic(s).

I hope you find this helpful. If it helps maximize its value, minimize any confusion or eliminate errors, I would be pleased to respond to your questions, suggestions or comments at vchiappe@willamette.edu.

My sincere thanks to LexisNexis for putting this Question and Answer series project together and, most particularly, for giving me the opportunity to participate.

Professor Vincent Chiappetta
Salem, Oregon
June 15, 2007

TABLE OF CONTENTS

Page

QUESTIONS

1

1. Which of the following BEST describes the generally accepted policy objective supporting United States trademark law?

    A. Prohibiting unfair competition.

    B. Avoiding impairment of producer goodwill.

    C. Providing consumers reliable information regarding goods or services.

    D. Providing incentives to invest in product innovation.

2. Your client, Perfect Goods, Inc., wishes to adopt the trademark "Eureka" for its new line of bicycles. Does the fact that the mark does not specifically identify Perfect Goods, Inc. as the source of those bicycles prevent it from adopting the "Eureka" mark?

ANSWER:

3. Which of the following provides the BEST justification for trademark law's pursuit of the purpose identified in Question 1?

    A. Facilitating interstate commerce.

    B. Reducing market transaction costs.

    C. Protecting producer goodwill associated with product innovation.

    D. Reducing customer search costs.

4. Which of the following BEST describes the primary intended beneficiary of United States trademark law?

    A. The market.

    B. The trademark owner.

    C. The trademark creator.

    D. The individual consumer

Cheap Shirts, Inc. makes and sells t-shirts bearing the "Golden" trademark used by your client on its beer products. Your client wants to bring a trademark infringement lawsuit. Your investigation reveals that no customers think your client is the manufacturer of the t-shirts or, indeed, that there is any connection whatsoever to your client or its products other than the presence of the mark. They are purchasing the shirts exclusively to convey their adoption of your client's wildly successful brand message about seeking the good life.

5.   Explain to your client why their trademark complaint may be problematic in light of trademark law's policy objectives.

ANSWER:

Your client, Tents-for-Urban-Warriors Co., makes specialty tents for camping. They have decided they need a good trademark for their products and have asked you for advice.

6.   Which aspect of your client's business is BEST SUITED to trademark protection?

A.   The use of special reflective colors to limit heat build-up in their tents.

B.   Their ecology-friendly advertising message.

C.   Their company logo.

D.   Their marketing plan to target new "urban-warrior" campers.

7.   Which of the following is MOST CRITICAL to your client obtaining domestic (United States) trademark rights?

A.   Registration of the mark.

B.   Use of the mark.

C.   Novelty of the mark.

D.   The marketing message conveyed by the mark.

8.   Which of the following MOST ACCURATELY describes your client's rights in their trademark?

A.   A property right.

B.   A right appurtenant.

C.   The right to prevent unfair competition.

D.   The right to prevent competition.

9.   Which of the following names is commonly used to reference the primary federal trademark statute?

A.   The Restatement of Unfair Competition (Third).

B.   The Landry Act.

C. The Lanham Act.

D. The Federal Trademark Act of 1812.

10. You are the legislative aid to a Senator who plans to propose an amendment to the federal trademark statute. Which Constitutional provision should the Senator indicate supports taking the Congressional action?

A. The Intellectual Property Clause.

B. The Commerce Clause.

C. The Necessary and Proper Clause.

D. Article V.

11. Which BEST describes the reason for enacting the federal trademark statute?

A. To provide information to consumers.

B. To preempt state law.

C. To harmonize state law.

D. To supplement state law.

12. Which of the following is a UNIQUE requirement for bringing an infringement claim under federal trademark law as opposed to under a state trademark statute?

A. A distinctive mark.

B. Use of the mark in interstate commerce.

C. Use of the mark.

D. A likelihood of confusion.

13. If the federal trademark statute does not explicitly cover an existing common law doctrine does that necessarily mean that it cannot be considered in an action under that statute?

ANSWER:

14. BigFour, Inc. uses the mark "Pret" on the accounting books it prints and distributes and the mark "Aporter" on the accounting services it renders to its clients. What are the legal differences between BigFour's rights in the "Pret" and the "Aporter" mark?

ANSWER:

15. LSF Corporation sells home electronics products bearing the mark "Fasto." Each of the products comes with a standard industry warranty. Can LSF Corporation claim service mark rights in the "Fasto" mark based on the services it provides under the warranty?

ANSWER:

16. Donster, LLC owns the certification mark "X-stuff" which it uses in connection with home electronic products. Which of the following BEST describes those who can use Donster's "X-stuff" mark on their goods?

    A. Donster.

    B. Everyone making home electronic products.

    C. All home electronic producers certified by Donster.

    D. All home electronic producers meeting Donster's certification standards.

17. How do certification marks further the objectives of trademark law?

ANSWER:

18. Which of the following BEST describes the difference between a collective mark and a trademark?

    A. A collective mark refers only to products made by trade unions.

    B. A collective mark refers only to products meeting collective standards.

C. A collective mark identifies the user as a member of an organization.

D. A collective mark identifies the collective as the source of a product

Ultra, Inc. performs a range of business management tasks such as sales tracking, inventory control, accounting, and personnel management under the "Exacta" mark. All of Ultra's services meet the extremely high standards of reliability established by the Alliance of Business Product Producers (the "ASPP") of which Ultra is a member. Ultra uses both the ASPP membership badge and the ASPP-compliant-logo in its Exacta advertising. Assume that "Exacta," the ASPP membership badge and the ASPP-compliant-logo all qualify as marks.

19. What kind of mark is "Exacta?."

    A. A trademark.

    B. A service mark.

    C. A collective mark.

    D. A certification mark.

20. What kind of mark is the ASPP membership badge?

    A. A trademark.

    B. A service mark.

    C. A collective mark.

    D. A certification mark.

21. What kind of mark is the ASPP-compliant-logo?

    A. A trademark.

    B. A service mark.

    C. A collective mark.

    D. A certification mark.

22. What kind of mark is "Ultra" and why?

ANSWER:

23. Mightyburgers, Ltd. sells hamburgers under the "Mighty-burger" name. It has developed a uniquely shaped and colored, widely recognized box in which it delivers every Mighty-burger. Each burger-box also sports the "Best Burgers" seal of approval showing the hamburger's compliance with the Burgers of America standards for low-fat hamburger content.

Assuming they all otherwise would qualify as marks, which of the following is NOT serving as a mark on these facts:.

A. Burgers of America.

B. Mighty-burger.

C. The burger-box.

D. Best Burgers.

24. Why is distinctiveness required in trademark law?

ANSWER:

25. Which of the following is NOT a category of "distinctiveness" in trademark law?

    A. Generic.

    B. Determinative.

    C. Suggestive.

    D. Arbitrary.

26. Which of the following is NOT a category of "distinctiveness" in service mark law?

    A. Generic.

    B. Determinative.

    C. Suggestive.

    D. Arbitrary.

27. Which of the following can NEVER serve as a trademark?

    A. The color red for steel bolts.

    B. Four musical notes played in a particular sequence for entertainment products.

    C. The words "sweet and crunchy" for a cereal which is sweet tasting and crunchy.

    D. The word "jeans" for pants made of denim material.

28. Which of the following is LEAST relevant to determining whether a mark should be classified as generic?

    A. The consumer's motivation when purchasing.

    B. The dictionary definition of the term.

   C. The class of goods involved.

   D. Primary significance of the term to the relevant public.

29. Which of the following is MOST LIKELY to be classified as generic?

   A. The word "sours" for a sour tasting candy.

   B. The word "apple" for personal computers.

   C. The word "copier" for electronic copy machines.

   D. The word "exxirl" for cosmetics.

30. Which of the following is MOST LIKELY to be classified as generic?

   A. The words "corn pillows" for a cereal which is made from corn and shaped like a pillow.

   B. The words "shoe warehouse" for a large store selling shoes in high volume from a large store at discount prices.

   C. The words "memory box" for computer disc drives.

   D. The words "kids' stuff" for children's toys.

31. Which of the following is MOST LIKELY to be classified as fanciful?

   A. "Well-Baked" for a bakery.

   B. "Orange" for a Midwestern United States airline.

   C. "Exxon" for gasoline products.

   D. "Argonaut" for an interstate bus service.

32. Which of the following is MOST LIKELY to be classified as arbitrary?

   A. "Well-Baked" for a bakery.

   B. "Orange" for a Midwestern United States airline.

   C. "XYZYX" for a cleaning service.

   D. "Argonaut" for an interstate bus service.

33. Which of the following MOST LIKELY to be classified as arbitrary?

   A. "Apple" used for personal computers.

   B. "Apple" used for apple pies.

   C. "Apple" used for apples.

   D. "Apple" used for apple sauce.

You represent BigIdea Co., the recent inventor of a unique, break-through portable electronic product for real-time downloading and displaying digital video. They are contemplating using the trademark "Travid" (an invented term).

34.   Explain to your client why "thermos" (also originally an invented word) used by the original maker of vacuum-insulated containers is no longer protectable as a trademark and what that experience indicates BigIdea Co. should do to avoid the same thing happening to their proposed "Travid" mark.

ANSWER:

35.   Assume your client decides to press on with the "Travid" mark for its product. It turns out that despite following your advice, the worst eventually happens and it has lost its ability to claim it as its trademark. What might BigIdea do at this point if a competitor were to start using the "Travid" mark on a competing product?

ANSWER:

36.   The use of "Easy-On" as a trademark for a house paint product will MOST LIKELY be classified as:.

    A.   Generic.

    B.   Fanciful.

    C.   Suggestive.

    D.   Descriptive.

37.   Explain why using "EZ-On" rather than "Easy-On" for the house paint will not avoid the problem under Question 36.

ANSWER:

38.   The use of the word "Pounce" as a trademark for cat food treats will MOST LIKELY be classified as which of the following?

    A.   Generic.

    B.   Descriptive.

    C.   Suggestive.

    D.   Arbitrary.

39. Which of the following is LEAST HELPFUL in distinguishing between a "descriptive" and a "suggestive" classification?

    A. The dictionary meaning of the mark.

    B. Whether imagination is required to reach a conclusion regarding the nature of the related goods.

    C. Whether competitors use the term to describe their product.

    D. Whether competitors are likely to need to use the term to describe their product.

40. To confirm your understanding of the "spectrum of distinctiveness," identify how each of the following would MOST LIKELY be classified and why:.

    A. "Diamond" for diamond gemstones.

    B. "Diemonde" for diamond gemstones.

    C. "Diamond" for a baseball team.

    D. "Diamonds.com" for diamonds sold over the internet.

    E. "Diamond" for an internet access service.

    F. "Quick" for an internet access service.

    G. "Quick" for a cuticle scissors.

    H. "I-crit" for consulting services.

    I. "I-crit" diamond gemstones.

41. Your client, BestBeer, LLC, has decided to use the letters "BYO" as the trademark for its new beer product sold only in pre-packaged twelve packs. Advise BestBeer on the wisdom of adopting the "BYO" mark based on its likely classification on the spectrum of distinctiveness.

ANSWER:

42. Imports, S.A. has selected the French word "café" for its premium ground roast coffee. How will that mark MOST LIKELY be classified on the spectrum of distinctiveness?

    A. Fanciful.

    B. Suggestive.

    C. Descriptive.

    D. Generic.

43. How would the word "cohiba" MOST LIKELY be classified if used in connection with cigars?

    A.   Fanciful.

    B.   Arbitrary.

    C.   Descriptive.

    D.   Generic.

44. What does it mean for a mark to be inherently distinctive?

ANSWER:

45. Trademark law uses what mechanism to make the "inherently distinctive" (or not) determination?

ANSWER:

46. Which of the following categories of marks is NOT inherently distinctive?

A. Arbitrary marks.

B. Fanciful marks.

C. Suggestive marks.

D. Descriptive marks.

47. CatSnacks, Inc. has developed a new cat-food product which is made from a variety of high-quality meat ingredients. They are trying to decide between two marks: "Meaty Blend" and "Royal Cat." Explain which mark you think is the better choice based on distinctiveness considerations and why those considerations merit serious attention.

ANSWER:

48. Which of the following BEST explains why as a policy matter certain classes of marks are not treated as inherently distinctive?

A. Those classes of marks take less effort to think up and, therefore, deserve less protection.

B. Those classes of marks do not provide useful information to the consumer.

C. Permitting a claim to rights in those classes of marks impairs efficient consumer search and producer competition.

D.   Those classes of marks have a non-trademark association with the entire product class.

49.   Which of the following is MOST LIKELY to be found inherently distinctive?

    A.   "Brite" for a delivery service.

    B.   "Brite" for a floor polish.

    C.   "Lumber & Pulp" for wood products.

    D.   "Big Burger" for a hamburger restaurant.

50.   Which of the following can NEVER be distinctive?

    A.   "Brite" for a delivery service.

    B.   "Brite" for a floor polish.

    C.   "Lumber & Pulp" for those wood products.

    D.   "Best Burger" for a hamburger restaurant.

51.   Which of the following is MOST LIKELY to be found inherently distinctive?

    A.   "Sweet and Crunchy" for a breakfast cereal which tastes sweet and is crunchy.

    B.   "Baker's Pride" for bread products.

    C.   "Tender morsels" for cat food treats.

    D.   "HI-Octane" for petroleum products.

52.   Your client wants to use the words "Vision Center" as its trademark for its optometry and eyeglass fitting services. Which of the following BEST describes what they must show to demonstrate the phrase is sufficiently distinctive to serve as their trademark?

    A.   Usage as a trademark.

    B.   Extensive use.

    C.   Independent primary meaning.

    D.   The public views the phrase primarily as a source identifier.

53.   Which of the following requires secondary meaning to be sufficiently distinctive to serve as a trademark?

    A.   "Speedy Delivery" applied to delivery services.

    B.   "President" applied to delivery services.

    C.   "Delivery couriers" applied to delivery services.

    D.   "Zastro" applied to delivery services.

Dental Corp. has adopted the phrase "Gentle Dental" as the mark for its dental care services. It has brought suit against a competitor, Teeth, Ltd., which has subsequently adopted the same phrase to describe its competing dental services. The court has classified the mark as descriptive.

54. Which of the following is LEAST relevant to the finder of fact determining whether or not "Gentle Dental" has developed secondary meaning?

   A. The amount spent on advertising featuring the phrase.

   B. Testimony of actual consumers that they view the phrase as a source indicator.

   C. Substantial, prominent use of the phrase other competitors.

   D. Customer surveys indicating consumers view the phrase as a source indicator.

55. Assume Dental Corp. has successfully demonstrated "Gentle Dental" has developed secondary meaning and is protectable as a trademark. Does that mean Dental Corp. can keep Teeth Ltd. from using the phrase in connection with its dental services?

ANSWER:

GreatCola, LLC has used the mark "Lite Cola" for a year in connection with its low-calorie cola soft drink product. It has decided to sue SecondCola, Inc., a later adopter of the "Lite Cola" mark, for trademark infringement. GreatCola has a survey which shows that customers associate the phrase "Lite Cola" with GreatCola's particular soft drink.

56. Advise GreatCola on how distinctiveness will affect the likelihood of success if it brings a lawsuit against SecondCola.

ANSWER:

57. Explain to GreatCola why a descriptive mark can become distinctive through secondary meaning while a generic mark cannot?

ANSWER:

58. If a court were to classify that GreatCola's mark were generic would GreatCola be able to obtain any relief against SecondCola?

ANSWER:

59. Miracle Company plans to introduce a new, patented treatment for eliminating face wrinkles. Miracle is considering the following four possibilities for the product's trademark: "Wrinkle Remover," "Wrinkle Away," "Young Again," and "Vitrex." Based exclusively on trademark distinctiveness considerations which mark or marks should Miracle most seriously consider and why?

ANSWER:

60. Which of the following may qualify for use as a mark?

    A. The word "cow."

    B. The color brown.

    C. A drawing of a tree.

    D. An abstract composition of shapes and lines.

    E. A smell.

    F. A sequence of musical notes.

    G. A photograph of an airplane.

    H. A graphic composed of a drawing, a photo and a word

Computer Universe, Inc. makes gray colored laptop computers. It would like to protect the gray color as its trademark.

61. How might we BEST go about determining whether Computer Universe's use of the color gray satisfies the distinctiveness requirement?

    A. Determine whether the mark is distinctive.

    B. Apply the classification schema of the spectrum of distinctiveness.

    C. Apply the policy goal implemented by the spectrum of distinctiveness.

    D. Apply a special test tailored to non-word marks.

62. Which of the following BEST identifies the central concern regarding whether to treat the color gray as distinctive?

    A. It is not a word.

    B. Colors cannot be trademarks.

    C. It is unclear how it should be classified on the spectrum of distinctiveness.

    D. A color has a pre-existing independent significance to observers.

63. Which of the following categories on the spectrum of distinctiveness most closely corresponds to the distinctiveness concern raised by Computer Universe claiming the gray color of their laptops as a trademark?

21

    A. Generic.

    B. Descriptive.

    C. Suggestive.

    D. Arbitrary.

64. Given the above determinations, what do you believe will be required for Computer Universe to claim gray as a trademark for its laptop computers?

ANSWER:

You represent the upscale men's fashion design house, StudsDuds LLC. They have decided to use the black color of the fabric used in their upcoming winter season's line of men's suits as the trademark for that collection.

65. Explain to your client whether the color black can serve as a trademark, and, if so, under what conditions and with what risks.

ANSWER:

66. Would your analysis change if StudDuds proposed instead to use a removable all black rectangular tag hanging from the middle button of its suit jackets?

ANSWER:

67. Which of the following forms of mark is LEAST LIKELY to require proof of secondary meaning to demonstrate distinctiveness?

    A. The number "909" for a denim jeans product.

    B. The picture of a pine tree for pine scented air-fresheners.

    C. The graciously curved shape of a teapot spout.

    D. A specially colored box in which the teapot is sold.

68. Which of the following is LEAST likely to influence a court's decision regarding whether product packaging is inherently distinctive?

    A. How the packaging would be classified under the spectrum of distinctiveness.

    B. Whether the packaging is unique, unusual or unexpected in the market.

    C. Whether the packaging includes color.

D. Evidence that consumers automatically view the packaging as a source identifier.

69. Which of the following is MOST LIKELY to be deemed inherently distinctive?

    A. A cow-shaped tag affixed to paint products.

    B. A cow-shaped tag affixed to milk products.

    C. The shape of a blender.

    D. The word "Stay-Prest" on an otherwise blank rectangular tag affixed to wrinkle-free clothing.

70. Which of the following is MOST LIKELY to be deemed inherently distinctive?

    A. The shape of a beverage bottle.

    B. The overall appearance of a line of children's clothing.

    C. The décor of a chain retail company's sales outlets.

    D. An ornamental spout on a teapot.

71. Which of the following BEST describes the effect of product packaging being found NOT to be inherently distinctive?

    A. The mark claimant must show it is distinctive.

    B. The mark claimant must demonstrate secondary meaning.

    C. It is treated in the same way as product design.

    D. It cannot serve as a trademark.

72. HomeBreads Corporation proposes to use a blue circle with the words "Fresh and Tasty" in the center as its trademark for its new bread product. It will be printed on the plastic in which the bread is wrapped. Provide your assessment of whether their proposed mark can and will qualify as a trademark.

ANSWER:

Tools, Incorporated makes a variety of small tools. It has just developed a new hammer with a specially designed head. It wants to protect the hammer head design as a trademark for the hammer product.

73. Which of the following BEST identifies the barrier Tools faces in claiming the design of the hammer head as a trademark?

   A. Only words can serve as trademarks.

   B. Product design marks are not inherently distinctive.

   C. Product designs can never serve as a trademark.

   D. It may adversely affect competition on the product merits.

74. Assume that Tools can demonstrate that its hammer head design has come to be uniquely associated in consumers' minds with its particular product. Which of the following BEST describes why Tools may still not be able to product the design as a trademark?

   A. Trademark protection would not further the basic purpose of trademark law.

   B. Trademark protection for a functional design provides undue competitive advantage to the Tools.

   C. Trademark protection is never afforded to marks which are not inherently distinctive.

   D. Trademark protection is never afforded to functional product designs.

75. Which of the following is LEAST relevant to finding Tool's hammer head design is functional?

   A. The hammer head design required substantial investment.

   B. The hammer head design enhances the performance of the hammer.

   C. The hammer head design improves the longevity of the hammer.

   D. The hammer head design affects the cost of manufacturing the hammer.

76. Assume Tools has decided to pursue protecting its hammer head design as a trademark despite the risk it is functional. It reasons that although the design's primary effect is to dramatically improve its efficacy as a hammer there are a significant number of alternative designs which provide the same or better performance available to competitors. How does the existence of those alternatives affect the functionality determination?

25

ANSWER:

Port-ALL LLC has invented a new container shape that simultaneously enhances grip thus enhancing the ability to carry the container while not impairing the efficiency of storage by increasing the dead-space around the container. Port-ALL has obtained a utility patent on its container design.

77. How does their patent affect their ability to protect the shape of the container as a trademark?

ANSWER:

78. How does the policy relationship between trademark law and utility patent law affect the above analysis?

ANSWER:

79. Which of the following circumstances makes it MOST LIKELY that a patented product feature may be entitled to trademark protection despite the patent?

A. The patent has expired.

B. The feature is incidental to the invention.

C. The feature has developed secondary meaning.

D. Developing the feature required substantial investment

104 Flavors, S.A. invented, obtained a utility patent on and has enjoyed exclusive use of the uniquely effective shape of its ice cream scoop for the last 20 years. Their current market research shows that customers strongly associate the scoop design with their products, not only because it has been the only scoop with that design in the market during that time but because they invested heavily in advertising encouraging customers to make the source connection. Their patent is about to expire and they would like to protect the scoop shape as a trademark to prevent its use by others in the ice cream business.

80. Can they protect the scoop design as a trademark?

ANSWER:

81. Is 104 Flavors entirely without recourse regarding competitive adoption of their scoop design if it is found to be functional?

ANSWER:

BigDrinks Limited has designed a new beverage container.

82. Under which of the following circumstances is the design of the beverage container most likely NOT to be functional?

A. If the design improves the ability of the container to keep the beverage cold..

B. If the design reduces the costs of storing and shipping the beverages.

C. If the design makes it difficult to pour the beverage.

D. If the design reduces the cost of materials used in manufacturing the container.

83. Which of the following is MOST LIKELY to be found functional in connection with a silverware design?

A. It's purely ornamental design.

B. The word "silverware."

C. A picture of a knife and fork.

D. The phrase "Eat Elegantly"

Farmal Corporation makes a wide range of farm equipment, tractors, plows, combines and the like.

84. Which of the following characteristics of their farm equipment is MOST LIKELY to be found aesthetically functional?

A. The materials used to make the equipment.

B. The color of the equipment.

C. The internal gearing design used in the transmissions.

D. The weight of the machinery.

85. Which of the following is LEAST LIKELY to be considered in determining whether the above identified characteristic of Farmal's equipment is, in fact, *aesthetically* functional and therefore barred from serving as a trademark?

A. That the design serves a significant non-trademark function.

B. That the exclusive use of the design would put competitors at a significant non-reputation-related disadvantage.

  C. Effect of the characteristic on use, purpose, cost or quality.

  D. The availability of alternatives

UberCars Ltd. has developed an extremely innovative body design for its new sports car. The design increases the aerodynamics of the car at very high speeds (over 100 mph). They are seriously considering obtaining a utility patent on the design. Additionally, UberCars recent marketing surveys show that consumers find the design tremendously appealing visually and very strongly associate it with UberCars' new sports car. UberCars would like to protect the appearance of the sports car as its trademark.

  86. Explain how functionality considerations will affect their ability to protect the car's sleek shape as a trademark.

ANSWER:

  87. Of what relevance to claiming rights in the design is the survey evidence that consumers very strongly associate the design with UberCars sports car?

ANSWER:

MightyFlakes, LLC has developed a specially shaped and specially colored box for their breakfast cereals.

  88. How do functionality considerations their ability to protect that special color scheme as a trademark?

ANSWER:

NewMark, Inc. has spent considerable time and money creating a logo to use as its trademark. The logo is clearly distinctive, poses no functionality problems and is completely unlike any other existing mark.

89.   Explain why neither the substantial investment in creating the logo nor its clearly non-functional originality is insufficient to support NewMark's claim of trademark rights.

ANSWER:

Your client, Rainstuff, Inc., has developed a new line of travel umbrellas. It wants to claim trademark rights in the mark "Dry Wherever."

90.   Which of the following BEST articulates the test for determining if there is sufficient USE to trigger trademark rights?

      A.   The circumstances show that Rainstuff has a good faith intent to use the mark as a trademark.

      B.   The circumstances show Rainstuff's use of the mark has made a significant market impression.

      C.   The circumstances show Rainstuff's has used the mark in good faith as a trademark.

      D.   The circumstances show Rainstuff's use of the mark has generated secondary meaning.

91.   In which of the situations below is Rainstuff MOST LIKELY to have engaged in sufficient use to establish trademark rights in the "Dry Wherever" mark?

      A.   Management has decided to adopted and use the "Dry Wherever" mark.

      B.   Labels have been ordered bearing the "Dry Wherever" mark.

      C.   Advertising has been created and prepared for publication using the "Dry Wherever" mark.

      D.   A few travel umbrellas bearing the "Dry Wherever" mark have been offered for sale.

92.   Which of the following is MOST LIKELY to constitute sufficient use to establish Rainstuff's rights in "Dry Wherever" as a trademark?

   A. Putting "Dry Wherever" labels on the umbrellas.

   B. Three labeled umbrellas were ordered by and sold to a retailer.

   C. Shipping 10,000 labeled umbrellas between two Rainstuff warehouses.

   D. Giving five labeled umbrellas to each of three acquaintances of Rainstuff's President.

93. Which of the following MOST LIKELY constitutes sufficient use by Rainstuff to establish trademark rights in "Dry Wherever"?

   A. They announce and show "Dry Wherever" labeled umbrellas at a major trade fair, but make no sales.

   B. They sell 1,000 "Dry Wherever" labeled umbrellas to their wholly-owned retail distribution subsidiary.

   C. They make discount sales of "Dry Wherever" labeled umbrellas to a few friends of the company President.

   D. They sell 100 "Dry Wherever" labeled umbrellas to an independent retailer solely to claim rights in the mark.

94. Four different companies (A, B, C and D) are introducing new products into different markets bearing different newly created logos. They each hope their activities will be sufficient use to give them trademark rights in their respective logos attached to their products. Which of the following "uses" is MOST LIKELY to be sufficient to establish trademark rights in the related logo?

   A. Company A sells 100,000 marked products to its wholly owned retail chain subsidiary for resale to the public.

   B. Company B sells a single marked product to an end-user in a market in which approximately 100 sales are made annually.

   C. Company C sells a single marked product to an end-user in a market in which approximately 10,000 sales are made annually.

   D. Company D sells a single marked product to its wholly owned retail chain subsidiary for resale to the public in a market in which approximately five sales are made annually.

Your client AllDrinks, Ltd., has adopted "Tamaway" as its mark for a new cola beverage it plans to offer in its shopping mall beverage bars.

95. Which of the following is MOST LIKELY to satisfy the trademark use requirement?

   A. Putting "Tamaway" on the cup in which the new beverage is served.

   B. Including "Tamaway" as part of the menu entry identifying the new beverage.

    C. Including "Tamaway" prominently in current television advertising announcing something new is "coming soon."

    D. Having counter personnel inform consumers that they have received a "Tamaway" cola when delivering the drink.

96. Does the "affixation/connection" analysis change if AllDrinks had instead proposed to use the "Tamaway" mark to identify its beverage bar *services* rather than a new cola drink?

ANSWER:

GreatBuys sells very high volumes of illegal pharmaceutical products to the public. It affixes the word "Amand" to each product capsule and to all product packages.

97. Is that use of the "Amand" mark sufficient to support GreatBuys' claim to trademark rights?

ANSWER:

Fabgizmos, LLC sells a variety of electronic equipment under the "Big E" trademark. Its use of the "Big E" mark is indisputably sufficient to satisfy the "good faith use as a trademark" and "affixation/connection" requirements.

98. Which of the following BEST identifies what ELSE must be true about Fabgizmos' USE for them to claim trademark rights in the "Big E" mark?

    A. Their sales and advertising activities must constitute bona fide use in commerce.

    B. They must actually sell electronic products labeled with the "Big E" mark to the public.

    C. They must have created the "Big E" mark.

    D. They must be the first to use the "Big E" mark in their market.

Each of the following four companies (A, B, C or D) all want to use the mark "ZetaProof" on their new ski products.

99. Ignoring geographic considerations, which of them has the BEST claim to trademark ownership?

    A. The management of Company A has decided to adopt "ZetaProof" as a trademark.

    B. Company B has actually offered ski products marked "ZetaProof" to the public.

    C. Company C was the first to offer ski products marked "ZetaProof" to the public.

    D.   Fritz Van Zeta, who thought up the "ZetaProof" mark but has yet to start the business which he will call Company D.

Alpha starts using the mark "GaZow" on its clothing products in 1999. In 2002 it changes the mark to a logo consisting of "BigZow" printed in a white circle. In 2004 it again changes the mark by changing "BigZow" to "B-Zow" still printed in a white circle and adding the words "Fab Rags" below the logo. Finally, in 2006 Alpha removes the words "Fab Rags" below the logo leaving only the logo consisting of "B-Zow" printed in a white circle.

100.   Assuming the use of each mark satisfies the good faith use as a trademark requirement, which of the following is the MOST LIKELY date Alpha can claim trademark use of the logo consisting of the word "B-Zow" in a white circle?

    A.   1999.

    B.   2002.

    C.   2004.

    D.   2006.

Before coming to you on July 1, 2006, your client had already started using the mark "CARBOTA" on its new line of industrial ovens. After a few months of use, it has received a letter from Carbota, Ltd., which explains that they are using the identical "CARBOTA" mark on their oven products and demand that your client immediately cease their use. Your investigation has turned up the following facts through today (July 1, 2006):

Your client's first offered ovens bearing the "CARBOTA" mark for sale to the general public on June 4, 2006 with the first sale occurring on June 10, 2006. Carbota Ltd. was incorporated on April 15, 2005. They started selling their oven products on May 1, 2005 under the mark "Kartoomb" (with no relevant reference to Carbota, Ltd.) Their Board of Directors decided to change the mark to "CARBOTA" on April 15, 2006 as part of the launch of a new line of updated oven products. Carbota, Ltd. announced the adoption of the new "CARBOTA" product line on May 1, 2006 with a significant publicity campaign, but offered no specific details regarding the related products. They first offered new oven products bearing the "CARBOTA" mark for sale to the public on June 5, 2006 and the first sale took place June 6, 2006. In all cases the mark is affixed directly and prominently to the front of the oven. No other relevant users of the CARBOTA (or substantially similar) marks exist, past or present and there are no relevant trademark registrations.

101.   Assume your client and Carbota, Ltd. are selling nationally in competition with one another, so there are no product or geographic market issues. Assess your clients chances of overcoming Carbota Ltd.'s trademark claim based their use.

ANSWER:

102. Would the analysis change if your client was advertising and selling their ovens only in Oregon and Carbota, Ltd. only advertised and sold in California?

ANSWER:

103. Would the analysis change if Carbota, Ltd. was only using the mark in connection with refrigerators, not ovens?

ANSWER:

Megabits Corporation has decided to adopt the word "Quastral" as the mark for its new line of network server electronics.

104. Advise them regarding how the "good faith use as a trademark" requirement affects their rights to claim trademark rights in "Quastral" and what actions should be taken in that regard.

ANSWER:

LightSpeed Co. uses the mark "Way Quick" on its internet speed accelerator software. It affixes the mark directly to the software package and the CD on which it is delivered. LightSpeed also can unquestionably claim the first good faith use of the mark in the relevant geographic and product market starting on January 6, 2005. A competitor started using the same "Way Quick" on their competing product in June 2005. LightSpeed's marketing department has done a series of consumer surveys attempting to assess the level of harm from the competitor's adoption of the mark. Those surveys show that consumers only developed a strong particular association between the mark and LightSpeed's product in July 2005.

105. Which of the following is LEAST LIKELY to support LightSpeed's superior claim to the "Way Quick" mark as against the competitor?

    A. LightSpeed's prior good faith use of the mark.

    B. LightSpeed's affixation of the mark to the product container.

    C. Classification of "Way Quick" as suggestive.

    D. LightSpeed's ability to show secondary meaning.

106. If LightSpeed cannot claim superior rights over the competitor by virtue of its prior good faith use as a trademark, is there any possible alternative on which it might still claim superior rights?

ANSWER:

107.   What rights does LightSpeed have against other subsequent adopters?

ANSWER:

108.   Sometimes the claimant of a mark is not itself the user but instead relies on use by another related party. Which of the following is LEAST LIKELY to support such a claim of "derivative" use?

A.   A parent company's reliance on use by its wholly-owned subsidiary.

B.   A licensor's reliance on use by its quality-controlled licensee.

C.   A band member's claim to independent rights based on use by the band in which he was a member.

D.   A company's claim based on use by the public of a publicly created name for its product.

FixIT, Incorporated makes staplers for home and office use. FixIT has used the mark "Mitiox" on its staplers since June 1, 2001, when it first started selling its staplers in Salem, Oregon. Over the years it has expanded its sales activity which now takes place throughout Oregon as well as Washington and Idaho. The "Mitiox" mark is not registered at either the state or federal level.

109.   Which of the following BEST describes FixIT's primary rights in the "Mitiox" mark?

    A.   The right to prevent all uses.

    B.   The right to prevent all uses which infringe.

    C.   The right to prevent use by competitors.

    D.   The right to prevent use likely to confuse consumers.

110.   Starting first with the PRODUCT "footprint" of the mark — the protection against its use by others on products, ignoring for now the geographic market issue — which of the following BEST describes the PRODUCT footprint of FixIT's "Mitiox" trademark?

    A.   Bars all use in connection with staplers made by other producers.

    B.   Bars all use in connection with staplers and all other goods likely to result in consumer confusion.

    C.   Bars all use in connection with all types of fastener products.

    D.   Bars all use in connection with all types of office supplies.

111.   In which of the following cases would FixIT's trademark rights be LEAST LIKELY to prevent the use of their unregistered Mitiox mark by an unauthorized third party? (Assume in each case that the use of the mark started after FixIT's expansion described in the initial facts above.)

    A.   Use in New York, New York on staplers.

    B.   Use in Seattle, Washington on staplers.

    C.   Use in Portland, Oregon on staplers.

    D.   Use in Salem, Oregon on staplers.

112.   Which of the following additional facts would be MOST helpful to FixIT's trademark claim against a subsequent adopter of the "Mitiox" mark for staplers the New York City geographic market?

A.   FixIT has definite plans to expand into the New York market next month but has taken no steps to do so.

B.   FixIT has given 10 Mitiox staplers to friends of its president who live in New York.

C.   There is a lot of business interaction between New York and Oregon.

D.   FixIT has done nothing in the New York market; however, New York stapler wholesalers regularly visit the Northwest trade shows where FixIT regularly shows its Mitiox staplers.

113.   Which of the following would be SUFFICIENT for FixIT to prevent use of the "Mitiox" mark by a subsequent adopter on staplers in the New York City geographic market?

FixIT has never marketed or sold its staplers in New York, but it can prove that:

A.   One key New York stapler wholesaler strongly associates the "Mitiox" mark with FixIT's staplers.

B.   Five significant New York stapler retailers strongly associate the "Mitiox" mark with FixIT's staplers.

C.   Fifty New York stapler end-users strongly associate the "Mitiox" mark with FixIT's staplers.

D.   One thousand New York residents recognize the "Mitiox" mark as indicating FixIT's staplers.

114.   FixIT is preparing to enter the Florida stapler market next month for the first time. It, of course, desires to use its "Mitiox" mark. There are no consumer associations between your client's products and the mark in that geographic market. It has just discovered that a small exclusively local company has just adopted the Mitiox mark on that company's line of staplers sold only in the southern part of the State. Explain what effect it would have on your analysis if you could prove that before the Florida producer adopted the "Mitiox" mark they knew about not only FixIT's Northwest use but also about its imminent planned expansion into Florida.

ANSWER:

115.   FixIT has no current plans to expand its stapler business into California. It does, however, view that geographic market as a natural fit with its existing business and has expressed concerned that someone else might adopt the Mitiox mark before it is ready to enter. Do you recommend FixIT rely on the *zone of natural expansion* doctrine to protect its California priority?

ANSWER:

O'wine LLC has been selling wine under the "Avert" mark throughout Oregon since August 18, 2001. It does not sell its wine or any other product under the "Avert" mark in any other geographic market. No one else has used the "Avert" mark on any product in any geographic market, including Oregon. There are no relevant registrations of the "Avert" mark.

116. Considering only the above facts, how would you RANK the following cases in order of your client's BEST to WORST likelihood of preventing third party use of the "Avert" mark?

    A. Use in connection with wine in California.

    B. Use in connection with wine glasses in Oregon.

    C. Use in connection with wine glasses in California.

    D. Use in connection with cars in Oregon

Company A has been selling watches under the "Paradigm" mark throughout Oregon since April 15, 2001. Another company, Company B, has been selling watches under the "Paradigm" mark throughout Georgia since June 30, 2001. Neither Company A nor Company B sells watches or any other product under the "Paradigm" mark in any other geographic market. No one else has used the "Paradigm" mark on any product in any geographic market. There are no relevant registrations of the "Paradigm" mark.

117. Considering only the above facts, in which of following cases is Company A LEAST LIKELY to be able to prevent the use of the "Paradigm" mark by Company B?

    A. Company B's sales of watches under the "Paradigm" mark in Oregon.

    B. Company B's sales of watches under the "Paradigm" mark in Georgia.

    C. Company B's sales of watches under the "Paradigm" mark in Maine.

    D. Company B's sales of watches under the "Paradigm" mark in Arizona.

118. Between Company A and Company B, which has the STRONGER claim to the "Paradigm" mark in Arizona?

ANSWER:

119. Assume that Company B has no actual sales activity in Arizona but has used a website to make its sales in Georgia since the very beginning of their business. The site clearly targets only Georgia consumers and Company B has never accepted an order or made an Arizona sale through the site. Usage statistics show that there are a few hits to the site each week resulting from Arizona users' search engine inquires including either or both of the words "watches" and "paradigm." They also show that although the number of searches originating in Arizona including both "watches" and "paradigm"

is extremely small, the number is slowly growing. How do these facts affect your analysis of Company B's trademark rights in Arizona?

ANSWER:

For the past four years Burnt, Inc. has been selling toasters under a logo consisting of a blue circle containing a white "lightening" symbol. It currently sells in the states of Michigan, Illinois and Indiana and its use is clearly sufficient to give it rights in the logo in those geographic markets.

120.   Which of the following BEST describes Burnt's rights regarding trademark use of the logo in Michigan?

   A.   Prevent the use of the logo on toasters and related products.

   B.   Prevent the use of the logo on toasters and other small kitchen appliances.

   C.   Prevent the use of the logo on toasters.

   D.   Prevent all use of the logo.

121.   Which of the following BEST describes Burnt's rights regarding use of the logo in Michigan under the trademark law?

   A.   Prevent all copying of the logo.

   B.   Prevent all use of the logo as a trademark on toasters.

   C.   Prevent all confusing use of the logo as a trademark on toasters.

   D.   Prevent all bad faith use of the logo as a trademark on toasters.

122.   Which of the following BEST describes Burnt's rights regarding use of the logo on toasters in Michigan?

   A.   Prevent all use of the logo.

   B.   Prevent all use of the logo likely to cause confusion.

   C.   Prevent all confusing use of the logo and similar logos.

   D.   Prevent all use of the logo and similar logos likely to cause confusion.

123.   Burnt is planning to expand its business into Iowa. Can Burnt safely assume that the logo is available as a mark in Iowa if no one is currently using it on toasters in Iowa?

ANSWER:

124.   Burnt has made no offers or sales in Iowa, nor is there any consumer association between the logo and Burnt's product offerings in the State. Advise Burnt on how it should

proceed to minimize conflicts with others and to maximize its own claims to the logo in connection with its proposed toaster product in Iowa other than by registration.

ANSWER:

Introductory Note: In all of the following Questions references to a federal registration refers to registration on the Principal Register. The Supplemental Register is discussed in Topic 10 — Registration: Process; Basic Requirements and Benefits.

TotoL Corporation uses the mark "Floquet" on its home linens products. It was the first to use the mark throughout Utah. It has recently expanded into Nevada, was the first to use the mark in that State and now sells throughout the State. Regional Four Corners (including Arizona and New Mexico) publications and television carry its advertisements.

125. Which of the following BEST describes the GEOGRAPHIC footprint (scope) of TotoL's trademark rights in the "Floquet" mark?

    A. Utah and Nevada.

    B. The Four Corners area.

    C. Utah, Nevada and those geographic areas where potential consumers associate the mark with TotoL's products.

    D. Utah, Nevada and those geographic areas where consumer confusion would be like likely if adoption by a junior user were permitted.

126. Which of the following BEST describes why TotoL should federally register its "Floquet" mark if it is considering expanding geographically in the future?

    A. Without a registration, geographic priority depends on actual use.

    B. Without a registration, open geographic territories are first-come, first-served with regard to trademark rights.

    C. Without a registration, it cannot prove it holds valid rights in the mark.

    D. Without a registration, its rights in the mark can be contested.

127. Which of the following BEST describes the *geographic* footprint benefits of TotoL's obtaining a federal registration of their "Floquet" mark?

    A. Federal registration allows the "Floquet" mark to become incontestable.

    B. Federal registration gives TotoL priority throughout the United States.

C. Federal registration constitutes constructive use throughout the United States as of the date filing of the application.

D. Federal registration constitutes use throughout the United States as of the date of registration

Poundem, LLC sells hammers used by professional construction contractors. It started using the color orange on the heads of its hammers in Georgia on June 1, 2002. It expanded into North and South Carolina in July 2004, continuing to use orange on the heads of its hammers as its mark. It applied for a federal registration for that mark (orange colored hammer heads) on June 30, 2005. It obtained the related federal registration on July 15, 2006. It started selling hammers with the orange head mark in Oregon on September 1, 2006. You have confirmed that the mark and registration are valid and that there were no relevant prior applications or registrations of any kind, anywhere.

128. Which of the following BEST describes the geographic territories covered by Poundem's registration of the mark?

A. The entire United States.

B. Everywhere Poundem has actually used the mark.

C. Everywhere Poundem has used the mark or customers associate the mark with Poundem's hammers.

D. Everywhere in the United States no one else can claim prior good faith use of the mark as a trademark.

129. In addition to the above facts, there are no pre-use Oregon consumer associations between the orange-hammer-head mark and Poundem. Which of the following is the latest date on which a good faith adopter would have priority against Poundem despite Poundem's federal registration?

A. A competitor who started selling hammers with orange heads in Oregon on July 1, 2004.

B. A competitor who started selling hammers with orange heads in Oregon on July 1, 2005.

C. A competitor who started selling hammers with orange heads in Oregon on July 1, 2006.

D. A competitor who started selling hammers with orange heads in Oregon on July 1, 2007.

130. Would the answer to Question 129 change if Poundem's federal registration has not yet issued?

ANSWER:

Poundem recently discovered that Junior, Ltd. had adopted and was using the orange-hammer-head mark throughout Oregon in March 2005, after Poundem's adoption of the mark on June 1, 2002, but before the filing and issuance of Poundem's federal registration. Junior adopted the mark in good faith and without knowledge of Poundem's use. Prior to Junior's adoption no one was using the mark in Oregon nor where there any Oregon consumer associations between the mark and any relevant product, including Poundem's hammers.

131. Which of the following BEST describes Poundem's ability to limit Junior's use of the mark?

A. Poundem can require Junior to stop using the mark if it would cause confusion when Poundem actually expands into Oregon.

B. Poundem can prevent Junior from using the mark outside the geographic area in which Junior had use or consumer-association-based rights to the mark on the date Poundem applied for its registration.

C. Poundem can prevent Junior from using the mark outside the geographic area in which Junior had use or consumer-association-based rights to the mark on the date Poundem applied for its registration, plus a zone of natural future expansion.

D. Poundem cannot prevent Junior from using the mark anywhere in the United States.

132. The facts are as stated in the Question immediately above EXCEPT Junior knew about Poundem's use when it adopted and started using the mark in Oregon. How might Junior's knowledge affect its rights to the mark?

ANSWER:

133. The facts are as stated in the Question immediately above EXCEPT that not only does Junior know of Poundem's use, but Poundem's mark has now become incontestable (it is the year 2011). ("Incontestability" is discussed in Topic 12 — Registration: Incontestability, but for this Question treat it as meaning Poundem's rights to the mark on hammers are conclusively treated as valid.) How might incontestability affect Junior's rights to the mark?

ANSWER:

134. Back to the less confusing times of Question 131, so no knowledge or incontestable marks. The facts are the same as stated in Question 131 EXCEPT Junior filed and received a federal registration BEFORE Poundem had applied for a federal registration. How does Junior's prior federal registration affect the parties' respective rights to the mark?

ANSWER:

135. How might the "loser" in Question 134 alter (or have avoided) that outcome?

ANSWER:

136. One last round with Poundem and Junior. The facts are the same as in Question 135 above, EXCEPT rather than a federal registration Junior obtained an *Oregon* state trademark registration before Poundem filed for its federal registration. How does that Oregon state trademark registration affect the parties' respective rights in the mark?

ANSWER:

WellShod Corp. holds a valid federal registration for the word "horse" which it uses as the trademark on the work shoes it manufactures and sells. It was the first to adopt the mark in the United States and the first to register the mark. It is currently selling its shoes throughout Kentucky, Tennessee and southern Indiana, Illinois and Ohio. It has recently discovered that Little Guys Co., a small local manufacturer of work shoes, is also using the word "horse" on its products. Little Guys adopted the mark three years after WellShod had filed for its federal registration, it sells in very small volumes exclusively in Prairie City, Oregon and its products cannot be found anywhere beyond a 100 mile radius of that city. There are no consumer associations between the mark and WellShod's products anywhere in the Northwest, including Prairie City, Oregon.

137. Which of the following BEST describes WellShod's rights against Little Guys?

   A. WellShod can immediately force Little Guys to stop using the mark.

   B. WellShod can stop Little Guys from using the mark when WellShod expands into Little Guys' geographic market.

   C. WellShod can stop Little Guys from using the mark when WellShod's expansion into Little Guys' geographic market is probable.

   D. WellShod cannot stop Little Guys, as first local user, from using the mark in Prairie City.

YourMoney, Inc. wants to federally register the stylized leopard drawing that it is using for its financial consulting services.

138. Which of the following BEST describes how much use YourMoney must show to support a use-based federal application?

   A. Good faith use as a mark in commerce.

    B.   Some use in commerce and/or recognition though-out the United States.

    C.   Use in commerce and/or recognition in a significant portion of the United States.

    D.   Use in commerce plus a showing of at least substantial regional consumer awareness.

139.   As a policy matter why does federal trademark law let registrant's claim national rights when their lack of actual use or consumer associations means that can be no possibility of consumer confusion?

ANSWER:

WriteALL LP manufactures and sells pens under the word mark "Sword." It started selling its pens on January 6, 2004 in the greater Detroit, Michigan metropolitan area. Since that time it has expanded its market to include all of Michigan plus northern Illinois, Indiana and Ohio. WriteALL's success led it to consider the possibility of further geographic expansion. WriteALL's President has come to you for advice concerning how to best avoid future trademark problems as it enters new markets.

Your investigation has turned up the following additional facts: There are two other manufacturers currently selling their pens under the "Sword" word mark in the United States. One has been selling its pens in the Dallas-Fort Worth, Texas area since March 15, 2004. They are entirely unaware of WriteALL's activities in the mid-West. The other is a company created by a former WriteALL distributor which just terminated its distribution contract and started selling its own pens in Southern Indiana and Illinois.

140.   What is your advice regarding how best to maximize WriteALL's geographic rights in the "Sword" mark?

ANSWER:

Casters Limited has decided to adopt a yellow bee as the trademark for its new line of fishing gear. A trademark search has revealed no existing users of that or any similar mark anywhere in the United States on any goods. Casters is not, however, ready to launch its new line, which still requires some time consuming and expensive preparatory steps. Casters is concerned that someone will adopt the "yellow bee" mark while they are finishing those preparations.

141.   You advise them:

    A.   To put a few yellow bees on their prototype products and offer them for sale.

    B.   To put a few yellow bees on their prototype products and apply for a federal registration.

    C.   To file a federal intent-to-use registration.

    D. Not to worry.

142. To follow your advice in Question 141, which of the following will be key?

    A. That the circumstances demonstrate Casters created the mark.

    B. That the circumstances show Casters' intent to use is bona fide.

    C. That the circumstances show Casters' use is imminent.

    D. That Casters can demonstrate active preparations to use.

143. Casters has filed its intent-to-use application for the yellow bee mark on fishing gear and received notice of allowance under Lanham Act § 13(b)(2) (15. U.S.C. § 1063(b)(2)). Explain to Casters what else, if anything, is required to "perfect" its trademark rights in the mark.

ANSWER:

Azurherb Company has filed a federal intent-to-use application (ITU) on the word mark "Raft" for its new line of banjos. After that filing, but before Azurherb's application has been published for opposition, another company, Senior User, Inc., adopts and starts using the "Raft" mark on banjos in New Jersey. Azurherb's application is then published and Senior User, Inc. starts an opposition proceeding claiming prior use. (Note: An opposition proceeding allows a third party to challenge a registration prior to its issuance. *See* Question 135 above).

144. Which of the following BEST describes the outcome of the opposition proceeding?

    A. Senior User wins as senior actual user of the mark.

    B. Senior User can obtain a concurrent registration for New Jersey.

    C. Azurherb wins.

    D. Azurherb wins if and when it files a statement of use which is accepted by the PTO.

145. Why is "use in commerce" required for federal registrations, whether use-based or intent to use?

ANSWER:

Smith et al, LP, an accounting partnership, has been using the mark "WofN" in connection with its national financial and tax consulting services since 1998. They have decided to federally register the "WofN" mark.

146. Briefly describe to Smith et al the basic process for registering its mark on the federal Principal Register.

ANSWER:

147. Explain why the above Question refers to registration on the federal "Principal Register" rather than simply "a federal registration."

ANSWER:

148. Which of the following is LEAST relevant to the registration of Smith et al's application to register its "WofN" mark?

    A. Use of the mark in commerce.

    B. Distinctiveness of the mark.

    C. Functionality of the mark.

    D. That the mark is a service mark.

149. Which of the following is MOST problematic to the registration of Smith et al's "WofN" mark?

    A. Use of the mark in commerce.

    B. Distinctiveness of the mark.

    C. Functionality of the mark.

    D. That the mark is a service mark.

150. Are there any other restrictions against which the "WofN" mark must be tested in order to be approved for federal registration?

ANSWER:

Smith et al have now successfully navigated the myriad requirements and has now obtained a federal registration on the Principal Register for its "WofN" mark.

151.   Which of the following BEST describes the term of that registration?

A.   For as long as Smith et al continues to use the "WofN" mark.

B.   Ten years.

C.   Ten years plus an unlimited number of ten year extensions provided Smith et al timely files all required renewal applications together with related use affidavits.

D.   Indefinitely provided Smith et al timely files all required renewal applications and all necessary use affidavits.

152.   Which of the following actions can result in Smith et al's loss of its Principal Register federal registration?

A.   Cancellation.

B.   Opposition.

C.   Filing a Section 15 Declaration.

D.   Filing a Section 8 Declaration.

153.   Which of the following is NOT a benefit of federal registration on the Principal Register?

A.   Nationwide constructive use.

B.   Enhanced remedies.

C.   Automatic incontestability.

D.   Prima facie evidence of validity and exclusive right to use

For the last four years Italian Pies Company has operated several pizza restaurants in the Chicago metropolitan area under the mark "Most Excellent WOP Pizza." The restaurants have been highly successful and Italian Pies has decided to expand its business into other areas of the country. Their lawyer has told them they should apply for a federal registration as soon as possible.

154. Which of the following is MOST LIKELY to preclude federal registration of the "Most Excellent WOP Pizza" mark?

   A. The word "Excellent" is descriptive.

   B. The word "WOP" pejoratively refers to those of Italian ancestry.

   C. The word "pizza" is generic.

   D. Italian Pies use is limited to the Chicago metropolitan area.

155. Explain to Italian Pies how the issue raised by the answer to Question 154 will be assessed.

ANSWER:

156. What policy arguments support the prohibition against federal registration of such marks?

ANSWER:

157. Which of the following BEST describes the effect if Italian Pies' "Most Excellent WOP Pizza" mark is ultimately determined unregisterable under federal law?

   A. Italian Pies will have state law rights in the mark.

   B. Italian Pies can enforce the mark as an unregistered mark under the Lanham Act.

   C. Italian Pies will have no federal rights in the mark.

   D. If Italian Pies continues to use the mark they face federal sanctions

BuffDesigns LLC has been using a picture of a fully nude, well-muscled man as its trademark for its men's shower body gel and shampoo over the last five years. Those products are sold in large volumes in the Northeast United States. No one else has or is using the mark or confusingly similar renditions on any goods or services, nor are there any relevant federal registrations. BuffDesigns has decided to seek a federal registration for their nude man mark.

158.   Which of the following is MOST LIKELY to cause problems with BuffDesigns' effort to register the mark?

   A.   Lanham Act § 2(a).

   B.   Lanham Act § 2(d).

   C.   Distinctiveness.

   D.   Use.

159.   Which of the following is LEAST relevant to making the determination on the issue identified in the previous Question?

   A.   The targeted customer group.

   B.   The general public.

   C.   Contemporary attitudes.

   D.   Dictionary definitions.

160.   Would it be relevant to the registerability inquiry that the picture of the fully nude man was the famous "figure in a circle" drawn by Leonardo da Vinci?

ANSWER:

161.   Is it relevant or perhaps even dispositive that BuffDesigns' internal memoranda reveal that it adopted the naked-man mark expressly to shock the public and thus draw extra attention to its products in the marketplace?

ANSWER:

162.   Assume BuffDesigns was acting without any attempt to shock or offend in adopting the naked man mark. It has filed an application which proceeded to publication. BuffDesigns has received a timely notice of an opposition. Which of following is its BEST argument that the opposer lacks *standing* to bring the opposition?

   A.   The mark has significant aesthetic merit.

   B.   The opposer will not be damaged.

   C.   The opposer is not shocked or offended by the mark.

   D.   The mark is incontestable.

Many Magazines, Inc. has applied for a federal registration of the American flag as a trademark for one of its magazines. Everyone agrees that the magazine, which has been on the market for a year, is an utterly tasteless and wholly offensive pornographic rag.

163. Which of the following is the STRONGEST argument for prohibiting the registration on these facts?

    A. The mark consists of the American flag.

    B. The magazine is utterly tasteless and wholly offensive.

    C. The mark disparages United States veterans.

    D. The mark brings the American flag into disrepute.

164. Would the outcome be different if the mark consisted of the flag of the small island nation of Tuvalu?

ANSWER:

165. Would the outcome be different if the mark consisted of the Texas state flag?

ANSWER:

166. Would the outcome be different if the mark consisted of the initials "CIA?"

ANSWER:

167. Would it affect the outcome if Many Magazines, Inc. could demonstrate that the consuming public strongly associated the American flag mark specifically with its associated magazine — that is, the flag mark had become distinctive of their particular product?

ANSWER:

DrinksofallKinds, Corp. is using the mark "FRESH FRUIT" on its artificially flavored juice drinks. The drinks contain no fruit, and certainly none that is fresh. There is strong evidence that the mark has developed secondary meaning regarding DrinksofallKinds beverages — uniquely identifying and distinguishing them from all other products in the class.

168. Which of the following will MOST LIKELY prevent DrinksofallKinds from federally registering the mark?

A.   The mark is deceptive.

B.   The mark is misdescriptive of the product.

C.   The mark is deceptively misdescriptive of the product.

D.   The mark is descriptive of the product.

169.   The facts are as stated in Question 168 above, EXCEPT DrinksofallKinds is using the mark "CRUSHED FRUIT" *but* the fruit is actually squeezed. The container also clearly says "without pulp." How does that mark fair regarding "deceptiveness" for registration purposes?

ANSWER:

170.   The facts are as stated in Question 168 above, EXCEPT DrinksofallKinds is using the mark "GLASS FRUIT" rather than "FRESH FRUIT." How does that mark fare regarding "deceptiveness" for registration purposes?

ANSWER:

The Trop-fruit Company makes tropical fruit drinks. The drinks are produced in Florida and are made exclusively from local Florida grown tropical fruit juices.

171.   Trop-fruit has decided to use the mark "ICELANDIC" on its fruit drink products. Which of the following is the BEST argument that the mark can be federally registered?

A.   Consumers will view the mark as a geographic identifier.

B.   The drinks are not from Iceland.

C.   Consumers do not make a goods/place association between tropical fruit drinks and Iceland.

D.   The drinks are from Florida and consumers do not associate Iceland with tropical fruits.

172.   The facts are as stated for Question 171, EXCEPT Trop-fruit has selected the mark "Pace" which is the name of the town in Florida where its drinks are made. Which of the following is the BEST argument that the mark can be federally registered?

A.   The mark is the name of an actual town.

B.   Pace has a meaning besides being the name of a town.

C.   Most consumers will not understand the mark as having geographic significance.

D.   The mark is primarily geographically descriptive.

173. Assume that the vast majority of consumers recognized Pace, Florida as the tropical drink capital of the United States and therefore assume (correctly) that the mark describes the geographic origin of the drinks. Does that mean that Trop-fruit can never federally register the "Pace" mark?

ANSWER:

174. Consumers recognize the "Pace" mark as indicating a product's geographic origin when used on tropical fruit drinks. However, rather than being used by a single local tropical juice, the Pace Camber of Commerce is using the "Pace" mark to certify the geographic origin of any producer's tropic fruit drinks which are, in fact, produced in their city — the tropical drink capital of the United States. Which of the following is the BEST argument that the Pace Chamber of Commerce can obtain a federal registration?

    A. The mark is not primarily geographically descriptive.

    B. The mark is primarily geographically descriptive.

    C. The mark has secondary meaning.

    D. The mark is not deceptive.

175. Enough of "Pace." The facts are as stated before Question 171, EXCEPT that Trop-fruit has selected the mark "Hawai'i" as the trademark for its tropical fruit beverages. Which of the following is MOST LIKELY to bar Trop-fruit's effort to federally register the "Hawai'i" mark?

    A. The mark is geographic.

    B. The mark is a geographically descriptive.

    C. The mark is deceptively geographically misdescriptive.

    D. The mark is deceptive.

Bellacitta S.A. operates a fashionable Italian-style restaurant in Los Angeles, California. It serves food based on recipes strongly evocative of Roman cuisine. In fact, the recipes come from a master chef who is fifth generation American of original Irish heritage and all of the ingredients are purchased locally. Additionally, none of the restaurant's cooks are from Rome (or ever been there) nor did they train under Roman or Roman-trained chefs. The restaurant operates under the name "Tratorria Roma." A survey shows that beyond question the relevant consumers believe both that the food is "authentically Roman" and strongly associate the mark with Bellacitta's restaurant.

176. Discuss Bellacitta's ability to overcome a claim that the "Tratorria Roma" mark cannot be registered in light of the geographic prohibitions contained in Lanham Act § 2 (15 § U.S.C. 1052).

ANSWER:

Assume that Bellacitta overcomes the geographic prohibitions and obtains a federal registration of the "Tratorria Roma" mark. It now wishes to bring a trademark infringement suit against a new Italian "usurper" restaurant operation which has recently opened up under the same mark. The defendant has challenged the mark as being geographically deceptively misdescriptive and therefore invalid.

177. Which of the following best describes the effect of Bellacitta's federal registration on the geographic mark invalidity defense?

   A. It creates a rebutable presumption that the mark is valid.

   B. It creates a rebutable presumption that the mark is valid provided there is secondary meaning.

   C. It creates a conclusive presumption that the mark is valid.

   D. It has no effect on the issue.

178. Would the outcome be different if Bellacitta only held an intent-to-use registration on the mark at the time it wants to bring the infringement suit?

ANSWER:

179. Assume that the court finds that Bellacitta's "Tratorria Roma" mark is geographically deceptively misdescriptive and its registration is invalid. Does that mean Bellacitta now cannot prevail on an infringement claim against its nearby Los Angeles competitor?

ANSWER:

Vino Veritas Ltd. has created a new wine. It is certain that the rich color and complex taste would have greatly appealed to Thomas Jefferson. Consequently, it would like use the phrase "Thomas Jefferson's Favorite" superimposed on his portrait as the mark for the new wine.

180. Which of following posses the MOST LIKELY problem to Vino Veritas obtaining a federal registration of the mark?

   A. The mark contains a personal name.

   B. The mark contains the portrait of a person.

   C. The mark contains the name of a deceased United States President.

   D. The mark suggests an association with Thomas Jefferson.

181. Assume that instead of the Thomas Jefferson mark Vino Veritas has proposed using the mark "Bill Gate's Favorite" (without a portrait) on its new wine. Assuming all of

the following are true, which is the LEAST relevant to determining whether the alternative mark can be registered under Lanham Act § 2(a) (15 U.S.C. § 1052(a)) as "falsely suggesting a connection with persons, living or dead?."

A. Bill Gates has never heard of Vino Veritas much less its new wine.

B. Many people are named Bill Gates.

C. A particular person named Bill Gates is the richest man in the world.

D. The rich person Bill Gates is actually named William Gates, Jr., but everyone refers to him "Bill Gates."

182. Having been discouraged by the outcome in Question 181, Vino Veritas has instead picked "Julio's Favorite" as the mark for its new wine. Assuming all of the following are true, which is the MOST relevant to determining whether the alternative mark can be registered under Lanham Act § 2(a) (15 U.S.C. § 1052(a)) as "falsely suggesting a connection with persons, living or dead?."

A. There is a well-know singer named Julio Iglesias.

B. There are many people whose first name is Julio.

C. Consumers will not connect Julio Iglesias to the mark.

D. Julio Iglesias is rarely referred to by only his first name.

183. Assume consumers do make the necessary association between Julio Iglesias and the "Julio's Favorite" mark. How does the registerability analysis of the mark under Lanham Act § 2(a) (15 U.S.C. § 1052(a)) differ from the analysis under Lanham Act § 2(c) (15 U.S.C. § 1052(c)) — both of which involve marks consisting of or comprising personal names?

ANSWER:

184. The facts are as stated in Question x183, EXCEPT Vino Veritas can prove that consumers make no association between Julio Iglesias and the "Julio's Favorite" mark. Does that mean the mark "Julio's Favorite" entirely avoids the Lanham Act § 2(a) (15 U.S.C. § 1052(a)) prohibition against marks "falsely suggesting a connection with persons, living or dead?"

ANSWER:

185. Would a demonstrated consumer connection between Julius Caesar (Julio Caesare) and the "Julio's Favorite" mark support a rejection under Lanham Act § 2(c) (15 U.S.C. § 1052(c)) as consisting of a person's "name, portrait, or signature?"

ANSWER:

186. What is the difference between the prohibitions under Lanham Act §§ 2(a) and 2(c) (15 U.S.C. §§ 1052 (a) and (c)) and the "right of publicity?"

ANSWER:

The indefatigable Vino Veritas has decided to give the wine mark one more try. This time it has come up with the last name of the sole shareholder and chief executive officer of the company — "Green." The shareholder/CEO has explicitly endorsed the wine and consented in writing to the use of her name.

187. What remaining name-based registration problems still exist under Lanham Act § 2 (15 U.S.C. § 1052)?

ANSWER:

188. Which of the following facts is NOT relevant to overcoming that difficulty?

A. The shareholder/CEO gave explicit written consent to use her name.

B. Consumers know that the Green family is involved in wine-making.

C. The word "green" also means the related color.

D. Green is a common family name in the United States.

189. Assume that the Patent and Trademark Office determines that consumers assume the Vino Veritas "Green" mark refers to the wine-making family and the company's sole shareholder. Does that mean that the mark cannot be registered?

ANSWER:

190. Could Vino Veritas have made this same argument with regard to the problems with registering the "Julio's Favorite" mark?

ANSWER:

191. Before we leave Julio — could a mark consisting of the first name "Julio" be registered despite the Lanham Act § 2(e)(4) (15 U.S.C. § 1052(e)(4)) prohibition against registration of marks which consist of "primarily merely a surname?"

ANSWER:

192.   Time to bring the Vino Veritas saga to a conclusion. Assume Vino Veritas makes the necessary showing and obtains registration of the "Green" mark. Does that federal registration preclude another wine producer named Joe Green from using his name to identify himself as the producer of his wine products?

ANSWER:

193.   Fleet Vehicles LLC has come up with a fabulous new automobile dashboard design. The design makes it far more convenient for the driver to see everything "at a glace" and reduces the cost of manufacturing the car. Fleet would like to federally register the dashboard's appearance as a trademark. Which of the following is MOST likely to raise problems with obtaining that registration?

   A.   Product design cannot be registered.

   B.   Lanham Act § 2(e)(1) (15 U.S.C. § 1052(e)(1)).

   C.   Lanham Act § 2(e)(5) (15 U.S.C. § 1052(e)(5)).

   D.   Fleet Vehicles cannot satisfy the requirements of Lanham Act § 2(f) (15 U.S.C. § 1052(f)).

194.   A final "quick test" to confirm understanding of the range, not the details, of the Section 2 prohibitions. Identify if there is a potential Section 2 concern with federally registering each of the following marks and, if so, the general nature of any concern(s).

   A.   "Hardy" for beef produced by George Hardy.

   B.   The coat of arms of the City of Lake Oswego, Oregon for hiking shoes made in but not by that city.

   C.   "Quick" for calendars.

   D.   "Redskins" for a football team.

   E.   "Ben Franklin" for banking services.

   F.   "Alaska" for ice cream produced in Maine.

   G.   "Peyton Manning" for athletic equipment from an unaffiliated producer.

   H.   "Georgia" for a band.

   I.   "Paris" for a perfume made in Paris.

   J.   The color "yellow" for safety tape.

K.   "Ronald Regan" for security services.

L.   "VFW" for a striptease club.

M.   "Kodiak" for camera supplies made in Indiana.

N.   "Burgundy" on a wine from Oregon used after 2002

Cereals Company has been using the mark "Sweet and Crunchy" on one of its cereals which is, in fact, sweet and crunchy.

195. Which of the following BEST describes what it means if Cereals' "Sweet and Crunchy" mark is "incontestable"?

    A. The mark is presumed valid.

    B. The validity of Cereals' mark cannot be challenged.

    C. The validity of Cereals' mark can only be challenged on limited grounds.

    D. Cereals' registration cannot be cancelled.

196. Which of the following is NOT required for Cereals to claim that its "Sweet and Crunchy" mark is incontestable?

    A. A federal registration.

    B. Proof of secondary meaning.

    C. Five years of trademark use following registration.

    D. Timely filing of a Section 15 Affidavit.

197. Why is the correct answer to the Question immediately above not required for incontestability?

ANSWER:

Assume that Cereals uses the "All Bran" mark on another of its cereals. That mark has become incontestable.

198. Assuming that the cereal is made entirely of bran, which of the following challenges is MOST likely to defeat Cereals' claim to incontestability under Section 15 of the Lanham Act (15 U.S.C. § 1065)?

    A. That "All Bran" is generic.

    B. That "All Bran" is descriptive.

    C. That "All Bran" is deceptive.

  D. That "All Bran" is deceptively misdescriptive.

199. The facts are as stated in Question 198 immediately above EXCEPT the cereal only contains 40% bran, the rest being other ingredients. On these facts which of the following challenges is MOST likely to defeat Cereals' claim to incontestability under Section 15 of the Lanham Act (15 U.S.C. § 1065)?

  A. That "All Bran" is generic.

  B. That "All Bran" is descriptive.

  C. That "All Bran" is deceptive.

  D. That "All Bran" is deceptively misdescriptive

Dentistry Associates is actively using the "Gentle Dental" mark. The mark is incontestable. A competitor, NovKain P.A., has recently starting using the phrase "gentle dental" in connection with its services. Dentistry Associates has sued NovKain for infringement.

200. Which of the following BEST describes the effect of the incontestable status of Dentistry's mark on the lawsuit?

  A. It means the mark is presumed valid.

  B. It means the mark is presumed valid except in certain circumstances.

  C. It means the mark is conclusively presumed valid.

  D. It means the mark is conclusively presumed valid except in certain circumstances.

201. The facts are as stated in the Question immediately above. Which of the following challenges is MOST likely to be of assistance to NovKain's defense?

  A. The mark is descriptive.

  B. NovKain is using the mark descriptively.

  C. Dentistry Associates has abandoned the mark.

  D. NovKain is a good faith prior user of the mark.

202. The facts are the same as stated in Question 200 above EXCEPT that Dentistry Associates intentionally filed fabricated evidence in support of its showing of secondary meaning to obtain its federal registration. How would NovKain's proof of that fact to overcome incontestability MOST LIKELY affect the validity of the "Gentle Dental" mark in the lawsuit?

  A. The mark is invalid.

  B. The mark is presumed valid.

  C. The mark is conclusively presumed valid.

  D. The mark is conclusively presumed valid except in certain circumstances.

Electromos LLC uses the mark "I-Vid" on its portable video viewer. The "I-Vid" mark is incontestable. The public has started using the word "I-Vid" to describe the class of portable video viewers. In response, a number of Electromos' competitors have adopted the term "I-Vid" in the reference their portable video viewer products. Electromos has decided to bring suit against one of those competitors, Comelately Corp.

203. Which of the following is MOST likely to be of assistance to Comelately's challenge to incontestability?

    A. The mark is generic.

    B. The mark is descriptive.

    C. Comelately is using the mark descriptively.

    D. Comelately is a good faith prior user of the mark.

204. The facts are as stated in Question 203 above EXCEPT that Comelately has prevailed on the defense to incontestability identified in the answer to that Question. Which of the following BEST describes the validity of Electromos' mark?

    A. The mark is presumed valid.

    B. The mark is presumed valid but subject to challenge.

    C. The mark is presumed invalid.

    D. The mark is invalid

GF Inc. uses the mark "Hearty" on its soups. The "Hearty" mark is incontestable, the necessary affidavit was timely filed identifying those goods and there are no defenses or defects available to challenge its incontestable status. Twofer Company has just started using the "Hearty" mark on its whole grain bread products. GF has brought a suit for trademark infringement against Twofer.

205. Which of the following BEST describes what GF should show regarding the "Hearty" mark to prevail in its trademark infringement lawsuit?

    A. That GF has relevant valid rights in the "Hearty" mark.

    B. That there are no viable defects or defenses regarding the incontestability of its mark.

    C. That its rights in the mark are incontestable.

    D. That the "Hearty" mark is validly registered.

206. How would a showing that GF has incontestable rights in the "Hearty" mark affect the final outcome on infringement by Twofer?

ANSWER:

Oops, Incorporated registered its "Bright" mark seven years ago. The mark is admittedly descriptive and does not have secondary meaning. Although Oops has been using the mark continuously following registration on its car polish products and there are no other issues regarding its incontestable status, Oops has yet to file the necessary Section 15 Affidavit.

207. Which of the following BEST describes the status of Oops' rights in the "Bright" mark and its related registration?

    A. Oops does not have incontestable rights in the mark or its registration until it files the Affidavit.

    B. Oops cannot obtain incontestable rights in the mark or prevent its registration from being cancelled.

    C. Oops cannot obtain incontestable rights in the mark but may be able to prevent its registration from being cancelled.

    D. Oops has incontestable rights in the mark but cannot prevent its registration from being cancelled.

208. The facts are as stated in Question 207 above EXCEPT assume that a competitor has just filed an action to cancel Oops' registration for the "Bright" mark based on its acknowledged descriptiveness and lack of secondary meaning. What result?

ANSWER:

209. Would the outcome in the above cancellation action be different if Oops' car polish actually left a dull, scratched surface when applied?

ANSWER:

210. If Oops' mark were cancelled as a result of the above action does that *ipso facto* mean Oops has no rights in the "Bright" mark?

ANSWER:

211. Can certification marks become incontestable and the related registrations immune from cancellation?

ANSWER:

Freeborn Ltd. makes and sells men's casual and dress slacks under the mark "Opusdiem." Its current geographic market covers Massachusetts, Connecticut and New York. Secundo Inc. has started selling men's casual slacks under the same "Opusdiem" mark in Boston, MA.

212. Assuming "use in commerce," which of the following must Freeborn allege about its "Opusdiem" mark to bring a federal trademark infringement action based on confusion under the Lanham Act?

    A. It is federally registered.

    B. It is valid.

    C. It is incontestable.

    D. It is inherently distinctive.

213. Assuming (for now) Freeborn's claim against Secundo is covered by the Lanham Act can it also bring a state trademark infringement claim?

ANSWER:

214. Which of the following BEST describes what Freeborn must prove to succeed in its confusion-based claim against Secundo?

    A. Harm to goodwill.

    B. Actual consumer confusion.

    C. Diversion of consumer trade to Secundo.

    D. Likelihood of consumer confusion.

215. How does the central inquiry identified in Question 214 immediately above vary depending on whether Freeborn brings a claim under federal or state law, or with regard to a registered or unregistered trademark?

ANSWER:

All Lawns, Inc. manufactures and sells a variety of lawn mowers under the "Swift" mark. All Lawns has been in business for 3 years and advertises and sells its mowers exclusively, but throughout, Indiana, Ohio and Michigan. It has used the "Swift" mark on its mowers the entire time. It does not have a federal registration for the mark. The President of All Lawns, John Seed, wants to bring a confusion-based trademark infringement action against a company named Just Grass Co.

216.   Assume Just Grass is advertising and selling lawn mowers under the "Swift" mark exclusively in Salem, Oregon. What advice do you give?

ANSWER:

Assume for the following questions that Just Grass is advertising and selling its lawn mowers in **Indiana** under the "Swit" mark (without the "f").

217.   Which of the following is LEAST relevant to determining whether the necessary level of confusion exists?

A.   That All Lawns has valid rights to the "Swift" trademark in Indiana.

B.   The "Polaroid" factors.

C.   The product "footprint" (scope) of All Lawns' rights in the "Swift" trademark.

D.   A demonstrable lack of existing actual consumer confusion.

218.   Briefly describe the analysis used to determine whether All Lawns' confusion-based infringement claim against Just Grass will succeed.

ANSWER:

219.   Which of the following BEST describes the effect if All Lawns can prove that Just Grass specifically adopted the "Swit" mark on its lawn mowers to confuse consumers?

A.   It is a factor.

B.   It is a key factor.

C.   It is determinative.

D.   It is irrelevant.

220.   Which of the following consumer groups is LEAST relevant to All Lawns' making the necessary showing of consumer confusion?

A.   Lawn mower purchasers.

B.   Potential lawn care equipment purchasers.

    C. People who have or may have lawns.

    D. The consuming public

The big question (finally). First a quick clarifying statement of the facts: All Lawns, Inc. manufactures and sells a variety of lawn mowers under the "Swift" mark. All Lawns has been in business for 3 years and advertises and sells its mowers exclusively, but throughout, Indiana, Ohio and Michigan. It has used the "Swift" mark on its mowers the entire time. It does not have a federal registration for the mark. Just Grass is using "Swit" as its mark on competing lawn-mowers sold in Indiana. There is no evidence that Just Grass intended to confuse.

221.   Which of the following BEST describes All Lawns' confusion-based trademark infringement case against Just Grass on the merits?

    A. Great case.

    B. Good case but there are some significant issues.

    C. Weak enough case that should try to negotiate a compromise settlement.

    D. Forget it.

222.   The facts are as stated in Question 221 above, EXCEPT Just Grass can prove that its lawn mowers are of a significantly higher quality than All Lawns' mowers. Now which BEST describes All Lawns' confusion-based trademark infringement case against Just Grass on the merits?

    A. Great case.

    B. Good case but there are some significant issues.

    C. Weak enough case that should try to negotiate a compromise settlement.

    D. Forget it.

223.   The facts are as stated in Question 221 above, EXCEPT Just Grass marks its lawn mowers as follows: "Just Grass/**SWIT**." Now which of the following BEST describes All Lawns' confusion-based trademark infringement case against Just Grass on the merits?

    A. Great case.

    B. Good case but there are some significant issues.

    C. Weak enough case that should try to negotiate a compromise settlement.

    D. Forget it.

224.   The facts are as stated in Question 223 above, EXCEPT Just Grass is advertising and selling patio furniture under the "All Grass/**SWIT**" mark in Indiana. Now which of the following BEST describes All Lawns' confusion-based trademark infringement case against Just Grass on the merits?

    A.   Great case.

    B.   Good case but there are some significant issues.

    C.   Weak enough case should try to negotiate a compromise settlement.

    D.   Forget it.

225.   On the facts of Question 224 above, which of the following factors raises the MOST serious concern for All Lawns in its confusion-based trademark infringement lawsuit?

    A.   The marks.

    B.   The marketing channels involved.

    C.   The nature of the purchase decision.

    D.   Related goods.

226.   Briefly outline the argument All Lawns would make to overcome the problem you identified in Question 225.

ANSWER:

227.   How would the existence of an All Lawns internal memoranda showing it had near-term plans to expand into patio furniture business affect its chances of success on the merits?

ANSWER:

228.   How would the U.S. Patent and Trademark Office assess the confusion issue if Just Grass filed an application to federally register its "All Grass/**Swit**" mark for patio furniture?

ANSWER:

229.   Searches, LLC operates an internet search engine. To enhance its revenues Searches has started a "sponsored advertisement" program. For a fee Searches will show the program participant's advertisements along with the search results whenever the search request includes an identified trademark. That trademark may belong to the participant or another (including competitors). Which of the following is Searches' BEST defense if it is sued by the owner of a valid trademark claiming that showing a competitor's advertisement triggered by the owner's mark in a consumer search request constitutes confusion-based trademark infringement?

    A.   The mark is not being used as a trademark.

    B. The plaintiff's mark is invalid.

    C. Searches is not selling any goods or services.

    D. Searches has not actually sold the mark

Regular Jeans, Inc. makes low cost jeans "for the masses." Its product development group has recently developed a pocket stitching design it would like to use on a new line of Regular Jeans products. Unfortunately, they have discovered that Fancy Jeans, an upscale designer clothing company, already holds a valid, federal trademark registration on the stitching design covering jeans.

230.   The Regular Jeans Vice-President of Marketing has had an inspiration. In order to avoid any possible consumer confusion as a result of the stitching, every pair of the company's new jeans will carry a conspicuous detachable notice expressly stating that the jeans are made by Regular Jeans and that Fancy Jeans has no connection either directly or by way of sponsorship or affiliation with the product. Which of the following is the BEST assessment of the Vice-President's plan with regard to possible confusion-based trademark infringement claims?

    A. It solves none of the infringement concerns.

    B. It solves some of the infringement concerns.

    C. It solves all of the important infringement concerns.

    D. It solves all of the infringement concerns.

231.   Would it change the answer to the previous Question if Regular Jeans can show that designer jeans purchasers are very sophisticated, careful shoppers and able to tell the difference between the two companies' product even with the presence of the stitching on both?

ANSWER:

Local Wines LLC is a small producer of pinot noir wines. It has been selling its wines locally in Washington State for the last 10 years under the valid but unregistered trademark "Veritas." Local has just discovered that six months ago MegaWines, Co., a national wine company, released a new pinot noir wine also under the "Veritas" mark. MegaWines adopted the mark with no knowledge of Local's mark (or Local itself for that matter). Although there is considerable consumer confusion, it is not that consumers believe that MegaWines' product comes from Local but that they believe all Veritas wine is produced by MegaWines.

232.   MegaWines has written to demand that Local cease using the "Veritas" mark based on the resulting consumer confusion. Which of the following describes the MOST LIKELY outcome if MegaWines were to sue Local?

    A. MegaWines wins because consumers are confusing Local's wine with its wine.

B.   MegaWines wins because it did not intend to cause confusion.

C.   Local wins because it is the senior user of the "Veritas" mark on wine.

D.   Local wins because it has lost sales.

233.   Instead of selling a competing wine under the "Veritas" label, MegaWines is buying Local's "Veritas" wine, relabeling and reselling it as its own product under the "Faustus" mark. Which of the following BEST describes the claim Local can bring under the Lanham Act?

A.   Reverse confusion trademark infringement.

B.   Forward confusion trademark infringement.

C.   Reverse passing off.

D.   Likelihood of confusion trademark infringement.

234.   Enzo Chip is running a very unsuccessful café/bar/grill just off of Exit 192 on Interstate 5 south of Portland Oregon. He realizes that the problem is that at each of the next three exits there are various national chain restaurants along with additional local options. Consequently, most if not all of his potential customers are waiting until those exits to get off to eat. He has come up with the idea of putting up a sign at his Exit 192 that indicates it leads to several of those same national chain eateries. He has no intention of using any of those chains' well-known marks in any other way, on his restaurant or otherwise. In fact, not only does his restaurant have an unmistakable non-chain appearance, he will prominently and proudly proclaim in his signage that he is entirely unaffiliated with any chain. Any problems with his plan?

ANSWER:

GenericCandy, LLP makes and sells at wholesale a variety of candy products which are specifically designed to look like well-known candies made by others. It is careful to only duplicate candies whose appearance is not protected by a valid trademark. However, to increase its sales volumes it has its sales staff employees encourage the retailer purchasers of the legal "look alike" candies to package them in containers which copy the protected trade dress and other marks of the original candy makers. Some of the retailers respond favorably to the idea, selling the GenericCandy products they purchase in infringing packaging.

235.   Which of the following is a potential trademark problem for GenericCandy LLP?

A.   Reverse confusion.

B.   Forward confusion.

C.   Vicarious infringement.

D.   Contributory infringement.

236. The facts are as stated in Question 235, EXCEPT GenericCandy's sales staff employees do not suggest the use of infringing packaging. Instead several individual retailers think up the packaging idea on their own and commit the infringement. How does that change the analysis regarding GenericCandy's liability?

ANSWER:

237. The facts are as stated in Question 235, EXCEPT rather than GenericCandy having its sales staff employees encourage the use of infringing packaging, several of the sales staff employees themselves secretly package the GenericCandy product using the protected trade dress and marks of the original manufacturers before delivery to the purchasing retailers. GenericCandy has no knowledge of the sales staff employees' activities. How does that change the analysis regarding GenericCandy's liability?

ANSWER:

238. BestStuff, Inc. sells electronic products. Many of the products it wishes to sell are produced by major manufacturers which only sell to their authorized distributors. Those manufacturers have expressly and repeatedly refused to authorize BestStuff because they do not like BestStuff's discount and volume sales business model. BestStuff acquires those manufacturers' products by purchasing surplus from their authorized distributors. BestStuff leaves all of the manufacturer's trademarks in place and advertises and sells them as "original" products. Does BestStuff's unauthorized resale of those manufacturers' products support a confusion-based claim for trademark infringement?

ANSWER:

Topcaps Co. makes baseball-style caps, each of which bears the "Ersatz" trademark on a tag attached to the interior of the headband. Each cap also has a third party trademark printed in large letters on the front above the bill. The caps are sold to a wide variety of consumers who purchase primarily based on their individual interest in the third-party mark printed on the cap. Topcaps' Vice-President of Marketing is convinced that because every Topcaps' cap carries the "Ersatz" mark there is no risk of liability for trademark infringement.

239. BigRigs Ltd., whose very well known "Rhino" trademark for work clothes graces Topcaps' most popular cap, has brought a trademark infringement suit against Topcaps. Which of the following describes the MOST LIKELY outcome if BigRigs brings a confusion-based trademark infringement claim against Topcaps?

    A. Topcaps will very likely win.

    B.   Topcaps will probably win.

    C.   BigRigs will probably win.

    D.   BigRigs will very likely win.

240.   Would the above analysis change if the plaintiff in the suit against Topcaps was Harvard University objecting to the use of "Harvard" on a new Topcaps' product offering?

ANSWER:

Anduin Rivers, Inc. makes and sells high end fishing equipment under the word mark "Pont." It has been using the mark for the past 10 years and holds an incontestable federal registration for fishing and related equipment. Anduin's "Pont" fishing equipment is much prized among avid anglers but few others recognize the mark. Anduin has discovered that another company, Quintex LLC, has started making and selling small standard kitchen appliances nationwide under the "Pont" name. There is no evidence that any consumers believe that Quintex "Pont" kitchen appliances are in any way associated with Anduin, but Anduin is convinced that Quintex adopted the "Pont" mark to trade on Anduin's goodwill.

241.   Which of the following BEST describes Anduin's chances of winning a confusion-based trademark infringement action?

    A.   Anduin will likely win.

    B.   Anduin may win but there are some difficulties with its case.

    C.   Anduin may win but there are serious difficulties with its case.

    D.   Anduin will lose.

242.   Which of the following offers Anduin the BEST chance of prevailing on the alternative theory that Quintex's use constitutes trademark dilution under federal law?

    A.   That Anduin cannot show a likelihood of confusion.

    B.   That Anduin holds an incontestable federal registration for the mark.

    C.   That the "Pont" mark is well-known to the consuming public.

    D.   That the "Pont" mark is inherently distinctive.

243.   Briefly explain the policy behind the creation of the "dilution" cause of action in trademark law.

ANSWER:

244.   Which of the following is LEAST relevant to Anduin's ability to demonstrate the "fame" of its "Pont" mark?

    A.   That Anduin holds an incontestable federal registration for the mark.

B.   The duration and extent of Anduin's use of the mark.

C.   The degree of consumer recognition of the mark.

D.   The nature of the goods on which the mark is used.

245.   Which of the following facts is the MOST problematic to Anduin's ability to prevail on its dilution claim?

A.   The mark is extremely well-known among fisherman, but not recognized by others.

B.   The mark is used nationally.

C.   The mark is registered on the federal Principal Register.

D.   The mark is only used on fishing equipment

Mauer, Ltd. has been making, advertising and selling "Tough-Sac" garbage bags nationally for 25 years. Mauer holds an incontestable federal registration for the "Tough-Sac" mark. The "Tough-Sac" product is widely recognized by United States consumers as a highly reliable, durable and sought after garbage bag. A maker of sport-bags, Totes Company, has just introduced a new gym bag bearing the mark "Tough-Bag." Mauer has brought a dilution claim against Totes in the Second Circuit.

246.   Does it matter that Mauer's mark was not originally inherently distinctive (that is, that "Tough-Sac" has become distinctive only through extensive use generating secondary meaning)?

ANSWER:

247.   Which of the following is the BEST description of Mauer's claim?

A.   Dilution.

B.   Dilution by tarnishment.

C.   Dilution by blurring.

D.   Dilution — tertium quid.

248.   Which of the following is NOT required for Mauer to prevail on its dilution claim?

A.   That its "Pont" mark is famous.

B.   Actual dilution.

C.   The likelihood of dilution.

D.   The absence of a defense.

249.   Assess Mauer's chances of prevailing on a dilution by blurring claim against Totes use of "Tough-Bag" on its gym bag.

ANSWER:

250.   If Mauer prevails on its dilution claim against Totes what is the measure of its damages?

ANSWER:

251.   What happens if Totes had started using the "Tough-Bag" mark on its gym bag BEFORE Mauer's "Tough-Sac" mark had become famous?

ANSWER:

252.   A local grocery store, WeHaveItAll, Ltd., has recently begun carrying Maurer's "Tough-Sac" garbage bags. Its management decides to try to capitalize on the "Tough-Sac brand name by running an advertising campaign which prominently features Tough-Sac garbage bags as a special sale item. Can Mauer prevail in a dilution action against WeHaveItAll with regard to the advertising campaign?

ANSWER:

253.   Which of the following is NOT a defense to dilution liability?

   A.   Nominative fair use in connection with comparative advertising.

   B.   Descriptive fair use on another's product.

   C.   News reporting.

   D.   Use in connection with a non-competitive product

Ultra Corporation sells a very expensive and high quality watch aimed at the "successful professional" under the mark "Glory." The mark has become nationally known by the consuming public. Ultra holds a federal registration on the mark for watches and jewelry products.

254.   In which of the following cases is Ultra MOST likely to prevail on a dilution claim?

   A.   A magazine publishes an advertisement for very expensive, high quality but extremely tasteless "Glory" underwear targeted at the "successful professional" as part of a feature mocking the "successful professional."

   B.   A newspaper publishes an editorial criticizing what it labels "the disgusting "**Glorfy**-cation" of consumerism represented by the very expensive, high quality watches sold by Ultra to the successful professional.

C. A pornography shop uses "Glory" on its very expensive, "high end" video products.

D. An unauthorized, price discounting retailer begins selling used-but-original "Glory" watches made by Ultra which the retailer acquires in the after-market.

255. Instead of using "Glory" as a mark for its goods, a car dealership specializing in expensive automobiles adopts the trade name (business name) "Glory Motors." Which of the following BEST describes how that use might affect a dilution claim by Ultra?

A. It is not trademark use so no dilution claim can be brought.

B. It is not trademark use, but a dilution claim can be brought.

C. It is trademark use, but the requisite harm does not exist.

D. It is trademark use and the requisite harm does exist.

256. Ultra has decided to leverage the fame of its "Glory" mark by adopting a unique trade dress for its watch stores which among other features prominently includes multiple uses of the "Glory" mark. The trade dress is neither functional nor registered on the Principal Register. Which of the following BEST describes Ultra's ability to protect the trade dress of its stores against dilution?

A. It cannot; trade dress cannot qualify for dilution protection.

B. It cannot; trade dress cannot serve as a trademark.

C. It can, provided it can show the trade dress as a whole is famous.

D. It can, provided it can show the trade dress as a whole is famous apart from the "Glory" mark.

257. What jurisdictional requirement must be satisfied for Ultra to bring a dilution claim under the federal statute?

ANSWER:

Algarve Company uses the "Ocotillo" mark on its hand lotion products. Fred Squires has registered the domain name "Ocotillo.com."

258. If Algarve wants to bring an anticybersquatting action against Fred under the Lanham Act, which of the following is NOT one of the core elements of Algarve's case?

   A. That Algarve owns the "Ocotillo" mark.

   B. That the "Ocotillo" mark was famous before Fred's registration of the domain name.

   C. That Fred registered, trafficked in or used the domain name.

   D. That Fred has a bad faith intent to profit from the mark.

259. Must Algarve hold a federal registration for the "Ocotillo mark to bring the federal anticybersquatting action?

ANSWER:

260. Does the date of Fred's registration of the domain name have any affect on the action?

ANSWER:

261. Which of the following BEST describes why Fred's challenged "Ocotillo.com" domain name triggers liability under the statute?

   A. The domain name contains Algarve's "Ocotillo" mark.

   B. The domain name is identical or confusingly similar to Algarve's "Ocotillo" mark.

   C. The domain name is likely to cause confusion with Algarve's "Ocotillo" mark.

   D. Fred registered the domain name after Algarve's "Ocotillo" mark became distinctive.

262. Assess the likelihood that Algarve will prevail on the "nature of the domain name" requirement identified in the preceding Question.

ANSWER:

263. Which of the following BEST describes the other core requirement (beyond the relationship to the mark) of an anticybersquatting violation under the Lanham Act?

    A. Likelihood of confusion.

    B. Confusing similarly.

    C. Bad faith use of the mark.

    D. Bad faith intent to profit from the mark.

264. How does the court go about determining whether the requirement identified in the preceding Question has been satisfied?

ANSWER:

265. In which of the following situations is Algarve MOST LIKELY to prevail in its anticybersquatting lawsuit against Fred?

    A. Fred has posted a few pictures of his house on his "Ocotillo.com" website.

    B. Fred is a cactus expert and has an entire series of websites named after various kinds of cacti (including the ocotillo), each of which includes information about the related species.

    C. Fred keeps a current blog on the website which criticizes Algarve's hand lotion products.

    D. Fred runs a car repair business under the name Ocotillo LLC which he advertises on the website.

266. Algarve has prevailed in its anticybersquatting case against Fred, who had registered his domain name on June 23, 2001. Which of the following BEST describes the remedies available to Algarve in these circumstances?

    A. Injunction and a forfeiture, cancellation or transfer order regarding the domain name.

    B. Injunction; a forfeiture, cancellation or transfer order; and monetary damages under Lanham § 35(a)).

    C. Injunction; a forfeiture, cancellation or transfer order; monetary damages under Lanham § 35(a);) and statutory damages.

    D. Injunction; a forfeiture, cancellation or transfer order; and either monetary damages under Lanham § 35(a)) or statutory damages.

267. The facts are as stated in Question 266 immediately above EXCEPT that Fred had registered the domain name on June 23, 1998. Which of the following BEST describes the remedies available to Algarve under these circumstances?

    A. Injunction and a forfeiture, cancellation or transfer order regarding the domain name.

B.   Injunction; a forfeiture, cancellation or transfer order; and monetary damages under Lanham § 35(a)).

C.   Injunction; a forfeiture, cancellation or transfer order; monetary damages under Lanham § 35(a);) and statutory damages.

D.   Injunction; a forfeiture, cancellation or transfer order; and either monetary damages under Lanham § 35(a)) or statutory damages

Avila Enterprises, Inc. has used the "Corpat" mark on its kitchen supply products for over ten years. It has recently discovered that someone has registered the "Corpat.com" domain name. There is no information on the website and the registration information is false.

268.   Which of the following BEST describes how Avila can bring an *in rem* anticybersquatting action under the Lanham Act?

A.   Sue the owner as a "John Doe."

B.   Start an action under the Uniform Domain Name Dispute Resolution Policy.

C.   File an *in rem* action stating its inability to locate the true owner.

D.   File an *in rem* action stating its inability to obtain personal jurisdiction of the true owner.

269.   Which of the following BEST describes the predicate showing Avila must make in order to bring the *in rem* suit on the basis identified in Question 268 immediately above?

A.   Show it is unable to deliver service of process.

B.   Show it sent notice of the action to the address shown on the registration.

C.   Publish notice of the action.

D.   Show it was unable to identify the registrant despite reasonable efforts to do so.

270.   Which of the following BEST describes the court in which Avila can bring the above described *in rem* action?

A.   The federal district court jurisdiction in which the defendant resides.

B.   The federal district court jurisdiction in which the relevant domain name registrar is located.

C.   The state court jurisdiction in which the domain name resides.

D.   The state court jurisdiction in which the relevant domain name registrar is incorporated.

271.   Which of the following BEST describes the claims which Avila can make in its *in rem* lawsuit against "Corpat.com"?

A.   Anticybersquatting, infringement and dilution.

      B.   Anticybersquatting and infringement.

      C.   Anticybersquatting.

      D.   It cannot bring any claims because the "Corpat" mark is not federally registered.

272.   Avila has prevailed in its *in rem* lawsuit. Which of the following BEST describes the remedies it may request?

      A.   Injunction, monetary damages, statutory damages and a forfeiture, cancellation or transfer order.

      B.   Injunction, monetary damages or statutory damages and a forfeiture, cancellation or transfer order.

      C.   Injunction and a forfeiture, cancellation or transfer order.

      D.   A forfeiture, cancellation or transfer order

Pine Corporation is the owner of the federally registered and incontestable "Spruce" mark which it uses on its lumber products. BigGuys Ltd. has registered the "Spruce.com" domain name for a website.

273.   Pine Corporation brings a Uniform Domain Name Dispute Resolution action (UDRP action) against BigGuys which is the authorized dispute resolution mechanism under BigGuys' contract with the domain name registrar. Which of the following is Pine NOT required to prove in order to prevail on the merits?

      A.   The "Spruce.com" domain name is likely to cause confusion.

      B.   The "Spruce.com" domain name is identical or confusingly similar to its mark.

      C.   BigGuys has no legitimate interests in the domain name.

      D.   BigGuys' registration and use of the domain name were in bad faith.

274.   The facts are as stated in Question 273 immediately above PLUS BigGuys has no prior connection to the word "spruce," it did not set up or post anything on the associated website and it provided inaccurate contact details in its registration. Which of the following BEST describes the most difficult element of Pine's case against BigGuys?

      A.   The relationship between its mark and the domain name.

      B.   BigGuys' motivation in registering the domain name.

      C.   BigGuys' bad faith use of the mark.

      D.   BigGuys' interest in the domain name.

275.   The facts are as stated in Question 274 above EXCEPT as follows: BigGuys Ltd. makes clothing products. It adopted the "Spruce" mark for a new line of seasonal men's casual clothing. Shortly after introducing that product line BigGuys registered the "Spruce.com" domain name. It never set up or used an associated website and six months later

approached Pine about buying the domain name for $5000. Pine immediately started an UDRP proceeding against BigGuys and won. The UDRP panel ordered transfer of the domain name to Pine. Does BigGuys have any recourse?

ANSWER:

276. Briefly describe the arguments which will be made by the parties in the action identified in Question 275 immediately above and identify who you believe is likely to win.

ANSWER:

Prosit Corporation makes and sells a yellow-colored pale ale beer. It has been using the trademark "Amber Ale" on the product for the last 10 years. Six years ago Prosit obtained a federal registration for the "Amber Ale" mark.

277.   Which of the following was LEAST LIKELY an issue in the registration proceeding before the Patent and Trademark Office when Prosit sought to register the "Amber Ale" trademark?

    A.   Whether the mark was generic.

    B.   Whether the mark was inherently distinctive.

    C.   Whether the mark had secondary meaning.

    D.   Whether the mark was used in commerce.

Assume that the "Amber Ale" mark was ultimately determined to be descriptive but with secondary meaning. The Patent and Trademark Office therefore approved its federal registration and that the mark is now incontestable.

Smallbeers, LLC has just started making and selling its own yellow-colored pale ale in a small corner of southeastern Texas. Its product carries the following marking "Smallbeers Amber Pale Ale." Prosit has sued Smallbeers for infringement of its "Amber Ale" mark.

278.   Which of the following will be MOST relevant to Smallbeers' defense that it is not infringing Prosit's "Amber Ale" mark?

    A.   Smallbeers pale ale is amber colored.

    B.   Smallbeers was unaware of Prosit's trademark.

    C.   Prosit's mark is invalid because it is descriptive.

    D.   Smallbeers is only using the mark in a small area of Texas.

279.   What is the name of Smallbeer's most likely defense against Prosit's claim of infringement identified in Question 278 immediately above?

    A.   Tertium quid.

    B.   Good faith use.

    C.   Fair use.

  D. Nominative use.

280. Briefly explain the rationale behind the above exception (defense) to an infringement claim.

ANSWER:

281. Which of the following is LEAST relevant to Smallbeers' use of the defense in the case?

  A. Whether Smallbeers is using the mark for criticism or commentary.

  B. Whether Smallbeers use of "amber ale" describes its product.

  C. Whether Smallbeers use of "amber ale" confuses consumers.

  D. Prosit's rights in the mark are incontestable.

282. Which of the following BEST describes the role of consumer confusion in Smallbeers' use of the defense?

  A. It is irrelevant.

  B. If confusion exists, Smallbeers may lose on the defense.

  C. If Prosit proves confusion exists, Smallbeers loses on the defense.

  D. Smallbeers must prove no confusion exists to prevail on the defense.

283. Which of the following BEST describes the role of Smallbeers' motivation in using the words "amber" and "ale" in its product marking?

  A. It is irrelevant.

  B. It is evidence of possible consumer confusion.

  C. Bad faith is determinative.

  D. Good faith is determinative.

284. Briefly describe the arguments that Prosit and Smallbeers will likely make on these facts regarding the defense, which argument is more likely to prevail and why.

ANSWER:

285. Assume that Smallbeers was instead using the phrase "Smallbeers Amber Ale." Which of the following BEST describes the likely outcome?

  A. Smallbeers will win the case.

    B.   Prosit will win based on likelihood of confusion.

    C.   Prosit will win based on fair use.

    D.   Prosit will win based on sponsorship/affiliation confusion.

286.   If Smallbeers wants to mitigate the risk of using the phrase "Smallbeers Amber Ale" what might it do?

ANSWER:

Miracle Corporation makes a hand and face cream that they sell under the trademark "Smooth Skin." The mark is federally registered and incontestable. PGS, Inc. is contemplating introducing a new hand and face cream product.

287.   Which of the following proposed PGS advertising slogans is LEAST LIKELY to avoid infringement of Miracle's trademark based on the fair use defense?

    A.   "PGS's Argos hand cream gives you smooth skin."

    B.   "Get smooth skin from PGS."

    C.   "Get Smooth Skin From PGS.

    D.   "Smooth Skin From PGS."

Fred Renaldo is a famous wine-maker. He has labeled his wines "Renaldo" for over 20 years. The mark has clearly demonstrated secondary meaning, Fred obtained a federal registration and the mark is now incontestable. Fred's brother George Renaldo has recently given up his faltering career as a trademark lawyer and has started his own wine making business. George has decided to use the mark "Renaldo."

288.   Which of the following BEST describes George's right to use his family name on his wines?

    A.   George can use "Renaldo" because it really is his last name.

    B.   George can use "Renaldo" as a trademark.

    C.   George can use "Renaldo" to clearly identify himself as the wine's producer.

    D.   George can use "Renaldo" to clearly identity and distinguish himself from Fred as the wine's producer

WHYNOT, LLC makes and sells an expensive perfume under its federally registered, incontestable "Sweet Scent" trademark. The Sweet Scent perfume is normally sold only in high-end specialty stores at a premium price. LowCost Megastores, Inc., a California discount chain, purchases and resells the original Sweet Scent perfumes. In its weekly advertisements LowCost prominently features the following: "**Sweet Scent** perfumes as much as 80% off suggested retail." WHYNOT sues LowCost for trademark infringement in California.

289.   Which of the following is LowCost's BEST defense?

    A.   Fair use.

    B.   No likelihood of confusion.

    C.   Nominative use.

    D.   No likelihood of dilution.

290.   Would the BEST answer be different if the lawsuit where brought in another jurisdiction?

ANSWER:

291.   Which of the following is LowCost NOT required to show in making out its defense?

    A.   That WHYNOT's does not have a valid trademark.

    B.   That WHYNOT's goods cannot be identified without use of the mark.

    C.   That LowCost used only so much of WHYNOT's mark as necessary to identify the goods.

    D.   That consumers will not assume any endorsement, sponsorship or affiliation between LowCost and WHYNOT.

292.   Based on the facts to hand in Question 289 above, does LowCost have a viable defense?

ANSWER:

293.   Would the answer change if LowCost also advertised itself as "THE Sweet Scent Emporium?" Why or why not?

ANSWER:

Jake's automobile shop specializes in Trebant vehicle repairs. Jake wants to advertise that fact. Trebant is a valid, incontestable trademark of the manufacturer of Trebant vehicles. Jake has no connection with or authorization from the manufacturer.

294.   Order the following from WORST to BEST in regard to maximizing Jake's nominative use defense if he is sued by the manufacturer.

    A.   Jake's Trebant Repairs.

    B.   Jake's Automotive — Trebant repairs.

    C.   Jake's Trebant.

    D.   Jake's Automotive — the Trebant repair specialist.

Flam Perridle was the not particularly good drummer for the band Rock-Your-World. The band was very well-known for its spectacular live concerts. Although The Band LLC, the group's legal entity which owns the incontestable trademark "Rock-Your-World," continues to exist and the group's recordings remain on sale, they have not performed or recorded together for several years. Six months ago Flam's bank account was running dangerously low, so he assembled a group of musicians, none of them members of the original group, to take on tour. He titled the tour "**Rock-Your-World**, Flam on Tour." The tour has been underway for a month and has gone very well, including unexpectedly large crowds.

295.   At the behest of group's other original members The Band LLC has now sued Flam for infringing its "Rock-Your-World mark. How would a court MOST LIKELY rule?

    A.   For Flam, because there is no way to refer to his membership in the band without using the trademark.

    B.   Against Flam because he was only a member of the band and is never allowed to use the mark by himself.

    C.   For Flam, based on the fair use defense.

    D.   Against Flam, because consumers believe his tour was endorsed by the band.

Gooddeals LLC makes and sells caps and tee-shirts. Gooddeals business concept is to permit consumers to buy caps and shirts which show their support of favorite sports teams at very reasonable prices. Therefore, each of its products bears a trademark owned by a professional sports franchise or college team. Gooddeals does not have the approval of the trademark owners. Each Gooddeals product clearly bears the "Gooddeals" trademark and its product packaging expressly states that neither Gooddeals nor its products have any approval or other connection with the trademark owner. One of the trademark owners has sued Gooddeals for trademark infringement.

296.   Which of the following is Gooddeals' BEST defense on the above facts?

    A.   Trademark fair use.

    B.   Aesthetic functionality.

    C.   Not a trademark use.

    D.   No likelihood of confusion

Grandluxe Co. owns and uses the mark "Oro" for its line of extremely high-end home furnishings. The mark is federally registered and incontestable.

297.   As part of a laudatory feature article on the fabulously wealthy, a national news magazine repeatedly refers to such individuals as "living the much desired Oro life." Grandluxe brings a lawsuit for trademark infringement against the magazine. Which of the following is the magazine's BEST defense?

    A.   Trademark fair use.

    B.   Nominative use.

    C.   Freedom of speech.

    D.   Non-trademark use.

298.   Instead of a laudatory news magazine article, a critic of the wealthy has made and sold tee shirts carrying the slogan "Oro-freaks" in the international "no" symbol of a red circle with a diagonal line drawn through it. If Grandluxe sues the critic, which of the following is the critic's BEST defense?

    A.   Fair use.

    B.   Nominative use.

    C.   Freedom of speech.

    D.   Parody.

299.   The facts are as stated in Question 298 immediately above. Is it relevant to the critic's defense that there may be adequate alternative means to make his point that do not involve using Grandluxe's "Oro" trademark?

ANSWER:

300.   The facts are as stated in Question 298 above. Is it relevant that the critic is making money from the sale of the tee shirts?

ANSWER:

301.   The facts are as stated in Question 298 above. Is it relevant to the critic's defense that it has not published his "commentary" in a traditional outlet such as a newspaper or a magazine editorial?

ANSWER:

Outdoor Gear, Inc. makes and sells recreational vehicles under the "Muscle" trademark. The mark is federally registered and incontestable. The Friends of the Environment, a non-profit environmental group, is upset with the negative environmental effects of Muscle vehicles, particularly when used off-road in parks and wilderness areas. To make the point, Friends' produces a fake advertisement for a non-existent Muscle vehicle which includes a picture of a person driving that vehicle through a field of flowers under the caption "There's nothing "Muscle" won't do." Friends runs the advertisement in a number of popular "off-roading" magazines. After the advertisement has run Outdoor receives large numbers of phone calls, most of which are from customers asking where they can purchase the non-existent vehicle. Outdoor sues Friends for trademark infringement.

302.   Which of the following BEST describes the likely outcome of the case?

   A.   Outdoor will win based on Friends having taken the risk that the parody will fail.

   B.   Outdoor will win based on a traditional infringement "factors" analysis.

   C.   Friends will win based on the parody defense.

   D.   Friends will win based on its good faith intent.

303.   Which of following BEST captures the essence of the trademark First Amendment inquiry, thus making it a helpful "rule of thumb" in assessing the trademark free speech defense?

   A.   Permissible commentary.

   B.   Non-commercial use.

   C.   Likelihood of consumer confusion.

   D.   Non-trademark use.

304.   What does the answer to Question 303 immediately above indicate about the burden of proof regarding trademark free speech defenses?

ANSWER:

Ergo Inc. is a nationally recognized producer of organic foods under the extremely well-known "NatureSafe" mark. The mark is registered and incontestable. Lema Muckracker has started a new consumer advocacy group under the name "Nature's Not Safe with NatureSafe." The group's purpose is to publicize what it considers Ergo's environmentally unsound agricultural practices and audacity at claiming its products are organic. The group has very successfully used its name to collect substantial donations from passionate environmentalists.

305.   Proving which of the following will be MOST important to the group if Ergo sues claiming that use of "NatureSafe" in the organization's name violates Ergo's trademark rights?

   A.   No likelihood of confusion.

   B.   Non-commercial use.

   C.   Permissible commentary.

   D.   Fair use

Eric purchased a television set made by Zistro Corporation bearing the company's "Zistro" trademark. The set performed admirably in all respects. Eric decided to upgrade to a newer model. He sold his used "Zistro" television via an advertisement on Craig's List.

306. Which of the following BEST explains why Eric can resell the television with the "Zistro" mark attached without infringing Zistro Corporation's trademark rights?

    A. Fair use.

    B. Nominative use.

    C. Trademark exhaustion.

    D. No likelihood of confusion

TVsForLess sells genuine "Zistro" television sets at retail for substantial discounts. It purchases the televisions new from authorized Zistro retailers who have acquired them directly from the manufacturer, Zistro Corporation. TVsForLess leaves the televisions in their original packaging and resells them without any alteration, including leaving the "Zistro" trademark attached and visible on the packaging and the products. TVsForLess does not have Zistro Corporation's authorization to purchase or sell its products or to use its "Zistro" trademark.

307. If TVsForLess sells the televisions from a store named "The Zistro Preferred Center" which of the following BEST describes the applicability of the first sale doctrine to its activities?

    A. The doctrine permits the sales because the goods are genuine.

    B. The doctrine permits the sales provided there is no consumer confusion.

    C. The doctrine probably does not permit the sales on these facts.

    D. The doctrine is not relevant on these facts.

308. TVsForLess changes the name of its store to "TVs For Less" and specifically disclaims any involvement of, or affiliation with, the Zistro Corporation with large signs posted near the television set display and at the cashier. Which of the following BEST describes the applicability of the first sale doctrine to TVsForLess' activities in these circumstances?

    A. The doctrine permits the sales because the goods are genuine.

    B. The doctrine probably permits the sales because the disclaimers eliminate the possibility of post-sale confusion.

    C.   The doctrine probably does not permit the sales because of likely post-sale confusion.

    D.   The doctrine is not relevant on these facts.

309.   The facts are as stated in Question 308 immediately above except that TVsForLess has not posted any disclaimers stating Zistro Corporation's lack of involvement or affiliation. Which of the following BEST describes the applicability of the first sale doctrine to TVsForLess' activities in these circumstances?

    A.   The doctrine permits the sales because the goods are genuine.

    B.   The doctrine permits the sales because TVsForLess has taken no affirmative steps to imply Zistro involvement beyond selling genuine goods.

    C.   The doctrine does not permit the sales because TVsForLess has not disclaimed any Zistro involvement.

    D.   The doctrine does not permit the sales on these facts

Flashy Dan's Inc. specializes in clothing which "makes a visual impact." It purchases genuine clothing products from the original manufacturers and then independently adds "dramatic" new design elements in the form of appliqués. It then resells the modified clothing which continues to bear the original manufacturers' trademarks.

310.   How does the first sale doctrine apply to Flashy Dan's activities?

    A.   It permits the sales because the underlying articles of clothing are genuine.

    B.   It permits the sales because the trademark owner rather than Flashy Dan applied the trademark to the goods.

    C.   It does not permit the sales because Flashy Dan's does not have the trademark owners' authorization to make the modifications.

    D.   It does not permit the sales because Flashy Dan's use of the mark is misleading.

311.   Does it change the above result if Flashy Dan's can prove that in every case the consumer is getting a more valuable garment?

ANSWER:

312.   Which of the following is MOST LIKELY to change the above outcome and permit Flashy Dan's reliance on the first sale doctrine as a defense to a manufacturer/trademark owner's suit for infringement?

    A.   Consumers are aware that they are purchasing the goods from Flashy Dan's and not the original manufacturer or one of its authorized dealers.

    B.   Flashy Dan's adds its own "FlashD" trademark to each garment.

      C.   Flashy Dan's promotional and sales materials (including a large sign near the products) expressly state that Flashy Dan's has independently added the appliqués.

      D.   Flashy Dan's adds a notice to each garment's exterior and interior labels expressly stating that Flashy Dan has independently added the appliqués.

Little Bottles Ltd. purchases genuine shampoos from the manufacturers and rebottles them in smaller containers for travel. On each of its smaller containers it attaches a label with the relevant manufacturer's trademark and a notice that Little Bottles has independently repackaged the original product in a new container.

313.   Which of the following BEST explains why Little Bottles can rely on the first sale doctrine in a claim brought by the manufacturers for trademark infringement?

      A.   Little Bottles has not changed the product.

      B.   The trademark accurately describes the shampoo in the bottle.

      C.   The trademark accurately describes the shampoo in the bottle and Little Bottles has indicated it independently rebottled the shampoo.

      D.   Nominative use.

314.   The facts are as stated in Question 313 immediately above, EXCEPT that Little Bottles' repackaging harms the shampoo's ability to lather and clean by exposing it to the air during the rebottling process. It is not clear on purchase that the defect exists but it is readily apparent on use. Which of the following BEST describes the effect of that harm on the first sale outcome?

      A.   Little Bottles losses on its first sale defense because consumers will only discover the defect after their purchase.

      B.   Little Bottles losses on its first sale defense because it has not given notice of the changed effectiveness of the shampoo.

      C.   Little Bottles wins on the first sale doctrine if consumers are likely to connect the ineffectiveness to Little Bottles' repackaging of the shampoo.

      D.   Little Bottles wins based on the first sale doctrine because it gave notice of its rebottling.

315.   Instead of purchasing shampoo from the manufacturers, Little Bottles instead buys defective shampoo from the services used by those manufacturers to dispose of rejected product. Little Bottles then bottles the product in its own travel-size containers each labeled with the related manufacturer's trademark and clearly stating that the product was not approved by that manufacturer. Which of the following BEST describes the effect of the first sale doctrine on Little Bottles activities?

      A.   The first sale doctrine protects the sales because Little Bottles did not modify the product.

B.   The first sale doctrine protects the sales because Little Bottles gave accurate notice of the defect.

C.   The first sale doctrine does not protect the sales because Little Bottles repackaged the product without notice.

D.   The first sale doctrine does not protect the sales because the product is not genuine.

Parnelli Company makes "fresh" frozen pizzas under the "Nona" trademark. Because the pizzas' lose their "fresh" taste after two weeks Parnelli contractually requires all of its authorized distributors to dispose of all unsold pizzas after that time. Trescheap, which is not an authorized outlet, regularly obtains Nona pizzas from Parnelli authorized outlets and resells them under the "Nona" trademark. To keep its prices low Trescheap does not adhere to the Parnelli two-week disposal requirement.

316.   Can Trescheap use the first sale defense to overcome Parnelli's claim of trademark infringement?

ANSWER:

317.   Would the outcome change if Trescheap expressly notified its customers that it did not adhere to the Parnelli disposal requirements?

ANSWER:

318.   Assume that despite Parnelli's claims that the two-week disposal requirement is vital to maintaining the pizzas' taste, Trescheap proves that it actually has no effect (on taste or otherwise) to keep the pizzas for a month, the outside limit of Trescheap's own storage. Does that mean that Trescheap can rely on the first sale doctrine?

ANSWER:

319.   Can Parnelli stop Trescheap's activities by contractually requiring that its own distributors not resell Nona pizzas to Trescheap, or does first sale "free movement of goods" policy prevent such agreements?

ANSWER:

Power Mary's LLC specializes in refurbishing automobiles. It purchases used cars and restores them to "like new" condition replacing many worn parts with new parts acquired from the original manufacturers; although as a matter of fact the cars are not quite up to the standards of a new automobile. It then resells the modified cars with the original trademarks left in place.

320. Which of the following BEST describes the application of the first sale doctrine to Power Mary's activities?

   A. It permits the sales because Power Mary's is merely restoring genuine goods.

   B. It permits the sales because Power Mary's has done nothing inconsistent with the trademark.

   C. It does not permit the sales because consumers will assume the trademark owners are involved.

   D. It does not permit the sales because Power Mary's use is misleading.

321. What should Power Mary do to allow it to claim the benefits of the first sale doctrine?

ANSWER:

322. Suppose instead of using original parts Power Mary's uses cheaper, inferior quality parts that it manufactures itself. Power Mary's gives clear notice both on sale and affixed to the cars that "cheaper, non-manufacturer parts have been used in restoration." Which of the following raises the MOST LIKELY concern regarding Power Mary's reliance on the first sale defense?

   A. The replacement parts are not from the manufacturer.

   B. The notice is inadequate.

   C. The goods have lost their identity and quality.

   D. Refurbishment is not permitted.

323. Would the problem identified in Question 322 immediately above be eliminated if Power Mary's modifications produced a substantially better automobile?

ANSWER:

324. Suppose instead of a restoration business where Power Mary's purchases and repairs and refurbishes used cars which it then resells, Power Mary's reconditions and customizes cars for individuals who deliver their own car and specify the modifications to be made. Power Mary's makes the requested modifications and delivers the car back to the owner with the trademarks still affixed. Which of the following BEST describes the application of the first sale doctrine to a claim of infringement brought against Power Mary's by the trademark owner?

A. It permits Power Mary's activities.

B. It is of no assistance in the claim of infringement.

C. It is irrelevant.

D. It permits the sales if Power Mary's gives notice of the modifications it has made.

BigDeal Corp sells its toothpaste products in a number of countries around the world. It uses the same "Carat" trademark on all of its products. BigDeal has discovered that ReImp is purchasing its toothpaste at low cost in England and importing it back into the United States for sale.

325. In which of the following circumstances is BigDeal MOST likely to overcome ReImp's first sale defense to a suit to trademark infringement?

A. The imported toothpaste is sold by BigDeal's English subsidiary.

B. The imported toothpaste is identical to the toothpaste sold in the United States.

C. The imported toothpaste is identical to the toothpaste sold in the United States except it tastes different.

D. The imported toothpaste was not made in the United States.

No-Motors uses the "Vanti" trademark on the mountain bicycles it manufactures and sells in Washington, Oregon and Idaho. It brought a federal trademark infringement suit against NewCorp which was using the "Vanti" mark on its own mountain bike products in those and other geographic territories. No-Motors won the lawsuit.

326. Which of the following BEST describes the available remedies set out in the Lanham Act?

   A. Injunction, NewCorp's profits, No-Motors' damages, costs and attorneys' fees.

   B. Injunction, NewCorp's profits, No-Motors' damages and costs.

   C. Injunction, No-Motors' damages, and costs.

   D. Injunction and No-Motors' damages.

327. Which of the following BEST describes the effect on the basic Lanham Act remedies if No-Motors holds a federal registration on its "Vanti" mark?

   A. There are no remedies for unregistered marks.

   B. The remedies for registered marks are very different.

   C. The basic remedies are the same for registered and unregistered marks.

   D. The remedies are identical for registered and unregistered marks.

328. Which of the following BEST describes the likelihood that No-Motors will be granted a permanent injunction against NewCorp's continued use of the mark?

   A. Possible.

   B. Very likely.

   C. Very unlikely.

   D. Only if No-Motors demonstrates exceptional circumstances.

329. The facts are as stated before Question 326, PLUS No-Motors does not hold a federal registration in the "Vanti" mark. Which of the following BEST describes the permanent injunction likely to be issued (assuming one is issued) against NewCorp?

   A. Preventing any use likely to cause consumer confusion.

   B. Preventing any use of the "Vanti" mark on mountain bikes.

C. Preventing the use of the "Vanti" or similar marks on mountain bikes likely to cause confusion.

D. Preventing the use of the "Vanti" or similar marks on mountain bikes in geographic areas likely to cause confusion.

Oscelot Enterprises uses the mark "Cat" to identify its stationary supplies. It holds a federal registration for all kinds of stationary supplies and the mark is incontestable. Oscelot has recently discovered that one of its competitors, Stationers Inc. has adopted "Kats" as its mark for a new line of its stationary supplies. Oscelot has filed a trademark infringement suit against Stationers and moved for a preliminary injunction preventing Stationers from using its mark until final adjudication on the merits at trial.

330. Which of the following BEST identifies the public interest which should be taken into account when determining whether to issue the preliminary injunction?

A. Avoiding confusion.

B. Ensuring efficient, robust competition.

C. The balance between confusion and competition.

D. An equitable balancing of hardships.

331. Which of the following identifies the MOST crucial element to Oscelot's obtaining a preliminary injunction?

A. The necessity of preserving the status quo.

B. Likelihood of success on the merits.

C. Probable success on the merits.

D. That the balance of hardships favors Oscelot.

332. Explain how the showing identified in Question 331 immediately above affects the other factors applied by a court in deciding to issue a preliminary injunction.

ANSWER:

333. Based on the facts stated before Question 330 above which of the following BEST describes the outcome on Oscelot's request for a preliminary injunction?

A. Very likely.

B. Likely.

C. Very unlikely.

D. Not going to happen.

334. The facts are as stated before Question 330 above EXCEPT Oscelot has waited a year after discovering Stationers' use to bring a trademark infringement suit against Stationers. Which of the following BEST describes the outcome on Oscelot's request for a preliminary injunction?

    A. Likely.

    B. Unlikely.

    C. Very unlikely.

    D. Not going to happen.

335. The facts are as stated before Question 330 EXCEPT Oscelot has moved so expeditiously that there is no evidence of any actual consumer confusion or, for that matter, any harm to either Oscelot or its "Cat" mark. Which of the following BEST describes the effect of that quick action on availability of injunctive relief?

    A. No preliminary or permanent injunction will be available.

    B. No preliminary injunction, but a permanent injunction will be available.

    C. A preliminary injunction, but no permanent injunction will be available.

    D. Both preliminary and permanent injunctions are available.

John Furvitch makes his living writing, performing and selling recordings of humorous songs which discuss in a critical way the brand messages of various famous trademarks. He has been sued by the owner of one such trademark seeking a preliminary injunction against another such song.

336. What additional special consideration might affect the issuance of a preliminary injunction if John raises the parody defense?

ANSWER:

Bean Blossom Enterprises manufactures and sells very high-end pens under the "Scriz" trademark. It holds a federal registration on the mark for pens and other writing implements and the mark has become incontestable. It has just discovered that a new company, Duo, Ltd., has introduced a line of extremely similar pens bearing the "Scriz" mark.

337. Which of following BEST describes what Bean Blossom must show to prove that Duo is using a "counterfeit mark"?

    A. The Duo is acting in bad faith.

    B. That Duo's "Scriz" mark is indistinguishable from Bean Blossom's mark.

    C. That Duo knew Bean Blossom's "Scriz" mark was federally registered.

    D. It cannot prove the mark is counterfeit on these facts.

338. Which of the following BEST describes the outcome if Bean Blossom makes an *ex parte* request for the immediate seizure of Duo's pens and records?

    A. Bean Blossom cannot get such an order because Lanham Act § 34(d) (15 U.S.C. § 1116(d)) only applies to marks found to infringe.

    B. Bean Blossom cannot get such an order because Lanham Act § 34(d) (15 U.S.C. § 1116(d)) only permits seizure of the pens.

    C. Bean Blossom can get the order if it posts a bond.

    D. Bean Blossom can get the order if it shows the order is required to avoid immediate and irreparable harm.

339. If Bean Blossom had not federally registered its "Scriz" mark does that eliminate the possibility of pre-trial seizure of the goods?

ANSWER:

Orange Corp sells chocolate candy under the federally registered "Fantasy" trademark. It has won a trademark infringement lawsuit against Second Inc. for selling candy using the "Fantasy" mark.

340. Which of the following is NOT one of the monetary awards Orange can request under Lanham Act § 35(a) (15 U.S.C. § 1117(a))?

    A. Second's profits.

    B. Orange's damages.

    C. Punitive damages.

    D. Costs of suit.

341. Does the answer to Question 340 immediately above mean that Orange can never receive that monetary award under trademark law?

ANSWER:

342. Which of the following is LEAST relevant to Orange's ability to collect monetary damages for harm it has suffered?

    A. Forseeability.

    B. Causation.

    C. The fact of harm.

    D. The amount of harm.

343.   Which of the following BEST describes role of "actual confusion" in the award of monetary damages for harm suffered by Orange?

    A.   Proof of actual confusion is always required to demonstrate harm.

    B.   It is never required; infringement only requires a likelihood of confusion.

    C.   It is required to show the requisite bad faith.

    D.   It is good evidence of harm and causation.

344.   Why does Orange's inability to definitively demonstrate both causation and the amount of harm not necessarily preclude an award of damages for harm actually suffered?

ANSWER:

345.   The facts are as stated before Question 340 above, PLUS Orange can prove: Duo's candy is inferior to Orange's product and Orange would have made 75% of the sales made by Duo absent Duo's infringement. Which of the following is LEAST appropriate as compensation for the actual harm suffered by Orange as a result of Duo's infringement under these circumstances?

    A.   Orange's profits on its sales lost to Duo.

    B.   The costs of Orange's corrective advertising.

    C.   Duo's profits on the sale of its products.

    D.   Harm to the reputation of Orange's "Fantasy" mark.

346.   Which of the following is generally key to Orange obtaining the monetary award identified as the LEAST appropriate measure of its actual damages in Question 345 immediately above?

    A.   Duo's willful infringement.

    B.   That Orange actually suffered lost sales.

    C.   Orange's federal trademark registration.

    D.   Duo's knowledge of Orange's federal registration.

347.   Which of the following is the BEST policy justification supporting an award of defendant's profits under the Lanham Act?

    A.   Equitable recognition of the difficulty of proving actual damages.

    B.   The equitable theory of unjust enrichment.

    C.   Deterrence of infringement.

    D.   Punishment for willful infringement.

348. If a court awards Orange an accounting of Duo's profits under the Lanham Act, which of the following BEST describes the burden of proof?

A. Orange must prove Duo's profits.

B. Orange must prove Duo's sales, Duo must prove any reductions.

C. Orange must prove its reduction in sales; Duo must prove those sales were not lost to Duo.

D. Orange must prove Duo's sales and Orange's resulting lost profits.

349. The facts are as stated in Question 345, PLUS Orange has been awarded an accounting of Duo's profits. Which of the following BEST describes the basis on which Orange might receive up to a trebling of those profits under the Lanham Act?

A. Trebling is automatic once an accounting is granted.

B. Trebling is granted if necessary to fully compensate Orange.

C. Trebling only applies to compensatory damages for actual harm.

D. Trebling is granted when appropriate to deter/punish infringement.

Nateast Company uses the federally registered "Star" trademark on its medical equipment. It has won a Lanham Act trademark infringement lawsuit against NewMed Corp., its competitor, for use of the "Star" mark on competing products.

350. Which of the following BEST describes the effect on Nateast's request for monetary damages of its failure to give the required statutory notice of its registration?

A. Nateast can recover all monetary damages.

B. Nateast can recover all monetary damages from the time NewCorp. had actual notice of the federal registration.

C. Nateast can only recover compensatory damages for actual harm suffered.

D. Nateast can only recover damages if it can prove that NewMed willfully infringed.

351. The facts are as stated in Question 350 immediately above EXCEPT that Nateast has proven that NewMed's infringement involved its intentional and knowing use of a counterfeit mark. Which of the following BEST describes the effect of that finding on Nateast's claim for monetary damages?

A. Nateast is entitled to treble damages absent extenuating circumstances.

B. Nateast is entitled to treble the monetary damages awarded if required to fully compensate Nateast for actual harm suffered.

C. Nateast is entitled to treble the monetary damages awarded for periods after NewMed had actual notice of Nateast's federal registration.

D. Nateast is not entitled to any monetary damages because it did not provide notice of its federal registration.

352. The facts are as stated in Question 351 immediately above. Which of the following is NOT an additional remedy available to Nateast on these facts?

    A. Statutory damages.

    B. Attorney's fees.

    C. Prejudgment interest.

    D. Criminal fines.

353. Which of the following BEST describes the court's ability to assess costs and attorneys' fees in a regular (non-counterfeit mark) infringement case under the Lanham Act?

    A. The court must award costs and attorneys' fees to a prevailing plaintiff.

    B. The court may award costs and attorneys' fees to the prevailing party.

    C. The court may award costs to a prevailing plaintiff and attorneys' fees to the prevailing party in exceptional circumstances.

    D. The court may award costs and, in exceptional circumstances, attorneys' fees to the prevailing party.

Zastra Corporation has prevailed in an action for dilution of its famous "Z-TEC" mark.

354. Which of the following BEST describes its available remedies?

    A. A permanent injunction.

    B. A permanent injunction and monetary damages under Lanham Act § 35(a).

    C. Upon a showing of willfulness, a permanent injunction and monetary damages under Lanham Act § 35(a).

    D. A permanent injunction and, upon a showing of willfulness, monetary damages under Lanham Act § 35(a)

Diesel LLC makes and sells commercial trucks and related parts. For 20 years Diesel has used the "PowerT" mark on its heavy duty dump trucks. The mark is federally registered and incontestable.

355. Which of the following BEST describes what could cause Diesel to lose its rights in the "PowerT" mark?

    A. Failure to timely renew its federal registration.

    B. Diesel stops using the mark.

    C. The mark ceases to identify and distinguish Diesels' dump trucks.

    D. Expiration of the term of protection.

356. The facts are as stated in Question 355 immediately above PLUS the public has begun to call all dump trucks in the class made by Diesel a "PowerT." Which of the following BEST describes how this affects Diesel's rights in the "PowerT" mark?

    A. Loss of all rights in the mark through genericide.

    B. Generic abandonment arising from the "conduct of the owner."

    C. An infringer can challenge the mark's validity in an infringement lawsuit despite its incontestable status.

    D. Diesel's federal registration can be cancelled.

The facts are as stated in Question 355 above EXCEPT that Diesel stopped using the "PowerT" mark on its dump trucks three and one-half years ago. A competitor, NuTrucks Inc. has recently adopted the "PowerT" mark for its own dump trucks. Diesel has brought a trademark infringement action against NuTrucks. NuTrucks has raised an abandonment defense.

357. Which of the following BEST describes the abandonment defense?

    A. Diesel must prove its intent to (re)commence use of the mark.

    B. Diesel must prove it did not intend to abandon the mark.

    C. NuTrucks must prove Diesel's non-use of the mark.

    D. NuTrucks must prove Diesel's non-use of the mark and Diesel's lack of intent to resume such use.

358. What language in the Lanham Act definition of "abandonment" provides significant assistance to NuTrucks (as a federal trademark infringement defendant) in making out its abandonment defense on these facts?

ANSWER:

359. Rank the following from LEAST to MOST helpful to Diesel's countering NuTrucks' abandonment defense on these facts.

   A. The mark is federally registered and incontestable.

   B. Diesel's President's affidavit stating Diesel's bona fide intent to resume use of the mark.

   C. Evidence that Diesel has infrequently made and sold tee-shirts bearing the "PowerT" mark emblazoned on the front.

   D. Diesel's business plan showing future sales of a newly designed dump truck under the "PowerT" mark.

360. What additional piece of factual information is important to ascertaining the strength of the "MOST helpful" answer to the previous question?

ANSWER:

361. Assume that Diesel has stipulated both to its non-use of the "PowerT" mark for the last three and one-half years and that it had at the time of cessation of use, and now has, no intent to resume such use at any time in the foreseeable future. Instead Diesel proves that its infrequent tee-shirt sales bearing the mark reflect a continuing strong consumer association between the "PowerT" mark and Diesel's dump trucks. Which of the following BEST describes how a court might deal with that association on these facts?

   A. The association should be treated as "use" of the mark.

   B. Prohibit all use of the mark by NuTrucks.

   C. Permit use by NuTrucks with appropriate disclaimers.

   D. Permit use by NuTrucks only on its dump trucks.

362. What difference would it make to NuTrucks abandonment defense if Diesel had been prevented from making its "PowerT" dump trucks by newly imposed regulatory requirements?

ANSWER:

For 10 years Slice Co. used the "Glide" mark on the shaving razors which it manufactured and sold throughout the United States. Five years ago the company fell on hard times and consolidated its operations and sales in the Southeastern United States. At that time it also reduced its product lines, including elimination of the "Glide" razor and ceased all use of the mark. Although it is clear that Slice had no intention of ever resuming use of the "Glide" mark at the time it ceased use or for nearly four and one-half years thereafter, six months ago Slice launched a new shaving razor under the "Glide" name in its Southeastern market. Two months ago Burn Ltd. began using the "Glide" mark on a new line of shaving razors which it sells in the Northwestern United States. Neither party has federally registered the mark.

363.	If Slice sues Burn for trademark infringement under the Lanham Act which of the following BEST describes how abandonment affects the outcome of the suit?

A.	Slice wins because it did not abandon the "Glide" mark.

B.	Burn wins because Slice abandoned the "Glide" mark.

C.	Burn wins because Slice's rights only extend to the Southeastern United States.

D.	Slice wins because Slice's rights revert to "nationwide" on its resumption of use

The facts are as stated in Question 363 immediately above EXCEPT that when Slice stopped using the "Glide" mark five years ago it licensed Makem, Inc. to make and sell the Slice shaving razor nationwide under the "Glide" mark, subject to Makem's adherence to strictly monitored contractual quality standards.

364.	If Slice sues Burn for trademark infringement under the Lanham Act which of the following BEST describes how "abandonment" affects outcome of the suit?

A.	Slice wins because it did not abandon the "Glide" mark.

B.	Burn wins because Slice abandoned the "Glide" mark.

C.	Burn wins because Slice's rights only extend to the Southeastern United States.

D.	Slice wins because Slice's rights revert to "nationwide" on its resumption of use.

365.	The facts are as stated in Question 364 immediately above EXCEPT for the quality control proviso. Which of the following alternative quality control arrangements between Slice and Makem would be MOST helpful to Burn's abandonment claim?

A.	Slice's license to Makem contains an express contractual provision setting quality standards and giving Slice full rights to monitor the compliance of Makem's razors.

B.	Slice's license to Makem contains an express contractual provision setting quality standards and giving Slice full rights to monitor the quality of Makem's razors, but the provision has never been implemented by Slice.

C.	Slice's license to Makem contains no contractual quality or monitoring provisions, but the parties regularly inspect Makem's razors.

D.	Slice's license to Makem contains an express contractual provision setting quality standards but no right for Slice to monitor quality, but Slice has an excellent long-standing relationship with Makem as a licensed manufacturer of various other Slice trademarked products

Instead of abandoning or licensing the "Glide" mark, assume Slice decided to sell the mark.

366. List the following from MOST to LEAST LIKELY as a valid assignment of the "Glide" trademark by Slice.

    A. To a competitor for use on its much lower quality shaving razors.

    B. To a new company which plans to make and sell shaving razors.

    C. To the buyer of Slice's Glide razor business.

    D. To a competitor for use on its similar shaving razors.

367. Slice has sold the "Glide" mark to Floorit, LLC, a company that makes floor finishes. Slice stops using the mark after making the transfer. Six months after the sale transaction but before Floorit started using the "Glide" mark, one of Floorit's competitors started selling a floor polish product using the "Glide" mark. Which of the following BEST describes the outcome if Floorit sues its competitor for trademark infringement?

    A. Floorit wins because it is the owner of the "Glide" mark purchased from Slice.

    B. Floorit wins because it is the owner of the "Glide" mark as a result of its use.

    C. Competitor wins; because Slice did not exercise any quality control the mark is abandoned.

    D. Competitor wins because the assignment to Floorit conveys no rights.

368. The facts are as stated in Question 367 immediately above EXCEPT the competitor started selling a floor polish product using the "Glide" mark six months after Floorit had starting using the mark on one of its own floor polish products. Which of the following BEST describes the outcome if Floorit sues its competitor for trademark infringement?

    A. Floorit wins as the owner of the "Glide" mark by purchase from Slice.

    B. Floorit wins as the owner of the "Glide" mark by use.

    C. Competitor wins; because Slice did not exercise any quality control the mark is abandoned.

    D. Competitor wins because the assignment to Floorit conveys no rights.

369.   A court has ruled Slice's transfer of the "Glide" mark to Floorit is an assignment in gross. What rights does Slice have in the mark?

ANSWER:

Pressit Company uses the federally registered "Echo" trademark on its acclaimed olive oil products. It markets and sells its product exclusively in the United States. It holds no foreign registrations in the "Echo" mark. The Pressit Vice President of Marketing has just returned from a European trade show having discovered that Miracolo S.A. has obtained an Italian registration for the "Echo" mark and is using it on its own olive oil products produced and currently marketed and sold exclusively in Italy.

370. Which of the following BEST describes Pressit's ability to stop Miracolo's use of the "Echo" mark in Italy based on Pressit's United States rights in the mark in a United States court?

    A. United States trademark rights have no effect on use in Italy.

    B. Miracolo's use does not support extraterritorial application of Pressit's United States trademark rights.

    C. Miracolo's use supports extraterritorial application of Pressit's United States trademark rights.

    D. Pressit's United States trademark rights permit it to stop Miracolo's use in Italy under the Paris Convention.

371. Which of the following additional facts would MOST LIKELY change the outcome in the Question immediately above?

    A. Miracolo is a partnership owned and operated by United States citizens based and residing in New York, New York.

    B. Miracolo knew about Pressit's adoption and use of the "Echo" mark in the United States at the time it adopted the mark in Italy.

    C. Miracolo's Italian registration for the mark is invalid.

    D. Miracolo purchases the bottles it uses for its olive oil in the United States with the labels already attached.

372. Assume the following specific facts about Miracolo: Miracolo is an Italian company, owned and operated by Italian citizens resident in Italy. Miracolo owns valid Italian trademark rights in Italy. Miracolo sources, makes and sells it product exclusively in Italy. Its advertising is also entirely local to Italy but it does post those materials to

its internationally accessible www.echo.it company website. Which of the following BEST describes the likely REMEDIAL outcome in a successful suit by Pressit seeking extraterritorial enforcement of its United States trademark rights?

A.   Pressit will obtain no relief.

B.   Pressit will likely obtain an injunction prohibiting all sales of "Echo" olive oil by Miracolo.

C.   Pressit will likely obtain an injunction prohibiting sales of "Echo" olive oil by Miracolo in the United States.

D.   Pressit will likely obtain an injunction limiting Miracolo actions which may have a significant adverse effect on the United States marketplace.

373.   What advice should a lawyer give to clients concerned about foreign adoption of their United States trademarks?

ANSWER:

374.   Under the facts set out in Questions 370 and 372 above, which of the following BEST describes when the famous mark doctrine may help Pressit obtain relief against Miracolo's use in Italy of the "Echo" mark?

A.   Paris Convention protection of famous marks applies if Pressit's Echo mark is well known in the United States olive oil market.

B.   Paris Convention protection of famous marks applies if Pressit's Echo mark is well known in the Italian olive oil market.

C.   TRIPS protection of famous marks applies if Pressit's Echo mark is well known to Italian olive oil consumers.

D.   TRIPS protection of famous marks applies if Pressit's Echo mark is well known in Italy.

Pasta S.A. makes, markets and sells a variety of pasta products under the mark "Barrita." Pasta has registered the "Barrita" mark in Italy but no where else. Pasta's business activities are currently limited exclusively to a very small area of southern Italy. There is no evidence that any United States citizens have seen or heard of Pasta S.A. or its pasta products, much less purchased them. Pasta has just discovered that Spag LLC, a United States company, has recently registered and is using the "Barrita" mark on Spag's pasta products marketed and sold exclusively in the United States. Spag had no knowledge of Pasta's adoption or use of the mark at the time it adopted the "Barrita" mark in the United States.

375.   Which of the following BEST describes the outcome on the above facts if Pasta seeks relief under the Lanham Act regarding Spag's use of the "Barrita" mark in the United States?

A. Pasta will lose because it must have registered the mark in the United States to obtain rights under the Lanham Act.

B. Pasta will lose because it has no enforceable United States trademark rights under the Lanham Act.

C. Pasta will win because having registered the mark in Italy before Spag's adoption it has enforceable Lanham Act rights under the Paris Convention.

D. Pasta will win because having been the first to use the mark in a member country it has enforceable Lanham Act rights under TRIPS.

376. Which of the following BEST describes the effect if Pasta can prove Spag knew of Pasta's use of the "Barrita" mark prior to Spag's adoption and use of the mark in the United States?

A. It is of no consequence.

B. Because Pasta is not a prior user of the mark in the United States, Spag's knowledge does not constitute bad faith.

C. Spag's knowledge constitutes bad faith thus preventing Spag's adoption and use in the United States.

D. It is evidence of bad faith provided Spag was aware Pasta intended to expand into the United States.

377. Assume the facts are the same EXCEPT: Although Pasta only sells its products in Italy, it does so throughout the country. Additionally, Pasta has advertised its products specifically to the United States tourist trade by placing advertisements in United States media encouraging visitors to Italy to ask for and purchase its Barrita pasta products while there. The advertising has been successful and many United States tourists have asked for and purchased Barrita pasta in Italy, in restaurants at meals and in stores to take home with them. Which of the following BEST describes the effect of these facts on Pasta's Lanham Act case regarding Spag's use of the "Barrita" mark in the United States?

A. Pasta will certainly win.

B. Pasta has a good argument it should win.

C. Pasta has a weak argument it should win.

D. Pasta will certainly lose.

378. What advice should a lawyer give a foreign mark owner client who is concerned about third party adoption and use of their mark in the United States?

ANSWER:

Beverages Inc. makes "Nature's Own" (a federally registered trademark) orange juice from 100% natural orange juice. Beverages' competitor, Best Juices Ltd., has started running a new advertisement stating that "Beverages' Nature's Own orange drink contains no natural orange juice."

379.   Under which provision of the Lanham Act can Beverages bring a claim?

    A.   Section 43(a)(1)(A).

    B.   Section 43(a)(1)(B).

    C.   Section 43(c).

    D.   Section 32.

380.   If Beverages had sued Best Juices under the Lanham Act provisions governing false advertising PRIOR TO the 1988 Trademark Revision Act, which of the following would have been a barrier to its bringing a false advertising claim?

    A.   The false claim does not concern Best Juices' goods.

    B.   There is no likelihood of confusion as to source.

    C.   The use does not appear in an "advertisement."

    D.   Beverages is not the sole producer of competing goods.

381.   Assume that instead Best Juices' advertisement had falsely claimed that its OWN juice contained 100% natural orange juice when in fact it contained none. In that case which of the following facts posed the most significant pre-1988 Trademark Revision Act barrier to Beverages' ability to recover under a Lanham Act false advertising claim against Best Juices?

    A.   The false claim does not concern Beverages' goods.

    B.   There is no likelihood of confusion as to source.

    C.   The use does not appear in an "advertisement."

    D.   Beverages is not the sole producer of genuine all natural juice.

382.   Which of the following did the 1988 Trademark Revision Act NOT change regarding the Lanham Act false advertising cause of action?

A. The interstate commerce nexus requirement.

B. An action can now be brought based on misrepresentations about either the advertiser's or another's product.

C. It is no longer required to show actual diversion of sales to obtain relief.

D. Claims for "false advertising" from those related to "false designations of origin" are now explicitly separated in the Lanham Act

History now given its due, apply the post-1988 Trademark Revision Act Lanham Act when answering all of the following Questions.

Bitty Phone LLC makes cell phones. It has started running an advertisement which claims that its cell phones have the same range as those made by its larger rivals. The claim is false; Bitty's cell phones have a substantially smaller range than those made by the larger companies.

383. Which of the following may NOT bring a Lanham Act false advertising claim against Bitty Phone?

A. An end-user who purchased a Bitty cell phone in reliance on the advertisement.

B. A cell phone manufacturer which can prove it lost sales to Bitty because of its false claim.

C. A cell phone manufacturer which can show it likely suffered harm as a result of Bitty's false claim.

D. One of Bitty's larger competitors.

384. Which of the following BEST describes the special effect of a plaintiff in a Lanham Act false advertising claim against Bitty proving it suffered actual economic harm as a result of Bitty's misrepresentation about its cell phone's range?

A. The plaintiff will have standing.

B. The plaintiff can get an injunction.

C. The plaintiff can collect damages.

D. The plaintiff will win its case.

385. Which of the following is LEAST LIKELY to satisfy the Lanham Act requirement that Bitty's misrepresentation appear in "commercial advertising or promotion"?

A. Bitty sent its cell phone range claim to a short "hot prospect" list via email.

B. Bitty published the claim in a newspaper advertisement.

C. A Bitty sales person made the statement in a presentation to a large corporate client.

D. Bitty posted the claim on its website.

386. What outcome on the "commercial advertising or promotion" requirement if instead of coming from Bitty, the false cell phone range statement had been invented and posted by a very happy Bitty customer on his "Bitty-is-great.com" website?

ANSWER:

No-Drip Ltd. makes candles. In its advertising No-Drip specifically states that all of its candles will never drip when used. In fact, they frequently do drip, sometimes copiously. A competitor, Candles, Inc., decides to bring suit for false advertising under the Lanham Act.

387.   Which of the following does Candles' NOT have to prove regarding the challenged "never drip when used" statement to satisfy the elements of its false advertising claim?

    A.   That it is a literally false statement of fact about No-Drip's candles.

    B.   That it is a false statement of fact about No-Drip's candles.

    C.   That it has actually deceived or has a tendency to deceive relevant consumers.

    D.   That it is likely to influence consumer purchasing decisions.

388.   Tests show that No-Drip's candles frequently drip, sometimes copiously. Which of the following statements by No-Drip would LEAST LIKELY satisfy the "falsity" requirement?

    A.   "No-Drip candles never drip."

    B.   "Tests show that Non-Drip candles never drip."

    C.   "No-Drip candles rarely drip."

    D.   "Tests show that No-Drip candles rarely drip."

389.   Which of the following does NOT describe a Lanham Act false advertising consequence of No-Drips' good or bad faith when making the false claim that its candles "never drip"?

    A.   If No-Drip intended to deceive consumers when making the claim plaintiff Candles does not need to prove either deception or tendency to deceive.

    B.   If No-Drip did not intend to deceive consumers Candles must prove it suffered actual harm as a result of the false statement to recover monetary damages.

    C.   If No-Drip intended to deceive consumers some courts may infer causation and award Candles monetary damages without actual proof of such damages.

    D.   If No-Drip did not intentionally make the false statement it is not liable under the Lanham Act.

Pro-Fridge LLC makes refrigerators and freezers for restaurants as well as residential use. It competes with Home-Fridge Ltd. in the residential refrigerator and freezer marketplace. Pro-Fridge's recent residential advertising campaign plays on the following point: "Be a Pro — Not a single restaurant uses Home-Fridge's products. Why should you?" The statement about restaurant use is true but only because Home-Fridge does not make or sell refrigerators or freezers for restaurants.

390. If Home-Fridge brings a Lanham Act false advertising claim against Pro-Fridge which of the following is the BEST possible classification on the facts of Pro-Fridge's statement that "not a single restaurant uses Home-Fridge's products" from Home-Fridge's perspective?

   A. The statement is misleading.

   B. The statement is false by necessary implication.

   C. The statement is literally false.

   D. The statement is false.

391. Assume that Home-Fridge obtains its preferred classification in the Question immediately above. Which of the following BEST describes the burden regarding the deception element of its false advertising case?

   A. Home-Fridge must prove actual deception.

   B. Home-Fridge need only prove a tendency to deceive.

   C. Deception is conclusively presumed.

   D. Deception is presumed subject to rebuttal by Pro-Fridge.

392. Assume that the court classified the Pro-Fridge statement as "misleading." Which of the following BEST describes the burden regarding the deception element of Home-Fridge's false advertising case in that situation?

   A. Deception is presumed.

   B. Home-Fridge must prove actual deception.

   C. Home-Fridge must prove actual deception if it is seeking monetary damages.

   D. Home-Fridge need only prove a tendency to deceive.

393. Assume that Home-Fridge carries its burden on both the falsity and deception elements of its case. Which of the following facts is LEAST relevant to whether Home-Fridge actually prevails in its Lanham Act false advertising claim against Pro-Fridge based on the statement: "Be a Pro — Not a single restaurant uses Home-Fridge's products. Why should you?"?

   A. Home-Fridge has suffered no decline in its sales since the advertisement has been running.

   B. Consumers see no connection between the refrigerators and freezers used by restaurants and those which might best serve residential purposes.

   C. Consumers believe that professional restaurants use high quality refrigerators and freezers.

D. Consumers have asked Home-Fridge why no restaurants buy its products.

Producers LLC makes office furniture. Each piece in a collection is individually designed to present a pleasing and integrated whole. Every time a new Producers' collection is released for sale, LowCost Inc. copies the designs and almost immediately starts manufacturing and selling a virtually identical product line at much lower cost. Each LowCost product is clearly labeled as "A LowCost Product." There is no mention that the designs have been copied from Producers.

394. Producers has brought a lawsuit under the Lanham Act to stop LowCost's "free-riding" on its designs. Its suit alleges that the "A LowCost Product" label's failure to attribute the designs to Producers is a "false designation of origin" under Lanham Act § 43(a)(1)(A). Which of the following is MOST relevant to Producer's claim?

A. The design of the products does not implicate their geographic origin.

B. The LowCost label fails to identify Producers as the source of the designs.

C. Producers cannot copyright the functional aspects of its furniture.

D. LowCost is the manufacturer of the products it sells under its label.

395. Would the "false origin" outcome be different if LowCost had purchased products manufactured by Producers and relabeled them "A LowCost Product" before selling them into the market?

ANSWER:

396. Does Producers have any other possible intellectual property claims against LowCost on the original facts?

ANSWER:

Tom "The Rocket" Mann is a world class sprinter. It has come to Tom's attention that SwiftShoes Company, an athletic shoe manufacturer, has started running (sorry about that) a series of television commercials for "Tom Mann" shoes targeting the aspiring high school sprint star.

397.   Can Tom bring a right of publicity action under the Lanham Act?

ANSWER:

398.   Which of the following is LEAST relevant to Tom's ability to bring a right of publicity claim?

   A.   He has no claim because the advertisements do not involve his likeness.

   B.   He has a claim because the advertisement involves commercial use.

   C.   He has a claim because the use of his name was unauthorized.

   D.   He has a claim because use of his name is likely to cause him commercial harm.

399.   Which of the following BEST describes the relationship between the right of privacy and the right of publicity?

   A.   The doctrines involve entirely independent issues.

   B.   The doctrines overlap, with right of privacy providing the conceptual underpinnings for right of publicity.

   C.   The doctrines overlap, but right of privacy focuses primarily on intrusion/disclosure while right of publicity is concerned economic value.

   D.   The doctrines involve the same concerns and issues.

400.   Which of the following BEST describes why Tom's "celebrity" status as a world-class sprinter is relevant to his right of publicity claim?

   A.   If the plaintiff isn't famous then no harm has been done.

   B.   If the plaintiff isn't famous his persona has no protectable value.

   C.   If the plaintiff is famous the use of his persona is more intrusive.

      D.   If the plaintiff is famous his persona has significant commercial value.

401.   The following Answers list a collection of ALTERNATIVE SwiftShoes' advertisements in their series, all of which Tom claim violate his right of publicity. Which of the advertisements is LEAST LIKELY to support such a claim?

      A.   The depiction of sprinter starting blocks with the words "be like a rocket out of the blocks" as the caption.

      B.   Use of Tom's "Rocket Mann" nickname for the shoes.

      C.   Tom's photo placed in SwiftShoes' catalog next to the shoes.

      D.   A picture of an unidentified sprinter shown from the back wearing the "orange flame" decorated running shorts Tom usually wears in big meets.

402.   On Tom's death can his legal heirs continue to enforce the right of publicity in his persona against commercial users?

ANSWER:

JenA DaV is a well respected, nationally recognized performance artist. All of her performances are based on her unique mannerisms and style. Those mannerisms are captured using a special notation she uses when composing and documenting her works. It has recently come to her attention that a comedy group is performing skits based on her most successful and well known performances. The skits' humorous take on JenA's style and performance art as a genre has routinely brought in full houses.

403.   Which of the following is MOST likely to prevent JenA from prevailing on a right of publicity claim brought against the comedy group?

      A.   Copyright preemption.

      B.   A free speech defense.

      C.   Lack of misappropriation of her persona.

      D.   Lack of commercial harm.

404.   How will a court assess the merits of JenA's case with regard to the issue identified as most problematic to her right of publicity claim in the previous Question?

ANSWER:

405.   Which of the following additional uses of JenA's persona rights by the comedy group is LEAST LIKELY to be protected by a First Amendment defense to a right of publicity claim?

A. The comedy group puts JenA's standard publicity photo on the front of their season advertising brochure.

B. The comedy group uses JenA's name in the program notes to identify her as the creator and performer of the works on which the skits are based.

C. The comedy group uses a photo of JenA as a backdrop for the skits during their performance.

D. The comedy group shows clips of JenA performing the works in the lobby before they perform the skits.

406. If JenA wanted to bring a false endorsement claim under Lanham Act § 43(a) against the group for the use identified as most problematic in the prior Question, which of the following would she NOT need to prove as part of that case?

A. The use was "commercial."

B. The comedy group expressly represented she had endorsed their activities.

C. The public likely believes she endorsed the group's activities.

D. That she did not endorse the group.

407. If instead of JenA's actual publicity photo the comedy group had used a photo of a JenA "look alike" actress, would that change the analysis of her Lanham Act false endorsement claim?

ANSWER:

408. Could JenA bring a trademark infringement action under Lanham Act § 43(a) based on the use of her actual publicity photo in connection with the comedy group's advertisement?

ANSWER:

Nifty Bampo is a famous mystery author. Small Films Ltd. is a struggling independent film company. In order to boost attendance at its most recent offering, which is a comedy not a mystery, Small Films has added a "credit" to its publicity materials stating the movie is "A Nifty Bampo Story." Nifty has no connection whatsoever to the story, the screen play or the movie.

409. Which of the following offers Nifty the BEST chance of recovery against Small Films?

A. False advertising.

B. False endorsement.

C. Trademark infringement.

D. False attribution.

410.   Assume that rather than having no affiliation with the Small Films movie Nifty had written the screen play but that Small Films had altered his work while making the movie. How would that involvement and alternation affect Nifty's ability to bring a "false designation of origin/false attribution" lawsuit?

ANSWER:

411.   Assume that Nifty had written the screen play, it was used verbatim in making the film and Small Films refused to give Nifty credit as the author. Which of the following BEST describes the likely outcome if Nifty were to bring a Lanham Act § 43(a) "false designation of origin" case against Small Films?

A. Nifty would win.

B. Nifty would win based on passing off.

C. Nifty would probably win based on reverse passing off.

D. Night would probably not win.

PRACTICE FINAL EXAM: QUESTIONS

PRACTICE FINAL EXAM

QUESTIONS

Miracle Corporation produces a hand cream moisturizer product for use on dry skin. Each jar of its cream is labeled with the words "Sleek Skin."

412. Which of the following BEST describes the trademark status of the word "Miracle"?

    A. It is a trademark because it identifies the source of the hand cream.

    B. It is a trademark because it is arbitrary.

    C. It is not a trademark because it is the name of the company.

    D. It is not a trademark because it is not used as a trademark.

413. Which of the following BEST describes the trademark status of "Sleek Skin"?

    A. It cannot be a trademark because it does not identify Miracle as the source of the hand cream.

    B. It can be a trademark because it does not matter if a trademark identifies the actual producer.

    C. It is a trademark because it is not the producer's trade name.

    D. It is not a trademark because it is not the producer's trade name.

414. Which of the following posses the MOST significant barrier to Miracle claiming "Sleek Skin" as a trademark?

    A. "Sleek Skin" is not being used to signal source.

    B. "Sleek Skin" may not be distinctive.

    C. "Sleek Skin" is not a trade name.

    D. "Sleek Skin" is not yet federally registered.

415. Why couldn't Miracle use the words "hand cream" as its trademark for the product?

ANSWER:

416.   Which of the following is the BEST distinctiveness classification for the "Sleek Skin" mark?

    A.   Generic.

    B.   Descriptive.

    C.   Suggestive.

    D.   Fanciful.

417.   Why is the classification issue identified in the Question immediately above so important to Miracle's trademark rights?

ANSWER:

418.   Which of the following BEST describes what Miracle must do to show that "Sleek Skin" is distinctive if it comes out on the wrong end of the classification issue?

    A.   The mark is arbitrary.

    B.   Fair use.

    C.   The mark identifies and distinguishes its product.

    D.   Secondary meaning.

419.   Which of the following is MOST likely to be treated as an arbitrary mark with regard to Miracle's hand cream moisturizer product?

    A.   Azzat.

    B.   Aloe.

    C.   Pica.

    D.   601.

420.   Assuming the "Sleek Skin" mark is inherently distinctive, which of the following BEST describes when Miracle first obtained trademark rights in the mark?

    A.   When Miracle federally registered the mark.

    B.   When Miracle first put the mark on the cream jars.

    C.   When Miracle sold 10 jars of the labeled cream to a retailer.

    D.   When Miracle shipped 10,000 labeled jars of the cream from its plant in Georgia to its warehouse in New York.

Astro Enterprises has marketed and sold its "Kart" camping equipment throughout, but exclusively in, the Eastern United States for the last four years. It has not federally registered the "Kart" trademark.

421. Duo, Inc. has started selling camping equipment under the "Kart" mark in Arizona. Assuming that Astro holds valid trademark rights in the "Kart" mark, which of the following BEST describes the MOST LIKELY outcome of a trademark infringement suit brought by Astro against Duo?

   A. Astro wins because it has valid rights in the mark.

   B. Astro wins because Duo is selling camping equipment.

   C. Duo wins because its product is not within the scope of Astro's trademark rights.

   D. Duo wins because its sales are not within the scope of Astro's trademark rights.

422. The facts are as stated in the Question immediately above. Both Astro and Duo are rapidly expanding geographically. Neither has federally registered the "Kart" mark. Which of the following BEST describes which company will obtain the rights in the "Kart" mark in Nebraska?

   A. The first to use the mark in Nebraska.

   B. The first to develop consumer associations in Nebraska.

   C. Astro because it was the first to adopt the mark.

   D. Duo because it was the closest first adopter of the mark.

Gern LLC started marketing and selling its meat products in Iowa under the "Cape" trademark in 1995. In 1998 Gern applied for and received a federal registration for the "Cape" mark on meat products. In 1997 Twofer Co. independently adopted (without knowledge of Gern's use of the mark) and started using the "Cape" mark on its meat products which it marketed and sold in Oregon.

423. Assuming that Gern has valid rights in the "Cape" trademark, which of the following BEST describes the MOST LIKELY outcome of a trademark infringement suit brought by Gern against Twofer for use of the "Cape" mark?

   A. Twofer wins because its Oregon use started prior to Gern's federal registration.

   B. Twofer wins because it is not selling in Iowa.

   C. Gern wins because it has valid use-based rights in the mark.

   D. Gern wins because it has federally registered the mark.

424. The facts are as stated in the Question immediately above EXCEPT Twofer first started using the "Cape" mark in 2000. Assuming that Gern has valid rights in the "Cape" trademark, which of the following BEST describes the MOST LIKELY outcome of

a trademark infringement suit brought by Gern against Twofer for use of the "Cape" mark?

    A.   Twofer wins because its Oregon use started prior to Gern's federal registration.

    B.   Twofer wins because it is not selling in Iowa.

    C.   Gern wins because it has valid use-based rights in the mark.

    D.   Gern wins because it has federally registered the mark.

425.   Which of the following is NOT a benefit of a federal trademark registration?

    A.   Prima facie evidence of validity.

    B.   Protection against dilution.

    C.   Possible incontestability.

    D.   Constructive use.

Scuzt Ltd. makes chewing tobacco.

426.   What issue might Scuzt face if it tries to federally register the logo "Redmen" superimposed on a picture of a Native American as a trademark for its product?

ANSWER:

427.   Scuzt has instead decided seek a federal registration of the mark "Mild Chew" for its product. As it turns out Scuzt uses a particularly low grade of tobacco making its product both bitter and tough. Which of the following classifications is MOST LIKELY to bar its registration of the "Mild Chew" mark?

    A.   Deceptive.

    B.   Deceptively misdescriptive.

    C.   Descriptive.

    D.   None of these classifications will bar federal registration.

428.   Undaunted, Scuzt offers one final possibility for federal registration — "Virginia's Finest" — despite the fact that neither the product nor its ingredients come from Virginia. Evidence shows that consumers believe the product comes from Virginia and many purchase it based on that mistaken belief. Which of the following BEST describes the effect of that finding on Scuzt ability to obtain a federal registration?

    A.   It can be registered because it is merely deceptively misdescriptive.

    B.   It can be registered if Scuzt shows secondary meaning.

    C.   It can never be registered because it is deceptively misdescriptive.

D. It can never be registered because it is geographically deceptively misdescriptive.

Mona Co. makes, markets and sells gloves nationwide under its "Tramwell" trademark. Mona has not federally registered the "Tramwell" mark. Ersalts Enterprises has started making, marketing and selling its home furnishings under the "Tramwell" mark in New England.

429. Which of the following BEST describes Mona's possible trademark infringement actions against Ersalts?

   A. Mona can sue under both state law and the Lanham Act.

   B. Mona can only sue under state law because Mona did not federally register the Tramwell mark.

   C. Mona can only sue under Lanham Act because the Lanham Act preempts state trademark law.

   D. Mona cannot sue until it registers the "Tramwell" mark.

430. Assuming Mona has valid rights in the "Tramwell" trademark, which of the following BEST describes what Mona will need to prove to prevail in its trademark infringement lawsuit against Ersalts?

   A. Ersalts product falls within Mona's trademark rights.

   B. Ersalts sales fall within Mona's trademark rights.

   C. Ersalts use of the "Tramwell" mark is likely to cause consumer confusion.

   D. Ersalts acted in bad faith in adopting the "Tramwell" mark.

431. Which of the following is LEAST relevant to whether Mona will prevail in its trademark infringement lawsuit against Ersalts?

   A. That the two products are advertised by and sold in the same department stores.

   B. That consumers will assume Mona has expanded into furniture.

   C. The marks are identical.

   D. That furniture is an infrequent purchase.

Pazzo Ltd. makes, markets and sells tomato pasta sauce in Illinois, Indiana, Michigan and Ohio. It has used the mark "Danziano" (an Italian sounding but invented word of its own creation) on its pasta sauce for the last six years. It applied for and obtained a federal registration for the "Danziano" mark three years ago. Secondo Corp. started making, marketing and selling pre-grated cheese for use on pasta in Ohio and Pennsylvania under the "Danziano" mark four years ago. Two years ago it expanded its business into New York and New Jersey.

432. Pazzo has sued Secondo for trademark infringement under the Lanham Act. Assess Pazzo's likelihood of success on the given facts.

ANSWER:

433. Assume that instead of "Danziano" Pazzo had picked "Pomodoro" as its mark, the Italian word for "tomato," which was also adopted by Secondo. Assuming the rest of the facts remain as described above (including Pazzo's federal registration) how does the change in the mark affect Pazzo's chances of success in a trademark infringement suit against Secondo's use of the "Pomodoro" mark?

ANSWER:

434. The facts are the same as in the Question immediately above EXCEPT that Pazzo federally registered the "Pomodoro" mark 6 years ago and Pazzo made the required Section 15 filing. Which of the following BEST describes why the issue in the above Question "goes away" in light of that change in the facts?

A. The mark is federally registered.

B. The federal registration can no longer be cancelled.

C. The mark has become incontestable and cannot be challenged.

D. The mark has become incontestable and cannot be challenged on the relevant grounds.

435. The facts are as stated in the Question immediately above EXCEPT Pazzo's pasta sauces do not, in fact, contain any tomatoes. Any change in the analysis?

ANSWER:

Wizards, Inc. provides internet access services under the mark "Quik."

436. Which of the following BEST describes the distinctiveness classification of Wizards' mark?

A. Fanciful because of the unusual spelling.

B. Fanciful because consumers will not make the connection to "quick."

C. Suggestive because it requires a "leap of imagination" to connect the mark to the related service.

D. Descriptive because consumers will view the mark as equivalent to "quick."

Aworthy Corporation evaluates automobile quality. It publishes a monthly magazine under the "Aworthy" name in which it lists those automobiles which it has approved. It also permits the manufacturers to use the "Aworthy Approved" label in connection with their approved products.

437. Which of the following BEST describes the "Aworthy Approved" label?

A. It is a trademark.

B. It is a service mark.

C. It is a collective mark.

D. It is a certification mark.

438. Which of the following BEST describes what is required to maintain the "Aworthy Approved" label's mark status identified in the Question immediately above?

   A. Permitting all products which meet the requirements to use the label.

   B. Ensuring regular use on Aworthy's magazine.

   C. Ensuring all members regularly pay dues.

   D. Ensuring approved producers regularly use the mark.

Scents Enterprises makes colognes and perfumes. It has recently developed a unique new formula which has an unusual, pleasant and popular smell. Scents desires to use that new smell as the trademark for the related perfume product.

439. Can a smell serve as a trademark?

ANSWER:

440. Which of the following is likely the MOST serious difficulty which Scents will likely face in claiming the smell as a mark on these facts?

   A. Smells cannot serve as trademarks.

   B. Inability to signal source in the marketplace.

   C. Distinctiveness.

   D. Functionality.

441. Rather than use the smell of the perfume as its mark, Scents has decided to use a drawing of the common flower whose essence forms the primary ingredient in the formula. Which of the following BEST describes the MOST serious difficulty which Scents will likely face in claiming the flower logo as a mark on these facts?

   A. Distinctiveness.

   B. Descriptive classification.

   C. Inability to signal source.

   D. There is no serious difficulty.

Glassware Enterprises has developed a new highly artistic wine glass shape.

442. What additional facts are required to determine how utility functionality considerations are likely to affect Glassware's' ability to claim the new shape as the trademark for its wine glass products.

ANSWER:

443. Assume that on the facts the considerations described in the answer to the Question immediately above all heavily favor Glassware. What other functionality issue might also be relevant on these facts and how does it differ?

ANSWER:

444. How would Glassware obtaining a utility patent on the shape of the glass affect the functionality analysis?

ANSWER:

445. Would it help Glassware's case to show that consumers had come to strongly associate the shape of the glass with its particular products?

ANSWER:

Pharma Corp has developed a new package for its over-the-counter cold remedies. The new package consists of a unique gradation of colors from blue fading gradually into yellow. While it is preparing to implement the new packaging design over the next six months, Pharma wants to obtain trademark protection for its new color scheme.

446. Which of the following BEST describes how the availability of that protection will be assessed?

   A. Product packaging is always inherently distinctive.

   B. Product packaging always requires a showing of secondary meaning.

   C. Product packaging may be inherently distinctive.

   D. Product packaging cannot be protected as a trademark.

447. As it turns out there are very few pharmaceutical product packages which use a gradated color scheme and none which involve blue fading gradually into yellow. Which of the

following BEST describes the likely outcome regarding the protectability of Pharma's new package design on these facts?

    A. It can be protected because it is unusual and, therefore, inherently distinctive.

    B. It can be protected if Pharma can show secondary meaning.

    C. It can be protected because it is arbitrary and, therefore, inherently distinctive.

    D. It cannot be protected because it is trade dress.

448. Assume that it is determined that Pharma's new product package is distinctive and can, therefore, serve as a trademark. What other barrier to claiming trademark rights does Pharma face on these facts and how might it quickly resolve that problem?

ANSWER:

For the last four years Events Enterprises has sold "last minute" tickets to various arts and music events under the "Quik-Tix" mark, which it uses in all its advertising and other marketing and sales materials. The mark is not federally registered.

449. Which of the following BEST describes the MOST LIKELY significant impediment to Events claiming service mark rights in "Quik-Tix"?

    A. Distinctiveness.

    B. Non-use.

    C. Non-registration.

    D. Incontestability.

450. Assume that Events has overcome the problem identified in the Question immediately above and has obtained valid trademark rights in the "Quik-Tix" mark. Global Co., a competitor in the last minute ticket business, has begun using the following catchphrase in all its advertising: "Your provider of quick tickets." What defense will Global likely raise if Events sues it for infringement of its "Quik-Tix" trademark?

ANSWER:

451. Which of the following versions of Global's catchphrase is LEAST likely to infringe Events' "Quik-Tix" mark based on the defense identified in the Question immediately above?

    A. Quick Tickets.

    B. Global's Quick Tickets.

    C. Quick Tickets from Global.

    D. Quick tickets from Global.

Arial Company makes and sells hand-held electronic personal assistant devices (PADs) under the federally registered and incontestable mark "eFriends." CompD Inc. acquires genuine "eFriends" PADS from authorized Arial retailers and resells them from its own "CompD" retail outlets.

452. Which of the following is CompD's BEST defense if Arial brings a trademark infringement suit against CompD for selling the PAD products bearing the "eFriends" trademark?

    A. Nominative use.

    B. Fair use.

    C. First sale.

    D. It has no defense against an incontestable mark.

453. The facts are as stated in the Question immediately above EXCEPT that CompD's weekly advertisements for products available at its CompD outlets regularly include the "eFriends" PAD. Which of the following is CompD's BEST defense if Arial brings a trademark infringement suit against CompD for those advertisements using the "eFriends" trademark?

    A. Nominative use.

    B. Fair use.

    C. First sale.

    D. It has no defense against an incontestable mark.

454. The facts are as stated in Question 452 above EXCEPT that CompD sells the Arial PAD product in a special corner of its retail stores which is separately marked as the "eFriends Center." What additional difficulty does this further action raise regarding CompD's reliance on the above defenses and what should CompD do to address that problem?

ANSWER:

455. The facts are as stated in Question 452 above EXCEPT CompD modifies the "eFriends" PADs prior to resale. The nature of the modifications makes it unlikely that consumers will recognize that any deviations from a genuine product arise from CompD's changes. CompD prominently displays signs in its stores next to the products indicating that it has modified the products and specifically what modifications were made. Arial brings a lawsuit for trademark infringement based on CompD's resale of the modified

trademarked products. Which of the following BEST describes the likely outcome of that lawsuit?

A. CompD wins based on the first sale doctrine.

B. CompD wins based on the first sale doctrine and its notices of modification.

C. Arial wins because the products were modified.

D. Arial wins because the notices are not effective.

Bredwell Company makes and sells saddles and other riding equipment under the "Stower" trademark. It has successfully sued Gudnuf Inc. for infringing the "Stower" mark on competing products in its geographic market under the Lanham Act. The "Stower" mark is not federally registered.

456. Which of the following BEST describes the basic remedies available to Bredwell as a prevailing defendant under the Lanham Act?

A. Injunction.

B. Injunction and damages.

C. Injunction, an accounting of profits and damages suffered.

D. Injunction, an accounting of profits, damages suffered and costs.

457. Which of the following BEST describes what Bredwell must show to obtain an injunction against further infringement of the "Stower" mark by Gudnuf?

A. Failure to issue an injunction will likely result in consumer confusion.

B. The traditional equitable factors are satisfied.

C. Gudnuf acted in bad faith.

D. Monetary relief is inadequate.

458. If prior to the final decision in the case, Bredwell had sought a preliminary injunction against Gudnuf's use of the "Stower" mark, what additional factor would be extremely important to obtaining that relief?

ANSWER:

459. During the period of Gudnuf's infringement Bredwell sales decreased 15% from previous years. Which of the following BEST describes what Bredwell must show to obtain its lost profits on those sales as damages from Gudnuf?

A. The reduction in its sales was caused by actual confusion arising from Gudnuf's infringement.

    B.   The reduction in its sales was caused by actual confusion arising from Gudnuf's infringement and the amount of Bredwell's lost profits.

    C.   A reasonable basis for finding the reduction in its sales was caused by Gudnuf's infringement and a credible calculation of the amount of Bredwell's lost profits.

    D.   Gudnuf's bad faith and a credible basis for calculating the amount of Bredwell's lost profits.

460.   If Bredwell receives lost profit damages can it also obtain an accounting of Gudnuf's own profits — why or why not?

ANSWER:

461.   Which of the following BEST describes the likelihood that Bredwell will receive "enhanced" damages under the Lanham Act?

    A.   Damages are automatically trebled on an accounting.

    B.   Accounting damages will be trebled if Gudnuf willfully infringed.

    C.   Damages are enhanced when required to provide full compensation.

    D.   Damages are enhanced to punish Gudnuf's willful infringement and to deter future infringement.

462.   Which of the following BEST describes how Bredwell's claim for damages under the Lanham Act would be affected had it federally registered the "Stower" mark?

    A.   Bredwell cannot bring a Lanham Act claim if the mark is not registered.

    B.   Bredwell cannot claim damages if it does not give statutory notice of the registration.

    C.   Bredwell's damages are limited if it does not give statutory notice of the registration.

    D.   Bredwell can receive enhanced damages.

463.   Which of the following BEST describes when and who will receive an award of attorneys' fees under the Lanham Act?

    A.   Bredwell if it wins the lawsuit.

    B.   Bredwell if it wins the lawsuit and receives an accounting.

    C.   Gudnuf if it wins the lawsuit.

    D.   Gudnuf if Bredwell's case is frivolous.

Superior Products Enterprises makes and sells very high-end jewelry under its long-time federally registered and incontestable "Star" mark. Duper Stuff LLC has recently started selling what can charitably be called extremely tacky home décor knickknacks under the "Star" mark.

464. What problem does Superior face if it brings a traditional trademark infringement lawsuit against Duper and how would a dilution action avoid that issue?

ANSWER:

465. Which of the following BEST describes the key predicate requirement if Superior brings a federal dilution claim?

   A. That the "Star" mark be widely recognized among jewelry consumers.

   B. That the "Star" mark be widely recognized by the general consuming public.

   C. That the "Star" mark be famous.

   D. That the "Star" be inherently distinctive.

466. Which of the following BEST describes the nature of Superior's federal dilution claim against Duper?

   A. Dilution.

   B. Dilution by blurring.

   C. Dilution by tarnishment.

   D. Dilution by blurring and tarnishment.

467. Assuming Superior satisfies the requirements for bringing a federal dilution case against Duper must it show actual dilution to prevail, and if so how would it do so?

ANSWER:

468. On the facts given in the Questions above does Duper have a valid affirmative defense to Superior's federal dilution lawsuit under the Lanham Act?

ANSWER:

469. Superior wins its federal dilution action against Duper. Duper, however, shows it had no knowledge of Superior's "Star" mark. Which of the following describes Superior's MOST LIKELY remedy?

   A. Injunction.

   B. Injunction and damages.

   C. Injunction, an accounting of profits and damages suffered.

D.   Injunction, an accounting of profits, damages suffered and costs.

Heter Company has used the trademark "Honey Bee" on its kitchen utensil products for the last two years. Its mark is not federally registered. It is very well known in the kitchen utensil market but not otherwise. Heter has discovered that someone has recently registered the Internet domain name "HoneyBee.com." The related website contains one picture of a honey bee.

470.   Which of the following trademark cause(s) of action do the above facts support against the registrant of the HoneyBee.com domain name: (a) likelihood of confusion infringement, (b) initial interest confusion infringement, (c) federal dilution and (d) anticybersquatting?

ANSWER:

471.   Which of the following is MOST helpful to Heter's case if it brings an anticybersquatting suit against the domain name registrant?

A.   The registrant offers to transfer the mark to Heter at no charge when it is served in order to settle the lawsuit.

B.   The registrant can show no connection to or interest in honey bees.

C.   The registrant's address on its registration application is incorrect.

D.   Heter cannot bring an anticybersquatting suit because the "Honey Bee" mark is not federally registered.

472.   Is it relevant to Heter's anticybersquatting case that the "HoneyBee.com" domain name is not identical to Heter's "Honey Bee" trademark?

ANSWER:

473.   Which of the following BEST describes what Heter can do if it cannot locate the actual domain name registrant and, therefore, is unable to deliver service of process?

A.   Use long-arm personal jurisdiction.

B.   Send notice to the address on the domain name registration.

C.   Show it diligently attempted to find the registrant as the basis for an *in rem* anticybersquatting action.

D.   Show it cannot obtain *in personam* jurisdiction over the registrant as the basis for an *in rem* anticybersquatting action.

For 15 years CityWear Company used the "Striders" mark on a particular line of "professional" very expensive walking shoes which it manufactured, marketed and sold exclusively in California.

Fourteen years ago CityWear obtained a federal registration on the "Striders" mark for shoes and its rights became incontestable after five years. Five years ago CityWear stopped using the "Striders" mark entirely and its internal records at the time show no it had further interest in the mark. Ten months ago CityWear launched a new line of upscale walking shoes using the "Striders" mark, which it makes, markets and sells exclusively in California. Six months ago LensCo Ltd. began using the "Striders" mark on "throw away" sunglasses which it markets and sells to vacationers exclusively in the Southeastern seaboard resort areas of the United States. CityWear has sued LensCo under the Lanham Act for trademark infringement.

474. Which of the following BEST describes CityWear's rights in the "Striders" trademark *one year* ago?

    A. It had incontestable rights in the mark.

    B. It had presumptively valid rights in the mark.

    C. Its rights in the mark were presumptively invalid.

    D. It had no rights in the mark.

475. What arguments will CityWear and LensCo make in the lawsuit and who is MOST LIKELY to prevail?

ANSWER:

Risso LLC makes, markets and sells tomato sauce under its federally registered "Pomo" trademark. It markets and sells its product exclusively in the United States. Risso holds no foreign registrations in the "Pomo" mark. Dos S.A. is a Spanish corporation, wholly owned and managed by European Union nationals. Dos has recently obtained a Spanish registration for the "Pomo" mark and is using it on its own locally manufacturer tomato sauce. Dos markets and sells its Pomo tomato sauce only in Spain.

476. Which of the following BEST describes how Risso will fare if it asserts its United States trademark rights against Dos' Spanish use of the "Pomo" mark in a United States court?

    A. Risso will win because Dos is using the mark on an identical product.

    B. Risso will win based on the Paris Convention and TRIPS.

    C. Risso will lose because Dos is entirely foreign owned and operated and holds a Spanish registration for the mark.

    D. Risso will lose because United States trademark rights never apply extraterritorially.

Personal Electronics Inc. makes and sells high-end personal computers in the United States. It has started a new advertising campaign on its company products web-page which lauds its new operating system, Mega, for its "exceptional functionality." The page also contains the specific claim that "Tests have shown Mega OS is twice as fast as Zeno OS." The Zeno operating system is sold by Personal Electronics' primary competitor, Manzana Computing Ltd. The Mega system has the same functionality as virtually all high-end operating systems, including Manzana's Zeno system, which include features not found in lower-cost, more basic operating systems. Personal Electronics' tests showed Mega is twice as fast as Manzana's system on certain specific tasks. The tests also show that Mega generally operates only marginally more quickly than Manzana's system on most common end-user applications and is sometimes slightly slower on the most complex applications.

477. Which of the following is MOST relevant to whether Manzana has standing to bring a false advertising suit against Personal Electronics under Lanham Act Sec. 43(a)?

   A.   Manzana is a competitor of Personal Electronics.

   B.   Manzana can show that it is likely to be damaged by Personal Electronics' advertisement.

   C.   Manzana can show the advertisement is false.

   D.   Manzana does not have standing because it is not a consumer.

478. Which of the following BEST describes why Manzana may have a better chance of successfully challenging Personal Electronics' "twice as fast" claim than its "exceptional functionality" claim?

   A.   The "twice as fast" claim is literally false.

   B.   The "exceptional functionality" claim is true.

   C.   The "exceptional functionality" claim is not about Manzana's product.

   D.   The "exceptional functionality" claim is more subjective.

479. Explain what Manzana must prove to prevail on its Lanham Act false advertising claim regarding Personal Electronics' "twice as fast" statement including any relevant presumptions and remedial considerations. Conclude with your view of Manzana's likelihood of success on the given facts.

ANSWER:

Allison Fame is a well-known American singer and movie star. Silver Entertainment, a California corporation, has started running an advertising campaign for its food catering services which prominently features an actress which looks very similar to Allison singing a jingle in Allison's voice and style lauding the quality of Silver's catering services. Allison is upset and decides to sue.

480. Which of the following claims is the LEAST likely to be successful on the above facts?

   A. False designation of origin/reverse passing off.

   B. False endorsement.

   C. Right of publicity.

   D. Trademark infringement.

481. If Allison brought a right of publicity suit against Silver Entertainment which of the following would be LEAST relevant to her case?

   A. Commercial use.

   B. Misappropriation of her persona.

   C. Harm to her commercial interests.

   D. Intrusion into her life.

482. Which of the following BEST describes the DIFFERENCE between bringing a right of publicity and a false endorsement claim on these facts?

   A. Publicity involves individual persona, endorsement does not.

   B. Publicity is limited by First Amendment concerns, endorsement is not.

   C. Publicity does not require deception/confusion, endorsement does.

   D. Publicity requires use without consent, endorsement does not.

Quimpet makes and sells a particularly delicious candy bar under its unregistered "Delight" trademark. QuickTurn has made a business of buying, repackaging and reselling Delight candy bars in its own packaging under its unregistered "Just as Good" trademark.

483. Which of the following identifies Quimpet's BEST Lanham Act Section 43(a) claim against QuickTurn?

   A. False attribution.

   B. False endorsement.

   C. Trademark infringement.

   D. False advertising.

484. Instead of purchasing, repackaging and reselling Quimpet's Delight candy bars, QuickTurn has copied the recipe and production methods used by Quimpet for Delight candy bars and makes and sells its own "Just as Good" candy bar itself. QuickTurn

does not attribute either the recipe or the methods to Quimpet. Under these facts which of the following is Quimpet's BEST Lanham Act Section 43(a) claim against QuickTurn?

A. False attribution.

B. False endorsement.

C. Trademark infringement.

D. False advertising.

485. QuickTurn has used its own distinct recipe and methods to make its "Just as Good" candy bars but has identified them as "Quimpet-style candy." Why might Quimpet be better advised to bring a false designation of origin over-attribution claim than a trademark infringement action on these facts?

ANSWER:

ANSWERS

1. **The best answer is C.** Trademark law has roots in unfair competition law (**Answer A**) including the protection of a producer's goodwill (**Answer B**) and related investment in product innovation (**Answer D**), so its policy objectives are difficult to crisply articulate. However, the distinction drawn by the Supreme Court between patent and copyright on one hand and trademark on the other (see the answer to Question 10 above) indicates that trademark law only extends to certain kinds of unfair competition and producer goodwill. The currently prevailing view is that trademark law's specific purpose is to provide consumers with reliable information regarding a product or service (**Answer C**); specifically, by ensuring that the presence of a mark reliably indicates to consumers that the product/service is the one they expect based on prior experiences with like-marked products/services. This is sometimes referred to as trademark law's "source identifying" function. *See* Lanham Act § 45 (15 U.S.C. § 1127) which defines a mark as serving to "identify and distinguish" the mark user's goods from those of others; that is, to "indicate the source of the goods."

NOTE: Although "unfairness" is not the central theme of modern United States trademark law the concept remains highly relevant, both because it influences the application of trademark law and because it serves as the basis for other distinct "supplemental" doctrines. Those other doctrines are mentioned throughout this volume.

NOTE: This being a study aid hoping to improve your understanding and ability to apply trademark and unfair competition law (most pressingly on an exam but in future practice as well) a brief aside on the importance of policy (and this Topic) is in order. Although a firm grasp of the policy objectives is rarely important as a stand alone matter its value lies in responding to issues at the boundaries of legal regimes; that is when doctrinal application gets mushy — something to watch for both in exam questions and in "real life."

2. **NO.** Although one frequently sees references to trademark law's "source identifying function" (like in the answer to Question 1 immediately above) it is important not to read that phrase too narrowly. It does not mean literally a trademark must name the specific producer. In fact, the statute expressly indicates that the actual source may remain unknown to consumers. *See* Lanham Act § 45 (15 U.S.C. § 1127 (the definition of trademark: ". . . even if that source is unknown.") Rather the phrase merely means that because similarly marked goods come from the same source (under the control of the mark owner), a consumer can assume that all of them share the same characteristics — thus distinctly "identifying and distinguishing" them as a class from goods not bearing the mark and from another source. Consequently, although some marks do include all

or a portion of the producer's actual name (*e.g.,* Ford, Coca-Cola) it is not required that a mark identifies the actual source/producer.

NOTE: Frequently the actual producer's name is intentionally omitted to permit differentiation as, for example, Levi Strauss & Co. did when it started producing the "Dockers" line of casual slacks and Heinz has done regarding its pet foods.

3. **The best answer is D**. Most courts and scholars (including most likely your professor, but that's worth confirming — we're an idiosyncratic lot) have adopted **Answer D**, the Chicago school's economic justification of "reducing customer search costs." Specifically, because the mark reliably indicates that the associated goods or services will always have the same characteristics, consumers do not need to make that determination in other less efficient ways (for example, actual sampling or other forms of testing). **Answer A** articulates the Constitutional basis for Congressional action, but provides no specific details as to why trademark law might facilitate commerce. **Answer B** articulates the general transaction cost reduction rationale, but fails to identify how trademark law actually does so. Both being less precise than **Answer D**, they are not the best answer. **Answer C** is a commonly articulated justification. Clearly trademark law helps the owner "capture" the goodwill benefits of innovative product characteristics by uniquely signaling their existence. However, the Supreme Court has clearly stated that patent (and perhaps trade secret) not trademark law is the proper intellectual property vehicle for encouraging investment in products themselves. That view is explicitly implemented by trademark law's affirmative exclusion of functional product features — those which embody product innovation and improvements — from protection. *See* Topic 6 — Functionality. As a consequence it is more accurate to view incentives to innovation as a (perhaps) desirable by-product of trademark law, not its justification. So **Answer C** is not the best answer.

NOTE: Although incentives to product innovation are not the justification for trademark law, incentives still arguably play an important role in the regime. Specifically, trademark law can reasonably be viewed as providing incentives to invest in the creation and implementation of the marks themselves. *See* Vincent Chiappetta, *Trademarks: More Than Meets the Eye*, Spring 2003 U. Ill. J. L. Tech. & Pol. 35 (2003). Such an approach goes far to explaining recent non-confusion-based trademark expansions, such as dilution and anti-cybersquatting. *See* Topic 14 — Dilution and Topic 15 — Anticybersquatting.

4. **The best answer is A**. This question emphasizes how understanding the actual purposes of trademark law assists in resolving "close calls" in interpretation and application. Under the prevailing economic search cost reduction justification the regime's primary focus is clearly on enhancing the efficient operation of the market as a whole (**Answer A**). Although individual trademark owners are the normal trademark plaintiffs and thus may feel that trademark law is designed to further their particular interests as owners, those claims are only (generally) recognized if the regime's market information-search cost reduction objectives are implicated. For example, unless consumer confusion is likely trademark law will does not (normally) prevent others from using the mark despite

the owner's desire to stop the use. *But see* Topic 15 — Anticybersquatting. Therefore, although trademark law provides protection to owners' interests, that protection is better understood as a by-product of trademark law's reliance on their self interest to bring enforcement actions for the market's benefit, not from an actual concern for the owners as owners. So **Answer B** is incorrect. The same argument applies to trademark creators; who receive no rights as such (as opposed to being the mark owner) under trademark law. **Answer C** is, therefore, incorrect. Consumers present the most difficult case, as the search cost reduction rationale is clearly intended explicitly to assist them. However, trademark law focuses on them as a group, not as individuals. That distinction is brought home by the fact that the regime does not permit direct claims by consumers themselves. To the extent an individual consumer feels "unfairly" dealt with the remedy lies only in unfair competition law not trademark law. So although **Answer D** is close, it is not the best answer.

5. Trademark law seeks to ensure that the presence of a mark reliably signals to customers that the related product has the desired attributes thereby reducing their search costs. In this case, the mark is clearly not serving that function. No customer purchases the t-shirt under the misconception that the t-shirt will have the attributes signaled by the trademark. Rather the mark is serving exclusively as a means for the t-shirt buyer to inform others about themselves — specifically, that they have adopted and support your client's "good life" brand message. Permitting your client to bring a *trademark* action on these facts, therefore, does not further the purposes of trademark law and, arguably, interferes with First Amendment speech. Consequently, the action is likely to face serious difficulties before a court. This is, in fact, precisely the issue raised in these types of lawsuits, although the actual lie-drawing is usually complicated by real-world facts which generally are much murkier than in this problem. *See* Topic 16 — Defenses: Fair Use, Nominative Use Parody/Free Speech.

    NOTE: This analysis provides a further demonstration of how understanding underlying policy can help assess cases lying at the boundaries of the trademark regime.

6. **The best answer is C**. Trademark law focuses on information-search cost reduction. Functional product are left to other regimes (patent and trade secret law) so **Answer A** is incorrect. *See* Topic 6 — Functionality (which discusses how to determine whether a product feature is functional). Although reasonable arguments can be made that all the remaining answers involve useful information for consumers, trademark law focuses on specific indicators which reliably communicate information by identifying and distinguishing the associated products from those of other producers. The client's logo is the only answer which implicates that objective, so **Answer C** is better suited to trademark law than either **Answer B** (which is the information conveyed by the mark) or **Answer D** (which is the target group to whom the mark should become meaningful).

7. **The best answer is B**. United States trademark law establishes a system of indicators which reliably identify and distinguish associated products and services from those of others in the marketplace. To further that objective, United States law expressly requires

that a mark actually be *used* before any legal rights attach, making **Answer B** correct. *See* Topic 7 — Acquiring Rights: Use. Registration provides important *additional* benefits but still requires actual use of the mark before those rights can be claimed, so **Answer A** is incorrect. *See* Topic 9 — Registration: Constructive Use and Intent to Use. Although it may add strength to the mark, novelty (**Answer C**) is affirmatively not required to obtain United States trademark rights. Finally, although a mark conveys information to consumers, there is no requirement that it convey a specific kind of information.

NOTE: There are, of course, other requirements which limit the ability to claim trademark rights, such as distinctiveness. *See* Topic 3 — Basic Distinctiveness: The Spectrum of Distinctiveness Word Marks, Including Acronyms and Foreign Words.

NOTE: The United States "use" requirement is not universal. Many countries (including the European Union and much of Latin America) confer trademark rights on the first to register. The related "race" for local rights can be source of significant difficulties for an uninformed United States producer who later decides to expand into such jurisdictions.

8. **The best answer is B**. Because the purpose of trademark law is to help customers identify the source of a particular good in the marketplace, trademark rights are commonly described as being *appurtenant to* (connected with) the trademark owner's business, and most particularly, the products and services which it produces. *See Hanover Star Milling Co. v. Metcalf*, 240 U.S. 403 (1916). Although that arguably constitutes a limited form of property right (**Answer A**), because it does not have the commonly associated right of free transferability — it can only be validly assigned in connection with your client's tent business (*see* Topic 19 — Duration of Rights, Abandonment and Loss of Rights), **Answer B** is the more accurate response. Although trademark rights do prevent specific forms of unfair competition (**Answer C**) and, consequently permit the holder to prevent related competition (**Answer D**), neither answer accurately captures very limited nature of those rights under trademark law.

9. **The answer is C**. The federal Trade-Mark Act of 1946 is commonly referred to as the "Lanham Act" (anecdotally I'm told that was the name of the Senator who proposed the bill), so **Answer C** is correct. Battle-worn trademark lawyers, courts and academics are extremely fond of referring to the federal statute sections by reference to the section numbers in the Lanham Act — for example, Section 2 regarding limitations on federal registerable marks rather than 15 U.S.C. § 1052 which is the actual Federal Code reference. As you have no doubt already noted, throughout this work the Lanham Act reference is given first, followed by the actual statutory citation.

Tom Landry was a famous professional football coach, and despite his iconic stature, **Answer B** is incorrect. The ALI Restatements are the legal "glitterati's" summary of the law (frequently as it actually is, but occasionally they can't resist and focus instead what it sound be). The Restatement (Third) of Unfair Competition (1995) can be an extremely helpful reference regarding trademark and unfair competition law, but it is not a federal statute, so **Answer A** is incorrect. Although many other events took place in 1812, passage of a federal trademark statute was not among them. In fact there was no federal trademark statute until 1870 when Congress passed the first (ill-fated — see Question 10 below) federal effort. Although the Lanham Act has been subsequently amended, the 1946 statute still provides the basic framework for federal trademark law.

10. **The best answer is B**. In the Trademark Cases, 100 U.S. 82 (1879), the Supreme Court held that trademark law differed from patent and copyright law in that those regimes sought to encourage intellectual labor while trademark law does not and, consequently, **Answer A** which authorizes the former two regimes does not support Congressional trademark action. Congress responded by passing a new trademark statute under the Commerce Clause (**Answer B**), thus rooting trademark law in the commerce between the States — and, importantly, limiting federal trademark law's applicability only to "interstate" commerce (*see* Lanham Act § 45 (15 U.S.C. § 1127) defining "commerce" as "all commerce which may lawfully regulated by Congress"). **Answer C**, the Necessary and Proper Clause, may be indirectly implicated, but does not serve as the actual legal foundation. **Answer D**, which concerns amendments to the Constitution, has nothing to do with trademark law unless the populace demands the addition of a specific clause addressing this important topic as a new Amendment (I wouldn't hold my breath).

NOTE: Congressional power to enact trademark laws is co-extensive with the Supreme Court's reading of the Commerce Clause. Under present interpretations that poses little if any limitation on the application of federal trademark law to domestic activities. The application of United States trademark law to foreign activity is considered under Topic 20 — Extraterritorial Application and Trademark Treaties.

11. **The best answer is D**. The federal trademark statute generally supplements rather than preempts State trademark law so **Answer B** is incorrect. Nor does it impose requirements on State law, which continues to be a matter for the individual States, so **Answer C** is also incorrect. Although the purpose of federal trademark law, as with all trademark law, is to provide information to consumers about products — **Answer A**, the federal law does so by supplementing state law particularly with regard to helping facilitate its application to interstate commerce. So, for example, by providing national constructive use upon federal registration (*see* Topic 9 — Registration: Constructive Use and Intent to Use) it provides a more uniform and predictable set of rules for interstate activities. So although **Answer A** is correct, **Answer D** is the better answer. That said, not all of the provisions of the Lanham Act can be convincingly explained on this basis — for example, the limitations on the kinds of marks which are federally registered arguably reflect other policy objectives. *See* Topic 11 — Registration: Grounds for Refusal.

12. **The best answer is B**. Although, like State trademark actions, a federal action requires a distinct mark (**Answer A**) and use of the mark (**Answer C**), the need to rely on the Commerce Clause as the basis for federal action (see Question 10 above) means that

all federal infringement actions require interstate commerce as a jurisdictional requirement (**Answer B**). Finally, a likelihood of confusion (**Answer D**) is required to prevail in a confusion-based trademark action (but not others), federal or state, so it is not uniquely relevant to a federal infringement actions. So **Answer B** is the best answer.

NOTE: The interstate commerce jurisdictional requirement as it relates to extra-United States activities is discussed in Topic 20 — Extraterritorial Application and Trademark Treaties.

13. **NO.** Because the federal act rests on the foundations of common law trademark, the failure to expressly incorporate or reference such doctrines does not, standing alone, mean they are inapplicable. Consequently, although the failure to clarify how existing common law doctrines interact with specific new rights of the federal law (e.g., incontestable registrations) may be read as negating their application in that specific context, that does not mean a general failure to "incorporate" them into the federal regime was intended to eliminate them entirely.

14. The "Pret" mark is called a "**trademark**" because it applies to goods (the books), while the "Aporter" mark is called a "**service mark**" because it applies to services. **The important point is that the substantive legal rules applicable to trademarks and service marks are, for all practical purposes, identical.** The good news, therefore, is that once one has mastered the basic black letter rules for one kind of mark, they are well in hand for the other. That said, application of those rules — for example, determining whether a mark has been used in connection with goods rather than services — will vary somewhat because while the former are tangible, the latter are not. So it is worth watching out for that difference. Aside from that, an acceptable answer to the Question is "none."

NOTE: Unless otherwise indicated, when used in the remainder of this work the word trademark refers to BOTH trademarks and service marks.

15. **Probably not**. The "Fasto" mark clearly serves as a trademark with regard to LSF's home electronic products. Although the warranty services are clearly services, those services are most likely to be viewed as part of the "product" as they are not separately offered and sold to consumers. Consequently, the "Fasto" mark is unlikely to be indicating source of the services to consumers and will not qualify as a service mark.

NOTE: Had LSF been selling a separate extended warranty, and certainly if it provided separate repair services to clients beyond the warranty, then there would be a good argument that "Fasto" was also a service mark.

16. **The best answer is D**. A certification mark informs the buying public that the related good (or service) meets the related "certification" standards. *See* Lanham Act § 45 (15 U.S.C. § 1127). Only those meeting the standards, but all that do, must be permitted to use the mark. **Answer A** is incorrect because ownership of a certification mark has a somewhat non-intuitive relationship to the right to use. Regarding certification marks the mark owner — for example, The Good Housekeeping Institute or Consumers Union — acts *only* as the certifying authority and not only does not, but under the Lanham Act *cannot*, use the mark on its own goods. *See id.* **Answer B** is incorrect because those not meeting the standards cannot use the mark. **Answer C** is close, but still incorrect because the mark owner does not have absolute discretion regarding whom to certify. All that meet the standards (**Answer D**) must be permitted to use the mark and none that fail to qualify may, regardless of the certification mark owner's desires.

17. Unlike traditional trademarks, **certification marks** permit a third party to control use in order to provide reliable information to consumers that the third party has inspected

and found the goods to be in conformity to the announced standards. This reduces the need for individual consumer testing of specific goods and provides a reliably transferable signal across a number of producers' goods regarding particular characteristics.

18. **The best answer is C.** A collective mark can be used *either* to indicate membership in a group (for example, a member of a farming cooperative or a lawyer as a member of the American Bar Association) *or* by an organization's members to distinguish their goods from those of non-members (for example, "Union made"). *See* Lanham Act § 45 (15 U.S.C. § 1127). **Answer A** refers only to one subset of collective marks; those used by union members, so is incomplete. **Answer B** incorrectly states the test for use of a certification mark. **Answer D** is also incorrect. A collective mark identifies the producer as a member of the collective organization, not the actual source of the product in the trademark sense. Therefore, although a collective may advertise it's members' products as a group under the collective mark, if the collective uses a mark to identify its *own* (rather than its members') products, the mark is now a trademark. Consequently, in all cases a collective mark merely indicates the user is a member of the related organization and **Answer C** is the best answer.

19. **The answer is B.** "Exacta" identifies the product as produced by Ultra, Inc., not that Ultra is a member of a collective (**Answer C**) or that the services meets a third party's standards (**Answer D**). The issue, therefore, is whether the Ultra's product is a service (making "Exacta" a service mark) or a good making "Exacta" a trademark. Because the product involved is consulting services, **Answer B** (service mark) is correct and **Answer A** (trademark) in not.

20. **The answer is C.** The ASPP membership badge indicates membership in the ASPP and, consequently, is a collective mark telling consumers that Ultra belongs to the ASPP. The membership badge does not signify that Ultra's products meet the ASPP certification standards, so it is not a certification mark (**Answer D**). Nor does it identify and distinguish Ultra's particular services, so it is not a service mark (**Answer B**). No goods are involved in the facts, so in no event can the membership badge be a trademark (**Answer A**) but even if Ultra were selling a good, it does not identify and distinguish Ultra's particular goods.

21. **The answer is D.** The ASPP-compliant-logo indicates that Ultra's services meet the ASPP certification standards, so it is a certification mark. Unlike the ASPP membership badge, it does not indicate membership in the ASPP and, consequently, is not a collective mark (**Answer C**). In fact, Ultra must be allowed to use the ASPP-compliant-logo, whether or not it is a member if it meets the related standards. The logo does not identify and distinguish Ultra's particular services, so it is not a service mark (**Answer B**). No goods are involved in the facts, so in no event can the membership badge be a trademark (**Answer A**), but even if Ultra were selling a good, it does not identify and distinguish Ultra's particular goods.

22. **On the facts it isn't clear that "Ultra" is a mark of any kind**. Even assuming that Ultra could qualify as a mark on these facts it is merely the name of the company.

Clearly it is neither a collective mark (membership) nor a certification mark (meeting third party standards). Without some evidence that it is actually being used to identify and distinguish the company's services by the consuming public (in addition to "Exacta"), it is not serving the necessary trademark source identification function and therefore does not qualify as a mark. *See* Topic 1 — Justifications and Sources of Trademark Law.

23. **The answer is A**. "Mighty-burger" (**Answer B**) is clearly serving as a trademark — identifying and distinguishing the Mightyburger, Ltd. burger product. "Best Burgers" (**Answer D**) is also clearly serving as a certification mark — showing that the Mightyburger product satisfies the Burgers of America standards. The contest, therefore, is between the box (**Answer C**) and Burgers of America (**Answer A**). The box, although not a word, can nonetheless qualify as a trademark as a form of *"trade dress"* which includes not only the design or appearance of a product's packaging of a product, but the design or appearance of the product itself. There are limitations on such marks (*see* Topic 5 — Distinctiveness: Non-word Marks, Colors and Trade Dress), but on these facts we are to assume that the box qualifies. It is likely serving as a trademark for Mightburger Ltd.'s burger product. Although Burgers of America might serve as a collective mark — showing membership in that organization — merely being the name of an organization is insufficient. On these facts there is no indication it is being used in that way, or for that matter that it is ever used in that way, so **Answer A** is correct.

24. The purpose of trademark law is to reduce consumers search costs by ensuring that the presence of a mark quickly and reliably conveys information about the characteristics of the related product. See Topic 1 — Justifications and Sources of Trademark Law. To do so each mark must be "distinctive" — that is, capable of specifically identifying and distinguishing a particular producer's goods from those made by others. *See* Lanham Act § 45 (15 USC § 1127) (definition of trademark).

25. **The answer is B.** Whether a mark is "distinctive" (that is, able to identify and distinguish a specific producer's goods) is determined based on the "spectrum of distinctiveness." That spectrum runs in increasing distinctiveness through four categories: (1) generic (the word for the class/type/genus of good involved) which are never distinctive (applying by definition to all products in the class) and thus never protectable as trademarks, (2) descriptive (of the goods' qualities or use of the product) which are not inherently distinctive but may become so through use, (3) suggestive (requiring a leap of imagination to make the connection to the goods) which are inherently distinctive, and (4) fanciful (invented "words") and arbitrary (an existing word but having no connection — descriptive or suggestive — to the goods), both of which are also inherently distinctive. *See Abercrombie & Fitch Co. v. Hunting World, Inc.*, 537 F.2d 4 (2d Cir. 1976). **Answers A, C and D** all are categories on the spectrum. **Answer B** is my invention and is NOT a category of distinctiveness.

26. **The answer is B**. Just making sure we're on the same page regarding trademark and service mark law. Other than the fact that trademarks apply to goods and service marks to the provision of services, the basic legal rules are virtually identical (although the specific application of the rule may vary to take into account the fact that products are tangible and services are not). *See* Topic 2 — Service Marks, Certification Marks and Collective Marks. Therefore, answers (and the related explanations) to "rules" questions using the term "trademark" will generally apply to both trademarks and service marks. This being a rules (as opposed to application) question, the answer to this Question is **the same as the answer to Question 25**.

27. **The best answer is D**. Reaching the correct answer requires a two step understanding of distinctiveness. The first is that trademarks can consist of virtually anything *capable* of uniquely identifying and distinguishing a product. *See Qualitex Co. v. Jacobson Products Co., Inc.*, 514 U.S. 159 (1995) (*citing* Lanham Act § 45 (15 U.S.C. § 1127) which defines "trademark" to include "any word, name, symbol or device, or any combination thereof"). Consequently, there is no absolute bar to non-word marks such

as colors, sounds or pictures serving as trademarks because of their "ontological" nature (that is, what they are — e.g., colors, sounds and pictures, respectively). Even smells have been permitted as trademarks. Under that all inclusive test, none of answers is categorically excluded, including the color and the musical notes.

The second is that the mark — whatever its ontological nature — must, in fact, be *distinctive*. Trademark law distinguishes between marks which are (1) inherently distinctive (suggestive, arbitrary and fanciful marks); (2) those which are not (descriptive and other marks which have a primary non-trademark significance) but can acquire distinctiveness through use as a trademark; and (3) those which can never be distinctive (generic terms — that is, the term for the class of goods involved). **Answer A** (color), **Answer B** (sounds) and **Answer C** ("sweet and crunchy" which are descriptive of the product) are *not* inherently distinctive because they all have a primary non-trademark significance — respectively, as a color, musical notes and a description of the goods). However, that does NOT preclude them from ever serving as trademarks; they can acquire distinctiveness ("secondary meaning") through usage. *See* Topic 4 — Distinctiveness: Inherently; Secondary Meaning; Never. **Answer D**, the word "jeans," however is the generic term for the class of products involved (pants made of denim material). For policy reasons, it is precluded from *EVER* serving as a trademark, even if it where to acquire distinctiveness through use.

NOTE: As an historical aside, although "jeans" is *now* the generic term for denim pants, it actually comes from "Genes" meaning the sailors from Genoa who wore those pants (not DNA sequences). Denim (the now generic term for the fabric used) comes from "de Nimes" meaning "from Nimes," the town in France where that material was produced. Consequently, both terms were originally "descriptive." Although that meant they were not inherently distinctive, had the creators of the pants or the material been thinking in terms of trademarks they might have successfully made "jeans" and "denim" distinctive through usage. However, even had the terms became distinctive, if the public subsequently adopted them as the generic term for the related good the mark then loses its status as a trademark. *See* Question 34 below.

28. **The best answer is A**. A generic term is the name of the general class of goods involved — or, as sometimes stated by the courts, it answers the question "what the good is" rather than providing information about its source and specific characteristics. *See Official Airline Guides, Inc. v. Goss*, 6 F.3d 1385 (9th Cir. 1993). Therefore, the determination requires (1) identifying the class or genus of goods involved and (2) determining the meaning of the term (its "primary significance" to the consuming public) to see if it labels that class of goods. *See Kellogg v. National Biscuit Co.*, 305 U.S. 111 (1938); *Miller Brewing Co. v. Jos. Schlitz Brewing Co.*, 605 F.2d 990 (7th Cir. 1986). **Answer B** and **Answer C** are, therefore, both clearly relevant as they identify the class of goods involved and offer objective evidence regarding the term's meaning to the general public. In the (in)famous Ninth Circuit case, *Anti-Monopoly, Inc. v. General Mills Fun Group, Inc.* 684 F.2d 1316 (9th Cir. 1982), the court held that a term is generic if consumer purchases are "motivated" primarily by a desire to obtain the product (the board game "Monopoly" in the case) rather than by who makes it (they

want the Parker Brothers' version). Trademark owners and academics objected on the grounds that even though a mark may identify the good (especially a unique good), it may *also* be identifying source — or stated in terms of the facts of the case, a buyer may be motivated to make the purchase simply to obtain the game of Monopoly but may also recognize (despite not caring) that they are getting the Parker Brothers' version because the mark is present. Congress agreed and amended the Lanham Act to explicitly make the generic determination turn on the "primary significance . . . to the general public" not simply that the mark identifies the type of product. Lanham Act § 14 (15 U.S.C. § 1064 (3)). Although that distinction does not, as they say, "shimmer with clarity" it is at least clear that a generic classification requires determining what the term "means" to the consumer — specifically, does it merely label the product or does it (also) identify source. So, at long last, because the test is articulated in the same terms as **Answer D**, and **Answer A** has been formally rejected, **Answer A** is the "least" relevant.

29. **The answer is C.** **Answer C** is clearly the term for the class of goods involved and, therefore, generic (an obvious result under the "meaning" test discussed in Question 28; something your dictionary will no doubt confirm). **Answer A** (sours) is *descriptive* (describing the nature of the candy), but not the word for the specific category of good (that would be "candy" or, perhaps "sour candy"). **Answer B**, although a real word describing a class of goods (apples), it is *arbitrary* (having no connection to) when applied to the goods involved — personal computers. **Answer D** is a fanciful term — that is an invented word having no pre-existing independent meaning (like sour, apple and copier), and therefore not the word for the related class of goods (petroleum products).

    NOTE: Remember, however, that the test is what the word means to consumers. So if consumers were ultimately decide that "sours" means the entire class of sour tasting candy or "exxirl" refers to cosmetic products as a group, then that usage controls and the word becomes generic for trademark purposes. *See* Question 34 below.

30. **The best answer is B.** When determining whether a term is generic it is not sufficient that it be composed of generic terms, even when they are relevant to the goods. The classification determination involves taking the mark *as a whole* in the specific context. *See Official Airline Guides, Inc. v. Goss*, 6 F3d 1385 (9th Cir. 1993). **Answers A, C and D** are composed of generic terms (*e.g.*, corn, pillows, memory, box, kids, stuff) relevant to the goods. However each combination taken as a whole in the particular context is descriptive of the related product, not the generic name for the class of goods (cereal, disc drives and toys, respectively). Only the combination in **Answer B** ("shoe warehouse") is arguably the genus label for the class of goods involved (a large store holding and selling high volumes of shoes) and, therefore, the most likely to be classified as generic.

31. **The best answer is C.** A fanciful mark is one which has been invented — that is, the word which does not already have a pre-existing independent meaning. **Answers A,**

B and D all are words having such independent meanings. Although **Answer C** is now recognizable to many, it does not actually have any meaning apart from being recognizable as a brand of gasoline, having been invented for that use. It is, therefore, the only fanciful mark.

Whether a word is invented (fanciful) is determined objectively. Consequently, it is not relevant whether particular customers actually know the word exists. So although I'm sure you recognized "argonaut" others might not realize it as a "real" word. What matters, however, is that the dictionary does.

32.   **The best answer is B**. An arbitrary word mark is one which has a pre-existing independent meaning but no connection with the particular product class. As it neither describes nor suggests product characteristics, use or effects, its use is termed "arbitrary." **Answer A** is descriptive of the baking activity. **Answer C** is fanciful (invented and having no pre-existing independent meaning), not arbitrary (its pre-existing meaning has no connection with the goods). As the argonauts referenced in **Answer D** were travelers, the word arguably suggests or perhaps even describes the bus service. Consequently, **Answer B** is the best choice: "orange" is a pre-existing word with an independent meaning having no connection to airline services.

33.   **The best answer is A**. When determining arbitrariness (as with most distinctiveness issues), *context* is key. The same word ("apple" in this case) can be arbitrary in one context (**Answer A** — personal computers) while it is generic (**Answer C** — the category of goods) or descriptive/suggestive (pies and sauce made from apples — **Answer B** and **Answer D**) in others.

34.   On the stated facts, both "thermos" and "Travid" are invented words having no pre-existing independent meaning. Consequently, they would both start their trademark life under the "fanciful" mark classification. Distinctiveness in trademark law, however, is not immutably fixed based on the original classification but by the term's actual significance to the public at any given time. Regarding "thermos," although it started as fanciful the public came to adopt the newly invented term as the word for the category of goods involved — that is, the public began to call ALL vacuum-insulated containers "thermos" rather seeing the word as referring only to the containers from a particular producer. *See King-Seeley Thermos Co. v. Aladdin Indus., Inc.*, 321 F.2d 577 (2d Cir. 1963). That transformation by public use of a fanciful term into the generic, and thus unprotectable, name for the product category is somewhat inelegantly referred to as "*genercide*" in trademark law. (A current example of that process in action is the "Google" mark — increasingly the public talks about "googling" a topic.)

In order to prevent the same thing occurring to "Travid" your client must take affirmative steps to prevent the public from adopting it as the generic term for portable, real-time digital video players. The problem is particularly acute in their case as they are using a fanciful (invented) term in reference to a unique and novel product. In such cases the public will be searching for a convenient label for the new product class and unless another appealing substitute is simultaneously made available, consumers may settle on the "Travid" mark for lack of other obvious alternatives. Avoiding this problem in your client's case this will take some creativity. The public is hardly going to latch onto "portable real-time digital video player," so the client needs to think of something else to fill that void — say "RTDVD?" Additionally, they should emphasize that "the Travid is a portable, real-time digital video player (or RTDVD)" in their advertising and sales activities and ensure their competitors do the same. They should engage in on-going educational efforts to prevent public generic adoption and use (for example the makers of Xerox copiers periodically run advertisements which emphasize to the public that their copiers make — "a copy, not a Xerox"). Finally, they should object to any dictionary or similar definitions which genricize their mark and thus encourage that public view.

However, the client should understand that the matter is ultimately not within their control — if the public comes to view the "Travid" mark as the category genus, then the term is generic and no longer protectable as a trademark, as number of famous examples (thermos, aspirin, escalator and cellophane) attest.

They might also consider another kind of mark — for example an arbitrary or suggestive mark which, already having pre-existing meanings, make unlikely candidates for a class name. However, genericide can sometimes be a problem even for those kinds of marks. For example, the public has threatened to make "Coke" (which was arguably originally descriptive, although that is disputed by the Coca-Cola Company) the label for the entire class of cola drinks. The Coca-Cola Company's concern over that possibility is reflected by the waitron's question "Is Pepsi, OK?" — specifically designed to emphasize to the public that "Coke" is a particular cola drink, not the class.

35. **BigIdea may be able to bring an unfair competition lawsuit**. Even though Travid has become generic and trademark law will not prevent its use to identify competing products in the same class of goods, a use which involved passing-off the competitor's product as BigIdea's product would be a violation of unfair competition law. Consequently, the competitor could be required to take affirmative steps to ensure consumers understood they were not getting BigIdea's product, for example by adding an express disclaimer ("not associated with BigIdea") or the producer's own mark ("an XYZ travid") *See Kellogg Co. v. National Biscuit Co.*, 305 U.S. 111 (1938).

36. **The best answer is D**. "Easy-On" is not the term for the class of product (house paint) so it is not generic; consequently, **Answer A** is incorrect. Nor is it an invented term — it has a readily discernable pre-existing meaning (even if it is grammatically somewhat suspect). So it is not fanciful, making **Answer B** incorrect. Because it describes rather than suggests a characteristic of the product or its use — it is easy to apply — it will most likely be classified as descriptive rather than suggestive. Consequently, **Answer D** is better than **Answer C**.

37. The classification determination turns on the meaning (primary significance) of the mark to the consuming public. Although phonetic misspellings and acronyms result in words that are technically "fanciful" —they clearly have no pre-existing dictionary meaning

— their actual classification turns on substance rather than form; specifically, how they will be understood and used by the consuming public. Whenever such terms sound (and/or look) similar to the "real" term or are commonly used acronyms for the "expanded" meaning, it is assumed the public will understand the reference and the courts will treat them as equivalents. *See Soweco, Inc. v. Shell Oil Co.*, 617 F.2d 1178 (5th Cir. 1980). For example, because consumers will understand and treat "ROM" as the equivalent of "read only memory," it would be found generic for that class of semi-conductor chips. *See Intel Corp. v. Radiation, Inc.*, 184 U.S.P.Q. 54 (T.T.A.B. 1984). Consequently, because "EZ-On" sounds like "Easy On" and/or "EZ" is a common short-hand version for "Easy" it is highly likely a court will view them as equivalents and classify the former in the same fashion as the latter — that is as descriptive.

38. **The best answer is C.** The word "pounce" does not label the category of goods (cat food treats), so it is not generic and **Answer A** is incorrect. Nor does it describe the characteristics, use or results of the product, making it unlikely to be classified as descriptive. So **Answer B** is incorrect. The word does, however, suggests how the user (the cat) will react to the treat and is, therefore, likely to be classified as suggestive, **Answer C**. Because it is related to the product, albeit indirectly, it is unlikely to be classified as arbitrary (having no relationship to the product), so **Answer D** is incorrect.

39. **The best answer is C.** All of the answers describe tests used by the courts to distinguish between a descriptive and a suggestive mark. *See Zatarain's Inc. v. Oak Grove Smokehouse, Inc.*, 698 F.2d 786 (5th Cir. 1983). **Answer A** is very good evidence of how consumers will understand the term which can then be assessed for descriptiveness in light of the nature, use or result of the related good. **Answer B** is the primary test for suggestiveness — that rather than explicitly describing, it requires some imagination for the consumer to make the association between the term and the nature of the related good. **Answer C** and **Answer D** are used by the courts to assess descriptiveness. However, **Answer D** directly focuses on the actual question — would the term be helpful to describing competitors' products. In contrast, **Answer C** is ambiguous. Competitors *may* be using the term to describe their products, but they may also be adopting a successful mark. So **Answer D** is better than **Answer C**, making **Answer C** the least helpful.

40.   Answers:

   A. **Generic.** In this context, "diamond" is the name of the class/genus of the goods involved.

   B. **Generic.** The term "diemonde" may technically be invented (and, therefore, fanciful), however, in this context its phonetic (and visual) equivalence to "diamond" will likely lead to is classification as generic.

   C. **Suggestive.** The term "diamond" is not invented so it is not fanciful. Nor is it the generic for, or descriptive of, a baseball team. Rather it suggests where the team performs making it most likely to be classified as suggestive rather than arbitrary.

(Note that although the example probably involves a service mark not a trademark, but the analysis is the same.)

D. **An open issue**. The Patent and Trademark Office takes the position that adding ".something" (including ".com") to the generic term for the goods involved has no source identifying (trademark) role and the resulting combination (URL) retains the character of the root. Consequently, "diamond.com" would be treated as generic. On the other hand, the "1-800-"generic" phone number cases not only support an argument that such URL combinations are not generic (the public does not use the term to reference the genus of diamonds or the class of online diamond sellers) but that they should not even be viewed as descriptive of either diamonds sold over the internet or the online sale of diamonds (although the latter is a closer call). The result would likely be to treat such marks as suggestive. (NOTE: An alternative argument might be made that such marks are "functional" — as they are the means for shopping on line and therefore should not be protectable as marks at all. *See* Topic 6 — Functionality.)

E. **Arbitrary, although descriptive is also arguably correct.** Generic and fanciful classifications can be readily eliminated on the facts (the related service is internet access and the word "diamond" is not invented). At first glance the word has no obvious connection to an internet service, which would make "diamond" arbitrary in this context. It does not suggest the related service as it does with the baseball team (context is everything, see example C above). However, a plausible argument might be made that the non-gemstone meaning of "diamond" connoting superior or high quality might be viewed as descriptive in the same way that "A-1" or "Best" might be.

F. **Descriptive**. The word "quick" describes the qualities of the service (not, it is important to note, the class of service itself — internet access — which would have made it generic).

G. **Suggestive; perhaps arbitrary.** The word "quick" does not describe the nature or purpose of the scissors (sharp or trim). It might be argued that it is arbitrary in this context, but because it involves an indirect connection with cuticle scissors by reference to the "quick" of one's nails, suggestive may be the best classification.

H. **Fanciful, although descriptive or suggestive are also arguably correct.** The term "I-Crit" is invented and on that basis would be classified as fanciful. In this context, however, when it is said out loud it could be viewed as short for "I criticize" which is part of what a consultant does. Consequently, one could argue that it is descriptive, or because it is abbreviated in a non-traditional way and therefore requires a "leap of imagination" it is suggestive.

I. **Fanciful**. In this context there is no obvious connection to the product involved (diamonds), so the term "I-crit" is now most likely to be treated as invented (having no pre-existing meaning) and, thus, fanciful.

41. On their face, the letters themselves — BYO — do not comprise an existing word and, therefore, might be classified as a fanciful (invented word) mark. That would make it

inherently distinctive and fully protectable, without more, on distinctiveness grounds. The difficulty is that the letters BYO are a commonly used acronym for "Bring Your Own (Booze)." As with misspellings (EZ-On — see Question 37 above), the classification of an acronym turns on how the consuming public is likely to understand the mark.

In this case, the common understanding of the "expanded" version of the "BYO" mark must be assessed based on the relationship of that meaning to the related product. The classification, therefore, comes down to whether "bring your own" is best viewed as descriptive or suggestive of a pre-packaged beer product, with only the latter providing the comfort of inherent distinctiveness and the former requiring a showing of secondary meaning.

The tests for making the descriptive vs. suggestive determination do not provide a definitive answer on these facts. It is reasonable to argue that "bring your own" requires a "leap of imagination" to understand the mark involves a beer product, as other kinds of beverages may also be BYO. *Cf. Anheuser-Busch, Inc. v. Stroh Brewery Co.*, 750 F.2d 631 (8th Cir. 1984). Moreover, BYO does not describe a characteristic or use of beer itself. However, if one focuses on the particular packaging in this case BYO does have a descriptive connection to the particular product's purpose or use — taking beer to a party. In that same vein, another beer producer might need to use the acronym (or its expanded meaning) to describe their product — pointing out that their pre-packaged beer is the "perfect BYO product." It might be useful to determine if that use is actually occurring — although as noted in Question 39 some skepticism is healthy in assessing whether such use is in fact descriptive rather than merely reflecting the adoption of a successful mark. That all said, it seems likely that the mark would be found descriptive and thus unprotectable unless (and only if) BestBeer can demonstrate secondary meaning. Consequently, they should be clearly and explicitly advised of that risk in order to help them decide whether to stick with BYO or select another mark.

42. **The best answer is D**. Foreign words are generally classified based on their translated meaning in English; the assumption being that some non-de-minimis portion of the United States consumer population will know the foreign word and its meaning. On that basis, the French word (café) will be classified based on its English meaning (coffee) which makes it generic. So **Answer D** is correct and **Answers A, B and C** are not.

NOTE: Another reason for using the translated meaning of foreign words is international "comity" — because the United States would be upset if producers in other countries used English generic terms as trademarks ("computer" for example) it honors foreign meanings as a matter of reciprocity.

NOTE: The "translate before assessing meaning" approach is also used regarding infringement assessments, so the sight, sound, meaning test would apply the English language meaning of a foreign word mark. So if the word "café" were used as a trademark on clocks (making it arbitrary) there would nonetheless be a strong argument for finding likelihood of confusion if another clock manufacturer adopted the word "coffee" as a mark for their product. *See* Topic 13 — Infringement: Likelihood of Confusion.

43.   **The best answer is C, but there is reasonable support for A.** This question illustrates (for most of us, anyway) the problems with the "translate before assessing" test as the language involved gets more obscure. As it turns out "cohiba" meant "rolled tobacco" in the language of the Taino Indians. Applying the "translate before assessing" rule there is no question but the word is descriptive. So **Answer C** is technically correct under the rule. But who actually knows that? The "obscure" (or in this case "dead") language problem has caused courts to depart from the general rule when it is clear that no (or at least virtually no) relevant consumers actually know the translated meaning.

44. A mark is "inherently distinctive" when it is presumed capable of uniquely identifying and distinguishing the mark owner's goods without any additional demonstration that it satisfies that requirement — or said another way, such a mark automatically qualifies as capable of acting as a unique source identifier.

45. The **spectrum of distinctiveness** which acts as a classification scheme to determine which marks can never be distinctive, which can become distinctive and which are "automatically" — or inherently — distinctive.

46. **The answer is D.** The "spectrum of distinctiveness" classifies marks based on their distinctiveness. Generic marks can *never* be distinctive, much less inherently distinctive. Descriptive marks are not inherently distinctive, but can become distinctive through a showing of "secondary meaning" (a demonstration that consumers view them as a source identifier for the mark claimant's particular product). Arbitrary, fanciful and suggestive marks are all deemed inherently distinctive — that is, they require nothing further to enable them to uniquely identify and distinguish that particular product. **Answers A, B and C** identify the "inherently distinctive" categories on the spectrum of distinctiveness. Only **Answer D** — a descriptive mark — is not inherently distinctive (although it may eventually become distinctive through use).

47. The "Meaty Blend" mark is likely to be classified as a descriptive mark (describing the product's primary ingredients), whereas the "Royal Cat" mark will, at worst, be found suggestive. *See* Topic 3 — Basic Distinctiveness: The Spectrum of Distinctiveness; Word Marks Including Acronyms and Foreign Words. As a result "Royal Cat" is inherently distinctive and will automatically meet the distinctiveness requirement. "Meaty Blend," however, will require a special showing of distinctiveness before it can be protected as a trademark. That showing will likely require an extended period of usage before trademark rights can be claimed, leaving CatSnacks at risk during the interim.

48. **The BEST answer is C.** The classes of marks which are NOT inherently distinctive are generic and descriptive marks. It is true that such marks flow naturally from the related product and require "little effort to think up." The distinctiveness requirement, however, is not generally about incentives to create, but ensuring that marks clearly and reliably provide information to consumers. Consequently, **Answer A** is incorrect. **Answer B** is incorrect — generic and descriptive marks do (rather than do not) provide information about the related product (the class of product and salient information about product characteristics, ingredients or use) as reflected in **Answer D**'s "non-trademark"

association. That non-trademark association, however, lies at the root of the distinctiveness problem. Treating those classes of marks as inherently distinctive would permit a single producer to control the name and/or relevant descriptors for the entire product class. That "exclusivity" would impair information flow to consumers and harm intra-class competition by requiring other producers to use other less efficient and effective ways to identify and describe their products. **Answer C** is, therefore, the best answer.

49.   **The best answer is A**. Applying the spectrum of distinctiveness, **Answer A** is arbitrary, **Answer B** is descriptive (phonetic misspellings are viewed as equivalent to the "real word" when consumers will make the connection), **Answer C** is generic and **Answer D** is descriptive. Only **Answer A** (arbitrary) falls in an inherently distinctive category on the spectrum, as it is the only term which is neither generic nor descriptive.

50.   **The best answer is C**. "Lumber & Pulp" is generic for the related wood products and thus it can never be distinctive. Although descriptive terms (**Answer B** and **Answer D**) are not inherently distinctive, they may become distinctive through use. **Answer A** is arbitrary and thus inherently distinctive — that is, treated as distinctive without further inquiry.

51.   **The best answer is B (it's a close call which is the point — if you understand why, then full credit).** What makes the answer problematic is the frequent difficulty in determining whether a mark is properly classified as descriptive, which would make it NOT inherently distinctive, or as suggestive which would. This issue arises frequently in trademark cases with the plaintiff trademark owner arguing vigorously for the inherently distinctive "suggestive" classification and the defendant for the not inherently distinctive (and thus not automatically protectable) "descriptive" classification. *See Zatarain's, Inc. v. Oak Grove Smokehouse, Inc.*, 698 F.2d 786 (5th Cir. 1983). In my view (but not necessarily a court's): **Answers A, C and D** are all descriptive of characteristics of the related product, while **Answer B** only suggests (a baker would be proud of this loaf) and thus is the only inherently distinctive mark of the group.

52.   **The best answer is D**. On the facts "Vision Center" will be classified as descriptive, meaning it does not qualify as inherently distinctive. Usage as a trademark is always required in United States trademark law for a term to qualify as a trademark, but that does not make a descriptive mark distinctive. Your client must *also* show that it uniquely identifies and distinguishes its services in the public's mind. So **Answer A** is incorrect. That demonstration turns on showing that — normally through extensive use (**Answer B**) — the public perception of the mark has moved beyond its independent primary descriptive role (in this case indicating the nature of the services — **Answer C**) to take on "*secondary meaning*" as a unique product identifying trademark for the client's *particular* vision services (conveying information about those services beyond their being about vision, such as prompt, courteous, particularly effective — **Answer D**). So **Answer C** is the problem NOT the solution, and is incorrect. Although **Answer B** is the means for showing secondary meaning, it is not sufficient unless it has actually resulted in the public viewing the phrase as a source identifier (for the client's services).

Answer D is the best answer. *See Vision Center v. Opticks, Inc.*, 596 F.2d 111 (5th Cir. 1980).

53. **The best answer is A.** *Only* marks classified as descriptive require secondary meaning. **Answer A** is the only mark which fits in that category. **Answer B** is arbitrary and **Answer D** is (arguably) fanciful making them both inherently distinctive. That means they satisfy the distinctiveness requirement without any further showing required. **Answer C** (delivery couriers) is the generic term for the service and is not inherently distinctive. However, unlike descriptive terms generic marks can NEVER be a trademark, so a showing of secondary meaning "distinctiveness" will still not permit them to serve as marks.

NOTE: This difference between generic and descriptive marks makes classification critical. For example, had the mark "Vision Center" in Question 52 been classified as generic (as it arguably could have been), then it could not have served as a mark even with a showing of secondary meaning.

54. **The best answer is A** (although they are all relevant to some extent). The doctrine of secondary meaning is not about protecting the producer's investment in the trademark but ensuring that once a descriptive mark has taken on trademark significance to the consuming public that source signaling expectation will be met. Consequently, secondary meaning is best demonstrated by evidence regarding how the consuming public views the mark. *See Zatarain's, Inc. v. Oak Grove Smokehouse, Inc.*, 698 F.2d 786 (5th Cir. 1983). **Answer B** and **Answer D** are, therefore, the best proof of secondary meaning as they provide direct evidence regarding whether consumers view the term as descriptive or as a mark-indicator-of-source. **Answer A** and **Answer C** are both forms of circumstantial evidence which can support an inference of secondary meaning. **Answer C** is extremely probative of a lack of secondary meaning as prominent use by competitors over a long period of time makes it highly unlikely that the public associates the term with a specific producer. **Answer A** (significant advertising) indicates the mark owner's effort to generate secondary meaning. However, demonstrating the attempt to develop secondary meaning does not, without more, permit the inference that the effort was in fact successful. Consequently, although all four answers are relevant, **Answer A** is the LEAST relevant. *See* Restatement (Third) of Unfair Competition § 13, Comment (e) (1995).

NOTE: The doctrine of "secondary meaning in the making," which would protect as yet unsuccessful investments in efforts to create secondary meaning to give the claimant some time to either perfect its rights or fail, has been rejected by the Supreme Court on the grounds that a mark is either distinctive (and protectable as a trademark) or it is not. *See Two Pesos, Inc. v. Taco Cabana, Inc.*, 505 U.S. 763 (1992), *reh'g denied*, 505 U.S. 1244 (1992).

55. **NO.** Although Dental Corp.'s trademark rights do prevent Teeth Ltd. from using the phrase "Gentle Dental" as a trademark, the doctrine of trademark (not copyright) "fair

use" will allow non-trademark use of the phrase in its descriptive sense (we offer gentle dental care). *See* Topic 16 — Defenses: Fair Use, Nominative Use, Parody/Free Speech.

56. **Their distinctiveness position is problematic**. The distinctiveness of the phrase "Lite Cola" will be determined based on consumer perception of the phrase. That means the phrase will be tested based on the phonetic equivalent "Light Cola." If the mark is found descriptive of a low calorie, cola soft drink, it will not be inherently distinctive and GreatCola will need to demonstrate secondary meaning. It can use the survey to make that demonstration. However, surveys are notoriously difficult to defend so more information about the actual methodology and results will be required. *See Zatarain's, Inc. v. Oak Grove Smokehouse, Inc.*, 698 F.2d 786 (5th Cir. 1983). Consequently, some additional proof may be necessary to make their case for distinctiveness including evidence of non-use by others (which is unlikely given the prevalence of "lite" marks in the marketplace). Yet more problematic is that a reasonable chance exists a court will find the mark generic for a low calorie soft drink. *See Miller Brewing Co. v. Jos. Schlitz Brewing Co.*, 605 F.2d 990 (7th Cir. 1979) (finding the term "Lite" generic for low calorie beer). If so, then the phrase will be precluded from serving as a trademark even with evidence supporting a finding of secondary meaning.

57. **It is difficult to justify the different treatment on policy grounds**. Trademark distinctiveness rules seek to enhance efficient consumer search while minimizing the adverse effects on competition. The adverse effects on competition of granting trademark rights in either generic or descriptive marks argue against protection of either category. The core argument for permitting descriptive marks with secondary meaning to act as trademarks is that once consumers have come to see the term as identifying a particular producer's product, it is necessary to preclude confusing use by others to ensure the related source identifying expectations are met. However, that same argument supports protecting generic marks with secondary meaning. It might be argued that granting exclusive rights to use the generic term for the class of goods is more detrimental to competition because finding an effective substitute may be extremely difficult. But that argument applies equally to an adjective describing a critical characteristic of a product class (for example, bran for bran cereal). Finally, it might be argued that the doctrine of fair use mitigates the competitive harm caused by offering trademark protection to descriptive terms which have acquired secondary meaning. There is no reason, however, that fair use might not also be applied to mitigate the harm of permitting a generic term which has acquired secondary meaning to serve as a trademark. In sum, it is difficult to support the distinction — either the secondary meaning/fair use arguments support protecting both generic and descriptive marks or the competitive harms argue against trademark status for both.

That all said, the <u>rule</u> is clearly that generic terms can never be trademarks while descriptive terms can provided they have demonstrable secondary meaning. Consequently, drawing the line between generic and descriptive is crucial, making the decision as to whether "Lite Cola" falls into the former or the latter classification key.

58. **YES**. Courts may fill the "gap" and provide relief if a generic term becomes strongly associated with a particular producer. This can happen, for example, when the originator of the product class is protected by patent law and, consequently, is the exclusive user of the related mark for a long period of time. Not only does the public come to view the mark as the generic term for the new product (particularly if it is a fanciful term like "thermos" or "aspirin") but it also associates the term with the single producer. To alleviate this conundrum the courts have permitted use of the generic term by subsequent producers (upon expiry of the patent) but have also required such producers to take steps to clearly distinguish themselves and their product from the original producer and its product. *See Blinded Veterans Assn. v. Blinded American Veterans Found.*, 872 F.2d 1035 (D.C. Cir. 1989) (citing a number of cases to this effect). Because the generic term cannot technically serve as a trademark — meaning its use by others cannot be prohibited — this "rule" may be more appropriately viewed as part of "unfair competition" law.

59. **The key is how each mark's classification affects its distinctiveness**. "Wrinkle Remover" is likely to be classified as generic. That means it can never be protected as a trademark, making it a very poor choice. Even if it were classified as descriptive, it would still not be protectable until it obtained secondary meaning — requiring substantial time and investment while exposing Miracle to significant risk of third party adoption in the interim. "Wrinkle Away" is likely to be classified as descriptive with those attendant difficulties. However, there is a weak argument that it is suggestive (requiring a leap of imagination). If that argument were to prevail then "Wrinkle Away" would cross the distinctiveness line into inherently distinctiveness, making it immediately protectable. "Young Again" seems much more likely to be classified as suggestive thus avoiding the risk of a descriptive classification and, consequently a better selection. Finally, "Vitrex" appears fanciful (invented), meaning it would also be treated as inherently distinctive. Additionally, because it has no pre-existing meaning or association with the product it will be viewed as the most distinctive and, therefore, the strongest of the four marks. However, as the product is new and has no easily articulated class label ("wrinkle remover" is clunky to say), there is there is perhaps a risk that the public will adopt "Vitrex" as the generic term. On balance the best two choices (on a distinctiveness scale — commercial considerations aside) are "Young Again" and "Vitrex" with, perhaps, Vitrex having a slight edge despite the genericide possibility.

60. **They ALL can serve as marks.** Trademark law is largely indifferent to *form* permitting virtually anything which can uniquely identify and distinguish a particular product to serve as a mark. Specifically, the definition of trademark and service mark in Section 45 of the Lanham Act (15 U.S.C. § 1127) states that "any word, name, symbol or device, or any combination thereof" will suffice, and in the words of the Supreme Court "it is the source-distinguishing ability of a mark — not its ontological status as color, shape, fragrance, word or sign" that determines whether it *can* serve as a trademark. *See Qualitex Co. v. Jacobson Products Co., Inc.*, 514 U.S. 159 (1995).

    However, although a wide variety of non-word marks *can* qualify for protection as a mark, whether a particular non-word mark actually *does* qualify depends on whether it satisfies the distinctiveness requirement. Because many non-word marks have no ordinary "word" meanings to assist in that latter determination (consider, for example, Answers D, E and F to the Question) it can be an extremely challenging undertaking. That difficult task is addressed in the Questions below.

61. **The best answer is C.** There is no question that the color gray *can* serve as a trademark; however, many non-word marks (including colors) pose special problems in determining their distinctiveness. **Answer A** simply restates the goal, telling us nothing about *how* the non-word mark distinctiveness determination might be made. Some courts purport to do that by applying the spectrum of distinctiveness used for word marks (**Answer B**). *See Stuart Hall Co. v. Ampad Corp.*, 51 F.3d 780 (8th Cir. 1995). However, the spectrum's tests were developed specifically to assess how the word mark's meaning relates to the particular goods or services. Because a color (like many, but not all, other non-word marks) has no such "meaning" those tests frequently are not particular illuminating. For example, in this case, gray doesn't mean anything in particular in the "word" sense so cannot have a connotative connection to the product involved. Consequently, its "classification" must turn instead on the broader market context. On that basis it might be argued that the prevalence of gray personal computing products makes the color generic (the color is part of what it means to be a personal computing product in the consumers' eyes) or, perhaps, descriptive (the color gray indicates the "serious" and/or "performance" characteristics generally associated with such products). But one could just as reasonably argue that the color of a computer has nothing to do with its "computerness" and therefore it is arbitrary. **Answer D**, therefore, correctly states some special testing will be required to assess many non-word marks' distinctiveness, but it doesn't indicate anything about the nature of that test. That gap is best filled by recognizing that the non-word mark distinctiveness inquiry turns the same underlying trademark policy requirement which drove the creation of the spectrum of distinctiveness

for word marks — assessing whether the non-word mark is uniquely identifying and distinguishing Computer Universe's particular product. **Answer C** is, therefore, the best answer because it indicates that the test for determining the distinctiveness of non-word marks should focus directly on whether the mark is signaling source in the particular context.

NOTE: As alluded to in the answer, some non-word marks do have readily ascribable word meanings, such as recognizable images of actual things. The spectrum of distinctiveness arguably does provide useful guidance in such cases as its word-oriented tests can be applied to the meaning of the image. For example, the distinctiveness of the picture of a cow might simply correspond to the classification of the word "cow." Thus a cow picture would be generic for cattle, descriptive/suggestive for milk or leather boots and arbitrary for computers.

62.   **The best answer is D**. The distinctiveness issue turns on whether the gray color is identifying and distinguishing Computer Universe's particular computer products. The ontological nature of the claimed mark is not limiting in that regard (*see* Question 60 above). In particular, marks clearly do not need to be words, so **Answer A** is incorrect. Nor are colors precluded from serving as trademarks, making **Answer B** also incorrect. It is true that the spectrum of distinctiveness frequently does not resolve non-word distinctiveness inquiries, so **Answer C** is at least correct in that regard. However, the central distinctiveness issue with colors (as well as many other, but not all, non-word marks) is that they have a pre-existing, independent significance to an observer; that is, as a color. The crucial issue, therefore, is determining whether consumers view the grey merely as the color of the object (the computer in this case) or as a source identifier. *See Qualitex Co. v. Jacobson Products Co., Inc.*, 514 U.S. 159 (1995). Consequently, **Answer D** is the best answer.

NOTE: An additional point regarding the problem with relying on the spectrum of distinctiveness: Even when a color mark spectrum classification seems clear — for example, generic (orange for oranges), descriptive (orange marmalade), suggestive (for a tanning product) or arbitrary (an orange personal computer in a sea of gray machines) — unlike word marks that classification does not resolve the central distinctiveness issue — are customers seeing the color merely in that pre-existing independent sense (as a color) or as a trademark source identifier.

NOTE: There can also be a functionality problem with colors — either as a practical or aesthetic matter. *See* Topic 6 — Functionality; *Qualitex Co. v. Jacobson Products Co., Inc.*, 514 U.S. 159 (1995).

63.   **The best answer is B**. As noted in Question 61, arguments can be made that the color gray is generic (**Answer A**), descriptive (**Answer B**) and arbitrary (**Answer D**). However, the issue is not finding the appropriate classification but determining whether, given its preexisting independent meaning as a color, customers are treating the color merely as a color or as a trademark signaling source. That is the same concern raised when a descriptive term is claimed as a mark — are consumers viewing the term as

merely describing a particular characteristic (tasty, fresh) of the related product class or as a unique identifier for the particular producer's specific product. So **Answer B** is the best choice.

64. **A showing of secondary meaning will be required**. The connection to the descriptive word marks problem means that a color can be claimed as a mark only under the same circumstances — that is, proof that consumers have actually come to see the color as a source identifier rather than merely as a color. So Computer Universe will need to provide evidence that the color gray uniquely identifies and distinguishes its particular product in the consumer's mind. *See* Topic 4 — Distinctiveness: Inherently; Secondary Meaning; Never *See Qualitex Co. v. Jacobson Products Co., Inc.*, 514 U.S. 159 (1995).

65. **It will be very difficult to claim black as a trademark on these facts.** There is no legal limitation on color serving as a trademark, so there is no absolute bar to their using black as a the trademark for their winter collection. The crucial issue is whether the color will be treated as distinctive — that is, uniquely distinguishing and identifying their particular product line. Because colors can serve in another role (the color of the suits in this case) even a successful (albeit difficult) argument that the selection or use of black is arbitrary will not resolve the distinctiveness issue. Instead StudDuds must be prepared to demonstrate that the color black has taken on a trademark source-identifying "secondary meaning" with the consumer. Accomplishing that task will require time and investment, as well as robust evidence indicating the effort has been successful with customers. Consequently, StudDuds will not be able to protect the mark immediately against adoption and use by others. That permitted simultaneous competitive use by competitors may hamper, if not prevent, eventually establishing a valid claim. As it appears StudDuds does not plan to use the mark over several seasons (the facts only mentions the upcoming winter season) it is unlikely that any practically useful trademark protection will ever be available. Consequently, some other form of mark would likely be preferable.

66. **Yes**. Although color remains an important element in the proposed mark the actual claim is now to a combination "device" (the black colored rectangular tag). Additionally, the removable black tag device is not a part of the suit so the color's pre-existing independent meaning is no longer entangled with the good itself. Applying the spectrum of distinctiveness, the tag doesn't have any "word" meaning so it might reasonably be argued that it falls into the fanciful "category" and hence should be treated as inherently distinctive. On the other hand how do we know that consumers are seeing it as a source indicator? The answer (which supports and explains the fanciful spectrum classification) is that the *device* (a black rectangle) has no non-mark significance in this market context (either a word "meaning" connected to the product, serving as part of the product (its color) or otherwise). It is, therefore, reasonable to presume consumers can only interpret its presence as signaling source. In such circumstances it can be treated as inherently distinctive and no further proof of distinctiveness will be required. *Cf. Two Pesos, Inc. v. Taco Cabana, Inc.*, 505 U.S. 763 (1992).

Although the actual legal answer is far more intricate (as revealed in the Questions below) the above provides a (hopefully) helpful "rule of thumb" for determining the distinctiveness of non-word marks. If in the particular context the non-word mark has no relevant non-mark significance to consumers (a word meaning, the color of the good) it can be classified as inherently distinctive. If there is a possible non-mark significance then further distinctiveness inquiry is required, including generally a showing of secondary meaning to overcome the inference that consumers are viewing the mark in its non-mark role rather than as signaling source.

NOTE: It is important, however, to understand that even if the black rectangle device is treated as inherently distinctive that does not give StudDuds trademark rights in the color black standing alone. In particular, although its rights to the black device may extend to prevent other "confusingly similar" black devices — say a black circular tag — that is a consequence of the rules for determining infringement of the device as a whole, not that StudDuds has established independent trademark rights in the color black itself.

67. **The best answer is D**. Applying the basic rule of thumb, a number "909" (**Answer A**) and a recognizable image of a pine tree (**Answer B**) are non-word marks which have a possible non-mark significance and require additional distinctiveness inquiry. Specifically, the image of the pine tree could "follow" its word meaning thus classifying it as descriptive and the number (which would be very hard to categorize on the spectrum) may be viewed as a stocking inventory or other non-source signaling identifier. So both **Answer A** and **Answer B** will require a showing of secondary meaning to prove they are serving as a trademark for the particular producer's goods.

Answer C is actually part of the product while **Answer D** involves the product packaging. These latter two answers implicate the special rules developed for determining the distinctiveness of non-word *trade dress*. The Supreme Court has drawn a distinction between product design (the way the product itself looks — **Answer C**) and its packaging (**Answer D**). In *Wal-Mart Stores, Inc. v. Samara Brothers, Inc.*, 529 U.S. 205 (2000), the Court held that the although in the proper circumstances *product packaging* can be inherently distinctive (thus not requiring a showing of secondary meaning), as *product design* "almost invariably serves purposes other than source identification" its protection as a trademark *always* requires a showing of secondary meaning (that it is viewed by customers as identifying source). Consequently, **Answer C** will require a showing of secondary meaning. Only **Answer D** *may not* require such a showing, making it the best answer.

NOTE: The *Walmart* design/packaging distinction tracks the "no relevant non-mark significance" rule of thumb — product design always has a connection to the related goods (it is part of the product) while packaging design must be assessed based on the specific facts (whether it is viewed merely as packaging — a non-mark significance — or as a source signal).

NOTE: Product design marks, in particular, but also product packaging marks, can also raise functionality concerns. *See* Topic 6 — Functionality.

68. **The best answer is C.** For product packaging to be inherently distinctive requires that consumers automatically perceive it to serve as a source identifier (in contrast to the packaging gradually taking on that role through secondary meaning). **Answer D** states that test, so it will be influential in (indeed central to) a court's decision. **Answer A** and **Answer B** reflect the approaches used by the courts to make that determination and are both relevant. Some courts use the spectrum of distinctiveness while others "supplement" that test (in light of the difficultly in applying it meaningfully to non-word marks without word-meanings) with other considerations. *See Yankee Candle Company, Inc. v. Bridgewater Candle Company, LLC*, 259 F.3d 25 (1st Cir. 2001). Under either approach, however, the key is how the mark is perceived by consumers in the particular context. Courts "supplementing" the spectrum inquiry look to whether the packaging is unique, unusual or unexpected in that context. If it is then consumers are likely to view it as "distinctive" and attach source significance; whereas if it consists of common or basic packaging features they will likely ignore it. (Note that this is consistent with the rule of thumb approach, common characteristics will be viewed as serving a non-mark role, the packaging of the good, whereas unusual or surprising packaging features are unusual and surprising because they appear to have no non-mark significance in the context). **Answer C** — whether the *packaging* includes color (it almost always will) — is not relevant standing alone. What matters is whether that packaging color is unique, unusual or unexpected (having no apparent non-mark significance) in this context. (A color as part of the product, however, always raises distinctiveness issues as it clearly serves in a non-mark role — the color of the product.)

69. **The best answer is A. Answer C** involves product design so according to the Supreme Court in *Wal-Mart Stores, Inc. v. Samara Brothers, Inc.*, 529 U.S. 205 (2000) it can never be inherently distinctive. **Answers A, B** and **D** all involve non-product-design, non-word marks, meaning they may or may not be viewed as inherently distinctive depending on the specific facts. **Answer B** — the cow-shaped tag affixed to milk products — is an example of a non-word mark with a clearly ascertainable word "meaning" (cow). Given the connection to milk products, the tag (following its word meaning) is probably descriptive. In addition, if treated as part of the product packaging, a cow-shaped tag on a milk product will not likely be viewed as unique, uncommon or unexpected and/or as performing the non-mark role of packaging. **Answer D** — the word "Stay-Prest" (despite the unusual spelling — most consumers will immediately make the connection, so it should be treated as "Stay-Pressed") used in connection with wrinkle-free clothing is descriptive. The fact that it appears on a white tag is unlikely to create a distinct (unique, uncommon or unexpected) impression on consumers — it still looks like it is serving in the non-mark role of describing the product. **Answer A** — putting a cow shaped tag on paint products — takes the word "meaning" of the non-word mark out of the ordinary, arguing for an arbitrary and/or unique, uncommon or unexpected consumer reaction. Consequently, **Answer A** is the most likely to be found inherently distinctive.

70. **The best answer is C.** This question points out the frequent difficulty in distinguishing product design (which can never be inherently distinctive) from product packaging

(which may be). **Answer B** (the "overall appearance") is most clearly part of the product design and most easily excluded. **Answer D** is perhaps more problematic because of the "ornamental" nature of the spout, but still best viewed as part of the product design. **Answer A** and **Answer C** are more ambiguous. Regarding **Answer A**, the Supreme Court in *Wal-Mart Stores, Inc. v. Samara Brothers, Inc.*, 529 U.S. 205 (2000) specifically indicated that a soft drink bottle posed a difficult line-drawing issue: consumers may view the bottle as merely the container (packaging) or as part of the product (design) depending on the specific facts (is the bottle thrown away or is it a collectable or part of the drink "experience"). Regarding **Answer C**, the Court in *Wal-Mart* (alluding to *Two Pesos, Inc. v. Taco Cabana, Inc.*, 505 U.S. 763 (1992) which found the décor of a restaurant could be inherently distinctive) indicated that such décor was NOT product design but either product packaging or, perhaps, some *tertium quid* more akin to packaging. Based on the Court's holdings the best technical legal response is **Answer C.**

NOTE: Part of the difficulty with restaurant décor is that the product design vs. packaging dichotomy misses the fundamental point that a service not a good is involved. Once that point is recognized then it becomes easier (I think, anyway) to see that the décor may actually be part of the dining experience (service) and more properly viewed as part of its "design." As it, therefore, has an important non-mark role, a trademark claim should require a showing of secondary meaning.

71.   **The best answer is B**. Merely because product packaging is not inherently distinctive does not prevent it from being a trademark, so **Answer D** is incorrect. **Answer A** properly indicates that the burden is on the claimant to show distinctiveness but does not indicate specifically how that might be done. **Answer C** is, perhaps, technically correct but also does not provide the actual requirement that secondary meaning be shown. **Answer B** provides that missing information — the claimant must show the packaging has developed secondary meaning, that is moved beyond its non-mark role as packaging to take on a source signaling role in the consumer's mind.

      NOTE: Product design, in particular, and product packaging marks must also overcome any functionality concerns — *see* Topic 6 — Functionality.

72.   First, virtually anything *can* serve as a trademark and a blue circle with the words "fresh and tasty" pose no problems on that account. Second, it must be determined whether the proposal meets the distinctiveness requirement. Looking at the various components, clearly the color blue, the circle shape and the words "fresh and tasty" all potentially have non-mark significance (a color, a shape and descriptive of the bread products). However, the device viewed as a whole (the *combination* of the blue circle and the words) in this specific context might qualify as inherently distinctive. As it is not part of the bread product (it is affixed to the wrapper), it should be assessed as product packaging rather than product design trade dress. Applying the "expanded" distinctiveness packaging-test, the question is whether the device is sufficiently unique, uncommon or unexpected that bread consumers will view it as creating a distinct impression from mere packaging and thus signaling source. Although the blue circle alone might pass

distinctiveness muster, the overall device is a close call because of the descriptive words. A reasonable case can be made for distinctiveness based on the fact that the device as a whole is not essential to the plastic wrapper and therefore doesn't serve any non-mark packaging function. On the other hand, consumers might view the blue circle as merely helping the descriptive words stand out on the package and thus see the device as serving in an informational non-mark role. If the inherently distinctive argument fails, then proof of secondary meaning will be required to claim trademark rights in the device as a whole.

NOTE: Even if the device does qualify as a trademark (either because it is found inherently distinctive or HomeBreads demonstrates secondary meaning) the related rights will NOT prevent others from using the words "fresh" and/or "tasty" apart from the protected device, unless a separate showing of secondary meaning can be made regarding those descriptive terms.

73. **The best answer is D**. Trademarks are not limited to words, so **Answer A** is incorrect
     (*see* Topic 5 — Distinctiveness: Non-word Marks, Colors and Trade Dress). Nor is
     there an absolute bar to a product's design serving as a trademark (*see id.*), so **Answer
     C** is incorrect. **Answer B** correctly identifies that claiming product designs as trademarks
     raise special difficulties because they are not treated as inherently distinctive. However,
     that barrier can be overcome by a showing of secondary meaning, so although
     problematic it is not insurmountable. **Answer D** indicates a reason that the hammer
     head design might be absolutely barred from serving as a trademark — if its protection
     adversely affects competition on the product's merits. That concern is covered by the
     "functionality" doctrine. Because functionality is relevant on these facts and cannot be
     overcome, it is the best answer. *Cf. Vornado Air Circulation Sys. Inc. v. Duracraft Corp.*,
     58 F.3d 1498 (10th Cir. 1995), *cert. denied*, 516 U.S. 1067 (1996).

74. **The best answer is B**. If, as the question assumes, the feature uniquely identifies and
     distinguishes a particular producer's products or services, Tool's hammer in this case,
     affording trademark protection *will* further the basic purpose of trademark law (source
     identification), so **Answer A** is incorrect. **Answer C** is also incorrect. Trademark law
     does afford protection to marks which although not inherently distinctive have become
     so through acquiring secondary meaning (which is the case for Tool's hammer head
     design on these facts). The hammer head design may be functional — that is, related
     to its performance as a hammer — and it is true that trademark law does not permit
     protection of functional marks. So **Answer D** is a correct statement. However, it does
     not explain why such protection is withheld when secondary meaning has been shown.
     Answer B provides the answer. Even when protection may further the efficient source
     identification objectives of trademark law, when protection of a mark provides undue
     competitive advantage by interfering with competition on the product merits, the cost-
     benefit balances of intellectual property law dictate that function trump the information
     signal and trademark protection be withheld. Consequently, **Answer B** is the best
     answer.

75. **The best answer is A**. The functionality concern is ensuring trademark law does not
     adversely affect competition on the product merits; that is limits competitors' ability
     to make and sell products of equal (or better) usefulness, cost and quality. **Answers
     B, C and D** each describes a circumstance when a product design feature would have
     such an adverse effect on competitors. *See TrafFix Devices, Inc. v. Marketing Displays,
     Inc.*, 532 U.S. 23 (2001) (a design is functional when it is "essential to the *use or purpose*
     of the article or if it affects the *cost or quality* of the article," (italics added) citing the
     test articulated in *Inwood Laboratories, Inc. v. Ives Laboratories, Inc.*, 456 U.S. 844
     (1982) — referred to as the *Inwood* test). **Answer A,** investment may be relevant to

finding functionality, but only because it implies that the design implicates use, purpose, cost or quality. However, without that further finding, mere investment is not sufficient to find a design functional, so **Answer A** is the least relevant and thus the best answer to the Question.

76. **The "alternatives" issue remains unresolved**. In *TrafFix Devices, Inc. v. Marketing Displays, Inc.*, 532 U.S. 23 (2001) the Supreme Court held that a design is functional if it is "essential to the use or purpose of the article or if it affects the cost or quality of the article." The Court further held that "the functionality of the . . . design means that competitors need not explore whether [alternatives exist]. . . . The design . . . is the reason the device works. Other designs need not be attempted." Applying that test to these facts, the central issue is what it means for the design feature to be *"essential"* to the product's use or purpose. If it means that it is the only (or, perhaps, one of a very few) alternatives for obtaining the same result, then the existence of a significant number of alternatives would lead to a finding that the design is not functional. The argument is that offering trademark protection to one of many design alternatives does not seriously adversely affect competition on the product merits because competitors remain free to use the remaining alternatives. However, this reading (it seems to me) is very close to the "competitive necessity" view of "essential" — a position which appears to be rejected by the second part of the Court's holding quoted above. The alternative reading would be that "essential" means only that the feature is integral to the improved performance of the particular product ("it is the reason the device works"). In such cases, the feature would be functional despite the existence of alternatives. The argument here is harm to competition on the merits arises whenever competitors are precluded from freely choosing among *all* available designs which are relevant to a product's use, purpose, cost or quality; in effect, function trumps trademark whenever it arises. Moreover, the approach avoids problematic judicial determinations of how many alternatives must exist and how competitive they must be, by leaving competition on the merits exclusively to the marketplace.

Obviously, reasonable minds can and do differ as evidenced by the fact that courts have varied in their application of the *TrafFix* holding. Some courts have found that *TrafFix* "did not [render] the availability of alternative designs irrelevant" and that alternatives remain "part of the overall mix." *Valu Engineering, Inc. v. Rexnord Corp.*, 278 F.3d 1268 (Fed. Cir. 2002). Other courts have held that when product designs "are essential to the operation of the [product], they are functional as a matter of law, and it is unnecessary to consider design alternatives available in the marketplace." *Eppendorf-Netheler-Hinz GmBH v. Ritter GmBH*, 289 F.3d 351 (5th Cir. 2002).

NOTE: To further confuse matters, the grammatical structure of the *TrafFix* holding is ambiguous. Specifically, it is unclear in the phrase "essential to the use or purpose of the article or if it affects the cost or quality of the article" whether "essential" applies only to the "use or purpose" part of the test. If so, alternatives may remain relevant to "use or purpose" kinds of functionality but not to "cost or quality" functionality. *See Valu Engineering, Inc. v. Rexnord Corp.*, 278 F.3d 1268 (Fed. Cir. 2002).

77. The container design involves product design trade dress. A finding that the design was functional would preclude trademark protection (even with a showing of secondary meaning). The test for functionality is whether the design is "essential to the use or purpose of the article or if it affects the cost or quality of the article." *See TrafFix Devices, Inc. v. Marketing Displays, Inc.*, 532 U.S. 23 (2001). Utility patents are granted for novel, nonobvious useful innovation in the "functional arts" (useful arts). Consequently, obtaining such a patent on a product design feature is strong evidence that the related subject matter affects the product's use, purpose, cost or quality by virtue of the innovative solution on which the patent grant was predicated. *Id.* However, as noted in Question 76 above, if a court decides to permit evidence that alternatives exist, a patent will be probative but not dispositive of functionality.

NOTE: It might even be argued that filing a patent application, whether or not granted, is evidence of functionality. Because the functionality issue is whether the feature is functional not whether its functionality is sufficiently inventive to obtain a patent, the application itself could be viewed as strong evidence that at least the claimant views the feature as affecting use, purpose, cost or quality.

NOTE: The inclusion of the word "utility" is important. Patent law also covers design patents which are granted for new and original *ornamental* designs. *See* 35 U.S.C. § 171. Consequently, the grant of a design patent does not raise the same functionality (use, purpose, cost or quality) inferences inherent in utility patents. Such patents may, however, raise possible aesthetic functionality concerns — a subject treated in later Questions below.

78. Trademark law is designed to reduce consumer search costs by protecting marks which uniquely identify and distinguish the products of a particular producer and, therefore, can provide clear and reliable "short-cut" information about the related goods (and services) to consumers. That objective imposes few limitations on what can qualify as a trademark and argues for protection against use of confusingly similar marks for as long as the mark is acting as a unique identifier. Patent law grants utility patents to provide incentives to encourage product innovation. To ensure a net beneficial outcome of those incentives it contains a number of stringent requirements designed to guard against inappropriate interference with competition on the product merits. For example, patent law requires novelty to prevent a competitor claiming exclusive rights to existing product features. Additionally, patent law only affords an inventor a fixed term of exclusivity (generally 20 years from the date of application), after which time everyone is free to use the invention in competition with the patentee. Trademark law's functionality doctrine, therefore, can be understood as ensuring that patent law's cost-benefit balancing limitations cannot be evaded. By prohibiting trademark rights in product design features which affect competition on the product merits the doctrine "channels" such subject matter out of trademark law, leaving protection to the more restrictive requirements of patent law.

This understanding of the functionality doctrine argues forcefully for taking an expansive view. To ensure that the patent "bargain" controls competition on the merits every product design feature which affects the use, purpose, cost or quality of the related good should be rejected as the "wrong stuff" for trademark protection. That outcome supports the narrower reading of *TrafFix* discussed in Question 76, that if the claimed feature has any effect on use, purpose, cost or quality the appropriate social bargain is offered under patent, not trademark, law and alternatives are simply irrelevant. *See TrafFix Devices, Inc. v. Marketing Displays, Inc.*, 532 U.S. 23 (2001); *Qualitex Co. v. Jacobson Prods. Co., Inc.*, 514 U.S. 159 (1995); *Kellogg Co. v. National Biscuit Co.*, 305 U.S. 111 (1938); *Vornado Air Circulation Sys. Inc. v. Duracraft Corp.*, 58 F.3d 1498 (10th Cir. 1995), *cert. denied*, 516 U.S. 1067 (1996).

79. **The best answer is B.** The existence of a patent on a product feature strongly indicates that the feature is functional and, therefore, cannot serve as a trademark. The Supreme Court has, however, indicated (but did not hold; specifically reserving the issue of whether patenting prohibits a trademark claim) that where a feature is only incidental to the patent (**Answer B**) a claimant might be able to prove it is not functional and protectable as a trademark. *See TrafFix Devices, Inc. v. Marketing Displays, Inc.*, 532 U.S. 23 (2001). *See also Vornado Air Circulation Sys. Inc. v. Duracraft Corp.*, 58 F.3d 1498 (10th Cir. 1995), *cert denied*, 516 U.S. 1067 (1996) (articulating the patent "test" as requiring the claimed mark to be a "described, significant inventive aspect of the invention"). It is irrelevant to that the patent has expired (**Answer A**). The functionality issue is not whether the feature is protected under a patent, but that the fact of patenting indicates an effect on competition on the product merits. *See id.* That developing the feature required substantial investment (**Answer D**) is, at best, irrelevant, and may actually indicate greater concern over supplementing natural cost barriers to competition with additional legal interference with competitive use. That the feature has developed secondary meaning (**Answer C**) is problematic in terms of possible confusion; however, although that may justify some mitigation it does not justify granting full trademark rights in the feature. *See id.*

80. **Their chances of protecting the scoop design as a trademark are poor in light of the functionality doctrine.** First, the existence of the utility patent will be strong evidence that the design is functional. Additionally, the facts indicate that the scoop shape has a significant effect on the product's use and is not merely incidental to the patent. Finally, the design's *uniquely* effective nature renders the already somewhat problematic "alternative design" argument against functionality unlikely to succeed. Consequently, although 104 Flavors can show strong secondary meaning (the customers' strong source identification of the feature with their product) that will not overcome the functionality-competition-on-the-merits concerns which require that trademark protection be withheld. *See TrafFix Devices, Inc. v. Marketing Displays, Inc.*, 532 U.S. 23 (2001).

81. **NO, all is not lost.** Although a showing of even strong secondary meaning will not give them trademark rights (and their efforts to generate that meaning may actually be viewed cynically by the court — having deliberately caused the problem), it does raise a serious concerns over consumer confusion, something trademark law vigorously seeks

to prevent. Consequently, it may be possible to convince a court to order competitors adopting the feature to take steps to prevent any confusion, such as adding disclaimers regarding any association with 104 Flavors. *See Kellogg Co. v. National Biscuit Co.*, 305 U.S. 111 (1938). *But see TrafFix Devices, Inc. v. Marketing Displays, Inc.*, 532 U.S. 23 (2001) (which appeared unmoved by the lingering confusion argument, perhaps because the plaintiff failed to make a serious showing of actual secondary meaning?)

82. **The best answer is C.** Functionality focuses on marks which may adversely affects competitors' ability to make and sell products of equal (or better) usefulness, quality and cost. **Answers A, B and D** all involve product designs which if protected as trademarks could prevent a competitor from matching the performance, quality or cost of the mark holder's containers (remember, competitive necessity is *not* required). **Answer C**, however, points in the opposite direction, involving a design which makes the container less rather than more useful as a beverage container. Consequently, it more likely serves other purposes — for example offering a more attractive first impression. That said, **Answer C** might implicate aesthetic functionality (coming up in the immediately following Questions) so although it is the least likely answer of the four to raise concerns, it is not entirely clear of functionality concerns.

83. **The best answer is A**. The question makes two distinct points. First, although various kinds of marks which impair competition are denied trademark protection, functionality only addresses marks which interfere with competition *on the product merits* — that is, granting trademark rights will interfere with other competitors' ability to make and sell equivalent (or better) products. **Answer B** clearly involves the absolute prohibition on claiming trademark rights in the generic term for the class of goods. **Answer C** may be similarly treated as generic, assuming the picture non-word mark is given its word meaning. And **Answer D** might be barred as descriptive, although it is perhaps suggestive. The policy driving their exclusion from trademark protection is to avoid interference with competitor's use — specifically the ability to identify or describe their products. None of these marks, however, affects a competitor's ability to compete on the product merits; to make an equally functional product of comparable use, purpose, cost or quality. Consequently, none of them implicates the functionality doctrine.

Second, although the design's "purely ornamental" nature (**Answer A**) makes direct application of the utilitarian functionality test (use, purpose, cost or quality) problematic, the doctrine of *aesthetic* functionality must also be considered. The courts have recognized that permitting trademark claims to a product's "aesthetic" appearance ("the noble instinct for giving the right touch of beauty to common and necessary things," *Qualitex Co. v. Jacobson Prods. Co., Inc.*, 514 U.S. 159 (1995)) — can also create non-reputation-based impairments to robust competition on the product merits. As there is a possibility that the ornamental design of the silverware may be treated as functional under the "aesthetic" rubric, **Answer A** is the best answer of the four. *Cf. Wallace Intl. Silversmiths, Inc. v. Godinger Silver Art. Co., Inc.*, 916 F.2d 76 (2nd Cir. 1990), *cert. denied*, 499 U.S. 976 (1991).

84. **The best answer is B**. The pivotal difference between traditional "utilitarian" functionality and aesthetic functionality is whether the characteristic affects the use, purpose, cost or quality of the good (the "*Inwood*" test, after the case of that name) or merely involves other "significant non-reputation-related disadvantage" (aesthetic appeal). Or, as the Supreme Court stated the point, aesthetic functionality is the "central question" when "there is no indication that the [product feature has] any bearing on the use or purpose of the product or its cost or quality." *TrafFix Devices, Inc. v. Marketing Displays, Inc.*, 532 U.S. 23 (2001). **Answers A, C and D** all go to matters which are likely to implicate the products use or purpose (gearing design), purpose, cost (materials, gearing and weight) or quality (materials, gearing), thus implicating the utilitarian functionality test. Although **Answer B** (color) may affect such matters (for example whether it shows dirt), it is nonetheless the most likely to involve other significant non-reputation-related disadvantage — in particular, purely aesthetic desirability.

Although the above draws a crisp distinction between "utilitarian — *Inwood*" functionality (use, purpose, quality and cost of the product) and "aesthetic" functionally (a *Qualitex* "touch of beauty"), that line does not, as law professors delight in saying, "shimmer with clarity." The ornamental silverware in Question 83 provides a good example of why straight-forward classification is so problematic. Whether even an admittedly purely ornamental silverware design is tied to its use, purpose, cost or quality or merely aesthetic depends on how the "function" of silverware is defined. Is that function simply moving food from plate to mouth while standing up tolerably well to related (ab)use or does it also involves how it fits into the overall dining experience. If customers only buy silverware for the former purpose, then appearance is merely an aesthetic not utilitarian functionality concern. However, if they buy silverware in part because of the particular appearance to meet the latter function, then protection of the ornamental design adversely affects competition on the product merits and it should be treated as any other utilitarian aspect of the product. *See Wallace Intl. Silversmiths, Inc. v. Godinger Silver Art Co., Inc.*, 916 F.2d 76 (2nd Cir. 1990) *cert. denied*, 499 U.S. 976 (1991) (adopting a similar position although articulating it in terms of hindering competition on the merits by limiting the range of adequate alternative designs).

85. **The best answer is C**. The Court has indicated that aesthetic functionality bars trademark protection when a product design serves "a significant non-trademark function," *Qualitex Co. v. Jacobson Prods. Co., Inc.*, 514 U.S. 159 (1995). So **Answer A** is not only likely to be considered, but is a key to determining whether the color of the farm equipment can serve as a trademark. Additionally, the Court has specifically held that "[i]t is proper to inquire into [whether trademark protection results in] a 'significant non-reputation-related disadvantage' in cases of aesthetic functionality . . . ." *TrafFix Devices, Inc. v. Marketing Displays, Inc.*, 532 U.S. 23 (2001). So **Answer B** is also directly relevant. **Answer A** and **Answer B** define the aesthetic functionality inquiry as needing to determine whether the color of Farmal's equipment is important to consumers' decisions to purchase (serve a significant non-trademark function) and, if so, whether its protection as a mark would lead to significant disadvantage to

competitors. **Answer D** reflects what appears to be the key difference between utilitarian functionality (purpose, use, quality, and cost) and aesthetic functionality (appearance) under current Supreme Court doctrine. The Court has indicated that in the former (utility) cases, competitive necessity as indicated by lack of feasible equivalent alternatives may not be required for the product feature to be barred as functional. *See TrafFix Devices, Inc. v. Marketing Displays, Inc.*, 532 U.S. 23 (2001); Questions 76 and 77 above. However, in aesthetic functionality inquiries the concern is only avoiding a *significant* non-reputation-related disadvantage. Consequently, even if the color of the farm equipment is relevant to consumers, the availability of alternative colors may indicate the requisite degree of adverse competitive effect does not exists. *Id.; Qualitex Co. v. Jacobson Prods. Co., Inc.*, 514 U.S. 159 (1995) (noting that aesthetic functionality "should not discourage firms from creating aesthetically pleasing mark designs, for it is open to their competitors to do the same"). *See also* Restatement (Third) Unfair Competition § 17, Comment c (1995). So **Answer D** is relevant to determining the aesthetic functionality of the color. Under that same analysis, **Answer C** is by definition irrelevant. Although the Court's distinction between utilitarian and aesthetic functionality make the design feature's effect on use, purpose, cost or quality relevant to determining *which kind* of functionality is at issue, once it has been determined that aesthetic functionality is the "central question," use, purpose, cost and quality effects are no longer especially relevant. *Id. But see* the Note on the complexity of making that determination at the end of the answer to the preceding Question.

NOTE: The Supreme Court has provided an interesting example of aesthetic functionality regarding the color of farm equipment. It mentions, without commenting on the merits, that the green color of farm equipment might be aesthetically functional if farmers would not accept other non-matching colors because it would offend their aesthetic sensibilities. *See Qualitex Co. v. Jacobson Prods. Co., Inc.*, 514 U.S. 159 (1995).

86. Protecting the shape of the car as a trademark raises two functionality concerns. The first, and most problematic, is that on the facts the design affects the use and quality of the car by increasing its high-speed performance. Seeking and, certainly obtaining, a utility patent will exacerbate that problem by making it extremely difficult to convince a court that the design is not functional; requiring UberCars to convincingly demonstrate that the design is merely incidental to the functionality of the claimed invention — something they cannot do. There are two possible counter-arguments. The first is that because improved performance only occurs at extremely high speeds, in particular speeds at which the car should not generally be driven in ordinary use, the design should not be considered functional. However, because the car is a "sports car" the enhanced performance at high speed is likely a key characteristic in consumer purchases. The second is that the design (even if patented) is not "essential" to the product's use or purpose because alternatives exist. The availability of that argument, however, is seriously undermined by the Supreme Court's holding in *TrafFix* that once a determination is made that the design affects use, purpose, cost or quality "there is no need to proceed further to consider if there is a competitive necessity for the feature." *See TrafFix Devices, Inc. v. Marketing Displays, Inc.*, 532 U.S. 23 (2001).

Even if UberCars were to avoid a utility functionality bar to trademark protection, aesthetic functionality must also be addressed. The issue is whether the design is serving a significant non-trademark function. The results of the survey indicate that the answer is affirmative — that consumers like the design for "touch of beauty" reasons — that is, it makes the car look fabulous. Consequently, it will be necessary to show that prohibiting competitive use will not put competitors at a *significant non-reputation-related disadvantage.*" The key issue in that determination will be whether design alternatives exist. However, unlike utility functionality it will not be necessary to show that the design delivers equivalent performance, merely that those designs are adequate to avoid a significant non-reputation-related disadvantage — that consumers view them as acceptable aesthetic alternatives.

NOTE: The functional bar problems in trademark law argue strongly in favor of pursuing patent protection if it is available. That result demonstrates how trademark law's functionality doctrine helps ensure that the right balances are preserved within intellectual property law as a whole by channeling functional subject matter towards patent law and its cost-benefit balances targeting that particular kind of innovation. *See* Question 78.

87. Product design is never considered inherently distinctive. The survey indicates that the design may have developed the necessary secondary meaning essential to overcoming that difficulty. Nonetheless, because function trumps signaling, UberCars will still not be able to claim trademark protection for the design unless they can prevail on the functionality issues. However, if UberCars does not succeed and is prevented from claiming trademark rights, the survey's evidence of secondary meaning may require any competitors who adopt the design ensure that consumers understand there is no connection with those competitors' products and UberCars or its "original" version of the car.

88. **This is an open issue**. The earlier problems all involved a feature of the actual product (for example, materials, color, shape), thus implicating product design. The cereal box in this case is separate from the product and involves product packaging trade dress. The Supreme Court has specifically indicated that product design and product packaging should be treated differently regarding distinctiveness, with only the latter capable of being inherently distinctive. *See Wal-Mart Stores, Inc. v. Samara Brothers, Inc.*, 529 U.S. 205 (2000); Topic 5 — Distinctiveness: Non-word Marks, Colors and Trade Dress. The Court has not, however, explicitly addressed whether different tests apply regarding functionality.

In favor of separate tests regarding "utility" functionality (use, purpose, cost and quality) is the *Samara* observation that product design is part of the product while product packaging is not. Consequently only the former directly implicates competition on the actual product merits. On the other hand, product packaging clearly indirectly affects competitors — for example by reducing the costs of display, storage, handling or shipping of the product. To permit trademark protection, therefore, would allow a single competitor to gain an advantage on the merits and thereby hinder competition. So it is reasonable to assume that the *Inwood* utility test (use, purpose, cost or quality) would be extended to packaging as well. The same general argument applies to the appearance of product packaging. To the extent that a product's packaging plays a "significant non-trademark" role in the consumer purchase decision, thus putting competitors at a "significant non-reputation-related disadvantage," trademark protection should be withheld.

While awaiting clarification, the best approach is to perform the complete functionality analysis. On the facts of the problem, the utility functionality inquiry would focus on whether the specially shaped cereal box has any indirect effect on the use, purpose, cost or quality (including display, storage, etc) of the cereal. If so, then trademark protection should be withheld for the shape. The special coloring of the box is unlikely to raise utility functionality concerns, but does implicate aesthetic functionality. On that latter issue, the question is whether consumers have a significant non-trademark/non-reputation-based preference for buying cereal in a box with those specific colors. Even assuming that the colors are particularly attractive, it seems unlikely that such a consumer preference would overcome a preference based on the cereal product merits. And even if that were the case, it would still be necessary to determine whether other equally appealing colors (or package designs) are available to competitors.

NOTE: It should always be remembered that definition of purpose is vital to the functionality inquiry. If part of a cereal *product* is looking at the box while eating, then arguably the box is not mere packaging but part of the product itself, thus avoiding the need to address the issue of packaging functionality at all.

89. Although a mark must be distinctive, non-functional and pose no likelihood of confusion with existing marks, under United States law obtaining trademark rights *also* requires *use* of the mark as a trademark. *See* Trade-Mark Cases, 100 U.S. 82, 94-95 (1879); Lanham Act § 45 (15 U.S.C. § 1127) (defining "trademark" in terms of "use"). (The converse is, of course, also true — actual use alone would be insufficient to claim trademark rights in a mark which is not distinctive, functional or conflicts with an existing mark.)

The justification for requiring actual use is that, unlike patent and copyright law which generally foster investment in the creation of new or original works (inventions and expression, respectively), trademark law seeks to improve market information by helping customers efficiently identify and distinguish products having the desired characteristics (*see* Topic 1 — Justifications and Sources of Trademark Law). Until an otherwise qualifying mark is actually used in the market as a trademark it cannot furthered that market information objective and, therefore, does not provide the related social benefits. *Cf. Hanover Star Milling Co. v. Metcalf*, 240 U.S. 403, 412-414 (1916). Moreover, granting rights over a potential mark without actual use prohibits its adoption and use by others. The use requirement thus also prevents the non-productive reservation or warehousing of marks.

NOTE: Other nations do not require actual use, instead employing a first to register system. Although such systems avoid the issues of sufficiency and priority of use (much more to come below), they do raise other "race" related concerns — consider, for example, the problems that have arisen from the internet domain name first to register system. In part to reflect applicable treaty obligations, Lanham Act § 44 (15 U.S.C. § 1126) contains special provisions permitting foreign nationals to obtain United States trademark rights without requiring any showing of actual use in United States commerce.

90. **The best answer is C.** The "actual use" test requires the circumstances demonstrate the mark has been used in a way which advances trademark law's the source signaling objectives, rather than simply in an effort to "reserve" the mark. "Good faith use as a trademark" best captures that requirement, making **Answer C** the best answer. The reference to "circumstances" emphasizes that the determination turns on the particular facts, so each determination must be made based on the "totality of the circumstances." *See Johnny Blastoff, Inc. v. L.A. Rams Football Co.*, 188 F.3d 427, 433 (7th Cir. 1999), *cert. denied*, 528 U.S. 1188 (2000). (Although some courts have not specifically adopted the totality of the circumstances test, it usefully captures the actual inquiry . . . a rose by any other name.)

Good faith intent to use clearly cannot satisfy the *actual* use requirement (no use of any kind has actually occurred), so **Answer A** is incorrect. Although actual use is required, that use does not need to have created a *significant* market impression. It is sufficient that the use implicates trademark law's the source signaling function. So **Answer B** is incorrect. **Answer D** addresses a different use-related inquiry; whether a non-inherently distinctive mark has acquired secondary meaning *distinctiveness* through use. Distinctiveness, however, only concerns whether a mark *can* act as a trademark. *See* Topic 3: Basic Distinctiveness: The Spectrum of Distinctiveness; Word Marks Including Acronyms and Foreign Words. The actual use requirement determines whether an otherwise qualifying mark (one that is distinctive) is being used as a trademark (actually signaling source in the marketplace) and therefore entitled to protection. Generally the amount of use necessary for secondary meaning will be substantially more than that required to demonstrate actual trademark use. So **Answer D** is incorrect.

NOTE: A brief elaboration on the last point above in the context of these facts may help clarify. Although the issue is not raised, the "Dry Wherever" mark would likely be classified as suggestive rather than descriptive as it requires a "leap of imagination" to connect the mark to the product. That classification would make it inherently distinctive and the issue is whether there is good faith use as a trademark. However, if the mark were classified as descriptive then no trademark rights could be obtained until the mark acquired secondary meaning distinctiveness through extended use, well beyond that required to satisfy the good faith use as a mark standard.

91.   **The best answer is D**. Protection requires good faith use as a trademark. Although a variety of preparatory (and expensive) steps are obviously necessary to support such use (for example, those set out in **Answers B** and **C**), until the mark is actually used in the marketplace in connection with specific products (or services) no source signaling can occur and no trademark rights will accrue. Only **Answer D** involves an actual market use of the mark on the product, so it is the sole answer which involves activities which might trigger trademark rights. Whether that use (offering the labeled product for sale) is sufficient is a separate question (addressed below), but it nonetheless remains the best answer of the four.

NOTE: The stringency of the use requirement poses a conundrum for those like Rainstuff preparing to launch a new trademark. The related preparatory investments necessarily come before the use necessary to claim trademark rights, so they involved considerable risk. To solve this problem the Lanham Act permits short-term, place-holder registrations based on bona fide intent to use the mark in the reasonably imminent future. However, transforming an intent-to-use reservation into enforceable trademark rights still requires subsequent actual use within a reasonably short period of time. *See* Topic 9 — Registration: Constructive Use and Intent to Use.

92.   **The best answer is B**. Sufficient use to qualify as good faith use as a trademark must implicate the marketplace source identifying function of trademark law. Merely marking the umbrellas without any indication of actual market use is, therefore, clearly insufficient, so **Answer A** is incorrect. Despite the large quantity involved, **Answer C** involves exclusively internal use so it also does not constitute the kind of use

supporting a trademark claim. (Would the answer be different if the umbrellas had been shipped from one warehouse to another in trucks prominently with a picture of the umbrellas bearing "Dry Wherever" mark on the side panels? Hold that thought). **Answer D** does involve transactions with persons outside the company. However, the transactions do not involve arms-length market transactions, and there is no indication that the mark played any role whatsoever. Those transactions are, therefore, unconvincing evidence of "good faith use as a trademark." **Answer B,** however, directly implicates actual market activity. Even though it only involves three labeled umbrellas sold to a single retailer and there is no indication the retailer has yet to sell them on to end-users products, the offer and sale reflects an actual market transaction with an independent market participant involving the mark. So **Answer B** is the best answer. The crucial point being that the use requirement is less about absolute volumes (although they can be a relevant fact) than the *bona fides* of the market transaction — do the circumstances indicate it is "real" or merely a pretext to lock-in trademark rights?

NOTE: The Lanham Act's definition of "use in commerce" as "the bona fide use of a mark in the *ordinary course of trade . . .*" supports requiring activity of the kind consistent with the transactional norms of the relevant industry. Lanham Act § 45 (15 U.S.C. § 1127). Although the Lanham Act definition technically only applies to rights under the federal regime, courts nonetheless treat it as stating the basic test for sufficient use. *See Allard Enters., Inc. v. Advanced Programming Res., Inc.*, 146 F.3d 350, 357 (6th Cir. 1998).)

93. **The best answer is A**. Although actual sales are undoubtedly strong evidence of good faith market use as a trademark they are not required. *See Planetary Motion, Inc. v. Techsplosion, Inc.*, 261 F.3d 1188 (11th Cir. 2001). The test only requires that the totality of the circumstances indicates sufficient bona fide market use to trigger the trademark source signaling function. **Answer B** does not involve any external market activity implicating the mark's source identifying function and, therefore, is not adequate use. **Answer D** does involve a sale to an independent market participant; however, although the relatively large order might normally indicate otherwise, the facts expressly state the sale took place *only* to reserve the mark. Because the mark was not used in good faith, the transaction is a "sham" or, more kindly, a "token" sale and insufficient to support a trademark claim. *See Blue Bell v. Farah*, 508 F.2d 1260, 1267 (5th Cir. 1975); Lanham Act § 45 (15 U.S.C. § 1127) (defining "use in commerce" as "the bona fide use of a mark in the ordinary course of trade, *and not made merely to reserve a right in a mark*"). The discount sales to friends of the company President in **Answer C** also raise significant "token sale" (non-bona fides) concerns. Additionally, the nature of the buyers and the limited number and small size of transactions also raise *de minimis* issues; that the amount of activity does not reflect ordinary course market activity in the industry necessary to demonstrate the source identifying role of the mark to the *public. See Paramount Pictures Corp. V. White*, 31 U.S.P.Q.2d 1768 (Trademark Tr. & App. Bd. 1994).

Consequently, although **Answer A** does not involve any actual sales transactions, it is the only answer which involves public market source identification activity — a *major* trade show announcement involving promotion of products labeled with the "Dry Wherever" mark. *See New England Duplicating Co. v. Mendes*, 190 F.2d 415, 418 (1st Cir. 1951) (evidence of adoption and sufficiently public use of the mark in its source identification capacity adequate to establish rights through use). The key, however, remains the overall circumstances. So advance promotion or advertising without actual identification of the related products or only a few private showings to limited numbers of prospects might prove inadequate. *See id.* (use must be "sufficiently public"); *Marvel Comics Ltd. v. Defiant*, 837 F. Supp. 546, 549 (S.D.N.Y 1993).

94.   **The best answer is B**. Good faith use as a trademark requires looking at the totality of the circumstances. **Answer A** involves internal, non-public use which does not implicate trademark law's source identifying objectives. Consequently, despite a high absolute number of marked products having been sold to a retail chain expressly for public resale, the fact that they are made to a wholly owned subsidiary makes the use inadequate to support trademark rights (the subsequent public resale by the retail chain subsidiary would, of course, qualify, but they have yet to take place). **Answer D** also involves a purely internal transaction, so even thought the single product is a significant proportion of the aggregate public market, the mark is not *yet* being used to identify source. Consequently, that use is also insufficient. The key to choosing between **Answers B** and **C** is that the "totality of the circumstances" requires looking beyond the absolute numbers of marked goods sold to the relevant market. On that basis, although a court could find either **Answer B** or **Answer C** sufficient, as a comparative matter ("most likely") **Answer B** is the better response. In a market involving only a few sales a year, a single sale to an end user is considerable market activity, whereas in the context of the market in **Answer C** it is arguably *de minimis*.

95.   **The best answer is B**. Good faith use as a trademark not only requires actual public market activity but that a sufficient connection exist between the mark and the related product so that consumers make the signaling association necessary to accomplish the mark's source identification function. Physical affixation to the product obviously provides a very clear connection. In some situations, however, such physical affixation is highly problematic. In this example it is impossible (well almost, physicists might find a way) to attach the "Tamaway" mark to the liquid cola drink. Those exigencies have led the law to relax the "fixation" requirement. Specifically, the Lanham Act definition of "use in commerce" permits mark placement not only on the goods but on their containers, on affixed tags or labels as well as use in associated displays and, when those alternatives are impractical, in "documents associated with the goods or their sale." Lanham Act § 45 (15 U.S.C. § 1127).

Answer A may appear the most desirable approach in this context as it involves marking the "container" which, along with affixed tags or labels, are generally the preferred alternatives to direct affixation. However, unlike a bottle "container" the cup in which the beverage is served has an ambiguous connection to a beverage served at a beverage bar. It is unclear that the customer will see the mark as identifying the particular beverage, the cup, the beverage bar or, for that matter, as a mark at all. **Answer D** suffers from the same "connection" difficulties. Because it happens post-transaction and ambiguously ("what did you say?") the necessary customer association between mark and drink are highly problematic. In contrast, **Answer B** — use of the mark as part of the menu entry (an associated display) — effectively makes a very clear connection between the mark and the new cola beverage. *See* Lanham Act § 45 (15 U.S.C. § 1127)) (definition of "use in commerce" — permitting use in an "associated display"); Restatement (Third) Unfair Competition § 18 cmt. d (1995) (listing "menus and other advertising uses calculated to inform prospective purchasers of the association between the designation and the user or the user's goods and services"). **Answer C** is the least likely to satisfy the affixation-connection portion of the use requirement as the advertising does not identify any actual product, only that "something new" is coming soon. Consequently, the advertisement probably does not even constitute use as a trademark, much less a use which sufficiently connects the mark to the new beverage. (All may not be lost for a claimant under **Answer C**. The doctrine of analogous use may provide some assistance. *See* Question 106 below.)

96. **Technically yes; in substance probably not.** Although trademarks and service marks are generally treated identically, this is one area where some, albeit not very significant, substantive differences exist. In particular, the non-tangible nature of services has required more generous approach to the "affixation/connection" aspect of the use requirement. Because with services there is nothing to affix the mark to (including containers) the test only requires that "the mark be used or displayed in the sale or advertising of the services." Lanham Act § 45 (15 U.S.C. § 1127) (definition of "use in commerce"). However, in application the inquiry remains essentially the same — does the use or display make it readily apparent that the mark is identifying the source of the related services (that is, serving as a service mark).

NOTE: It is, of course, also necessary that the use be sufficient to meet the good faith use as a mark requirement — that is, the offer or sale of the related services implicates the market source identification function of the mark. So use on pre-availability promotional or advertising materials which do not actually describe the service may not suffice even though that use might otherwise technically meet the affixation/ connection "use or display in the sale or advertising of the services" requirement.

97. **No.** GreatBuy's use includes the preferred method of ensuring consumer association — the physical labeling of the product and the packaging. Additionally, the high volume of actual public market sales satisfies the basic use as a mark requirement. The difficulty lies with the "good faith" requirement. Although that requirement generally is used to differentiate actual market use from sham/token efforts to reserve a mark, it has also been relied on to withhold trademark production based on the policy argument that illegal sales cannot be in good faith.

Withholding protection does raise the problem that consumers (who may not realize the goods are illegal) may actually associate the "Amand" mark with GreatBuys' product and, therefore, expect the related characteristics when it is present. The result would be confusion if the unprotected mark were adopted and used by another producer of legal goods. As a practical matter a court would likely resolve that concern by requiring some form of disclaimer.

NOTE: Just in case you jumped to conclusions about the "pharmaceuticals" involved, the same policy argument would apply to a large national pharmaceutical manufacturer who failed to obtain FDA approval for their new high-blood pressure drug before placing the product on the market.

98.   **The best answer is D**. As trademarks must identify and *distinguish* the products of a particular producer it is not enough to show good faith use as a trademark. There must also be no existing uses which are likely to cause confusion. Stated affirmatively, the trademark rights in a mark belong to the *first* user of the mark in the relevant market. That user can prevent all subsequent adoptions likely to cause confusion. *See Zazu Designs v. L'Oreal, S.A.*, 979 F.2d 499 (7th Cir. 1992); *Blue Bell v. Farah*, 508 F.2d 1260 (5th Cir. 1975); *New England Duplicating Co. v. Mendes*, 190 F.2d 415 (1st Cir. 1951). **Answer D**, which addresses this additional "first in time" use requirement is therefore the best answer.

Bona fides of FabGizmos' use is already covered by the stated facts — for the client's activities to be sufficient means they are bona fides. So that is not an *additional* requirement ("what ELSE"); making **Answer A** incorrect. It is not necessary to sell a product to trigger trademark rights — other kinds of use can be sufficient (*see* Question 93 above), but in any event that concern is also covered by the facts, so **Answer B** is also incorrect. "Creation" of the mark, **Answer C**, might reasonably be equated with priority of use. "First is time," however, requires only first use as a mark, not the actual creation of the mark itself, so **Answer D** is better than **Answer C**. (If FabGizmos did not create the mark that may raise other ownership issues such as claims for copyright infringement by the author of the work.)

NOTE: As indicated by the "in their market" qualifier, and discussed further below, the "first in time" requirement includes both a product (on what) and geographic (where) component which which together form the mark footprint. So it may be possible to have the same mark on different products or in different regions on the same product. *See* Topic 8 — Use: Product/Service and Geographic Reach (Footprint).

NOTE: Additionally, first use can be either actual or constructive (through federal registration), and a constructive use-registration trumps subsequent actual use. This Topic deals only with the actual use, while Topic 9 — Registration: Constructive Use and Intent to Use addresses the effects of a federal registration.

99.   **The best answer is C**. A claim to trademark ownership depends on "actual prior use in commerce;" that is, first sufficient good faith use as a trademark in the relevant market. *Tally-Ho, Inc. v. Coast Community College Dist.*, 889 F.2d 1018 (11th Cir. 1989). The mere decision to adopt a mark is not sufficient — market activity not intent governs trademark ownership — so **Answer A** is incorrect. In **Answer B** and **Answer C** both companies are using the mark in commerce. However **Answer C** clearly states Company C was first, so Company C has the better claim. Fritz as creator of the mark may have

other kinds of ownership claims (say under copyright law — although they don't sound particular good), but as his yet-to-be-created Company D has not used it on goods, neither he nor it can make any trademark claims. Therefore, **Answer D** is incorrect.

100. **The best answer is B**, but there is a reasonable argument for **Answer C.** Clearly on the facts Alpha can claim rights as of 2006 (their first use of the specific logo "B-Zow" in a white circle) — so **Answer D** provides the "worst case" date. The question is whether Alpha can claim "credit" for its earlier use of different marks; that is, can they "tack" on that prior use to claim earlier priority (which would be important to cut off claims by interim adopters of the final logo). Tacking is permitted when "the two marks are so similar that consumers generally would regard them as essentially the same." *See Brookfield Communications, Inc. v. West Coast Entertainment Group*, 174 F.3d 1036 (9th Cir. 1999).

Under that test, tacking back to **Answer C** (2004) seems very likely. Although the earlier version included the additional words "Fab Rags," they are unlikely to affect distinct consumer identification of the B-Zow in a white circle fanciful construction as a stand-alone logo. More significant difficulties arise with claiming use based on the earlier versions. **Answer A** (1999) seems highly unlikely. GaZow and BigZow have relatively little in common in terms of sight, sound and meaning (*see* Topic 13 — Infringement: Likelihood of Confusion discussing substantial similarity as part of the test for likelihood of confusion) and the addition of the white circle makes a consumer connection even more problematic. **Answer B** (2002) does use the white circle logo construction, so the question is whether consumers will make the necessary association despite the change from "BigZow" to "B-Zow." It might be argued that such a slight change — a contraction — has no effect on customer perception (it may even be the result of consumer usage). If so, then Alpha would be able to tack back to 2002 and **Answer B** would be the best answer. But it is also possible that the change was the result of Alpha's desire to affirmatively seek to break from the past and it would be essential to see how consumers reacted to the change.

101. **Your client may just squeak through**. In order to claim trademark rights in "CAR-BOTA," Carbota Ltd. must demonstrate they were the first to use the mark in good faith as a trademark. There is no issue on the facts related to affixation/connection as all uses involve conspicuous attachment directly to the related product. So the central "use" issue is first good faith use as a trademark. Because there is no other relevant use or any registrations, the crucial question is whether your client or Carbota, Ltd. can claim priority based on their actual activities. There is no evidence your client engaged in any market activity prior to their first public offer for sale on June 4, 2006. However, no actual sale is required so the offer-use is sufficient to claim June 4, 2006 as their first use, rather than June 10, 2006 when the first sale was made. The question is whether Carbota, Ltd. can claim a priority date before June 4, 2006 based on an earlier first good faith use as a trademark.

The date of their corporate formation (April 15, 2005) under the name Carbota, Ltd., will not stand. Their use as a business (trade) name does not create trademark rights and there is no indication of any use at that time in connection with product offerings (if there had been, then Carbota, Ltd. might raised an *analogous use* claim, discussed in Question 106). On the facts, the May 1, 2005 date does not involve use of "CARBOTA" as a mark, but it might be asserted based on tacking linking back to the use of "Kartoomb." However, because "Kartoomb" bears little resemblance to "CARBOTA" the tacking argument is unlikely to succeed (that is not to say there is no risk; a consumer survey might be useful). The first evidence related to trademark use of the "CARBOTA" mark is the Board's adoption decision on April 15, 2006 in connection with the new product line. Neither intent to use nor planning qualifies as use, so those activities provide no support for a trademark claim as of that date. The May 1, 2006 product announcement and related publicity campaign, however, do pose significant concerns. However, a "coming soon" campaign is not the same as actual "ordinary course" trademark use in the market — so it will be important to determine whether there was sufficient product association and whether the activity was merely a precursor bad faith effort to reserve the mark. The only firm evidence of actual use is their June 5, 2006 offer for sale. Again, there is no need for an actual sale, so the June 6, 2006 date is not relevant. If the May 1 announcement date holds up, your client is in trouble. Otherwise, the client's June 4, 2006 use as a trademark predates Carbota, Ltd.'s June 5, 2006 use and that one day advantage gives the client priority and rights to the mark.

102. **YES**. Use only confers trademark rights to the extent of the use. Consequently, even if Carbota, Ltd. could claim priority based on first use (May 1, 2006) it may not have any valid rights in your client's geographic market. The issue of the geographic scope of trademark rights is discussed in Topic 8: Use — Product/Service and Geographic Reach (Footprint) and Topic 9: Registration: Constructive Use and Intent to Use.

103. **YES**. Again, because use-based trademark rights only reflect the extent of the use, it must be determined whether Carbota Ltd.'s use in connection with refrigerators gives them rights with regard to ovens. The issue of the product scope of trademark rights is discussed in Topic 8 — Use: Product/Service and Geographic Reach (Footprint) and Topic 9: Registration: Constructive Use and Intent to Use.

104. Ah, prized is the client who contacts to their lawyer <u>before</u> acting (compare to Question 101 above). Best to encourage that kind of activity by giving them not only sound but practical advice. Obtaining trademark rights requires being the (i) first to (ii) actually use the mark in the marketplace in the "ordinary course" (in lieu of sham or token use to reserve the name, (iii) in a way which associates the mark with the related product in the consumers' minds (affixation/connection).

Priority (being "first") is the vital first step. If others are already using the (or a similar) mark (on the same or similar products in the relevant geography — those particulars are taken up Topic 8 — Use: Product/Service and Geographic Reach (Footprint) and Topic 9: Registration: Constructive Use and Intent to Use), then no amount of use by a subsequent adopter will create rights (in fact, it will be an infringement). The initial step, therefore, is a trademark search to determine whether any relevant prior claimants exist (including prior registrants claiming constructive use). NOTE: As a practical matter such searches do pose difficult problems, such as how to find small, local businesses. Professional searchers often resort to huge telephone directory databases, but even that can come up short.

Assuming the search indicates no priority problems, Megabits should as quickly as possible engage in sufficient use to trigger trademark protection. That involves two requirements: ensuring that consumers connect the mark to the related good (affixation/ connection) and sufficient good faith use as a mark to trigger the source identification function. The cleanest method of ensuring the affixation requirement is met is to attach the mark directly and prominently to the product. However, it is also permitted to attach the mark to related containers or via tags or labels or, if those methods are impracticable, by use in associated documents. In this case, however, it is best to avoid all uncertainties and attach the mark directly to the network server as well as in advertising. The second requirement is best satisfied by offering (and, hopefully, actually selling) the marked servers to the public in the ordinary course of the network server trade. That approach, however, requires waiting until the product is ready to be rolled-out with the attendant risks of an interim adoption by another. Nonetheless, the client should NOT yield to temptation and engage in "token" sales activity, such as internal shipping or "sales" to affiliated companies or others solely to reserve the mark. A better alternative (although less desirable than full product launch) would be an incremental launch involving real public distribution. As a last resort they might consider a pre-launch promotional campaign but they should make sure it includes an actual product specifically associated with the mark.

NOTE: The real-world solution to the Catch-22 problem of investment, then use, then rights is an intent-to-use registration which creates a limited time "reservation" of the mark while the necessary preparations for use are being made. *See* Topic 9 — Registration: Constructive Use and Intent to Use.

NOTE: Because the scope of the question was limited to use, there was no need to determine if there were other barriers to adopting the term as a trademark. In particular, it should always be considered whether the mark is barred by functionality or faces distinctiveness problems. In this case functionality is not an issue (the mark is entirely unrelated to the product or its design — it is not part of "what makes it work"). Regarding distinctiveness, my vote would go for fanciful (made up) making it inherently distinctive and avoiding the need for a showing of secondary meaning.

105.   **The best answer is D**. **Answer A** and **Answer B** are both required to claim superior rights in the mark. However, on these facts there is an additional problem which makes neither of them, standing alone, sufficient. "Good faith use as a mark" requires that the mark actually perform source signaling for consumers. That requires not only sufficient prior good faith use and affixation/connection, but that the mark itself is *distinctive* at the time of the use. On these facts it is a close call. If "Way Quick" is viewed as being suggestive (requiring a leap of imagination), then the mark was inherently distinctive when first adopted and used. That would give LightSpeed's

trademark claim priority from January 6, 2005 which is before and, therefore, superior to, the competitors June 2005 adoption. However, if "Way Quick" is classified as descriptive, then it will only be sufficiently distinctive to qualify as a trademark once it has acquired secondary meaning. LightSpeed's surveys show that only occurred in July 2005, after the competitor starting using the mark. The issue is how the two uses can be reconciled in such circumstances. Most courts resolve the problem by requiring that the senior user (LightSpeed) show secondary meaning (trademark use) prior to adoption by the junior user. Under that rule LightSpeed has no valid claim against the competitor. Consequently, **Answer C** is also necessary to support LightSpeed's claim to superior rights, making **Answer D** (perhaps somewhat ironically) the least likely to do so.

NOTE: This rule hardly seems to further the policies of trademark law. If despite subsequent development of secondary meaning the junior user continues to use the mark, consumers (by definition) will thereafter be confused. Perhaps a better rule might be to permit continued descriptive use by the junior user with appropriate disclaimer. *See* Topic 16: Defenses — Fair Use, Nominative Use, Parody/Free Speech.

106.   **Analogous use and tacking**. The concept of analogous use arises in the registration context, but may have applicability in this situation as well. The courts have held that even though a senior claimant does not have prior trademark rights, it may still have standing to oppose the registration of the mark by another if it can demonstrate "analogous rights." Analogous rights requires a "substantial impact" on the consuming public, that is, a showing that it identifies the mark with the senior user as a supplier despite the absence of good faith use as a trademark. Such non-trademark identification might arise from the regular appearance of producer's non-mark trade name in associated advertising or press articles related to its goods or from extensive use in pre-availability promotion despite the lack of any specific product identification (as discussed in Questions 95 and 101 above). On these facts, LightSpeed might claim that its consistent use of the "Way Quick" phrase (even though descriptive) in connection with its particular product was open and notorious, aimed at the relevant consumers and informed those consumers of the availability of LightSpeed's product under the mark (the basic requirements for proving analogous use). If LightSpeed can prevail on the analogous use issue, it may then be able to argue that use should be tacked on to its post-secondary meaning rights, carrying them back to before the competitor's adoption.

There are two difficulties with this creative argument. First, and most significant, is that it is difficult to see how on these facts LightSpeed could show the necessary public association without also demonstrating secondary meaning. If they can, it seems that analogous use merely serves as an alternative to secondary meaning "in the making," a doctrine specifically rejected by the courts. Second, the analogous use doctrine has primarily been used defensively to oppose the registration of the mark by another. In this case analogous use is being used to create trademark rights in the claimant. On one hand, they are only being used to extend independently demonstrated trademark rights back in time. On the other, that permits LightSpeed to effectively reserve the mark without compliance with the intent-to-use registration requirements (including the time limitations and notice such a registration provides). *See* Topic 9: Registration — Constructive Use and Intent to Use.

107. **It is unclear.** The most reasonable argument seems (to me) to be that LightSpeed's showing of secondary meaning and trademark rights should cut off any further subsequent adoptions as they would be likely to confuse consumers. *See* Question 105 above.

108. **The best answer is C.** The concept of derivative use rests on the fact that although trademarks signal source that does not mean the consumer must know the actual producer. Therefore, provided that nature and characteristics of the goods bearing the mark are consistent, use by another may qualify as use by the trademark claimant. That connection is particularly non-problematic when the actual user is controlled by the claimant. *See* Lanham Act §§ 5 & 45 (defining related company use inuring to the benefit of the owner in terms of control over nature and quality) (15 U.S.C. §§ 1055 & 1127). Both **Answer A** and **Answer B** make such control likely so they should generally support a related derivative claim, although it may be necessary to confirm that such control was in fact exercised, Neither **Answer C** nor **Answer D** can depend on this "control" logic so some other justification is required. As trademark law focuses on the consuming public, it is reasonable to assume that when the public itself has created the mark and its connection to a particular product (as it did with both "Coke" — a shortened version of the original "Coca-cola" — and the Volkswagen "Bug"), it will not be mislead if the trademark rights are assigned to the related producer. So **Answer D** is likely a good derivative claim. **Answer C**, however, is problematic. Although the band member was a part of the original "source," to permit a single member subsequently to use the mark for his/her individual goods or services is very likely to cause confusion. Such derivative use claims are generally denied. *See Robi v. Reed*, 173 F.23 736 (9th Cir. 1999); *HEC Enters., Inc. v. Deep Purple, Inc.*, 213 U.S.P.Q. 991 (C.D. Cal. 1980); *Boogie Kings v. Guillory*, 188 So. 2d 445 (La. App. 1966). *But see* Topic 16 — Defenses: Fair Use, Nominative Use, Parody/Free Speech.

109. **The best answer is D**. Trademark law protects owners of marks against use by others which would impair the mark's ability to uniquely identify and distinguish the mark owner's goods. *See* Topic 1 — Justifications and Sources of Trademark Law. Generally, that objective is fostered by prohibiting confusing uses — that is, uses which interfere with consumers' ability to rely on the mark as signaling a unique source. Because trademark law seeks to prevent confusion *before* it happens rather than after the fact, the actual infringement standard is "likelihood of confusion." *see* Topic 13 — Infringement: Likelihood of Confusion. The right to prevent all uses goes well beyond that objective, so **Answer A** is incorrect. **Answer B** is a tautology, the question is what constitutes an "infringing use," so it is incorrect. **Answer C** and **Answer D** are closely related, with competition frequently contributing to a likelihood of consumer confusion. However, sometimes use by those not in direct competition with the trademark owner can also cause confusion (in particular, with regard to "related goods"). Additionally, in order to maximize desirable competition in some instances trademark law will permit use even by competitors, provided it does not cause confusion (for example, consistently with the fair use exception). Consequently, **Answer D** — preventing only those uses which are likely to cause consumer confusion — is better than **Answer C**.

Professor Robert Lind of Southwestern School of Law refers to a mark's *"footprint"* to capture the concept of a mark's maximum reach (geographic and product) — that is, the full extent of a mark owner's rights to prevent uses likely to cause confusion. I use that convenient label in the remainder of the questions in this Topic.

NOTE: You might (and should) wonder, if consumer confusion is the primary concern of trademark law, what justifies the regime's non-confusion based rights such as intent-to-use registrations (by definition there is no use, so there can't be any confusion), anti-dilution and anticybersquatting (both of which explicitly do not require confusion). *See* Topic 9 — Registration: Constructive Use and Intent to Use, Topic 14 — Dilution, and Topic 15 — Anticybersquatting, respectively. Some argue that those rights are designed to avoid incipient, initial interest or potential future confusion. I believe (although it is hardly a mainstream view so watch this on an exam), however, a better explanation is that trademark law *also* seeks to affirmatively encourage the creation of powerful trademark signals which communicate information clearly and efficiently to consumers. Consequently, the regime will protect the related investments (in selection and publicizing the mark) when the social benefits outweigh the costs. Because "incentive" balancing turns on factors other than confusion, it explains the existence and appropriate scope of non-confusion based trademark rights. *See* Vincent Chiappetta, *Trademarks: More Than Meets the Eye*, Spring 2003 U. ILL. J. L. TECH. & POL. 35 (2003).

110.   **The best answer is B**. Trademark law gives FixIT the right to prevent all uses of the "Mitiox" mark which are likely to cause consumer confusion. **Answer B**, further refines although not fully satisfactorily, that statement in light of the particular facts. As it turns out it is the BEST of the four listed answers. The mark owner's actual product use — that is, the type(s) of good(s) on which the mark has actually been used — provides the starting point for defining the related product footprint. However, despite its vital importance, that professional use does not define the full extent of that footprint. In addition to the specific products, the footprint also covers products which are closely enough "related" to those products to make consumer confusion likely. So although **Answer A** is clearly correct — third party staplers bearing the "Mitiox" mark are very likely to cause consumer confusion, it does not go far enough. **Answer C** and **Answer D** both provide possible "related goods" extensions. However, although they should be considered, it is far from certain on these facts that consumers are likely to make the erroneous (confused) assumption that "Mitiox" staplers and either other "Mitiox" fastener products (which is possible) or every "Mitiox" office product come from the same source. Consequently, **Answer B**, which states the "related goods" test rather than an unsupported conclusion, is the best answer. The details of what constitutes a "related" good — one within the mark's product footprint — are discussed in Topic 13 — Infringement: Likelihood of Confusion.

NOTE: The federal registration of a mark significantly affects a mark's geographic footprint; however, although there may be some evidentiary consequences arising from the stated product coverage in the registration, the product footprint analysis is generally the same for both registered and unregistered marks.

NOTE: Although this Question focuses on how to determine a mark's product footprint, the mark's overall footprint (the owner's *actual* rights to prevent use) is determined by the *combination* of its product and geographic footprint. For example, even though other uses on staplers clearly falls within the "Mitiox" product footprint, no consumer confusion would exist if two Mitiox staplers from different producers are sold in entirely separate geographic markets. So although FixIT has strong rights regarding staplers, it would be erroneous to say that mark's product footprint covers "***all*** use in connection with staplers." Geographic footprint is discussed in the following Questions.

111.   **The best answer is Answer A**. FixIT's trademark rights permit it to prevent use likely to cause consumer confusion. One part of that inquiry concerns the "footprint" created by its product use (on staplers) as discussed in Question 110 above. As all of the new adopters in this Question use the mark on the identical product, their use clearly falls within the "Mitiox" product footprint. The issue, therefore, is whether they fall within the "geographic" footprint of the mark. Under the general "use creates rights" theory of United States trademark law FixIT's use will be key to their geographic rights. As expected, geographic trademark rights generally go to the first actual good faith user as a trademark in the particular territory (remembering, of course, as with any rule there are exceptions — the effect of a registration and related "constructive" use is discussed in Topic 9 — Registration: Constructive Use and Intent to Use and, as we'll see in the Questions below where consumer associations may exist even absent actual use).

On these facts: FixIT first used the mark in Salem, Oregon and has gradually expanded its geographic use into all of Oregon, Washington and Idaho. Although the expansion of their rights took place over time, it was prior to all new (current) adoptions. FixIT's priority gives it rights in those geographic markets over all *subsequent* users within its product footprint. Consequently, FixIT will prevail in each of the situations described in **Answers B, C** and **D**. However, as there is no indication of FixIT's use of the Mitiox mark in New York City (or any connection with that market, for that matter), it cannot claim rights in that territory, even on staplers. Consequently, **Answer A** is easily their worst claim and, therefore, the best answer.

NOTE: Limiting trademark rights to specific geographic areas produces a competition for geographic rights in open territories. Because producers in different geographic markets can obtain rights in the identical mark on identical products, the same mark will "mean one thing in one market [and] an entirely different thing in another." *United Drug Co. v. Theodore Rectanus Co.*, 248 U.S. 90 (1918). Consequently, as mark owners contemplate geographic expansion a "race" is triggered with each competing to be the first to obtain rights for its version of the mark in "open" (unclaimed) territories. Federal registration is in large part designed to help mitigate the inefficiencies of that situation. *See* Topic 9: Registration: Constructive Use and Intent to Use.

112. **The best answer is D**. Although good faith use as a trademark is sufficient to establish geographic rights there is a key difference between testing whether enough use exists to provide any trademark rights and the geographic footprint of those rights once established. The subtle but important shift is from preventing unjustified appropriation as a mark to the proper scope of existing rights. That means the geographic footprint of existing use-based trademark rights focuses not on "warehousing/reservations" but on whether permitting another's use in the geographic region is likely to cause consumer confusion. Consequently, although satisfying the use in commerce test within a geographic market is sufficient to establish related rights, it is not necessary. All that is required is sufficient consumer *association* between the mark and the producer/owner in that market to make confusion likely if the subsequent use is permitted.

Merely prospective geographic expansion — such as **Answer A** — fails both tests. It does not constitute good faith use in New York nor does it, standing alone, offer any evidence of existing consumer associations in the new geographic market (New York, in this case) — something more active (say a pre-launch advertising campaign) is required. **Answer B** certainly does not suffice as good faith use; in fact it looks like "token use" as discussed in Topic 7 — Acquiring Rights: Use. The footprint question, however, is whether that use supports a claim of likely consumer confusion based on New York consumer association. Ten people are de minimis in a place like New York. Nor is there any evidence those ten people are likely to have any significant contact with stapler consumers (they are not, for example, office supply retailers). The contest is between **Answer C** and **Answer D**. **Answer D** edges out **Answer C** (in my view anyway, but reasonable minds can differ). **Answer C** supports the argument that significant numbers of New York business people (and potential customers) have seen Mitiox staplers while visiting Oregon (in their counterparts' offices or office supply stores). However, **Answer D** directly implicates individuals likely to buy staplers (the wholesalers) in a setting where the mark is relevant. The wholesalers are, therefore, very likely to be confused if they suddenly see "Mitiox" staplers from another producer in the New York market.

113. **Who knows?** Although the greater the numbers of those making the association the better FixIT's claim, no bright-line exists for determining the precise point at which *sufficient* association exists to trigger related geographic rights. It can be argued that **Answer B** is better than **Answer A** and **Answer C** is better than both **Answer A** and **Answer B**. They all involve stapler buyers in the relevant geographic market and are very likely to be confused) and 5 making the association seems more problematic than 1, and 50 seems more problematic than 5. However, the sufficiency question doesn't turn on which answer involves the most consumers. Who is to say that one (perhaps large volume) wholesaler isn't more relevant than either five retailers or fifty end-users? And even had they all been wholesalers, at what point have "enough" consumers confused — at 1, at 5 or at 50? And of what relevance are the *potential* consumers, like the 1000 in **Answer D**? A *de minimis* threshold of consumer association seems necessary to ensure actual benefits from the rights (balancing the possible confusion against the value of permitting actual use by another to signal source), but where that line should be drawn is hardly clear. Consequently, determining how much consumer association is *sufficient* to grant geographic rights *absent* actual use therefore will be a difficult judgment call based on the particular facts.

114. The geographic footprint analysis always starts from the same basic considerations. FixIT's lack of good faith use as a mark and the absence of any consumer association in Florida mean they have no demonstrable confusion-based claims over a *prior* local user of the same mark even on the same product. However, courts will frequently look at the good faith of the junior adopter in cases such as this one. *See United Drug Co. v. Theodore Rectanus Co.*, 248 U.S. 90 (1918). If FixIT can shown that the junior local geographic adopter was acting with bad faith intent to interfere with, or capitalize on, its mark (or goodwill), a court may be convinced to rule in fixIT's favor (on unfair competition grounds) notwithstanding the absence of any demonstrable confusion-based priority. Combining the Florida adopter's knowledge of both FixIT's previous Northwest use and its plans for imminent expansion into Florida with no other explanation for their selecting the Mitiox mark makes for a strong case.

NOTE: There is a strong relationship between the "bad faith" geographic doctrine and the recent excitement over cybersquatting (third party use of a trademark as part of a domain name thus preventing the trademark owner from doing so). In both cases the concern is less about likely consumer confusion, than the the unfairness to/unjustified interference with the mark owner. The importance of bad faith/unfairness in anti-cybersquatting is explored in Topic 15: Anticybersquatting.

115. The "zone of natural expansion" doctrine permits a mark-owner to claim rights in geographic areas into which it is likely to expand (the theory being, perhaps, that it

makes sense to preempt adoptions likely to cause future conflicts) without inquiry into actual use or existing consumer associations. On that basis, FixIT can certainly make a good argument that the proximity and ties between California and its existing Northwest market as well as the commercial fit with its business makes that market a "zone of natural expansion," giving it current rights and, therefore, priority over any future adopters. However, because the doctrine has the effect of permitting the "reservation" of a mark without any showing of use, likely confusion or even "unfairness" to the mark holder, as well as its ambiguous application (how is the zone actually defined?), it is far from generally accepted. *See* Restatement (Third) of Unfair Competition § 19, comment (c) (1995). Therefore, it is probably best viewed as a fall-back argument. A better approach would be to build a record (if possible) of how FixIT's Northwest use has generated significant consumer associations between the mark and its product and, if those associations do not exist, FixIT would be well advised to take steps to create them.

NOTE: The best approach (as it almost always is) to maximize geographic priority is a federal registration which triggers nation-wide constructive use and related priority. *See* Topic 9 — Registration: Constructive Use and Intent to Use.

116. **The answer, from best to worst case, is: B, A, C, D**. The order reflects how the mark owner's *use* affects a mark's product and geographic footprint as well as how the two variables interact with regard to the owner's related rights. On the facts O'wine only expressly has the right to prevent the use of the "Avert" mark on wine in Oregon. **Answer B** is within that geographic footprint, but requires a determination of whether use on a different product (wine glasses) is likely to cause consumer confusion. As wine and wine glasses are commonly used and purchased together, it is not unreasonable to infer a strong possibility of consumer association and, therefore, confusion. *See* Topic 13 — Infringement: Likelihood of Confusion. In contrast, **Answer A** involves the actual product (wine) thus obviating the need for the "related" goods inquiry; however, it involves a geography in which you client has made no actual use of the mark on wine or any other product. Obtaining the necessary geographic rights would depend on evidence of existing consumer associations — which are not explicitly stated but may be reasonably inferable given the proximity and business relationships between the two states. **Answer C** requires both the related product confusion inference and a showing of existing associations, so it is yet a more difficult case to make. Finally, **Answer D** involves the mark's express geographic footprint, so it is a strong case in that regard. However, it is an example of when product "unrelatedness" is determinative. It is so unlikely that consumers will "make the leap" from wine to cars, that the case is a clear loser.

NOTE: There might be a claim for dilution in Answer D; however, the given facts offer little support.

117. **The best answer is B**. On the facts Company A has clear geographic priority regarding the Paradigm mark on watches in Oregon, while Company B has geographic priority regarding the Paradigm mark on watches in Georgia. Consequently, **Answer A** describes

when Company A is MOST likely to prevail, so it is incorrect. On *only* the above facts neither company has any actual use nor is there any reason to suppose consumer association with either company in Maine or Arizona. So both markets are "up for grabs." **Answers C** and **D**, therefore, describe open territory with the rights going to the first to stake a valid claim. The winner of that race is unclear on the existing facts, so neither situation is particularly strong for Company A. However, **Answer B** involves no ambiguity. The rights to the mark on watches in Georgia belong to Company B making it the case in which Company A is LEAST likely to prevail.

118. **There is no way to tell on the given facts**. It is important to always answer questions on exams and in practice based on analysis rather than on hopeful inference. The question asked which has *the stronger claim* not which *most likely has the stronger claim*. A claim to geographic priority requires either first use or evidence of existing consumer associations. The former can be resolved on the given facts — neither company as any use-based rights in Idaho. The latter cannot. The answer, therefore, depends on something which is not known — whether either company can show existing consumer associations in Arizona.

NOTE: On these facts it is also entirely possible that both companies can show some level of consumer association. In that case it is very difficult to resolve the priority issue — do the rights go to the company which can show the strongest associations or that it was the first to develop the associations? And what about the resulting confusion generated by the conflicting associations?

119. The internet has added a new dimension to the "open" geography race; that is, how does a web site accessible by anyone, anywhere change the priority determination. The issue remains unresolved; however, as trademark law's objectives haven't changed, the basic analysis should remain the same: geographic rights should follow from either use or consumer associations which will generate confusion if use by another is permitted.

In that framework, the central issue is not whether the web site *can* be accessed but whether it constitutes use or has generated problematic consumer association between the mark and the claimant's product. Regarding "use," the lack of actual Arizona customers is not fatal. However, the fact that the site clearly targets only Georgia consumers and Company B does not take Arizona orders makes it very difficult to argue that Company B is offering its watches for sale in Arizona.

However, the usage statistics do raise associational possibilities. They show some Arizona consumers are being directed to and accessing the site. They do not show, however, that these consumers are "current" or even potential watch buyers or whether their experience at the site (do they linger and read?) is sufficient to make any trademark impression. Although some inferences might be drawn, without more it seems problematic to assume any significant Arizona consumer association exists. That conclusion is supported (albeit not confirmed for the same reasons) by the small absolute numbers of combined searches relative to what one might expect if consumers made the necessary association. The evidence of a growing trend might be helpful in demonstrating that an association might be forming, however, "extremely small" and "slowly" seem short of the level required to conclude that the "Paradigm" mark was associated with Company B watches in Arizona.

120. **The best answer is A.** The facts state that Burnt has established used-based priority rights in the logo for toasters. Those basic rights are certainly sufficient to support **Answer C**. The product footprint of those established rights, however, extends to other uses which are likely to cause consumer confusion, so **Answer C** does not go far enough. On the facts **Answer B** seems a likely possibility, but remains an unresolved question of fact. Consequently, **Answer A** which states the related products "rule" is the better answer. In all events, that rule does not cover all uses so **Answer D** is incorrect.

121. **The best answer is C.** The trademark right to prevent use extends only to uses which are likely to cause consumer confusion as to source. **Answer A** which only involves "copying" does not implicate that concern. Although copying could give rise to a copyright violation, without any trademark use it does not violate Burnt's trademark rights. The remaining answers all involve uses on a product and in a geographic area clearly within the footprint of Burnt's existing trademark rights. The question, therefore, raises the issue of more nuanced limitations. Because **Answer B** only refers to toasters rather than third party toasters, it does not eliminate the possibility that the use is in connection with Burnt's toasters. Such fair/nominative use is permitted even on toasters provided it does not give rise to confusion (for example, of sponsorship or affiliation). *See* Topic 16 — Defenses: Fair Use, Nominative Use, Parody/Free Speech. So **Answer B** is overly broad. **Answer D** also involves relevant product and geographic use. In this case, however, the statement is too limiting. The trademark issue is whether the use is likely to cause confusion. Although bad faith may be a relevant factor (*see* Topic 13 — Infringement: Likelihood of Confusion), if the use is not likely to cause confusion (evil heart, weak abilities) it is not a violation. Any confusing use is prohibited, regardless of the user's good faith (although it may affect the related remedies), making **Answer C** the best of the four answers.

122. **The best answer is D.** All of the fact patterns involve uses on a product and in a geographic area clearly within the footprint of Burnt's trademark rights. **Answer A** is clearly incorrect as there may be relevant defenses (*see* the answer to Question 121 immediately above). **Answer B** is clearly a correct answer, stating the basic rights of the trademark owner. However, the remaining two answers raise an important additional refinement of the mark owner's confusion-based rights — the right to prevent use of *variations on the mark* which are likely to cause confusion. *See* Topic 13 — Infringement: Likelihood of Confusion. Consequently, although correct **Answer A** does not go far enough. As between **Answer C** and **Answer D, Answer D** is the more accurate, covering not only actual confusion but uses *likely* to cause consumer confusion.

123. **No.** Rights to the mark include both geographic and product footprints. Non-use in connection with the specific product (toasters) is important (use would definitely preclude Burnt's use), it is insufficient to confirm the mark is available. In particular,

there may be an existing use in connection with related products — for example, other small kitchen appliances — which may give rise to a claim that Burnt's use on toasters is likely to cause consumer confusion. Additionally, it is possible that someone in another geographic market has generated strong consumer associations in Iowa between the logo and their products.

124.   The crucial issue (as noted in the previous Question) is identifying whether any prior uses or associations exist. Therefore, Burnt should do a search for any potentially problematic product use or associations (including related goods) in *any* portion of Iowa, as even if the use is extremely limited (say to a particular town), at best it will cause difficulties in that location and at worst may have generated consumer associations between the mark and that product in other parts of the State. If such uses show up then steps will need to be taken to obtain the related rights before commencing its own use.

If the search comes back "clean" — showing Iowa is unclaimed geographic territory in the relevant product footprint — because Burnt has neither use nor consumer associations in Iowa, it is involved in a *priority* race with other possible adopters of the mark. That means it needs to take steps to limit possible adoptions in Iowa prior to its own actual use. Although the "zone of natural expansion" doctrine provides a possible argument given its existing Mid-western business' proximity to Iowa and, perhaps, its imminent plans to actually expand, the doctrine is not widely accepted. It should, therefore, take immediate steps to either develop or strengthen consumer associations between the mark and their products within Iowa. For example, it might consider pre-launch marketing prominently employing the logo on their toasters targeting distributors as well as end-users.

Burnt should, however, understand there is no assurance it will actually be able to claim rights in the logo in Iowa until it has in fact engaged in good faith use in the State. This problem with use-based trademark rights is an important justification for the federal registration regime and related constructive use. *See* Topic 9 — Registration: Constructive Use and Intent to Use.

125. **The best answer is C**. The facts state that TotoL has first-user priority throughout Utah and Nevada which gives it full geographic rights in both those states. Therefore, **Answer A** is correct as far as it goes. However, **Answer A** does consider any additional geographic rights which arise from consumer associations outside TotoL's primary market. *See* Topic 8: Use: Product/Service and Geographic Reach (Footprint). **Answer B** adds areas in which those associations *may* exist because of TotoL's regional advertising activity. However, geographic rights do not arise from the advertising activity alone; only when the necessary association has in fact been created. Absent that evidence, **Answer C** is the better answer — limiting rights to where such associations actually exist. Although **Answer D** is correct regarding TotoL's overall trademark rights in the "Floquet" mark (based on the combination of its product and geographic footprint) — the question only asks about the *geographic* footprint. Geographic rights only require association in consumer's minds with regard to some product or service, whereas a likelihood of confusion also considers the nature of the junior adopter's products or services. **Answer C** is, therefore, the best answer to the question as asked.

NOTE: Differentiating between the geographic footprint (scope) and the product-related footprint (scope) of a mark is crucial to understanding registration-based constructive use, which only concerns the former.

126. **The best answer is B**. A key difficulty in relying on use-based rights is the "race" to acquire open geographic territories. In particular, the first to either use the mark or able to demonstrate sufficient consumer association generally obtains the exclusive rights in the related geographic territory. *See* Topic 8 — Use: Product/Service and Geographic Reach (Footprint). Consequently, when TotoL decides to expand geographically it may discover that its use of the "Floquet" mark has been "blocked" by interim adopters. A federal registration mitigates that concern considerably. It grants the registrant constructive (deemed) use throughout the United States from the date of application (whether or not there is actual use or even consumer association), thereby "reserving" future rights to the mark in all open territories. **Answer B** focuses expressly on the race created by the use-based first-come, first-served system. **Answer A** is almost correct; however, it omits the fact that geographic priority may also be based on proof of consumer association (**Answer B** is not phrased in terms of "use" to emphasize that the geographic rights can — and frequently do — extend beyond the mark owner's actual market). A federal registration does provide additional benefits, including prima facie evidence of validity and incontestability — the issues alluded to in **Answer C** and **Answer D**. Those issues are, at best, very indirectly relevant to geographic expansion concerns. Having a valid mark only means the owner has rights in the mark,

but it is still use and constructive use from registration which define the geographic scope of those rights.

NOTE: Although a federal registration helps prove a mark's validity it is not the only way to prove validity — demonstrating prior good faith use as a mark is sufficient. Nor does a federal registration, even an "incontestable" registration, guarantee validity. A registration is only prima facie evidence of validity, *see* Lanham Act §§ 7(b) & 33(a) (15 U.S.C. §§ 1057(b) & 1115(a)). And although a registration may become "incontestable" after five years (it is subject to ordinary validity challenge until then), even after that time its validity can still be challenged on certain grounds. *See* Topic 12: Registration: Incontestability. So neither **Answer C** nor **Answer D** is factually correct as stated.

127.   **The best answer is C.** As state in **Answer C**, under the Lanham Act § 7(c) (15 U.S.C. § 1056(c)) federal registration constitutes constructive use as of the date of the application, conferring nationwide priority against all users after that date (provided, of course, the registration actually issues). Such constructive use, therefore, "solves" the open geographic market use-based race issues regarding expansion. However, although such constructive use serves as the basis for *claiming* priority in the mark in all "open" geographic markets as of the date of the filing, it does NOT guarantee *actual* priority throughout the United States. There may be prior users in some geographic regions existing on the date of application, so **Answer B** is incorrect. Nor does the registration constitute actual use throughout the United States, merely constructive use, so **Answer D** is incorrect (Question 137 below deals with the remedial differences which may arise from that distinction). Finally, only a federal registration can become incontestable (after five years of continuous use). However, as explained in the previous Question, incontestability only means that the owner has strong rights in the mark, it does not provide any extra geographic scope to those rights. So **Answer A** is incorrect.

NOTE: Constructive use is contingent on actual registration but provided the registration is granted it relates back to the *date of the application*, not merely the date of registration. That not only gives incentives to early filings but avoids penalizing the applicant for any delays in processing the registration at the Patent and Trademark Office (including the possible interim adoption by others while the application is pending).

128.   **The best answer is D.** Although registration is deemed constructive use everywhere in the United States, the registrant's rights do not extend to territories in which others have adopted and used the mark in good faith *prior to the date the application was filed. See* Lanham Act §§ 7(c)(1) & 33(b)(5) (15 U.S.C. §§ 1065(c)(1) & 1115(b)(5)). So even with a federal registration prior good faith users still have priority claim to the mark. That is true whether they are senior in absolute terms — prior to any use by Poundem of the mark — or junior in time to Poundem's first use in Georgia, but started using elsewhere prior to Poundem's filing of its application. If there are, in fact, no other prior good faith users, then **Answer A** would be correct. However, as that is not known on the given facts **Answer D** — which specifically mentions the exception — is the better answer. **Answer B** and **Answer C** are both incorrect. Although good

faith use as a trademark *somewhere* is a prerequisite to registration, registration's constructive use makes the applicant's actual use or ability to prove consumer associations irrelevant to claiming priority in "open" geographic territory after the date of application.

NOTE: In case you are wondering: The color orange is, indeed, problematic on distinctiveness grounds (as are all colors). *See* Topic 4: Distinctiveness — Inherently; Secondary Meaning; Never. Specifically, being the first user would not be sufficient to claim trademark rights in the color; rights could only be obtained with first use *after* a demonstration of *secondary meaning*. However, the facts state that both the mark and the registration are valid, so the secondary meaning issue is assumed to have been resolved.

129. **The answer is A**. Without a federal registration, the absence of its use and consumer association in Oregon means Poundem has no trademark rights in that State. Obtaining a valid registration for the mark triggers constructive use and related first-user priority over any adopter *after the date the application was filed. See* Lanham Act §§ 7(c) (constructive use) & 22 (constructive knowledge) (15 U.S.C. §§ 1057(c), 1072); *Dawn Donut Co., Inc. v. Hart's Food Stores, Inc.*, 267 F.2d 358 (2d Cir. 1959).

So the crucial date on these facts is June 30, 2005 (the date the application was filed (NOT January 15, 2006, the date the application was granted). The only date which falls before the date of filing is July 1, 2004, so **Answer D** covers the sole use prior to Poundem's constructive Oregon use triggered by its federal registration, making it the correct answer. The uses in **Answers A, B** and **C** all are subsequent to the date the application was filed, so Poundem has priority based on its registration.

130. **Yes**. In order to obtain federal constructive use rights Poundem's federal registration must issue. So if the application is still merely pending, Poundem has no claim to the mark, or rights to prevent its use by others, in Oregon. However, once the registration issues then constructive use will relate back to the date of application, giving Poundem the right to prevent use by all subsequent adopters. If Poundem's registration is ultimately denied (say for lack of distinctiveness) then Poundem has no use, constructive or otherwise, in Oregon and all of the users in Question 129 would have priority over Poundem (assuming anyone could obtain rights in the mark).

131. **The best answer is B**, but **Answer C** is worth arguing for if you are Junior's attorney. On the facts, Poundem has at least first use-based rights in the mark throughout Georgia and the Carolinas, independent of its federal registration. Because those rights allow it at a minimum to prevent Junior from using the mark in those markets, **Answer D** is incorrect. However, as Poundem's registration-triggered constructive use only dates from the filing of its application, it cannot displace a good faith adopter whose use in an open territory started prior to that date. On the facts, Junior is such a user. Its first use-based rights extend at least to use in Oregon, so **Answer A** is incorrect (in fact, Junior can prevent Poundem from using the mark in Oregon). **Answer B** and **Answer C** address how much additional geographic territory Junior's prior Oregon use carves

out of Poundem's "national" registration rights. **Answer B** treats Junior as "frozen" on the date Poundem's application was filed, limiting Junior's rights to areas in which Junior can show actual use or in which then existing associations would risk confusion if Poundem started using the mark. **Answer C** adds a zone of natural expansion (territory Junior would likely enter in the ordinary course of its business, whether or not there are existing consumer associations in that territory). Although support can be found for both positions (and therefore they should both be considered on an exam and in real life), **Answer B** avoids the highly questionable proposition of permitting post-registration expansion by a junior user into open markets (those in which there was no existing use or consumer association on the date the application was filed) making it, my opinion, the better legal position. *See Thrifty Rent-A-Car System v. Thrift Cars, Inc.*, 831 F.2d 1177 (1st Cir. 1987); Restatement (Third) of Unfair Competition, § 19, comment (c) (1995). However, full credit for either answer, provided you saw and understood the issue.

NOTE: On the facts there is no indication of Junior's bad faith, nor does the mark become incontestable until June 30, 2011 (far in the future, unless you are reading this after that date — in which case I'm amazed at longevity of this work), so neither of those issues are raised. They are, however, dealt with immediately below, so press on.

132.   On the facts, Junior's first use was before the date Poundem's registration was filed so it "beat" the related constructive use. However, Junior's knowledge of Poundem's use prior to adopting the mark raises the question of whether Junior's use satisfies the "*good faith*" requirement for claiming use-based priority. Under the common law rule, mere knowledge would not likely be enough. Poundem would probably have to demonstrate that Junior's adoption involved some form of affirmative bad — unfair competition, such as a desire to benefit from Poundem's goodwill and/or interfere with its future expansion. *See* Topic 7 — Acquiring Rights: Use. So the answer would likely remain the same as set out in Question 131 — Junior would have the rights to the mark in Oregon plus any additional geographic areas where consumer associations between the mark and Junior's product existed prior to the date Poundem filed its application for federal registration.

133.   Lanham Act § 33(b)(5) (15 U.S.C. § 1115(b)(5)) sets out a junior user good faith "defense" in connection with incontestable marks. It specifically requires the remote junior user (someone adopting the mark after another's first use in another territory, but before federal registration's constructive use triggered) have adopted the mark "without knowledge of the registrant's prior use" and "the mark must have been continuously used" prior to [the federal registration]" (that bit in the brackets is more complicated in the statute and worth a look, but the basic idea is the adoption must be prior to and use continuous through the date a federal registration triggered constructive use priority). The statutory test applied when an incontestable mark is involved is therefore arguably more restrictive than the common law test, making mere "knowledge" (rather than bad faith — unfair competition) sufficient to eliminate the junior user's priority. *See Thrifty Rent-A-Car System v. Thrift Cars, Inc.*, 831 F.2d 1177

(1st Cir. 1987). Under that strict reading of the statute, Junior's mere knowledge would mean it loses all rights to the mark once Poundem's federal registration becomes incontestable — so it should have taken action (seeking at least a concurrent use registration) before the five years triggering uncontestable status expired.

NOTE: If this seems a bit anomalous, it is. The best explanation for permitting then revoking use by Junior upon Poundem's registration becoming incontestable despite the resulting consumer confusion may be that incontestability is a way of "quieting title" thus putting the burden on other users to contest prior to that time or "forever after holding their peace." *See* Topic 12 — Registration: Incontestability.

134. Even though it is the junior user of the mark in time, as the first federal registrant statutory constructive use now favors Junior's claims to any open geographic markets. A strict application of the statute would, therefore, give Junior all of that territory and limit Poundem (the senior adopter and user) to the markets in which it could show actual use, existing consumer associations between the mark and its products, and, perhaps a zone of natural expansion. *See Wiener King, Inc. v. Wiener King Corp*, 615 F.2d 512 (C.C.P.A., 1980). Obviously, this first-in-time risk encourages early registration by senior users, which not only serves their interests but avoids conflict by providing early notice to other potential adopters. *See id.*

135. Poundem could start a cancellation proceeding at the Patent and Trademark Office (heard by the Trademark Trial and Appeal Board (the TTAB)) under Lanham Act § 14 (15 U.S.C. § 1064) claiming priority. The TTAB would examine the issue under Lanham Act § 2(d) (15 U.S.C. § 1052(d) which addresses conflicts with previous uses). However, as no actual conflict exists in the open territories it would likely use the "good faith" approach, meaning Poundem might have to show that Junior knew about its use and/or plans to expand and, thus, on unfair competition grounds Poundem should have priority. *Cf. id.* (The cancellation action based on prior use can only be brought before the registration has become incontestable.)

An important mechanism helps prevent this situation from arising, at least for diligent senior users. Trademark applications are published in the Official Gazette prior to issuance (*see* Lanham Act § 12 (15 U.S.C § 1062)) and any party wishing to contest the registration can commence an opposition proceeding (*see* Lanham Act § 13 (15 U.S.C § 1063)), coupled with a counter-application for registration, arguing that they have prior rights and the first registration should be denied (*see* Lanham Act § 2(d) (15 U.S.C. § 1052(d)). In such situations of contested priority, the PTO can start an interference proceeding under Lanham Act § 16 (15 U.S.C. § 1066) to sort out ownership. In such cases concurrent registrations reflecting the right to use in the different territories can be granted, provided such dual registration is not likely to cause confusion. *See* Lanham Act § 2(d) (15 U.S.C. § 1052(d)). So the result in this case might be two registrations, one giving Poundem a "national" federal registration minus Junior's Oregon and consumer association-based rights and the other to Junior covering only Oregon and those rights.

136. The answer turns on the specifics of the State registration statute and, in particular, how it deals with rights obtained from a federal registration. If the State registration statute is expressly subject to the federal Lanham Act (as many are), then Junior's Oregon registration would only serve as notice of its asserted interests somewhere in Oregon, rather than defining its substantive rights throughout the state. *See National Assn. for Healthcare Communications, Inc. v. Central Arkansas Area Agency on Aging, Inc.*, 257 F.3d 732 (8th Cir. 2001). However, if the State registration statute purports to create rights based on state-wide constructive use then preemption needs to be considered. If the State statute is found to conflict with the Lanham Act or its objectives, it would be preempted. There is a good argument that is the case whenever a State statute purports to give more than common law rights based on use or consumer association, as doing so would interfere with the Lanham Act's stated national constructive use priority over everyone other than prior users or federal registrants. *See* Lanham Act § 7(c) (15 U.S.C. § 1057(c)); *Spartan Food Systems, Inc. v. HFS Corp.*, 813 F.3d 1279 (4th Cir. 1987).

137. **The best answer is C.** Federal registration constructive use clearly gives WellShod rights in the mark over Little Guys, on the facts a post-registration adopter and thus not entitled to rights even as a good faith junior user (Lanham Act § 22 (15. U.S.C. § 1072) gives all post-registration users constructive notice, so they can no longer be acting in good faith without knowledge). So clearly **Answer D** is incorrect. Trademark law's concern over avoiding consumer confusion would clearly support **Answer B**, allowing WellShod to stop Little Guys from using the same mark once there is a likelihood of confusion. The issue is whether WellShod must wait until it actually expands into the Prairie City market. The prevailing doctrinal rule, albeit subject to criticism, is that until it is *probable* that the registrant (WellShod) will actually enter a geographic market, a user who adopted the mark after registration (presumably without *actual knowledge* otherwise there are unfair competition concerns raised) should be permitted to continue to use the mark (provided no consumer confusion is likely to result from, say, overlapping consumer associations). *See Dawn Donut Co., Inc. v. Hart's Food Stores, Inc.*, 267 F.2d 358 (2d Cir 1959). That makes **Answer A** incorrect and **Answer C** a better answer than **Answer B**.

There are two criticism of the *Dawn Donut* approach. The first is that with an increasingly mobile and technologically linked society the notion of isolated geographic markets is an historical anachronism (you might consider your knowledge of local doings in Prairie City, Oregon when assessing this argument). *See Circuit City Stores, Inc. v. Carmax, Inc.*, 165 F.3d 1047 (6th Cir. 1999) (Jones, J., concurring). The second is that permitting continued use by the junior user may serve to enhance confusion when the senior user/registrant actually enters the market. Permitting continued use more firmly entrenches the existing local association between the mark and the junior user making it even more confusing when the senior user/registrant's products appear. Even if these criticisms are insufficient to support abandoning the rule entirely, they must council in favor of very circumspect application — demanding extensive inquiry into whether there really is no association with the owner-registrant's product in the "local" market (reflecting the interconnected modern world argument) and a very generous approach to the probability of the owner-registrant's future expansion (even a possibility being, perhaps, enough to start disconnecting the mark from the junior user).

138. **The answer is A**. Lanham Act § 3 (15 U.S.C. § 1053) states that service marks are registrable in "the same manner and with the same effect as are trademarks, and when registered they shall be entitled to the protection provided in this chapter in the case of trademark." So once again, trademark and service mark law parallel one another. Lanham Act § 1(a) (15 U.S.C. § 1051(a)) states that only "use in commerce" is required for federal registration (there are other requirements and limitations related to the mark itself and registration process). The Act's definition of "use in commerce" tracks the common law definition for establishing trademark rights (some view it as a codification of those rules) with the additional "clarification" that such use must be in the "ordinary course of trade." *See* Topic 7 — Acquiring Rights: Use. Consequently, sufficient use of the mark in such a way as to have trademark rights in *any* geographic portion of the United States is sufficient to permit registration and the resulting nationwide constructive use and related priority. **Answers B, C** and **D**, therefore, all overstate the use requirement. Only **Answer A** is correct.

    NOTE: "Commerce" is itself defined in the Lanham Act as "all commerce which may be lawfully regulated by Congress — that is interstate commerce. *See* Question 145, below.

139. The common law "race" for open territory is highly inefficient. It leads to numerous, extremely complex disputes over nuanced factual issues such as which party has first sufficiently penetrated the contested market to claim priority. It can also result in a mark identifying one source of a product in some parts of the United States while identifying another in others, an increasingly problematic outcome as the national market becomes more and more integrated both commercially and technologically. National registration mitigates those difficulties (but does not entirely eliminate them as the above Questions reveal) by allowing a form of national "reservation" by the first user in commerce. Additionally, the existence of a registration record permits relatively straight-forward searching thus reducing unintended conflicting adoptions. Finally, the use in commerce and good faith requirements and (arguably) the *Dawn Donut* rule help minimize the adverse effects of warehousing and land-grab problems which arise from pure first-to-register-race systems (such as recently seen regarding internet domain names and cybersquatting).

    NOTE: The United States registration system is not the prevailing model in the international community. Many countries prefer the administrative simplicity of first-to-register systems.

140. Under common law (without federal registration) rights in a mark extend only to territories in which the mark is being used plus areas in which consumers associate the mark with the claimant's product. That means WriteALL can currently claim rights only in Michigan, northern Illinois, Indiana and Ohio plus perhaps some surrounding areas. It also means the existence of the two other users pose potential difficulties to

future expansion. Although both are junior adopters of the "Sword" mark, if they can establish they are the first good faith users in their respective territories the "Sword" mark on pens belongs to them in those geographies. On the facts, there is no reason to suspect the good faith of the Dallas/Forth Worth user, so it will be necessary to negotiate with them if WriteALL wishes to enter that market. The former distributor, however, is certainly aware of WriteALL's gradual expansion in the mid-west and may even know of its current plans. Its recent adoption of the mark in areas which seem like logical next markets for WriteALL makes its claim subject to bad faith negation of its rights Additionally, it may be possible to demonstrate that WriteALL has priority based on pre-existing consumer associations in part, if not all, of those markets. Nonetheless the fact remains that the former distributor is the local actual first user and it will, therefore, be necessary for WriteALL to "unseat" them.

In all events, WriteALL should immediately seek a federal registration. Once the registration issues, WriteALL can claim construction use throughout the United States and related priority in all remaining "open" territories from the date of its application. The result will be to foreclose both additional geographic expansion by the two existing users as well as any subsequent adoptions, even in good faith. Any delays in registering not only risk such expansion or new adoptions, but a registration by one of the junior users. If a junior user registers first, WriteALL will face the difficulty of convincing a court that the registrant's technical statutory priority to "open areas" should be ignored in light of their bad faith or other equities. If it cannot do so, WriteALL may find itself frozen in its existing Midwestern territories and, perhaps, a reasonable area of future expansion.

141.   **The best answer is C**. You should probably tell them not to worry (**Answer D**), but only because that advice is coupled with a good reason not to do so. **Answer A**, putting the mark on Casters' existing prototype products, is insufficient for two reasons. First, it likely constitutes token use rather than good faith use as a trademark and, consequently, will not give them any trademark rights. Moreover, even if it were sufficient to support trademark rights, those rights would only extend to the geographic areas in which they sell those products and places where consumer associations between the mark and their product could be demonstrated, a territory which may or may not be sufficient for their existing plans, to say nothing of possible future expansions. **Answer B** is a bit better, but still not good enough to avoid worrying. A federal registration solves the geographic problem by giving Casters priority throughout the United States based on constructive use. The difficulty is that as the proposed use on prototype products is still likely only token use, so it will not support a federal registration which requires "use in commerce" (ordinary course). **Answer C** provides the answer to the conundrum of having to use a mark before it can be protected (to say nothing of federally registered) while needing time and wanting to protect investments made to "gear up" for that use. The federal "intent-to-use" registration makes it possible to file and "reserve" a mark based solely on the applicant's bona fide intent to use the mark in the (near) future. *See* Lanham Act § 1(b) (15 U.S.C. § 1051(1)(b)).

142. **The best answer is B**. Filing an intent-to-use (ITU) application requires a "bona fide intention, under circumstances showing the good faith of the applicant . . ." Lanham Act § 1(b) (15 U.S.C. § 1051(1)(b)). Although it is important to ensure that others involved in the creation of the mark don't have claims (for example, under copyright law or contract) and Casters must affirm in its ITU application that it is entitled to use the mark in commerce (*id.*, at (3)(A) and (D)), it is not necessary that it have created the mark. So **Answer A** is incorrect. All that is required is reason to believe that Casters has a bona fide intent to use. Circumstances showing imminent use, including active preparations to use, provide excellent support for that conclusion. However, neither is necessary. Consequently, **Answer C** and **Answer D** both overstate the requirement, making **Answer B** the best answer.

NOTE: An affidavit that merely states the applicant's good faith intent may be suspect if not supported by some corroborating evidence in the affidavit (for example, that the applicant did an availability search and/or that management has adopted the mark). Of course the more the circumstances indicate possible ulterior motives (filing of ITU applications on many marks for the same product being a classic example), the stronger the counter showing of good faith required.

143. An intent-to-use application only acts as a temporary reservation. Obtaining actual rights as a federally registered mark requires that within six (6) months after the notice of allowance Casters file a verified statement of use in commerce (which, of course, means Casters must have actually starting using the mark in the ordinary course of trade by that time). *See* Lanham Act § 1(d), 15 U.S.C. § 1051(d)). Only following examination and acceptance of that "use" statement does the mark actually become registered. If use in commerce is delayed Casters may obtain on simple request one additional six-month extension and, for good cause shown, additional extensions up to a total of 24 months from the date of allowance of the ITU. Any failure to timely file for an extension or a necessary use statement will result in abandonment of the registration (unless the applicant can satisfy the PTO that the delay was unintentional) and a failure to obtain registration related rights in the mark.

144. **The best answer is D.** The PTO has, correctly I believe, taken the position that because under the statute constructive use "relates back" to the date a federal application is filed, that an ITU registrant can overcome even actual use in good faith subsequent to that date. However, because the ITU does not "mature" into an actual registration which triggers constructive use until the filing and acceptance of a verified statement of actual use, the applicant cannot obtain actual judgment until after that date. *See Zirco Corp. v. American Telephone & Telegraph Co.*, 21 U.S.P.Q.2d 1542, 1544 (T.T.A.B. 1991). So **Answer D** is not only correct, but better than **Answer C** which does not address those timing and filing issues. It is correct that Senior User wins if Casters fails to perfect its ITU through use; however, Senior User does not win because it is the senior actual user but because it would then be the *only* one with rights. So **Answer A** is incorrect. **Answer B** would be correct if Senior User had started using in good faith *before the date Casters filed its application*. In this case, however, Senior User only started using

after that date (and, consequently, after Casters' constructive use), so **Answer B** is incorrect on these facts.

NOTE: The above analysis giving priority to the ITU applicant also applies to situations in which the subsequent user (Senior User) files its own use-based application. *See Larami Corp. v. Talk to Me Programs, Inc.*, 36 U.S.P.Q.2d 1840 (T.T.A.B. 1997). However, because jurisdictional limitations prevent courts from hearing cases which are "unripe" for decision, the prior ITU applicant (or any applicant for that matter) must wait until after its ITU registration has been perfected and issues before claiming its constructive use-based prior rights. *Id.*

145.   Use is required in all circumstances to acquire (or perfect) trademark rights. *See* Topic 7 — Acquiring Rights: Use. However, obtaining *federal* trademark rights, including under a registration) must be consistent with Congressional power to act. The Supreme Court has held that Congressional power with regard to trademark law (and, therefore, to enact the Lanham Act) is found in the Commerce rather than the Intellectual Property Clause meaning all rights under federal law are similarly limited. That requirement is reflected in the Lanham Act's definition of "commerce" as "all commerce which may lawfully be regulated by Congress." *See* Lanham Act § 45 (15 U.S.C. § 1127); Topic 1 –Justifications and Sources of Trademark Law. Consequently, the kind of use required to support a federal registration will vary with the Supreme Court's interpretation of the reach of Congressional power under the Commerce Clause (which is not particularly constrained under current jurisprudence).

146.   The applicant must file an application (in hard copy or electronically — which is now
        the preferred method) with the Patent and Trademark Office (PTO) together with the
        applicable fee (by mark and computed based on the number of international goods/
        services classifications covered). The application must contain the information specified
        in Lanham Act § 1(a) (15 U.S.C. § 1051(a)) including a drawing of the mark (typed
        for words — in this case "WofN"), a list of the goods or services on which the mark
        is used (financial consulting services) and, if a use-based application (as opposed to
        intent-to-use application, *see* Topic 9 — Registration: Constructive Use and Intent to
        Use) a statement that the mark is used in commerce, that to the best of the applicant's
        knowledge no other person has the right to use the mark in commerce (or such concurrent
        use exceptions as may exist — *see* Topic 9 — Registration: Constructive Use and Intent
        to Use) and a specimen showing the use of the mark in connection with the goods or
        services (a brochure or some other materials used in connection with the sale or
        advertising of the services). The applicant must also verify that all provided information
        is correct. A trademark examiner will review the application and raise any objections
        in an office action to which the applicant is entitled to respond (there are time limitations
        related to filing responses). Once all objections have been resolved the PTO will publish
        the mark in its Official Gazette for opposition (charging the registrant the prescribed
        fee). *See* Lanham Act § 12(a) (15 U.S.C. § 1062(a)). If no one opposes the mark ("any
        person who believes that he or she would be damaged by the registration") by filing
        within the prescribed time period (30 days after publication, but subject to extension),
        the mark will be approved for registration and upon payment of the required fee a
        certificate will issue and notice of registration published. *See* Lanham Act § 13 (15
        U.S.C. § 1063).

147.   The federal registration system includes two registers — the Principal Register and the
        Supplemental Register. The trademark benefits, discussed in Topic 9 — Registration:
        Constructive Use and Intent to Use, and this Topic, both generally attach only to
        registrations on the Principal Register. *See* Lanham Act § 26 & § 28 (15 U.S.C.
        §§ 1094 & § 1096).

        The Supplemental Register permits registration of marks *capable* of identifying and
        distinguishing a producer's goods or services but, because they do not actually serve
        that function, are not registerable on the Principal Register — for example a descriptive
        mark which does not yet have demonstrable secondary meaning. *See* Lanham Act
        § 23(a) (15 U.S.C. § 1091). Because registration on the Supplemental Register does
        not provide extensive rights, the application process is not as complicated — in
        particular, the process does not involve publication for, or opposition, although

Supplemental Register registrations are published upon issuance and are subject to cancellation.

The Supplemental Register does not play a significant role in domestic United States trademark law. Its primary function is to facilitate United States citizens' registration of marks in *other jurisdictions* with less stringent trademark requirements, in particular those countries which permit a registration when applicants can demonstrate they has previously acquired rights in their "home" country. With the United States accession to the Madrid Protocol it is likely that even this limited Supplemental Register function will fade away.

148.   **The best answer is D**. On the facts "WofN" is a service mark. However, the Lanham Act explicitly states that service marks are treated the same as trade marks for federal registration purposes. *See* Lanham Act § 3 (15 U.S.C. § 1053). In order to federally register *either* a trademark or service mark the applicant must, among other things, show it is used in commerce, distinctive of the applicant's goods and non-functional. See Lanham Act §§ 1(a)(1) & 2(d) & (e) (15 U.S.C §§ 1051(a)(1) & 1052(d) & (e)). So **Answers A, B** and **C** are very relevant to the examination process and **Answer D** is the least relevant.

149.   **The best answer is B**. As noted in the preceding Question, it is not relevant to registration that the mark is a service mark, so **Answer D** is incorrect. On the facts "WofN" has been used in commerce — Smith et al's "national" accounting services clearly meet both the ordinary course of trade and Commerce Clause requirements, so **Answer A** is not an issue. Nor is the functionality of the word mark — it is not involved in what makes the "services" work, thus excluding **Answer C**. That leaves **Answer D**, distinctiveness. Although "WofN" may look like radio call letters to those in the eastern United States, it could be treated as an acronym for Adam Smith's "Wealth of Nations." An acronym is assessed based on whether the consuming public likely perceives it as such and, therefore, sees it as having the meaning of the underlying phrase. Although that is highly unlikely, the phrase does have a connection to the services involved. If consumers did make the connection the phrase is probably suggestive and, therefore, inherently distinctive. *See* Topic 4 — Distinctiveness: Inherently; Secondary Meaning; Never. And in all events, for registration purposes the PTO may treat a mark requiring secondary meaning which the applicant proves it has substantially, exclusively and continuously used as a mark on its goods in commerce for five years as *prima facie distinctive* with regard to those goods. *See* Lanham Act § 2(f) (15 U.S.C. § 1052(f)). Even though, on balance, distinctiveness is not an issue, it is the only one of the four answers which, on these facts, requires any real inquiry, so **Answer B** is the best answer.

NOTE: The same requirements apply to registration on the Supplemental Register except that the mark only need be "capable" of distinguishing the applicant's goods or services (meaning generally it has not yet developed the necessary secondary meaning). *See* Lanham Act § 23(a) & (c) (15 U.S.C. § 1091(a) & (c)).

150.   **Yes**. Lanham Act § 2 contains a variety of additional specific prohibitions against federal registration of certain types of marks. These include scandalous, disparaging, national symbols, personal names, geographic marks and marks likely to cause confusion with other marks. These prohibitions are discussed in detail in Topic 11 — Registration: Grounds for Refusal, but are unlikely to apply to the "WofN" mark.

NOTE: These prohibitions do NOT generally apply to registration on the Supplemental Register. *See* Lanham Act § 23(a) (15 U.S.C. § 1091(a)).

151.   **The best answer is D** (but for very technical reasons so it is worth reading the following closely). A federal registration has an initial fixed term of 10 years. Extension requires an application for renewal. Consequently, if no renewal application is filed the registration will expire despite continued use, so **Answer A** is incorrect. Conversely if an application for renewal is filed and granted the term may extend beyond the initial ten years, so **Answer B** is incorrect. **Answer C** is almost correct, but not quite. Renewal applications must generally be filed within one year before the expiration of the current 10 year term (with a six-month additional post-expiration grace period) together, of course, with the related fee. Each such application must include an affidavit of continued use (or excusable non-use) called a "Section 8 Declaration" in reference to the section of the Lanham Act in which the requirement is found (15 U.S.C. § 1058). Provided the applicant demonstrates continued use (the purpose of the renewal requirement and Section 8 Declaration is to clear out marks which are no longer serving their market information purpose) any number of renewals may be obtained. The problem with **Answer C** is that in order to obtain the full *initial* 10 year term, the registrant must *also* file a Section 8 Declaration during the sixth year of that initial term (subject to a six-month additional grace period). The failure to do so terminates the registration even before the renewal issue comes up. So **Answer D** is the better answer, as it includes that additional "first term" Declaration ("all necessary use affidavits" vs. "all related use affidavits").

152.   **The best answer is A**. Oppositions are filed *prior* to registration — their purpose is to prevent registration — so **Answer A** is incorrect. A Section 15 Declaration relates to establishing incontestable rights (which strengthen a registration), so **Answer B** is incorrect. *See* Topic 12 — Registration: Incontestability. Filing a Section 8 Declaration supports continued registration (although the *failure* to timely file can result in the registration lapsing), so **Answer D** is also incorrect. Cancellation proceedings can be brought by any party who "believes that he is or will be damaged" by a registration under Lanham Act § 14 (15 U.S.C. § 1064). Cancellation proceedings on grounds of genericness, functionality, abandonment, fraud and violations of § 4 (related to collective and certification mark limitations, *see* Topic 2 — Service Marks, Certification Marks and Collective Marks) or §§ 2(a), 2(b) & 2(c) (prohibitions on the registration of certain kinds of marks — scandalous, disparaging, national symbols, personal names — which are treated in Topic 11 — Registration: Grounds for Refusal) of the Lanham Act can be brought at any time *after* the date of registration. Proceedings on other grounds must be brought within five years *after* the date of registration (incontestability

is treated in Topic 12 — Registration: Incontestability). Consequently, only **Answer A** involves actions which terminate an existing registration, so it is the correct answer.

153.   **The answer is C.** Under the Lanham Act registration on the Principal Register triggers nationwide constructive use (*see* Topic 9 — Registration: Constructive Use and Intent to Use), is prima facie evidence of validity and exclusive right to use (*see* Lanham Act § 7(b) & 33(a) (15 U.S.C. § 1056(b) & 1115(a)) and provides enhanced remedies (*see* Topic 18: Remedies). So **Answers A, B and D** are all benefits of federal registration. Although registration makes incontestability a possibility, it is not automatic upon registration (*see* Topic 12 — Registration: Incontestability). Consequently, **Answer C** is not a benefit of federal registration and the correct answer to the question.

NOTE: In addition, under the U.S. Trademark Dilution Revision Act of 2006 (effective October 6, 2006) ownership of a valid federal registration bars any action for dilution by blurring or tarnishment under a state statute or common law. *See* 15 U.S.C. § 1125(c)(6); Topic 14 — Dilution.

154.   **The best answer is B.** "Excellent" being descriptive and "pizza" being generic with regard to the product do pose distinctiveness issues. However, Lanham Act § 6 (15 U.S.C. § 1056) permits (and requires) an applicant to disclaim unregisterable portions of their mark while still allowing registration of a composite mark as a whole. In this case, Italian Pies will have to disclaim rights to both "excellent" and "pizza" apart from the composite mark (which means that in an infringement action, confusion will be based on similarity of the challenged mark to the entire "Most Excellent WOP Pizza" mark), but that will not keep them from registering the mark including those words. **Answer A** and **Answer C** are, therefore, both incorrect. The client's actual use in the Chicago metropolitan area is sufficient to support a federal registration. Prior use by others in other areas may raise priority issues, but even if such users exist that will not likely preclude registration entirely, making **Answer D** incorrect. *See* Topic 9 — Registration: Constructive Use and Intent to Use. The fact that "WOP" (Without Papers) pejoratively refers to Italian-Americans, however, raises significant concerns under Lanham Act § 2(a) (15 U.S.C. § 1052(a)) which, among other restrictions, prohibits registration of marks which consist of "matter which may disparage . . . persons, living or dead, institutions, belief, or national symbols."

155.   In determining whether a mark "*may*" disparage (it need not actually disparage under the statute) the question is whether the mark may treat as "inferior, slight, deprecate, degrade, or affect or injure by unjust comparison" the referenced group. That question is, in turn, determined by how a substantial composite of the target group views the mark — in this case Italian-Americans. *See Harjo v. Pro-Football Inc.*, 50 U.S.P.Q.2d 1705 (T.T.A.B. 1999), *rev'd*, 284 F. Supp. 96 (D.D.C. 2003). There is some debate over whether that determination should be based exclusively on evidence regarding the target group's reaction or if evidence of how others see and use the mark is also probative of that group's likely feelings about the mark. *See id.*

NOTE: The proper time for making the "disparaging" determination also remains unresolved. The logical time would seem to be when the issue has been raised by a request to register — that is, the present. Under that approach the inquiry might look at past viewpoints, but only to inform the finder of fact concerning contemporary views (for example, as evidence of the meaning of a mark not in widespread current usage). A "today" assessment does mean that a previously disparaging term which no longer carries negative connotations would be currently registerable. The alternative approach would be to bar registration of any mark which has ever been disparaging. Whether that approach would produce significantly different outcomes is questionable. Even when testing disparagement "today" only the referenced group's perception matters — as opposed to the general public and that group is unlikely to view a previously disparaging mark as a thing of the past.

NOTE: A related issue is how to deal with a mark which was not disparaging when registered, but has now become so. Arguably relief would come via a cancellation action. That approach, however, raises a technical statutory issue. The statue reads that a disparaging mark "shall be refused registration." That language could reasonably be interpreted as applying the requirement at the time of registration. The counter argument is that federal registration should be treated as an on-going act (especially as registrations require renewals to stay in force), giving the language continuing applicability. Perhaps considering the policy reasons for the exclusion might help resolving the issue. Not surprisingly, that leads to the next Question.

156. There are a number of possible articulations but they essentially come down to two positions. First, the prohibition may reflect a social policy that disparaging marks should not be allowed, with the non-registerability provision reflecting a desire to affirmatively prevent *any* use of such marks. The difficulty with that argument is explaining why the Lanham Act merely makes the marks unregisterable rather than simply denying them all protection (or affirmatively barring their use as marks). In particular, the Act expressly creates an affirmative federal infringement action for unregistered marks (*see* Topic 18 — Remedies) without any exclusion (or even mention) of disparaging marks. Some have argued that the social policy against any use of disparaging marks means that the registration prohibition restriction should apply by implication to all provisions of the federal statute. That argument, however, seems circular — resolving the statutory omission by assuming the very policy that the statutory language calls into question.

Second, and alternatively, the prohibition could be viewed as limited to discouraging (or at least not encouraging) use of disparaging marks by withholding the benefits of a federal registration. Beyond that limited goal, however, the Lanham Act reflects the primary goal of trademark law– ensuring whatever marks are adopted can uniquely identify and distinguish a particular producer's product, explaining why the Act offers remedies against any consumer confusion, even regarding disparaging marks.

The other prohibitions on registration found in Lanham Act § 2 (15 U.S.C. § 1052), as discussed below, raise the same policy issue. The courts have not ruled on the question *in any context* so the matter remains unresolved (and thus material for a really messy "policy" question on an exam). For a court to find the Lanham Act imposed a general prohibition against disparaging (or other prohibited) marks would require addressing and resolving several additional issues. In particular, a general prohibition would arguably raise First Amendment concerns. And a finding that the First Amendment issue was avoided because although the federal statute prohibited such marks the states allowed them would, in turn, require resolving whether the federal statute preempts state law and, if so, whether Congress' had the power to do so.

157. **The best answer may be "who knows?" but, I'd personally go with Answers A and B.** There are no affirmative federal penalties for the use of a disparaging mark, so **Answer D** is incorrect. Beyond that the analysis enters the statutory interpretation — policy debate discussed in the answer to Question 156 immediately above demonstrating its very real practical effect. As noted, the courts have not determined whether the

prohibitions of Lanham Act § 2(a) (15 U.S.C. § 1052(a)) preventing registration also preclude claims arising under § 43(a) (15 U.S.C. § 1125(a)) for infringement of unregistered marks. Consequently, it is unclear whether **Answer B** or **Answer C** is the correct response regarding Italian Pie's federal statutory rights. For the reasons indicated in Question 156, I'd go with **Answer B**. However, the federal issue is resolved **Answer A** focuses on the existence of state trademark rights. I believe that because Lanham Act does not explicitly prohibit use of disparaging marks, to say nothing of there being no indication that Congress intended to preempt state protection, the better argument is that regardless of the outcome at the federal level, the States remain free to create rights under their statutory and common law. But who knows . . . .

158. **The best answer is A**. On the facts BuffDesigns use of the mark is easily sufficient to support a federal registration, so **Answer D** is incorrect. Regarding distinctiveness, as it takes a leap of imagination to connect the mark to the particular products (they make the user clean not well-muscled) it will likely be found suggestive and inherently distinctive (all in the trademark sense, of course). *See* Topic 4 — Distinctiveness: Inherently; Secondary Meaning; Never. In addition, under Lanham Act § 2(f) (15 U.S.C. § 1052(f)), BuffDesigns' five years of exclusive and continuous use provides prima facie evidence of distinctiveness for registration purposes. So **Answer C** is unlikely to raise any problems. The lack of any potentially confusingly similar uses or relevant registrations makes problems under Lanham Act § 2(d) (15 U.S.C. § 1052(d)) — prohibition on registration based on prior uses or registrations likely to cause confusion (mistake or deception) — highly unlikely, so **Answer B** poses little concern. *See* Topic 13 — Infringement: Likelihood of Confusion. However, there is a possibility of problems under Lanham Act § 2(a) (15 U.S.C. § 1052(a)) which prohibits federal registration of a mark which "consists of or comprises immoral, deceptive or scandalous matter . . .," terms which some might apply to a fully nude picture of a man. **Answer A** is, therefore, the best answer.

NOTE: Under the Trademark Dilution Revision Act of 2006, although the Patent and Trademark Office cannot on its own deny registration to a mark on likelihood of *dilution* grounds (either by blurring or tarnishment), that Act does permit third party opposition to, or actions to cancel, such a mark. *See* Lanham Act § 2(f) (15 U.S.C. § 1052(f)) (last two concluding sentences of the Section). Consequently, *all* existing uses — not just those involving a likelihood of confusion — must be considered before registration is sought.

159. **The best answer is A**. When making (the difficult) determination of whether a mark is "immoral . . . or scandalous" the PTO and courts engage in a two-step process. They first determine the likely meaning(s) of the mark and then determine whether it is "shocking to the sense of truth, decency, or propriety" or "offend the conscience or moral feelings" of "a substantial composite of the general public" in the "context of contemporary attitudes" and the particular usage. *See Harjo v. Pro-Football, Inc.*, 50 U.S.P.Q.2d 1705 (T.T.A.B. 1999), *rev'd* 284 F. Supp. 96 (D.D.C. 2003). **Answer D** (dictionary definitions) is part of the first inquiry — the likely meaning of the terms

used in the mark. *See In re Red Bull GmbH*, Serial No. 75788830 (Feb. 15, 2006); *id.* Although not dispositive (there may be various meanings and the particular usage will affect which is the more likely, *see id.*), it is clearly relevant. **Answer C** is relevant to the second inquiry — immorality or scandalousness is determined by contemporary reaction (words or images that may have been vulgar/offensive may have ceased to be so despite their meaning, *see In re Old Glory Condom Corp.*, 26 U.S.P.Q.2d 1216, 1218-1219 (T.T.A.B. 1993)). However, unlike disparagement which focuses on the referenced group the second step of the "immoral/scandalous" inquiry looks to the reaction of a substantial composite of *the general public*. Consequently, **Answer B** is relevant while **Answer A** is not, making **Answer A** the LEAST relevant to the inquiry.

NOTE: The "substantial composite of the general public" test means that it is not relevant that a particular segment of the public is terribly shocked or offended. The question is whether the public are large finds the mark immoral or scandalous. *Cf. In re Bad Frog Brewery, Inc.* (T.T.A.B. 1999) (involving a frog "giving the finger;" the majority found that although it would offend some, but because it involved a wide-spread practice in a context which would not offend the *general* public, the mark was not immoral or scandalous for registration purposes). Relief for specific groups only is available under the disparagement or disrepute prohibitions which focus on the perceptions of the target group.

160.   Some courts have deemed it relevant that a potentially immoral or scandalous mark has an independent "serious purpose" — in effect treating the issue similarly to the First Amendment obscenity inquiry. *See* In re Old Glory Condom Corp. 26 U.S.P.Q.2d 1216, 1217 (T.T.A.B. 1993). The federal registration inquiry, however, is focused whether *in the particular context* a substantial composite of the general public would find the mark shocking or offensive. On that basis, the relevance of the da Vinci source is not that it indicates "value," but only that public recognition and the particular nature of the drawing might reduce the adverse reaction to the nudity. Conversely, a clearly provocative or salacious image, whether or not done by a famous artist, would go the other way.

161.   **It is not dispositive, but it is relevant**. *See Harjo v. Pro-Football, Inc.*, 50 U.S.P.Q.2d 1705 (T.T.A.B. 1999), *rev'd* 284 F. Supp. 96 (D.D.C. 2003). The test is whether a substantial composite of the general public is shocked or offended, so even the strongest motives to do so will not prevent registration if the effort fails. Practically, however, when a scandalous challenge is raised it generally comes in the form of an opposition, meaning someone in the public sees the mark as problematic. *See Ritchie v. Simpson*, 170 F.3d 1092 (Fed. Cir. 1999) (applauding the PTO practice of not pre-judging public sentiment and instead allowing a mark to be published and permitting the public to raise any concerns). In most circumstances each side will proffer supporting evidence, leaving the PTO (or court) with a need to "break the tie." In such cases it is likely that demonstrating the applicant believed (despite its protestations now to the contrary) that the public would find the mark shocking or offensive will undermine the credibility of their position, thus tipping the scales against them.

NOTE: Conversely, the absence of intent to shock or offend will not overcome actual evidence that the mark had that effect on the public.

162.   **The best answer is C.** The standing issue does not go to the merits, so **Answer A** which is a (relatively weak, see Question 160 above) argument that the mark is not immoral or scandalous is irrelevant and, therefore, incorrect. **Answer D** is not only irrelevant to standing; it is totally irrelevant to registerability (addressing the validity of a mark which has been *registered* for at least five years). *See* Topic 12 — Registration: Incontestability. **Answer B** and **Answer C** address the two prongs of the Federal Circuit's test for standing in an opposition. That court held that the opposer must (1) have a real interest in the outcome and (2) a reasonable basis for believing damages will accrue. *See Ritchie v. Simpson*, 170 F.3d 1092 (Fed. Cir. 1999). The first seeks to ensure that the opposer has individual *bona fide* interests at stake. Those interests need not be commercial nor is it relevant that few or many share them (that is the test on the merits), however, they must be "real." The second requires only that the opposer allege reasonable (objective) grounds for the assertion he will be damaged if the mark is registered, not proof that he will in fact be damaged. On that basis, **Answer B** is not required for standing, whereas **Answer C** eliminates (actual damage) any legitimate interest the opposer would have in the outcome. As a result **Answer C** is the best answer (admittedly for very technical reasons).

163.   **The best answer is A.** As discussed in the previous Questions a *mark* the public ("everyone" qualifies) finds utterly tasteless and wholly offensive may be denied registration as immoral or scandalous under Lanham Act § 2(a) (15 U.S.C. § 1052(a)). However, in this case the mark is the American flag and the fact that all concur the *magazine* which the mark identifies is tasteless and offensive does not, by itself, prevent registration of the mark. So **Answer B** is incorrect. The argument that the mark disparages United States veterans misconstrues the prohibition against registering disparaging marks. Although veterans may find the association of the American flag with the magazine offensive, the *mark* (the flag) is not deprecating or degrading of veterans. Consequently, the Lanham Act § 2(a) (15 U.S.C. § 1052(a)) argument will not succeed and **Answer C** is incorrect. **Answer D** is a better position as Lanham Act § 2(a) (15 U.S.C. § 1052(a)) *also* explicitly prohibits registration of marks which might bring national symbols into disrepute. The use of the American flag (a national symbol) on a tasteless magazine certainly merits consideration. However, Lanham Act § 2(b) (15 U.S.C. § 1052(b)) expressly prevents the registration of any mark which "consists of or comprises the flag or coat of arms or other national insignia of the United States. . . ." As the mark in this case clearly falls within that provision, no further analysis is required. Consequently, **Answer A** is the strongest argument.

NOTE: The Lanham Act § 2(b) (15. U.S.C. § 1052(b) prohibition raises a question about the outcome in In re Old Glory Condom Corp. 26 U.S.P.Q.2d 1216, 1217 (T.T.A.B. 1993). In that case the TTAB permitted registration of a mark which included a modified but clearly recognizable American flag in the form of a condom on the grounds that it was not immoral or scandalous. Isn't the better argument that the national flag is never registerable as a mark, especially as the statutory provision prohibits not only registration of the flag but "any simulation thereof?"

164. **No.** Lanham Act § 2(b) (15 U.S.C. § 1052(b)) also expressly prohibits registration of flags, coats of arms or other insignia of "any foreign nations."

165. **No.** Lanham Act § 2(b) (15 U.S.C. § 1052(b)) also expressly prohibits registration of flags, coats of arms or other insignia of "any State or municipality" (meaning that marks consisting of city flag, etc. may also not be federally registered).

166. **The "CIA" mark is a closer call.** Most would recognize "CIA" as the acronym for the Central Intelligence Agency, part of the federal government. Consequently, the question is whether the mark involves registration of a mark consisting of "other insignia of the United States" which is prohibited under Lanham Act § 2(b) (15 U.S.C. § 1052(b)). The Patent and Trademark Office has indicated (through the TTAB) that it interprets "other insignia" to cover only indicators of "the same general class" as flags and coats of arms, such as the Great Seal, the Presidential Seal, and official seals of government departments; not other identifiers of "a service of facility of the Government." *See* In re United States Department of the Interior, 142 U.S.P.Q. 506, 507 (T.T.A.B. 1964). Applying that test, it seems likely that the prohibition does not apply in this case. Consequently, the better claim is under Lanham Act § 2(a) (15 U.S.C. § 1052(a)) — that the mark used on the tasteless and offensive magazine may bring the CIA "institution" into disrepute.

167. **No.** Although Lanham Act § 2(f) (15 U.S.C. § 1052 (F)) permits registration of certain marks otherwise subject to the Section 2 prohibitions upon a showing of distinctiveness, that exception does NOT apply to matter "expressly excluded in subsections (a), (b), (c), (d), (e)(3) & (e)(5)." So the prohibition against registering the American flag applies despite a showing of secondary meaning.

NOTE: The Lanham Act § 2(f) (15 U.S.C. § 1052(f)) "distinctiveness" exception to prohibition on registration, all involve subject matter prohibited because it is not inherently distinctive (descriptive and geographically descriptive marks and surnames) and thus require a showing of secondary meaning to serve as trademarks. Thus § 2(f) does not undo the policy prohibitions on "undesirable" marks (disparaging, national symbols, etc). It is merely clarifying that only marks which uniquely identify and distinguish a particular product qualify as marks, including for federal registration purposes. *See* Topic 4 — Distinctiveness: Inherently; Secondary Meaning; Never.

NOTE: The inability to register the mark does not necessarily mean that Many Magazine's cannot claim the American flag as a trademark. If the federal statutory prohibitions only apply to registration, then Many Magazines may be able to claim use-based rights (supported by their showing of secondary meaning) and, perhaps, even rights to bring an infringement action under Section 43(a) of the Lanham Act (15 U.S.C. § 1125(a)). *See* Question 156 above.

168. **The best answer is A.** First a quick bit of law, then its application to the facts. Lanham Act § 2(a) (15 U.S.C. § 1052(a)) bars the registration of marks which are *"deceptive."* Lanham Act § 2(e)(1) (15 U.S.C. § 1052(e)(1)) bars registration of marks which are either *"deceptively misdescriptive"* or merely *"descriptive"* of the product. Under Lanham Act § 2(f) (15 U.S.C. § 1052(f)) either deceptively misdescriptive or descriptive marks can be registered if secondary meaning can be shown, whereas deceptive marks are absolutely barred.

The test for the first category (*deceptive* marks) requires satisfaction of three conditions: (1) the term is misdescriptive of the product, (2) consumers are likely to believe the misdescription accurately describes the product, *and* (3) the misdescription is likely to affect consumer decisions to purchase the product. *See In re Budge Manufacturing Co., Inc.*, 857 F.2d 773 (Fed. Cir. 1988). The second category (*deceptively misdescriptive* marks) applies when *only the first two conditions* of the deceptiveness test are satisfied; that is, the term is misdescriptive and consumers are likely to incorrectly believe the mark describes the product when it does not, but that error is NOT likely to affect their purchase decision. The test for the third category (*descriptive* marks) is that the mark accurately describes a characteristic, ingredient or use of the product.

Using the "FRESH FRUIT" on artificially flavored juice drinks containing no fresh fruit is misdescriptive rather than descriptive. Not only is it inaccurate but on these facts consumers are likely to believe the misdescription. Furthermore, that belief is likely to affect their purchase decisions. Applying the tests, **Answer D** (descriptive) is not a proper classification and inapplicable to whether the mark can be registered. Under the Lanham Act § 2 (15 U.S.C. § 1052) structure, being merely misdescriptive (**Answer B**) does not bar (or even adversely affect) registration of a mark. The reason is that a mark may be technically misdescriptive but if in the particular context consumers do not believe the mark's descriptive meaning has any connection to the goods then the mark is probably best viewed as arbitrary (for example, "Orange" airlines which flies silver planes). So **Answer B** is incorrect. Nor, on these facts, is the mark properly categorized as deceptively misdescriptive (**Answer C**). Because consumers will believe the inaccurate description *and* that mistaken belief will affect their purchase decision, the mark should be treated as "deceptive" (**Answer D**). Under that classification, DrinksofallKinds' ability to demonstrate secondary meaning under Lanham Act § 2(f) (15. U.S.C. § 1052(f)) cannot keep the mark from being barred from registration. So **Answer D** is the best answer.

NOTE: Not that it particularly matters, but I find the above classification nomenclature appallingly opaque and confusing. In particular, it doesn't help me keep things straight to use a nasty sounding phrase like "deceptively misdescriptive" for marks which consumers incorrectly believe to be accurate descriptions of the product but which can nonetheless be federally registered because they have no adverse effects on purchase decisions. It seems more appropriate to apply "deceptive" only to those marks which actually harm (or manipulate) purchase decisions and label those which consumers erroneously believe to be descriptive but ignore as simply "misdescriptive" (and those that they don't believe as "arbitrary" or "non-descriptive"). But the existing nomenclature governs, so remember the important difference between *deceptive* marks (unregisterable) and *deceptively misdescriptive* marks (registerable with secondary meaning). (By the way, the naming system becomes even more Byzantine when the geographic mark formulations are added to the mix — they are coming soon below).

169. **The mark is probably best viewed as deceptively misdescriptive rather than deceptive and, therefore, would be registerable with a showing of secondary meaning.** The "CRUSHED FRUIT" mark is misdescriptive rather than descriptive on the facts (crushed is not the same as squeezed). Additionally, consumers will likely believe it accurately describes the contents, thus making it at least *deceptively misdescriptive* and registerable only with a showing of secondary meaning. The key question is whether that mistake *also* affects their purchase decision, thus taking the mark beyond merely deceptively misdescriptive to deceptive and absolutely unregisterable. It seems unlikely that consumer decisions would turn on the difference between crushed and squeezed when the label clearly says "without pulp" (although one never knows), so I'd be inclined to stick with deceptively misdescriptive but reasonable minds can differ.

NOTE: Truly deceptively misdescriptive marks are relatively rare. Generally, either consumers don't see any connection so they don't believe the misdescription and the mark is arbitrary, or the misdescription is sufficiently relevant to both cause consumers to believe the misdescription and for that mistaken belief to affect their purchase decision. Consider the commonly given example of a deceptively misdescriptive but not deceptive mark: "Glass Wax" (it's the common example because that is how the case came out, *Gold Seal Co. v. Weeks*, 129 F. Supp. 928 (D.D.C. 1955)). The mark was used on a product for cleaning glass that contained no wax. Although it can certainly be (and was successfully) argued that although consumers believe the product contains wax that mistake did not influence their purchase decision, I'd argue that chain of logic is very weak. Consumers may not have believed any wax was in the product or never considered it. But that is different than assuming consumers believed it did contain wax and then totally ignored that fact in their purchase calculation. It seems highly improbable (to me) that a consumer would believe a product included an important ingredient and then dismiss it as irrelevant. Some consumers may think it makes the product more effective while others may avoid the product because they think it will leave a film, but very few would find it irrelevant. I also think it would be disingenuous to argue the misdescription is irrelevant provided the consumer is ultimately pleased with the outcome *after* the purchase — the deception and manipulation occurs before that point. That would be tantamount to a rule which states that provided a duped customer is ultimately happy, a deceptive mark should be registerable.

170. **There is no issue.** "GLASS FRUIT" clearly inaccurately describes (misdescribes) the beverage product. However, in that context consumers will not believe it accurately describes the product, making the mark arbitrary/non-descriptive. Consequently, neither of the Lanham Act § 2 (15. U.S.C. § 1052) "deceptiveness" barriers to registration apply.

171. **The best answer is C.** Registration of "geographic" (place name) marks are governed by Lanham Act § 2(a) (15 U.S.C. § 1052(a)) (deceptive marks), 2(e)(2) (15 U.S.C. § 1052(e)(2)) (primarily geographically descriptive marks) & 2(e)(3) (15 U.S.C. § 1052(e)(3)) (primarily geographically deceptively misdescriptive marks). The test for *deceptive geographic marks* is the same as for other deceptive marks as outlined in the answer to Question 168 above. The test for *primarily descriptive geographic marks* consists of three elements: (1) the primary significance of the mark is geographic, (2) consumers are likely to make a "goods/place" connection (the goods are from that place) *and* (3) the mark actually identifies the origin of the goods. The test for *primarily geographically deceptively misdescriptive marks* has caused some consternation, but in substance tracks the test for other deceptive marks — that is, (1) the mark is geographically misdescriptive (the goods are NOT from that place), (2) that consumers are likely to erroneously believe that misdescription accurately describes the geographic origin of the goods and (3) that mistaken belief affects their purchase decision. Finally, Lanham Act § 2(f) (15 U.S.C. § 1052(f)) permits the federal registration of only a primarily geographically descriptive mark upon a showing of secondary meaning. Registration of either deceptive or deceptively misdescriptive geographic marks is always prohibited even if they have developed secondary meaning. Finally, Lanham Act § 2(a) (15 U.S.C. § 1052(a)) absolutely prohibits registration of "geographic indications" in connection *with wines or spirits* which refer to a place other than their origin, used on or after January 1, 1996, without any showing of deceptiveness and despite secondary meaning.

NOTE: Continuing my rant from the Note in the answer to Question 168 above regarding the category of "deceptively misdescriptive" marks: These geographic classifications further confuse the matter. If one works through the various definitions (all there is good reason to be ambivalent about undertaking that task), a deceptively misdescriptive mark can be registered provided the applicant demonstrates secondary meaning unless (horrors) it is geographically deceptively misdescriptive in which case it can never be registered. The point: pay close attention to whether the specific misdescription is geographic or something else rather than relying on the word "deceptively" which can be, well, deceptive.

Applied to these facts: Consumers will view "ICELANDIC" as a geographic identifier (**Answer A**), thus raising the "geographic mark" issue. That problem points against registration so **Answer A** is not the best argument in favor of registerability. **Answer B** eliminates the possibility the mark will be found primarily *geographically descriptive* — causing it to fail the third "actual origin" requirement — and thus enhances the possibility it can be federally registered. **Answer B** does not, however, eliminate the possibility that the mark may be barred as deceptive or primarily geographically deceptively misdescriptive — in fact, standing alone, it actually lends (non-definitive) support to those outcomes. **Answer C** eliminates the possibility of deception, as it negates the likelihood consumers will mistakenly believe that "ICELANDIC" describes the geographic origin of the drinks. *See In re Nantucket*, 677 F.2d 95 (U.S. Ct. C.&P.A. 1982). It does not, however, address the issue of the mark being found primarily geographically descriptive. **Answer D** resolves all geographic mark concerns — the actual origin being Florida means Icelandic is not primarily geographically descriptive and the lack of consumer association limits the possibility of deception — making it the BEST answer.

NOTE: The lack of any consumer connection between Iceland and the drinks makes the mark arbitrary and hence inherently distinctive. Even were some connection made (for example, that the drinks were cool and refreshing) the mark would be treated as suggestive (leap of imagination) rather than descriptive. *See* Topic 4 — Distinctiveness: Inherently; Secondary Meaning; Never.

172. **The best answer is C** (but B isn't a bad second choice). **Answer A**, Pace is the name of an actual town, raises the geographic mark issue and thus argues, albeit non-determinatively, against rather than for registration, so it is incorrect. As Pace is the actual geographic source of the goods, it cannot be barred from registration as being either deceptive or geographically deceptively misdescriptive. The issue, therefore, is whether it is barred from registration because it is primarily geographically descriptive under Lanham Act § 2(e)(2) (15 U.S.C. § 1052(e)(2)). **Answer D** states that conclusion, which bars registration. So **Answer D** cannot be the best argument *for* registration. The test for geographically descriptive marks requires that (1) the primary significance of the mark is geographic, (2) consumers are likely to make a "goods/place" connection (the goods from that place) & (3) the mark actually identifies the origin of the goods. Consequently, it is not sufficient that the mark accurately describes the geographic origin of the goods; consumers must perceive it as having primarily geographic significance *and* make the necessary goods/place connection. The fact that "pace" has a non-geographic meaning (**Answer B**) argues against the first of those requirements — that consumers will view the mark's primary significance as geographic — and, hence, favors registration. However, it does not definitively resolve the question as stated. The test is whether consumers view the mark as having a primarily geographic significance *in the particular context*. For example, despite the existence of a non-geographic meaning, consumers may still view "pace" as having a geographic significance if Pace, Florida is the publicly acknowledged tropical drink capital of the United States. **Answer C** specifically states the necessary conclusion, making **Answer C** the (slightly) better answer.

173. **No.** Lanham Act § 2(f) (15 U.S.C. § 1052(f)) specifically permits registration of *primarily geographically descriptive* marks if secondary meaning can be demonstrated. So if Trop-fruit can show that despite the geographic descriptiveness consumers have come to view the "Pace" mark as identifying and distinguishing its specific drink products — meaning its particular flavor or other characteristics as a drink as opposed to its geographic source — it can register the mark. *See* Topic 4 — Distinctiveness: Inherently; Secondary Meaning; Never.

However, and it's an important "however," registering the mark does NOT mean Trop-fruit can keep all others from using the mark. The trademark "fair use" doctrine prevents the appropriation by a single producer of accurate descriptive terms, including geographically descriptive terms. So others will be permitted to use the town name "Pace" to indicate the actual geographic origin of their products. *See* Topic 16 — Defenses: Fair Use, Nominative Use, Parody/Free Speech.

NOTE: In some instances geographically descriptive marks become so connected to a particular category of goods that they move beyond describing origin to serving as the generic term for the class of goods — for example, "Swiss" cheese (*see Schweizer-ishe Kaeseunion Bern v. Saul Starck, Inc.*, 293 N.Y.S. 816 (1937). In such cases the mark will not be registerable even with a showing of secondary meaning.

NOTE: To avoid leaving any misconceptions — Pace, Florida is a real town, but I have no idea whether it has any connection to the tropical fruit drink business, much less whether it might be (or not) perceived by the public as the "tropical drink capital of the United States."

174. **The best answer is B.** Lanham Act § 2(e)(2) (15 U.S.C. § 1052(e)(2)) states that a geographically descriptive mark can be registered *even without secondary meaning* if it qualifies for registration under Lanham Act § 4 (15 U.S.C § 1054) as a "certification mark" (that is a mark used by a third party to certify compliance with standards) indicating regional origin. *See* Topic 2 — Service Marks, Certification Marks and Collective Marks. As Pace Chamber of Commerce mark is geographically descriptive the certification mark will issue, making **Answer B** correct and **Answer C** irrelevant. **Answer A** is not true on the given facts which state the mark is primarily geographically descriptive. Because the mark accurately identifies the certified products' origin it is not deceptive and **Answer D** is, therefore, incorrect.

Geographic "certification marks" are frequently referred to as "indications of origin" and have been the source of much interest and controversy in the international marketplace due to their connection with "appellations of origin" (such as "Champagne"). As note earlier in Question 171, the Lanham Act § 2(a) (15 U.S.C. § 1052(a)) prohibition on registration of "geographic indications" used in connection with wines or spirits which refer to a place other than their origin expressly prohibits California wine growers cannot mark their bubbly "Champagne" — without he need for any further inquiry into deceptiveness.

NOTE: Had the "Pace" mark been geographically misdescriptive (used to certify drinks which do not come from Pace, Florida), the special treatment of certification marks under Lanham Act § 2(e)(2) does not apply. On those facts, the mark is either deceptive under Lanham Act § 2(a) (15 U.S.C. § 1052(a)) or geographically deceptively misdescriptive under Lanham Act § 2(e)(3) (15 U.S.C. § 1052(e)(3)), it will be denied federal registration despite its use as a certification mark and whether or not showing of secondary meaning can be shown.

175. **The best answer is C.** The mere fact that a mark is geographic raises the possibility that federal registration may be barred, but it is not dispositive. The other answers more specifically state when geographic marks may not be registered, so **Answer A** is

incorrect. On the facts, the drinks are made in Florida from Florida produce so the mark is not geographically descriptive (Hawai'i does not accurately describe the actual source of these goods), so **Answer B** is incorrect.

The issue, therefore, is whether consumers are likely to be deceived by the mark because (1) they believe the drinks come from Hawai'i (make a goods/place connection) & (2) that belief affects their purchase decision. Some decisions indicate that a geographic mark consisting of a place which is likely well known to consumers (it is neither obscure nor remote) is enough to presume the goods/place connection. *See In re Trans Continental Records, Inc.*, 62 U.S.P.Q.2d 1541 (T.T.A.B 2002). *But see In re Wada*, 194 F.3d 1297, 1300 (Fed. Cir. 1999) (burden on the person relying on the good/place association (examiner, opposer) to make the showing). However, that seems a bit over-reaching. Making the connection clearly does turn on whether consumers recognize the mark as having geographic significance (see Question 172, concerning the multiple meanings of "pace"). However, it *also* requires that the particular location points toward, or at least not away, from a logical goods origin connection. For example, Ohio is clearly recognized as a place but it is unlikely to be viewed as the origin of tropical fruit drinks. On these facts, consumers are not only going to recognize Hawai'i as a geographic place, but will associate tropical fruit drinks with that state thus making the necessary the goods/place connection. Regarding the second requirement (that the mistaken belief will affect purchaser decisions), the specific factual context again controls. In this case, the reputation of Hawai'i as a "tropical paradise" means that consumers likely will take that origin into account in making their purchase decision. Both **Answers C** and **D** are correct; however, **Answer C** is more precise and the better answer.

176.   The case involves a service mark. However, as is generally the case, the basic rules track those applicable to trademarks so the prohibitions on federal registration are the same. Additionally, the foreign language mark "Tratorria Roma" will be assessed in its translated form. *See* Topic 3 — Basic Distinctiveness: The Spectrum of Distinctiveness; Word Marks Including Acronyms and Foreign Words. The English version — roughly "Roman Restaurant" — clearly includes a key geographic term, so the various geographic prohibitions might apply.

On the facts none of the food (prepared or ingredients), the recipes, the cooks or their training come from, or have anything to do with, Rome. Consequently, the mark is not primarily geographically descriptive under Lanham Act § 2(e)(2) (15 U.S.C. § 1052(e)(2)). The issue, therefore, is whether the evocative association of the mark makes it either deceptive under Lanham Act § 2(a) (15 U.S.C. § 1052(a)) or geographically deceptively misdescriptive under Lanham Act § 2(e)(3) (15 U.S.C. § 1052(e)(3)). That showing requires BOTH: (1) consumers have made a services/place connection and (2) that belief affects their purchase decisions. Services/place associations can take a variety of forms. On one hand, consumers might believe the mark indicates that the food, the recipes, the ingredients or the chefs and/or their training are connected with Rome. Or they may only view the mark as evoking a sense of being in Rome. The former connections, given their likely influence on purchase decisions (blending the services/place and materiality requirements), may more readily lead to classification as a deceptive or geographically deceptively misdescriptive mark, than the latter "bringing to mind" evocations. *See In re Less Halles de Paris, J.V.*, 334 F.3d 1371 (Fed. Cir. 2003). That all said, the test remains whether the misdescriptive services/place association affects the related purchase decisions.

177. **The best answer is A**. Under Lanham Act § 7(b) (15 U.S.C. § 1057(b)) and § 33(a) (15 U.S.C. § 1115(a)), a federal registration is *prima facia* evidence of the validity of the registered mark, so **Answer A** is correct. That presumption can, however, be rebutted by evidence that the registration was improperly granted. Although courts have been inconsistent in determining the quantum of evidence required, the registration is not conclusive, making **Answer C** incorrect. A lack of secondary meaning might be a way to attack a valid registration and thus rebut the presumption, but the existence of the presumption does not depend on an affirmative showing of secondary meaning by the registrant in the lawsuit. And, in all events, secondary meaning is irrelevant to the registerability of a potentially geographically deceptively misdescriptive mark such as this one. So **Answer B** is incorrect. Finally, the presumption of validity arises from the existence of a federal registration so the registration has an effect on the assertion of the defense. **Answer D** is, therefore, incorrect.

NOTE: For the purists the presumption can become "incontestable" with the passage of time. However, the term "incontestable" does not quite live up to its full promise as a variety of invalidity defenses remain available. *See* Topic 12 — Registration: Incontestability. In this case, however, the necessary five year period making the registration incontestable has not yet passed, so those rules do not apply.

178. **Yes.** An intent-to-use registration does not benefit from the presumption of validity (or for that matter other federal registration-related rights) until it is "perfected" by filing of the necessary statement of use. *See* Topic 9 — Registration: Constructive Use and Intent to Use.

179. **Not necessarily**. The court decision means that the registration will be cancelled and the related benefits will disappear (such as the presumption of validity and constructive use). However, the question remains whether the fact that the mark cannot be federally registered also means Bellacitta cannot claim trademark rights based on its use. That issue is unresolved, although as argued in Question 156 above it seems unlikely the federal registration prohibitions extent to other federal, and particularly, state trademark rights. On the other hand, it can be argued that with regard to deceptive marks (as opposed, for example, to immoral, scandalous or disparaging marks) trademark law's market information strongly suggests they should not be protected as a general proposition and that the First Amendment concern is substantially mitigated if not eliminated.

180. **The best answer is D**. The use of person's names, portraits and even signatures can run afoul of Lanham Act § 2 (15 U.S.C. § 1052) prohibitions. Because Thomas Jefferson was a President of the United States the Section 2(c) special "presidential" prohibition should come to mind. However, that section only prohibits the use of the

"name, signature or portrait of a deceased President of the United States during the life of his widow" except with her consent, so it is inapplicable on these facts. Thus **Answer B** is incorrect. The Section 2(c) prohibition on registration of marks consisting of names, portraits or signatures only applies to those "identifying a particular living individual" (without written consent). So, Mr. Jefferson having long left us to our own devices, that provision would not bar registration of the mark and **Answer D** is also incorrect. The more general prohibition on "name" marks, reaching both the living and dead, is found in Section 2(e)(4) which prevents registration of any mark which is "primarily merely a surname." Although the mark in this case does contain a surname (Jefferson), its use as part of a greater whole makes that prohibition an unlikely barrier to registration of the entire mark (although the name standing alone might need to be disclaimed). **Answer A** is, therefore, a possible answer, but not the *best* answer. Section 2(a) contains the most applicable prohibition extending to marks that "falsely suggest a connection with persons, living or dead." In this case the phrase "Thomas Jefferson's Favorite" could be legitimately interpreted as meaning the famous President (who was a well-known wine aficionado) actually preferred this wine during his lifetime, a clearly false connection. Consequently, **Answer C** is the best answer.

181.   **The best answer is B** (although all the answers are relevant). The test for determining whether a mark should be refused registration as falsely suggesting a connection with persons, living or dead (note that either status is covered) involves four parts: (1) the mark must be the same or a close approximation of the person's name, (2) it must be recognized by consumers as such, (3) the person must be sufficiently famous that prospective purchasers will make a connection between that person and the mark, and (4) there must, in fact, be no connection between the person and the goods or services. *See Buffett v. Chi-Chi's, Inc.*, 226 U.S.P.Q. 428, 429 (T.T.A.B. 1985). **Answer A** is relevant to part 4 of the inquiry, as never having heard of the wine; there can be no actual connection between Bill Gates and the wine. **Answer C** is relevant to part 3 of the inquiry; being the richest man in the world makes it likely that consumers will recognize the reference in the mark as to *that* Bill Gates. **Answer D** is relevant to parts 1 and 2 of the test; Bill Gates is both a close approximation of the person's name and is readily recognized as such by the consuming public. **Answer B** is relevant to the inquiry — it cuts against part 3 of the test — that consumers will make the necessary connection — but on these facts the fame of the rich Bill Gates virtually ensures the connection will be made. So **Answer B** is the least relevant to the inquiry.

182.   **The best answer is C** (although all the answers are relevant). **Answer A** points against registration (fame increasing the likelihood of consumer association) while **Answer B** and **Answer D** argue for registration (many people having the first name Julio and that Julio Iglesias is rarely referred to only by his first name, making consumer association between him and the mark less likely). However, **Answer C** states as a conclusion that the required association does not exist, thus definitively eliminating the problem.

183.   The analysis under Lanham Act § 2(c) (15 U.S.C. § 1052(c)) largely tracks that under Lanham Act § 2(a) (15 U.S.C. § 1052(a)). Both sections apply to full names, shortened

names (Bill Gates), nicknames, etc. *See In re Sauer*, 27 U.S.P.Q.2d 1073 (T.T.A.B. 1993). They also only apply when consumers are likely to associate the particular person with the mark, either because of the person's fame or some public association with the particular good or service. *Id.* However, whereas under Lanham Act § 2(a) (15 U.S.C. § 1052(a)) that association must also imply a false connection between the identified individual (in this case Mr. Iglesias) and the goods (the wine), under Lanham Act § 2(c) (15 U.S.C. § 1052(c)) the registration is barred if no *written* (not merely oral) has been obtained, whether or not a false connection is made by the consuming public (for example, it may actually be Julio Iglesias' favorite wine, but without his consent Vino Veritas cannot use his name in its mark).

NOTE: Lanham Act § 2(a) (15 U.S.C. § 1052(a)) only refers to a *false* connection with a person (as well as institutions, beliefs or national symbols) whereas Lanham Act § 2(c) (15 U.S.C. § 1052(c)) specifically refers to "name, portrait, or signature." Consequently, any reference to an individual which leads consumers to make the connection will suffice under Section 2(a).

NOTE: There is one other difference not relevant on these facts but important to remember. Lanham Act § 2(c) (15 U.S.C. § 1052(c)) applies to persons both *living and dead*, whereas Lanham Act § 2(a) (15 U.S.C. § 1052(a)) applies *only to living* individuals.

184.   **NO**. The Lanham Act § 2(a) (15 U.S.C. § 1052(a)) prohibition is not avoided simply because no association is made by consumers with any single individual. *Any* association leading to a false connection will suffice. For example, there was a famous wine-maker named Julio Gallo and his direct association with wine-making makes it likely that wine purchasers will make the connection. Provided that Julio Gallo has no connection with Vino Veritas' wine, registration would be barred.

185.   **NO**. Lanham Act § 2(c) (15 U.S.C. § 1052(c)) ONLY applies to *living* individuals. Only Lanham Act § 2(a) (15 U.S.C. § 1052(a)) applies to both the living and the dead (which might bar the registration in this case if consumers actually erroneously believed Caesar had some connection).

186.   The Lanham Act prohibitions only preclude federal registration of marks which either falsely connect the person to goods or services or involve use of their name, portrait or signature without the person's consent. They do not address the more general question of whether the use of a person's name or likeliness may give rise to other claims, including as an unregistered mark or under rights of publicity which more generally prevent use of person's public persona for commercial benefit, even if not signaling source. *See* Topic 22: Right of Publicity, False Endorsement and Attribution.

187.   Unlucky Vino Veritas has now managed to run into the Lanham Act § 2(e)(4) (15 U.S.C. § 1052(e)(4)) prohibition against registration of names which are "primarily merely a surname."

188. **The best answer is A.** Answers **B, C** and **D** are all relevant to the Lanham Act § 2(e)(4) (15 U.S.C. § 1052(e)(4)) "primarily merely a surname" prohibition, albeit not dispositive. In particular, they all address the key issue: whether *consumers* are likely to identify the mark as a surname. **Answer B** and **Answer D** are evidence that consumers would recognize the mark as a surname (family name) while **Answer C** provides a reason they might not (the same argument might be made with regard to "green" meaning ecologically friendly in this context). Although **Answer A** is relevant to the Lanham Act § 2(a) & (c) (15 U.S.C. § 1052(a) & (c)) inquiries, it is not irrelevant to the "primarily merely a surname" prohibition, making it the best answer.

189. **NO.** The "primarily merely a surname" prohibition stems from two concerns. First, granting one producer control over family names (or any names for that matter) will interfere with the ability of others with that name to use it to identify themselves as producers. Second, like other marks which have independent pre-existing meanings (descriptive and geographic terms, for example), consumers may treat the personal name as a trademark. As with those other marks, Lanham Act § 2(f) (15 U.S.C. § 1052(f)) draws the balance by permitting registration of a recognized surname only if the applicant can demonstrate the surname "has become distinctive of the applicant's goods in commerce" — that is, acquired secondary meaning and is, therefore, serving in a trademark capacity. Secondary meaning does not, however, mean it is sufficient to show that consumers recognize the "Green" wine-making family produces the wine (a form of signaling source). Secondary meaning requires consumers use the name mark to identify the particular characteristics of the marked wine itself (for example, its taste, color and/or bouquet).

      NOTE: "Too much" secondary meaning can make name mark generic for the product or service; for example a "Murphy" bed which the public came to use to refer to any bed which folds into a wall. *See Murphy Door Bed Co., v. Interior Sleep Systems, Inc.*, 874 F.2d 95 (2d Cir. 1989).

190. **NO.** Lanham Act § 2(f) (15 U.S.C. § 1052(f)) secondary meaning exception, expressly does not apply to the "name" prohibitions under Lanham Act § 2(a) & 2(c) (15 U.S.C. §§ 1052(a) & (c)). That exclusion reflects the distinct policy reasons supporting these different name prohibitions. Registration is prohibited under Lanham Act § 2(a) & 2(c) (15 U.S.C. §§ 1052(a) & (c)) because such marks may mislead consumers or harm the interests of the individual involved. Secondary meaning does not resolve either of those concerns. In contrast, the prohibition under Lanham Act § 2(e)(4) (15 U.S.C. § 1052(e)(4)) reflects a lack of distinctiveness (the mark is not signaling information about the product to consumers) which is overcome by a showing of secondary meaning.

191. **Technically YES, but . . . .** Unlike the other name prohibitions which cover refer to "persons" and "names" Lanham Act § 2(e)(4) (15 U.S.C. § 1052(e)(4)) expressly refers to marks which are "primarily merely a *surname*" (family or last name). A "clear meaning" interpretation, therefore, would impose no barrier to registration of other kinds of name marks — such as first names. However, clearly identifiable first names (and

nicknames) raise the same policy concern: do consumers see them as a name or as a mark? On that basis there are good reasons to prohibit registration on non-distinctiveness grounds. The difficult question is where to find the justification in the Lanham Act as it does not appear anywhere in Section 2. The key is that to be a trade mark *at all* (not merely a registerable mark) the mark must be distinctive. That requirement is arguably set out in the introductory clause to Lanham § 1 (15 U.S.C. § 1051) which only permits registration of a "trademark" which, in turn, is defined as involving use "to identify and distinguish his or her goods." That takes the registration analysis back a step to the spectrum of distinctiveness, raising the secondary meaning problems for all forms of name marks. *See* Topic 4 — Distinctiveness: Inherently; Secondary Meaning; Never. Ah, but then why specifically single out surnames in § 2(e)(4)?

192. **NO, but . . . .** There are two concerns with giving trademark rights in names — ensuring it is acting as a trademark and the difficulty those rights pose for competitors' with the same name. *See* Question 189 above. The secondary meaning requirement resolves the former, but leaves open the latter. That problem is addressed by the trademark "fair use" exception which permits producers to use their actual names on their products, even if the name has acquired secondary meaning regarding products from another source. However, that right to use is limited by the requirement that the other users clearly indicate that the name/mark is being used *solely* to identify the actual producer by name, not as a mark, AND the use does not raise implications of sponsorship or affiliation by or with the mark owner. *See* Topic 16 — Defenses: Fair Use, Nominative Use, Parody/Free Speech.

193. **The best answer is C.** The dashboard involves product design which raises functionality concerns — the most likely barrier to Fleet's registration. *See* Topic 6 — Functionality. Although product design is suspect, it can be registered if it is not functional, so **Answer A** is incorrect. **Answer B** cites to the Section 2 prohibition against descriptive marks, which although arguably applicable, is not the actual concern. **Answer C** explicitly cites to the Section 2 functionality bar to registration, making it the better answer. **Answer D** — the Section 2 "secondary meaning" exception — expressly does not apply to the functional prohibition in § 2(e)(5) (15 U.S.C. § 1052(e)(5)), so it is not relevant to the inquiry.

194. The answers:

A. Primarily merely a surname.

B. Flags, coats of arms or other insignia of the United States, etc. . . . ; false connection with an institution.

C. No issue.

D. Matter which may disparage.

E. False connection with a person, living or dead.

F. Geographically deceptively misdescriptive or deceptive.

G. False connection with a person, living or dead; and a mark consisting of the name, portrait or signature identifying a particular living individual without written consent (Paris Hilton).

H. No issue.

I. Primarily geographically descriptive need for secondary meaning; false connection with a person, living or dead, and a mark consisting of the name, portrait or signature. identifying a particular living individual without written consent.

J. Functionality; lack of distinctiveness (fair enough, that's a Section 1 issue)

K. Name, signature, or portrait of a deceased President of the United States during life of his widow without consent (2007); false connection with a person, living or dead

L. Bring an institution into contempt or disrepute.

M. A mark which so resembles a mark registered . . . or previously used in the United States (although a Section 2 issue, the test is discussed in Topic 13 — Infringement: Likelihood of Confusion); maybe (but not likely) geographically deceptively misdescriptive.

N. Geographic indication on wines or spirits identifying a place other than the origin of the goods used after January 1, 1996; geographically deceptively misdescriptive or deceptive.

195.   **The best answer is C.** A federal registration is sufficient for a mark to be *presumed* valid, but that presumption can be overcome by any legal or equitable defense or defect. An "incontestable" mark is a federally registered mark which is *conclusively* deemed valid except for specific statutory reasons (more in the Questions below on those exceptions), as stated in **Answer C.** Consequently, **Answer A** does not go far enough while **Answer B** goes too far. **Answer D** is incorrect for two reasons. First, an incontestable mark can be cancelled in limited circumstances. Second, incontestability speaks to validity of the mark not merely its registerability.

196.   **The answer is B.** The right to claim incontestability is governed by Section 15 of the Lanham Act (15 U.S.C. § 1065). That section specifically requires that in order for a mark to be incontestable it must: (1) be registered on the Principal Register, (2) have been used in commerce as a trademark continuously for a period of five consecutive years after the date of registration, and (3) the claimant must have filed an affidavit within one year after the expiration of such five year period setting forth, among other things, the specific goods or services in connection with which the mark has been so used and is still in use (unsurprisingly, called a § 15 Affidavit). **Answers A, B** and **D** are, therefore, all required. It is not, however, necessary to show the mark, even a descriptive mark like "Sweet and Crunchy," has secondary meaning — despite the fact that such marks should not be registered (or even serve as common law trademarks) in the first instance. *See* Topic 11 — Registration: Grounds for Refusal. So **Answer C** is not required and the correct answer to the Question

NOTE: In addition to the above requirements Section 15 also requires that there be no pending proceeding regarding, nor have been a final adverse decision to, the claimant's ownership or right to ownership in the mark, both of which must be affirmed in the affidavit.

197.   When Congress passed the Lanham Act it made a policy decision that despite the concerns over granting a single producer control over a descriptive (and certain other) marks, it was more important to obtain the efficiencies of "quieting title" in registrations after the passage of a reasonable period of time (five years). As the Questions below reveal, Congress did take a number of steps to mitigate those costs by carving out a number of exceptions to incontestability. *See Park 'N Fly, Inc. v. Dollar Park And Fly, Inc.,* 469 U.S. 189 (1985).

198.   **The best answer is A.** Lanham Act § 15 (15 U.S.C. § 1065) sets out a number of exceptions to incontestability. Section 15(4) (15 U.S.C. § 1065(4)) specifically excepts the generic term for all or a portion of the goods or services for which the mark is registered. In addition, Section 15 cross-references to the certain grounds on which a

mark can be canceled under Section 14 (15 U.S.C. § 1064). Those exceptions include marks which have become generic as well as marks which are functional, have been abandoned, would be denied registration under Section 2(a), (b) or (c) (15 U.S.C § 1052(a), (b) or (c)) — which include immoral, deceptive and disparaging marks among others (*see* Topic 11 — Registration: Grounds for Refusal) — and marks being used to misrepresent the source of the goods or services. Most importantly, that list does NOT include either descriptive or deceptively misdescriptive marks.

On these facts "All Bran" might be classified as either generic or descriptive. Consequently, the mark is neither deceptive (**Answer C**) nor deceptively misdescriptive (**Answer D**) and those claims would fail on the merits whether or not they are permitted challenges to incontestable status (the former is, while the latter is not). The descriptiveness challenge is not among the permitted exceptions under the statute so **Answer B** cannot be raised, much less succeed. *See Park 'N Fly, Inc. v. Dollar Park And Fly, Inc.*, 469 U.S. 189 (1985). That leaves **Answer A** as the only possible (albeit weak) argument on the facts, making it the best answer.

NOTE: The exceptions to incontestability reflect an effort to mitigate the costs of quieting title to a registration. Although incontestability prevents challenges to descriptive marks, the exceptions expressly allow challenges to the more "damaging" marks consisting of generic terms, functional marks or marks likely to deceive consumers. Although not entirely accurate, a convenient rule of thumb is to think of incontestability as quieting title against challenges to marks which require secondary meaning while permitting them against marks which are barred from registration even with a showing of secondary meaning. There is at least one omission from the list of permitted challenges on that basis — marks which are primarily geographically deceptively misdescriptive which are denied registration under Lanham Act § 2(e)(4) (15 U.S.C. § 1052(e)(4)). The response is that although not explicitly excepted, such marks are covered under the permitted challenge of deceptive marks.

199.   **The best answer is now C.** On these facts the mark is either deceptive or deceptively misdescriptive. Although a challenge based on genericness (**Answer A**) is permitted under the statute, it will fail on the facts. The challenge based on descriptiveness (**Answer B**) is neither permitted nor sustainable on the facts. Of the remaining answers only a challenge based on deceptiveness (**Answer C**) is permitted, so it is a better answer than **Answer D**.

200.   **The best answer is D.** Lanham Act § 33 (15 U.S.C. § 1115) deals with the evidentiary effects of federal registration on the plaintiff's right to use the mark. Section 33(a) states that a *registered* mark is presumed valid subject to proof of "any legal or equitable defense or defect." Section 33(b) states that for *incontestable* marks the registration is conclusive evidence of "the validity of the registered mark and of the registration of the mark, of the registrant's ownership of the mark, and of the registrant's exclusive right to use the mark in commerce." However, even an incontestable mark is subject to the nine "defenses or defects" listed in Section 33(b). **Answer A** and **Answer B** are correct regarding the effects of registration but do not describe the further effects of

the mark becoming incontestable. **Answer C** describes the conclusive presumption but omits the exceptions, making **Answer D** the best answer.

201. **The best answer is B.** Lanham Act § 33(b) (15 U.S.C. § 1115(b)) lists nine exceptions to the conclusive presumption of validity. Those exceptions include, among others, that the mark has been abandoned (**Answer C**), the good faith trademark "fair use" defense (**Answer B**) and "prior user" defenses (**Answer D**). It specifically omits challenges based on the descriptiveness of the mark, thus eliminating **Answer A** as a possibility. *See Park 'N Fly, Inc. v. Dollar Park And Fly, Inc.*, 469 U.S. 189 (1985). On the facts, Dentistry is actively using the mark, so although an abandonment challenge is permitted **Answer C** is of no assistance. The analysis of **Answer D** requires three steps. *See* Topic 19 — Duration of Rights, Abandonment and Loss of Rights. First, the good faith prior user defense will permit use of even an incontestable mark, but only in the area of *prior* use. Second, for Dentistry's mark to be incontestable it must have been registered for at least five years. That registration predicate gives Dentistry constructive use priority throughout the United States from the date it filed the application. Finally, the facts state that NovKain has only recently started using the mark meaning its use in any part of the United States must be after the effective date of Dentistry's constructive use. That cuts off NovKain's good faith use everywhere in the United States and makes **Answer D** of no help. **Answer B** — the trademark "fair use" defense — requires the mark be descriptive of the good or service (which it is in this case) and that the defendant be using "fairly and in good faith only to describe [its] goods or services." Although more facts are required regarding the specific nature of NovKain's use (*see* Topic 16 — Defenses: Fair Use, Nominative Use, Parody/Free Speech), trademark fair use is easily its best option of the four answers.

NOTE: The trademark fair use defense is another example of Congressional mitigation of the costs associated with quieting title through incontestability — in this case permitting competitive use of otherwise unchallengeable descriptive marks provided the use is limited to the mark's descriptive (non-trademark) meaning. *See* Question 198 above.

202. **The best answer is B.** Fraud in obtaining registration of the mark is one of the permitted challenges to an incontestable mark in Lanham Act § 33(b) (15 U.S.C. § 1115(b)). Consequently, proof of Dentistry's fraud is a valid "defense or defect" to its claim to the incontestability conclusive presumption, meaning neither **Answer C** nor **Answer D** is correct. The Supreme Court has held that eliminating the conclusive presumption does not *ipso facto* make the mark invalid, so **Answer A** is incorrect. Instead the normal validity presumption applies, which in the case of a registered mark means that under Section 33(a) the mark is presumed valid subject to proof of any legal defense or defect. So **Answer B** is the best answer.

NOTE: On these facts, NovKain might move to cancel Dentistry's registration under Lanham Act § 11(3) (15 U.S.C. § 1064(3)) eliminates even the presumption of validity. More on the relationship between incontestability and cancellation in the Questions below.

203. **The best answer is A**. A challenge based on descriptiveness is not permitted against an incontestable mark under § 33(b) (15 U.S.C. § 1115(b)) so **Answer B** is incorrect. The facts offer no support to a claim that Comelately is a good faith prior user, making **Answer D** improbable at best. The contest is between **Answer A** and **Answer C.** On these facts it can be argued that Comelately's use is generic as the public has come to view the mark as the name of the class. The Section 33(b) list of exceptions does not specifically permit challenges based the mark being (or having become) generic. However, Section 33(b) bases the conclusive presumption is predicated on the mark being incontestable under § 15 (15 U.S.C. § 1065). § 15(4) (15 U.S.C. § 1065(4)), in turn, specifically permits a challenge to incontestability based on the generic nature of the mark. Consequently, **Answer A** is better than **Answer C** on these facts.

204. **The best answer is D** (this one is a bit tricky, sorry). As stated in the answer to Question 202 if incontestability is overcome neither the mark nor the registration will be *ipso facto* invalided, meaning the registration remains in effect and the mark is presumed valid but subject to proof of any legal or equitable defense or defect. **Answers A** and **Answer C** are, therefore, incorrect and **Answer B** is the best at this point in the analysis. However the facts in this case indicate that Comelately has demonstrated that the mark is generic. As generic terms can never qualify as mark Comelately has also proven that the "I-Vid" mark is invalid. **Answer D** best describes the validity of the mark.

NOTE: Not all challenges which overcome incontestability have this effect. For example, the trademark fair use defense permits non-trademark use rather than leading to invalidation of the mark. Similarly, a good faith prior user defense will only apply within the area of prior use leaving the mark valid elsewhere.

205. **The best answer is A**. The issue on these facts is whether GF can rely on the mark's incontestable status to show it has *relevant* valid rights. A federal registration is required for incontestability, but not enough to prove that status, making **Answer C** better than **Answer D**. It is the defendant's task to overcome the related conclusive presumption by showing a permitted defense or defect under Section 33(b), so **Answer B** which would require an affirmative showing by GF is incorrect. The difficulty arises from the fact the Section 33(b) expressly states that the conclusive presumption applies *only* to "the exclusive right to use the mark on or in connection with the goods or services specified in the [§ 15 affidavit]." As GF's affidavit refers only to soups incontestability of GF's rights does not resolve whether Twofer's use on bread products falls within the product footprint of GF's rights in the "Hearty" mark in the first instance. To prevail on that point GF must prove valid rights *beyond* its incontestable rights by demonstrating that Twofer's use will cause a likelihood of confusion. **Answer A** is, therefore, the best answer.

206. As indicated in the answer to Question 205 above the final outcome will turn on whether Twofer's use is likely to cause confusion. That determination will involve a "factors" analysis. *See* Topic 13 — Infringement: Likelihood of Confusion. One of the relevant considerations in that inquiry is the strength of the plaintiff's mark — how powerful

a trademark impression it is likely to make on consumers. Inherently distinctive fanciful, arbitrary and suggestive marks weigh more heavily in plaintiff's favor than descriptive marks, the likely classification of GF's mark. Although GF's mark's incontestable status prevents challenge to its basic validity (on soups), there is considerable debate regarding the effect of incontestable status on the mark's product footprint for confusion purposes. Some courts view incontestability as indicating that the mark should be presumed strong — with an equivalent expansive effect on footprint — while others follow the original classification with weaker ability to help consumers bridge the product gap (from soup to bread in this case). *Compare Dieter v. B&H Industries*, 880 F.2d 322 (11th Cir. 1989), *cert. denied.* 498 U.S. 950 (1990) (incontestable mark presumed strong, at least to the extent of having secondary meaning) with Lone Star Steakhouse & Saloon, Inc. v. Alpha of Virginia, Inc., 43 F.3d 922 (4th Cir. 1995) (treating an incontestable descriptive mark as weak and thus less likely to cause confusion).

207. **The best answer is C.** Lanham Act § 15 (15 U.S.C. § 1065) requires filing a § 15 Affidavit to obtain incontestable rights. However, that affidavit must be filed within one year after the expiration of the five consecutive years of post-registration continuous use. That did not happen on these facts so **Answer A** (filing will give them incontestable rights) and **Answer D** (they currently have incontestable rights) are both incorrect. Understanding why **Answer C** is correct and **Answer B** is not requires carefully differentiating between § 15 and § 14 (15 U.S.C. § 1064). The former concerns incontestability's quieting title in the validity of, and mark owner's exclusive right to use, the mark. The latter addresses the related but nonetheless independent issue of whether the related registration of the mark can be cancelled. Most relevant to this Question, there is no affidavit requirement under § 14. Consequently, although the failure to file prevents Oops from obtaining incontestable status under § 15, it does not prevent it from claiming the benefits of § 14 regarding efforts to cancel its registration.

NOTE: The § 14 "statute of limitations" on cancellations permits actions only within five years after the date of registration. It does not, however, absolutely bar cancellation actions, permitting actions based on the circumstances listed in the Section. Of particular importance are the exceptions in § 14(3) (15 U.S.C. § 1064(3)) — which are expressly incorporated by reference into § 15 (and, in turn into Section 33(b)) and, therefore, also constitute permissible challenges to incontestability). However, the latter incontestability list remains more expansive, so it is important to focus on what precisely is at issue — incontestable status claimed by the mark owner or a cancellation action brought by a third party. The overall effect of these differences (no affidavit, more restrictive lists of exceptions) is that the Lanham Act gives greater protection ("quieter" title) to registrations (and the related, more limited, presumption of validity) than incontestable marks.

208. **Oops will prevail.** The action has been brought five years after the date of Oops' federal registration and will be barred unless an exception applies. Lanham Act § 14 (15 U.S.C. § 1064) does not contain an exception permitting challenges based on descriptiveness,

so despite the fact that the mark is descriptive and without secondary the registration (and the related presumption of validity) stands.

209. **Probably**. There is now a good argument that the "Bright" mark is not descriptive but *deceptive* (it misdescribes the product and consumers are likely to believe that misdescription with an adverse effect on their purchase decisions — *see* Topic 11 — Registration: Grounds for Refusal). Lanham Act § 14(3) (15 U.S.C. § 14(3)) does permit cancellations brought after the five year quiet title period has run on such grounds through its cross-reference to Section 2(a) (15 U.S.C. § 1052(a)). Consequently, not only can the cancellation proceed but it is likely to succeed.

210. **No.** A cancellation action only affects (eliminates) the federal registration. Oops can still claim common law rights in the "Bright" mark based on its use. *See* Topic 11 — Registration: Grounds for Refusal (including the discussion of the effect of bars to federal registration on both common law rights and other rights under the Lanham Act).

211. **Yes.** Lanham Act §§ 14, 15 & 33(b) (15 U.S.C. § 1064, 1065 & 1115(b)) all refer to a "mark" which is defined to include "any trademark, service mark, collective mark or certification mark." Section 45 (15 U.S.C. § 1127). Consequently, the same basic quiet title rules apply to all kinds of marks. § 14 does, however, specifically permit post-five year actions seeking to cancel a certification mark which is being improperly used (lack of control, uses by the owner on its own goods or refusals to certify qualifying goods). By cross-reference Sections 15 and 33(b) also incorporate that exception as a permissible basis for challenging an incontestable certification mark.

212.   **The answer is B**. Although a federally registered mark (**Answer A**) provides a presumption of validity, it is not required to bring a federal trademark infringement action. Similarly, an incontestable mark (**Answer C**) provides further protection against claims of invalidity (*see* Topic 12 — Registration: Incontestability) but is not required. An inherently distinctive (**Answer D**) trademark can be (very) helpful to prevailing in an infringement action — limiting challenges to validity as well as helping prove likely confusion — it is not necessary to bringing an action. What is always required is that the plaintiff own a valid trademark (**Answer B**) — in this case that Freeborn can claim trademark rights "opus diem."

        NOTE: The Lanham Act provides a cause of action for both registered (Lanham Act § 32, 15 U.S.C. § 1114) and unregistered (Lanham Act § 43(a), 15 U.S.C. § 1125(a)) marks "used in commerce" (the basic federal jurisdictional requirement, see Topic 1 — Justifications and Sources of Trademark Law). Although both are generally referred to as trademark "infringements" the cause of action concerning unregistered marks is sometimes referred to as either a "false designation of origin" (the caption on the related Lanham Act section) or "common law infringement" (despite the fact that it is actually brought under the Lanham Act statute). Use of "false designation of origin" to describe unregistered mark infringements should not, however, be confused with the wider range of "unfair competition" claims authorized under Section 43, including the particular sub-species of claims addressed in *Dastar Corp. v. Twentieth Century Fox Film Corp.*, 123 S. Ct. 2041 (2003) which focus on passing off another's goods as one's own ("reverse passing off"). That issue is treated in Question 22 below.

213.   **Yes**. Federal trademark law does not preempt state causes of action; a trademark owner can also bring an action under applicable state common law or an applicable state trademark statute. *See* Topic 1 — Justifications and Sources of Trademark Law. Frequently both causes of actions are joined in a single lawsuit (in federal court) in order to maximize the remedial possibilities.

214.   **The best answer is D**. All of the answers are relevant, however **Answer D** best identifies the core confusion-based infringement inquiry. Both at common law and expressly under the Lanham Act, infringement turns on whether consumers are ***likely*** to be confused. That standard is driven by the central objective of trademark law — ensuring clear and reliable indicators that products or services bearing the mark consistently will have the same characteristics (signaling "source"). *See* Topic 1 — Justifications and Sources of Trademark Law. Accomplishing that purpose requires that unauthorized use of a mark be stopped before the market loses confidence in, or is actually harmed by, the resulting confusion. The existence of *actual* consumer confusion (**Answer B**) provides good

247

evidence of the requisite likelihood of confusion but is not required. **Answer A** (harm to goodwill) and **Answer C** (diversion of trade) reflect the central concern of the unfair competition law precursor to modern trademark law. *See Borden Ice Cream Co. v. Borden's Condensed Milk*, 201 F. 510 (7th Cir. 1912). Neither, however, is now required to make out trademark infringement, although they are relevant to the issue of damages. *See* Topic 18 — Remedies. Protecting against harm to goodwill or preventing diversion of trade are, therefore, perhaps better viewed as (desirable) by-products providing the particular incentive for a mark owner to bring an infringement claim and thus protect greater market interests.

215. **Practically, not at all.** The basic "likelihood of confusion" test is virtually identical under federal and state law as well as regarding a registered or unregistered mark.

216. **Forget the infringement suit, get a federal registration ASAP.** In order to bring the confusion-based trademark infringement action All Grass must own a valid trademark giving it relevant rights. That means that not only must the mark be distinctive and in use (as it is on these facts), but it must apply to the defendant's related geographic and product activities. In this case, although the products are in the same class of goods, because All Lawns does not have a federal registration its geographic trademark footprint is limited exclusively to territories affected by its use. As a result All Lawns' rights extend only to the area of actual use (Indiana, Ohio and Michigan) plus any additional geographic areas where it can demonstrate consumer association and (perhaps) a reasonable area of expansion. *See* Topic 8 — Use: Product/Service and Geographic Reach (Footprint). On these facts it seems highly unlikely that geographic footprint includes Salem, Oregon. Without relevant geographic rights All Lawns' infringement claim cannot succeed (how can anyone in Salem be confused if they have never heard of All Lawns' "Swift" mowers?). The real concern on these facts, therefore, is the race with Just Grass for the remaining open territory as the companies expand. Consequently, obtaining a federal registration is the most important next step; something which, hopefully, Just Grass has not already done. *See* Topic 9 — Registration: Constructive Use and Intent to Use.

217. **The best answer is D**. As discussed in the previous question without the relevant geographic rights no claim for infringement will lie, so **Answer A** is very relevant. The test for infringement is *likelihood* of consumer not *actual* consumer confusion. That means that even absent a showing of *existing* actual consumer confusion the likelihood of *future* consumer confusion can still justify finding infringement, making **Answer D** nondeterminative. To determine whether consumer confusion is sufficiently probable the courts use a variety of factors to determine whether on the specific facts the challenged use falls within the product footprint of the plaintiff's rights and is thus likely to confuse. Although the specific list of factors varies from jurisdiction to jurisdiction (so it is always important to confirm), the classic reference to that factors analysis refers to *Polaroid Corp. v. Polarad Electronics Corp.*, 287 F.2d 492 (2d Cir. 1961) — the "Polaroid" factors. So **Answer C**'s concern over the product footprint of All Lawns'

mark is clearly relevant and **Answer B** is a useful reference to how that determination is made, making **Answer D**, merely one of the factors, the least relevant.

218. The courts use different lists of factors for finding a "likelihood of confusion." Those lists are always explicitly stated to be "non-exclusive" and intended to be assessed as a whole. Although the jurisdiction's specific list should always be confirmed and followed in making the argument, there are three basic inquiries.

The first involves the *marks* themselves. In particular, the greater the similarity between the two marks in visual appearance, sound and/or meaning (the "sight, sound, meaning" test) and the strength (distinctiveness) of the plaintiff's mark (which affects its "recognizability" particularly when either slightly varied or combined with other features) the greater the likelihood consumers will mistake the defendant's mark for the plaintiff's.

The second looks at *basic product footprint* — the relationship between the goods or services involved. Use on the same goods or services is, of course, very likely to cause confusion. Normally, the crucial question is whether the defendant's goods are sufficiently *related* (connected) to the plaintiff's that consumers are likely to make the mark-source association despite the differences. One frequent consideration is whether consumers are likely to view the defendant's product as a likely product-line expansion for the plaintiff — say, from lawn mowers to lawn edgers.

The third involves the *market context*. This set of factors focuses on how the marks are actually seen and used by consumers, thus helping measure the likely effects of differences in the marks and the goods. The two core inquiries involve: (1) whether similarities in the way the goods are sold are likely to generate consumer source associations (for example, when the goods are sold side-by-side in the same stores or advertising is directed at the same consumer group, confusion is more likely, whereas when the goods are in different kinds of stores or addressed to different consumers, it is much less so) & (2) how likely consumers are to rely on the mark based on the cost or complexity of the product, consumer sophistication and the nature of the purchase decision (is it an impulse buy, a routine purchase made in reliance on prior experience or likely to involve considerable care in selection, including research and inquiry regarding comparative product characteristics).

NOTE: Frequently in infringement cases survey evidence is offered to demonstrate not merely the likely response of consumers but actual confusion. Survey evidence can be extremely powerful, however, not only is it relatively expensive but it is very difficult to produce a survey which is not decimated on methodology grounds.

219. **The best answer is A.** The courts frequently consider the defendant's intent to confuse, so **Answer A** is correct. The question is whether it is the best answer. Because infringement turns on the likely adverse consumer effects of the defendant's use, subjective intent without more is not determinative — even the blackest of hearts does not mean the intent to confuse was successful; that turns on the specific facts. So **Answer C** is incorrect. However, demonstrable intent indicates not only that an effort was made

but the defendant believed it could succeed. So intent cannot be seen as entirely irrelevant, making **Answer D** incorrect. Deciding between "key" factor (**Answer B**) and "a" factor (**Answer A**) is a close call, turning largely on how the factor is actually weighed by the courts. The better (I believe) use of intent in trademark law's market efficiency paradigm is as a thumb on the scales regarding interpretation of the other factors. For example, it would undermine the credibility of a defendant's litigation arguments and serve as a tie-breaker in close cases. So I would give **Answer A** the nod. Those more inclined to make bad actors bear the consequences of evil desires might, however, be more likely to load the scale more heavily — for example, by creating a presumption of likelihood of confusion when intent is shown, leaving it to the defendant struggling to demonstrate it failed in its objective. A counter argument is that such punitive desires are perhaps better dealt with as a remedial matter — distinguishing between its use in determining whether there is an infringement on the facts and dealing with infringements shown to be intentional. *See* Topic 18 — Remedies.

NOTE: The converse is also true — it is entirely possible to be any entirely innocent infringer. A pure heart (even armed with counsel's advice that no infringement exists) does not alter the infringement outcome when it is clear on the facts that consumers are likely (to say nothing of actually) confused.

220.   **The best answer is D.** Making infringement turn on likelihood of consumer confusion raises the issue of *which consumer?* As a general proposition the market information/ search cost reduction objectives of trademark law focus the inquiry on the likely consumers for the particular good covered by the mark is used. However, the "related goods" issue means that the net must be cast more broadly than actual past purchasers, to include not only potential future purchasers of the specific product but related products which may be within the mark's product footprint as well. In all events, the inquiry does not include the general consuming public which would include consumers who never have and never will be purchasing relevant goods. On these facts **Answers A, B** and **C** all identify potential purchasers, while **Answer D** involves many consumers who are irrelevant to the inquiry.

221.   **The best answer is A** (no wimping out on these kinds of facts, get a retainer and go for it — although it is always prudent to remember and remind the client that lawsuits are never without risk, especially when juries are involved). On these facts, All Lawns clearly has valid trademark rights in the relevant geographic region. The outcome, therefore, turns on likelihood of confusion based on the "factors" product footprint analysis. The common approach followed in judicial opinions is to assess the various factors sequentially, and then return for a final overall look at what those outcomes taken in aggregate indicate about the likelihood of confusion.

A good starting point is with the *marks themselves.* All Lawns' "Swift" mark is a common word with a pre-existing independent meaning, so it is not as strong as a fanciful mark. However, with regard to lawn-mowers it is, at worst, suggestive and perhaps even arbitrary, making it a relatively distinctive mark that consumers will likely remember it in that context. Comparing the two marks "Swift" and "Swit" reveals a close visual and sound relationship (applying the sight, sound, meaning test) suggesting a strong probability of likely confusion. (As a self-test, did you even notice they were different or, if you did, assume the latter was merely a typographical error?). The "mark" factors analysis heavily supports a likelihood of confusion.

Turning to the *product and market context*: The goods are competing lawn mowers so there is no "related" goods footprint problem. That also means they are likely sold in the same outlets, probably side-by-side, and advertised to the same consumers in very similar ways. So those factors also support infringement. The size and infrequency of the purchase coupled with consumers' relative lack of expertise and inability to self-test the product at purchase is more problematic. Those facts mean consumers will rely heavily on recommendations. That reliance could take the form of on site, purchase-time inquiries of sales staff making a clear distinction between the two products likely. On the other hand, it may involve information from other sources (friends or independent testing) obtained before the purchase decision, which could result in a mistaken purchase. Intent is not present to tip the balance, but given the extremely strong likelihood of confusion on the other factors, the distinct possibility of the latter kind of confusion is enough to strongly favor a finding of infringement.

222. **The best answer is still A.** One could argue that the consumer has suffered no harm from the confusion (they get a better lawn mower as a result of their mistake). However, trademark law is not ensuring that consumer's get a *good* deal, only that the mark ensures they got the deal they *sought* — that is, the product with the characteristics they *expected* based on the presence of the mark. The analysis in Question 221 still applies on its terms and the case on the merits remains "great case" (remembering that litigation involves uncertainties and surprises).

223. **The best answer is now B.** The basic geography, product and market context factors remain the same (strongly favoring All Lawns); however, the inclusion of the defendant's company name "Just Grass" in the composite mark raises some difficulties. First, how should the composite be approached — can All Lawns claim infringement by "dissecting" (separating) the mark into its two component parts and applying the sight, sound, meaning test simply to "Swit?" As a general rule the courts follow an anti-dissection rule, stating that the mark should be considered "as a whole." In looking at the "totality" of the mark, however, courts generally consider how the mark is likely to be viewed by the consumer. That means that, as in this case, not all portions of the mark will necessarily receive the same "weight." Here one could reasonably conclude that because "Swit" is in all capitals and darker letters ("Just Grass/**SWIT**") it will create the primary impression within the composite and should remain the primary focus in the factors analysis. However, the entire consumer impression context must be considered. For example, if "Just Grass" is a very well known "house mark" identifying a wide ranging family of garden products made by the company, its lead-off position in the composite may mean consumers will be strongly influenced by its presence in the composite despite the emphasis on "SWIT." That would make it very difficult to argue that "Swit" raises a likelihood of confusion. *Cf. AMF Incorporated v. Sleekcraft Boats,*

599 F.2d 341 (9th Cir. 1979). However, even on those facts it may be that although the house mark (a company's family of products mark) clarifies to consumers that the mower comes from Just Grass, they may still connect the "SWIT" mark to All Lawns and incorrectly assume that it is in some way involved, perhaps as a partner or sponsor of the product. *See* Topic 16 — Defenses: Fair Use, Nominative Use Parody/Free Speech, discussing the sponsorship, affiliation issues in that context. Consequently, although strong arguments for infringement can be made, there is now sufficient ambiguity to downgrade the assessment on the merits to "Good, but there are some significant issues."

224. **The best answer is now C.** There is a point at which legitimate optimistic assessment must be abandoned and these facts reflect the tipping point. The next Question explores why in more detail.

225. **The best answer is D.** All of the answers are relevant and at least somewhat problematic. **Answer A** (the marks) is generally favorable but poses the potential problems discussed in Question 223 — that although the prominence of the SWIT portion of the composite mark cuts strongly in favor of All Lawns' case there are concerns about the effects of the company name on the overall impression. Regarding **Answer B**, the products might sometimes be sold near each other (helpful to All Lawns' case), but more likely they will be found in different parts of the store or in separate stores (very problematic). The defendant will also argue that the non-routine nature of the purchase decisions (**Answer C**) will lead to specific consumer inquiry, including visual inspection of the lawn furniture, thus making the marks relatively unimportant in the ultimate purchase decision and, therefore, unlikely, to confuse.

However, the most serious concern is that Just Grass' use lies beyond the "related goods" reach of All Lawns' mark's product footprint. Lawn mowers and patio furniture may be so unrelated in consumers' minds that regardless of the other factors, they will not "bridge the gap" and assume that All Lawns has moved into the lawn furniture business. The sales channel inquiry (**Answer B**) is, of course, relevant in this regard, but the outcome of that inquiry is not the crucial issue. It is what that inquiry shows about the mark's "related product" footprint that controls, so **Answer D** is the best answer.

NOTE: The focus on unfair competition "diversion of trade" in the early days of trademark law meant the "related goods" issue had little importance — in such cases consumers didn't buy the infringer's product instead of the mark owner's so there was no claim. *See Borden Ice Cream Co. v. Borden's Condensed Milk*, 201 F. 510 (7th Cir. 1912). As the trademark policy justification shifted from protecting the producer to the consumer, the related goods — product footprint issue became much more relevant.

226. Although as indicated in the Answer to the previous Question, "relatedness" of the two goods is the key problem, the "likelihood of confusion" factors are inter-related, and need to be assessed as a whole. The actual inquiry is whether looking at all the factors consumers will likely (it need not in fact be the case) "bridge the gap" and make the association. All Lawns would, therefore, focus on facts which support that connection.

Of particular importance would be the "channels" of sale — whether the products are sold in the same outlets and/or advertised to the same target consumers ("everything for your yard"). Another factor would be that consumers will associate the goods because they are related in their use; in this case that one mows the lawn to enjoy the patio furniture. *See Death Tobacco, Inc. v. Black Death USA*, 31 U.S.P.Q.2d 1899 (C.D. Cal. 1993) (cigarettes and vodka viewed as "complementary" products by consumers). Additionally, the similarity of the marks can affect the likelihood of consumer connection. Specifically, All Lawns might argue that because its mark is strong (suggestive and/or well know) and the two marks (or at least the parts emphasized) are so similar ("Swift" and "Swit"), that less connection between the products is required for consumers to make a connection.

227. **Some, but not a lot**. The key to "likelihood of confusion" remains actual consumer perception not the plaintiff's individual future plans (or subjective views of the market). Although All Lawns' future plans may provide evidence of relatedness of the products, the crucial question is whether All Lawns' plans reflect a common characteristic of the "lawn products" marketplace or is just an isolated situation.

228. **The PTO would apply the same analysis**. Lanham Act § 2(d) (15. U.S.C. § 1052(d)) prohibits registration of a mark which "so resembles a mark registered . . . or previously used in the United States by another . . . as to be likely, when used on or in connection with the goods of the applicant, to cause confusion, mistake or to deceive." That language closely tracks the likelihood of confusion standard for infringement and, unsurprisingly, the above analysis would apply in making the registerability determination.

NOTE: The *ex parte* nature of a registration proceeding and the absence of an All Lawn registration to bring the matter to the PTO's attention means that All Lawn's may have to bring an opposition following publication. *see* Topic 10 — Registration: Process; Basic Requirements and Benefits.

229. **The best answer is A**. The facts indicate that the mark is valid, so **Answer B** is not Searches' best defense. **Answer C** is not factually accurate as Searches' is "selling" something — the sponsored advertisement program. **Answer D** is irrelevant, confusion-based infringement does not allege sale of a mark, but that its *use* by a non-owner is likely to cause consumer confusion. Various internet uses of trademarks, including the example in this case, as well as meta-tags (embedding a trademark in a website to increase the search engine's likelihood of indexing the site as a high ranked search response) or to generate pop-up advertisements have reenergized debate over the "use as a trademark" requirement such "use in commerce" being explicitly required under the Lanham Act) as a predicate to finding infringement. The issue is whether a use which does not involve direct display of the mark to consumers on or in connection with a good satisfies that requirement (can there be a likelihood of confusion in such circumstances?). The courts continue to struggle with the issue. *Compare Rescuecom Corp. v. Google, Inc.*, 456 F. Supp. 2d 393 (N.D.N.Y. 2006); *U-Haul Intl., v. WhenU.com*, 279 F. Supp. 2d 723 (E.D. Va. 2003) (use in commerce) with *800-JR Cigar*

Inc. v. GoTo.com, Inc., 437 F. Supp. 2d 273 (D.N.J. 2006) (no use in commerce). Consequently, the best defense (albeit problematic) among those listed is **Answer A** — that Searches use of the mark does not involve "use in commerce" as a trademark.

NOTE: Even should a court find that Searches' use is use commerce as a trademark, the plaintiff will still need to show that its use creates a likelihood of consumer confusion. The fact that the mark is not displayed on Searches (or another's) goods or services to consumers raises some significant difficulties in applying the traditional factors analysis. As a result other forms of confusion — for example, initial interest confusion — may be more amendable theories of infringement. *See* Question 234 below.

230.   **The best answer is B**. On the facts the plan seems very likely to resolve the likelihood of consumer confusion problem at the point of sale — the notice clearly states that the mark is not indicating the expected source. Consequently, **Answer B** is better than **Answer A**. The plan does not, however, take into account what might happen *after* the product is purchased, the detachable notice is removed and the jeans are worn in the marketplace. A post-sale observer of the Regular Jeans' product bearing the Fancy Jeans' stitching mark may, therefore, mistake it for a Fancy Jeans' product and erroneously assume that the observed characteristics are those of the original — arguably creating a likelihood of confusion. Some courts have found infringement in such cases under the doctrine of *post-sale* confusion. *See Lois Sportswear, U.S.A., Inc. v. Levi Strauss & Co.*, 799 F.2d 867 (2d Cir. 1986). So **Answer D** is incorrect. As the doctrine of post-sale confusion is not without its critiques, it might be argued that **Answer C** is better than **Answer B**. However, ultimately prevailing after a lawsuit is not the same as solving the potential infringement problem, so I'd stick with **Answer B**.

231.   **Perhaps.** Clearly if the potential consumers for a product are not going to mistake it for those of the competitor in the after-market it is hard to argue there is a risk of post-sale confusion. The question is whether the relevant group of potential consumers consists only of those who purchase the mark owner's product. Some courts have been unreceptive to that argument, looking instead to the likely reaction of the general public. *See Hermes Int. V. Lederer De Paris Fifth Ave.*, 291 F.2d 104 (2d Cir. 2000). Considering the consuming public at large — including those that don't have any interest in jeans — seems to move to the other extreme. The more appropriate group on these facts might be the class of potential buyers of jeans. However, Regular Jeans would still be in trouble even with that group because some of them (the non-sophisticated, non-designer jeans purchasers) are still likely to be confused by the presence of the stitching.

NOTE: The Question raises the issue of what public interests finding infringement in this case actually protects. What harm is caused by "regular" jeans consumers' confusion? It certainly could be argued that the effect is to deter them from becoming Fancy Jeans consumers because they are mistaken about the attributes of the Fancy Jeans product. However, what if that group is highly unlikely to buy designer jeans in any event — say because of the price? It might be argued that designer jeans buyers will no longer buy the Fancy Jeans product, but on the facts that will not be the result of their confusion but because other non-buyers do not value the brand — raising the (as yet unresolved) question of whether that is a legitimate trademark law concern.

232.   **The best answer is C.** These facts describe a case of "reverse confusion" — where the senior user's trademark loses its ability to identify its products because it is overwhelmed by confusion with similarly marked products of a junior user (usually, as in this case, a much larger and well known producer). The baseline issue in confusion-based trademark infringement is who owns the mark and thus will be harmed by confusion caused by subsequent adoption and use. In this case that is Local who is the senior user. It does not matter whether the confusion is "forward" (consumers buying MegaWines product thinking it comes from Local) or "reverse" (the converse), the mark owner has the right to prevent any likelihood of confusion which may interfere with the ability of the mark to reliably communicate information about its product to consumers. Because MegaWines does not own the "Veritas" mark, **Answer A** is incorrect. Although intent may be relevant to remedy it does not excuse the infringement or permit a likelihood of (or actual) confusion, so **Answer B** is incorrect. **Answer D** harkens back to the now less central unfair competition concern with diversion of trade. The doctrine of reverse confusion demonstrates how current trademark law's focus on ensuring clear and reliable source signals dramatically changes the infringement analysis. On these facts it would not be surprising to see Local's sales of its products actually increase, but that does not affect its right to prevent the confusion. So **Answer C** is the best answer — the senior user/owner of the mark will prevail.

NOTE: On the facts Local's mark may only be valid in a limited geographic footprint. That may affect the remedy (particularly the scope of an injunction), but does not deprive Local of its rights to enforce its mark within that footprint. *See* Topic 8 — Use: Product/ Service and Geographic Reach (Footprint).

233.   **The best answer is C.** On these facts there is no consumer confusion arising from the use similar trademarks by different producers of any kind (likelihood, forward or reverse), so none of **Answers A, B** or **D** is correct. The Lanham Act, however, *also* prohibits "false designations of origin" which are likely to cause confusion, mistake or deception. *See* Lanham Act § 43 (a) (15 U.S.C. § 1125 (a)). *The Supreme Court in Dastar Corp. v. Twentieth Century Fox Film Corp.*, 539 U.S. 23 (2003) stated in dicta that repackaging another's goods under one's *own* trademark may constitute such a violation, called "reverse passing off." **Answer C** is, therefore, the best (only correct) answer. *See* Topic 21: False Advertising and False Designation of Origin.

NOTE: In *Dastar* the Court went on to specifically hold that "origin" refers — at least in cases involving goods subject to copyright law — "to the producer of the tangible goods that are offered for sale, and not the author of any idea, concept, or communication embodied in those goods." *Id.* So reverse passing off claims can only be brought by the actual producer of the good, not the owner of related intellectual property rights. *See also Beckwith Builders Inc. v. Depietri*, 2006 DNH 106; 2006 U.S. Dist. LEXIS 67060, 81 U.S.P.Q.2D (BNA) 1302 (builders of home not the creators of the design are the "origin" of the home, so no false designation of origin for failing to credit the design creator).

234. **YES — initial interest confusion**. On these facts there is no likelihood that customers will eat at Enzo's restaurant under the mistaken impression that they are at one of the chains whose mark appears on the freeway exit sign. Consequently, it is impossible to argue that consumers are likely to be confused when making their purchase decision. The *"initial interest confusion"* doctrine focuses instead on the effects of temporary pre-sale confusion on purchase decisions. For example, on these facts consumers may have decided to eat at one of the advertised chains when they exited but then eat at Enzo's restaurant once they realize no chain is present. As a result of their confusion caused by Enzo's use of another's trademark he has gained trade.

The doctrine has been called into service in internet cases — particularly those involving use of a competitor's mark (or close derivative) in a domain name or search results (frequently with meta-tags, thus raising the "use" question discussed in the answer to Question 229 above) to bring in consumers. As with Enzo's situation, the site itself makes it clear that there is no connection with the mark or its owner, so no consumer is likely to be confused at time of purchase. *See Interstellar Starship Services, Ltd. v. Epix, Inc.*, 304 F.3d 936 (9th Cir. 2002); *Brookfield Communications, Inc. v. West Coast Ent. Corp.*, 174 F.3d 1036 (9th Cir. 1999).

There is a lively debate about the justification (or lack thereof) for initial interest confusion. Supporting the doctrine is the argument that the competitor's use of the mark does "confuse" and the possible diversion of consumers (the old unfair competition law focus) is sufficient harm to satisfy the "likelihood of confusion" requirement for finding infringement (the lack of confusion at the time of purchase being irrelevant). The counter argument is that such use merely provides additional options to consumers, while still leaving the choice between the marked good and the competitor to them based on full information. Consequently, such use does not cause any (substantial) harm to trademark law's consumer information objectives. The reply in rebuttal is that such uses unavoidably undermine the reliability of a mark by increasing the likelihood of false positives. As a result consumers will lose confidence in the mark as a means to obtain the desired product. For example, freeway travelers must factor in the possibility they will be stuck with Enzo's if they get off at a freeway exit even though the sign clearly indicates the presence of the desired chain restaurant.

NOTE: The traditional "factors" approach to confusion provides useful guidance when determining whether pre-sale initial interest confusion is likely; in particular, the strength/similarity of the marks and relatedness of the goods or services.

235. **The best answer is D**. On the facts GenericCandy is not itself violating or even using any third party trademark, so it cannot be liable for infringement of any kind (forward or reverse). **Answer A** and **Answer B** are, therefore, incorrect. The question is whether it can be held liable for the infringements by the retailers. The Supreme Court held in *Inwood Laboratories, Inc. v. Ives Laboratories, Inc.*, 102 S. Ct. 2182 (1982) that

"if a manufacturer or distributor intentionally induces another to infringe a trademark, or if it continues to supply its product to one whom it knows or has reason to know is engaging in trademark infringement, the manufacturer or distributor is contributorially responsible for any harm done as a result." The encouragement by GenericCandy's sales staff likely suffices to trigger contributory infringement under the first category of the Court's test, making **Answer D** correct. Vicarious infringement involves *respondeat superior* liability for agents' infringements. Here the independent retailers not Generic-Candy's own sales staff engaging in the infringement, so **Answer C** is incorrect.

NOTE: Unlike the federal patent statute, there is no Lanham Act provision which addresses either contributory or vicarious liability. Rather the doctrines are of judicial origin. The Lanham Act does, however, contain several "safe harbors" regarding indirect infringements by innocent publishers (print and electronic) which limit the remedy to an injunction. *See* Lanham Act § 32(2) (15 U.S.C. § 1114 (2)).

236. GenericCandy's only possible liability is still indirect — it is not committing any trademark violation on its own. Regarding contributory infringement (liability for infringement by the independent third party retailers), on these facts there is now no inducement by GenericCandy, so it cannot be liable on that basis. There is, however, a second category of contributory infringement possible under the *Inwood* test (discussed in the previous answer) based on knowledge of the third party infringement. The question is whether GenericCandy either knows or has reason to know (an objective test — would on the facts a reasonable person have known) of the retailers' infringements. If so, and it nonetheless continues to supply the infringers it will be liable. Nothing in the facts provides any basis for making that determination, so the outcome is indeterminate.

237. On these facts GenericCandy has not encouraged nor does it have knowledge (or, arguably, reason to know) of the infringement by its sales staff. It, therefore, cannot be held contributorially liable for those infringements. Because those sales staff employees constitute GenericCandy's agents (it exercises control over their activities which actions benefit it as principal), GenericCandy can likely be held liable under respondeat superior, vicarious liability for those infringements.

NOTE: Vicarious and contributory liability theories provide a more effective remedy against trademark infringements at swap-meet/open markets than going after the myriad individual sellers. If the mark owner can show either inducement, knowledge/reason to know, or agency, then it may be able to prevail in a suit against the owner/operator of the entire event. *See* Hard Rock Cafe *Licensing Corp. v. Concession Services, Inc.,* 955 F.2d 1143 (7th Cir. 1992) (rejecting the claim).

238. **Maybe, but it's a difficult case on these facts.** Clearly BestStuff is selling original goods, bearing the original marks put there by the mark owners, so the infringement problem is not likelihood of consumer confusion over the identity, characteristics or source of the labeled goods. The possible concern is that BestStuff's sale of marked goods implies that those manufactures are in some way affiliated with BestStuff despite

the fact it is not an authorized dealer. That "confusion" issue is addressed in (horrifying) detail in Topic 16 — Defenses: Fair Use, Nominative Use Parody/Free Speech.

239. **The best answer is D.** The central inquiry, as in all confusion-based infringement claims, is the likelihood of consumer confusion under the specific circumstances. The basic "factors" analysis strongly favors BigRigs. Its "Rhino" mark is strong (most likely arbitrary) and identical to the mark appearing on Topcaps' new product. The products, if not in direct competition, are very closely related making it very probable that consumers will make a connection between the mark on Topcaps' product and BigRigs. Regarding marketing channels the fact that Topcaps sales are dependent on purchaser interest in the mark on the cap makes it likely that there is substantial overlap, if not in actual distribution certainly in the marketing effort and the target consumers. Finally, the cap purchase is unlikely to involve careful scrutiny and, moreover, the facts state that the purchase is usually motivated by the presence of the Rhino mark.

The argument based on Topcaps' use of the separate "Ersatz" mark is not without merit. Consumers will see the "Ersatz" mark at the time of purchase and may realize that although the cap carries the "Rhino" mark it is actually produced by someone else. However, there are three good confusion-based counter-arguments. First, consumers may not notice the "Ersatz" mark, they may not recognize it as another's mark, or even if they see it and recognize it they may believe that there is some connection with BigRigs, such as sponsorship or affiliation. Second, even if consumers are not confused at the time of purchase, they may have been attracted to the product by the "Rhino" mark, giving rise to initial interest confusion. Finally, even if there is no point of sale confusion people seeing the cap in the market post-sale cannot see the "Ersatz" mark and may mistakenly believe the cap reflects the attributes of a BigRigs' product based on the very visible "Rhino" mark.

Consequently, it is very unlikely that Topcaps will win the case, eliminating **Answer A** and **Answer B**. Granted, whether BigRigs will "probably" or "is very likely" to win is a judgment call, but the above analysis gives the strong nod to the latter, making **Answer D** better than **Answer C**.

240. **Probably not, but perhaps it should.** The courts have generally been unsympathetic to defendants in all such situations, even in cases like this where there is a serious question regarding the relatedness of the goods. Harvard may produce a line of clothing (including, perhaps, baseball caps) bearing the University name. However, the mark's association is with educational services. That means few, if any, are seeing the use of the "Harvard" mark on Topcaps product as indicating anything about the cap's characteristics as a cap. Rather the purchase is motivated primarily by the desire to obtain an exemplar of the mark. Not only does the purchaser have this objective, but the same purpose is readily understood by others. Consequently, there is substantial doubt whether, either at the time of purchase or in the post-sale marketplace, consumers will make any connection between the presence mark and the product's source. In such situations trademark law has arguably been extended to protect the mark as a distinct commodity through an associated "merchandising right." This issue is one of most

difficult current problems in trademark law. If trademark law is designed solely to avoid consumer confusion, then there is little (if any) justification for prohibiting Topcaps' use in this context. Or stated the other way around, if trademark law is to prevent this use some justification beyond ensuring clear and reliable indicators of source must be found in support. *See* Topic 1 — Justifications and Sources of Trademark Law discussing the objectives of trademark law.

NOTE: Although Harvard University might bring a claim for trademark dilution (*see* Topic 14 — Dilution) that hardly resolves the policy conundrum. It merely raises the question of why the dilution right should exist if it is unconnected to any possible consumer confusion.

241.   **The best answer is D** (although an irrationally optimistic lawyer might make a case, with luck, for Answer C). On the facts Anduin clearly owns a valid trademark and its federal registration gives it national rights (certainly over Quintex and likely over all others). So basic validity and geographic footprint pose little or no concern. The difficulty arises from the factors analysis applied to determine if there is a likelihood of confusion based on the two companies' respective product uses. *See* Topic 13 — Infringement: Likelihood of Confusion. On the plus side "Pont" is a strong mark — being both inherently distinctive and well-known, and Quintex is using the identical word. Additionally, a case can be made that purchasers of small standard kitchen appliances rely heavily on the mark. The problem is that the differences between the goods and method/location of distribution factors point convincingly away from any likelihood of consumer confusion. There is at best a very indirect connection between fishing equipment and kitchen appliances. As a stretch the latter is used to prepare what is caught with the former; but that hardly makes it probable that consumers will "bridge the gap" and believe that Anduin has diversified into kitchen appliances. Additionally, although the goods might be sold in different sections of very large department stores, the fact that Anduin's products are "high-end" makes even such overlap unlikely. Finally, the lack of any actual confusion offers little help in overcoming the conclusion that there is no merit in Anduin's confusion-based infringement claim. The best assessment is that Anduin will lose, making **Answer D** the best answer.

242.   **The best answer is C**. As explained in the Answer to Question 241 above, Anduin cannot make out a case of likely consumer confusion, so they must look elsewhere for relief. A dilution claim is brought under 15 U.S.C. § 1125(c) (forming part of Lanham Act § 43, but not contained in the original Act as the federal dilution provisions were first adopted only in 1995). The Trademark Revision Act of 2006 amended § 1125(c) addressing and resolving a number of controversial issues which are discussed in the following questions.

NOTE: These Questions deal exclusively with the federal statutory provision, so any reference to dilution should be read as referring to the federal regime. Many states have their own "anti-dilution" statutes. Those state statutes are generally consistent with the federal requirements, but important differences exist (particularly regarding remedies), making confirmation of specifics extremely important in "real life."

As amended the federal right to prevent dilution provides that "the owner of a famous mark that is distinctive, inherently or through acquired distinctiveness, shall be entitled to an injunction against another person who, at any time after the owner's mark has become famous, commences use of a mark in commerce that is likely to cause dilution

261

. . ., regardless of the presence or absence of actual or likely confusion, of competition, or of actual economic injury" — referred to, for obvious reasons, as a "dilution" claim.

One thing that remains unchanged under the Trademark Revision Act is that a dilution claim explicitly does not require confusion; rather dilution focuses on whether the owner's mark is *famous*. *See* 15 U.S.C. § 1125(c)(1), as amended (the definition of dilution previously set out in 15 U.S.C. § 1127 was deleted by the Trademark Revision Act). Consequently, **Answer C** which explicitly addresses dilution's "famous mark" requirement is better than **Answer A** which is (fortunately for Anduin) irrelevant to such a claim. **Answer B** and **Answer D** are both relevant to determining fame (although the statute specifically does not require inherent distinctiveness), but the crucial issue is whether fame actually exists, so **Answer C** is the best answer.

243.   Confusion-based claims, obviously, prevent direct attacks on a mark's ability to uniquely identify and distinguish a particular product by prohibiting the same or similar marks on the same or related products. Dilution goes one step further by preventing "the lessening of the capacity of a famous mark to identify and distinguish goods or services . . . regardless of the presence or absence of the likelihood of confusion." 15 U.S.C. § 1125(c)(1), as amended. Commentators describe that extra step as preventing the gradual "whittling away" of a famous mark's communicative power as a result of proliferating use by third parties. For example, in this case although a consumer will not be confused by seeing the "Pont" mark on kitchen appliances (they understand there are two unrelated sources involved) the additional use creates another consumer association with the "Pont" mark beyond its original connection with Anduin's fishing equipment. If such non-competing, non-confusing uses are permitted to multiply (say on cars, music, etc) the original unique and powerful association with Anduin's products may become increasingly blurred in consumers minds with the myriad other product messages, eventually reducing the "Pont" mark's power to call to mind the Anduin product characteristics. In short, dilution recognizes that if "everything becomes a Cadillac, nothing is a Cadillac."

244.   **The best answer is D**. A key element in Anduin's dilution claim is whether the "Pont" mark is "famous" as defined in 15 U.S.C. § 1125(c)(2)(A), as amended. That Section instructs the courts to consider "all relevant factors" when making the fame determination, including specifically: the duration, extent and geographic reach of publicity; the amount, volume and geographic extent of sales; the actual public recognition of the mark; and whether the mark is registered. **Answers A, B** and **C** are specifically included in that list and will be important considerations in determining whether the "Pont" mark is famous; they are all directly relevant to whether consumers are likely to recognize the mark as "something special." The specific nature of the goods on which the "Pont" mark is used — in this case fishing equipment — is not directly relevant to whether the mark is famous and, therefore, **Answer D** is the least relevant consideration and the best answer to the Question.

NOTE: Although the nature of the goods does not preclude or confirm fame of the associated mark, it can have an indirect effect on fame by influencing how many customers become familiar with the mark (the more widely purchased the good, the more likely it is to generate high public awareness).

245. **The best answer is A**. The question of "niche" (limited) market fame has been troublesome in dilution actions, with some courts holding that the mark must be "a household name" to qualify while others have been willing to consider lesser renown, although frequently requiring in such cases that the defendant's use involve a closely related niche market (presumably to increase the likelihood of consumer overlap and therefore recognition across markets). The Trademark Dilution Revision Act of 2006 resolved the issue in favor of "national" fame — requiring that to be famous a mark must be "widely recognized by the general consuming public." Consequently, Anduin's biggest problem in making out a dilution claim on these facts is proving its mark is well known to the *general public*; that is to those outside the fishing equipment niche market. **Answer B** and **Answer C** both are listed as relevant considerations under the 2006 Revision Act, so although far from conclusive they at least help in that regard. The fact that the mark is only used on fishing equipment makes it less likely that it has national recognition (the narrower the consumer base, the less likely to generate public awareness), so **Answer D** is unhelpful. However, **Answer A** affirmatively states that the mark is only known in Anduin's niche market thus destroying Anduin's claim to fame (sorry about that).

246. **NO (not any more)**. Uniquely among the federal circuits the Second Circuit had focused on the language in pre-amendment 15 U.S.C. § 1125(c)(1) which stated "[i]n determining whether a mark is *distinctive* and famous, a court may consider factors, such as . . . ." The Second Circuit alone read the explicit inclusion of "distinctiveness" in that sentence to require not only that the mark at issue be famous but that it *also* be inherently distinctive, rather than having acquired distinctiveness. *See TCPIP Holding Co., Inc. v. Haar Communications, Inc.*, 244 F.3d 88 (2d Cir. 2001). The Trademark Dilution Revision Act of 2006 now has expressly resolved that issue by amending the statute to read ". . . a famous mark that is distinctive, inherently or through acquired distinctiveness, ..." So that issue has now disappeared and either kind of mark will support a dilution action.

247. **The best answer is C**. The Trademark Dilution Revision Act of 2006 also specifically addressed the debate over the kinds of dilution claims which may be brought. Amended 15 U.S.C. § 1125(c)(1) now expressly states that dilution claims can be *either* in the form of blurring or tarnishment. That not only made clear that dilution by tarnishment is a valid claim (the Supreme Court had implied that perhaps it was not) but also eliminated the possibility that some other form of dilution might exist. So although **Answer A** is correct, it is not as specific as the other answers and therefore not the best description of Mauer's claim. **Answer D** is incorrect as other forms of dilution claims have been eliminated. The Act now specifically defines "dilution by blurring" as "association arising from the similarity between a mark . . . and a famous mark that impairs the distinctiveness of the famous mark." This definition confirms, as indicated in the answer to Question 243 above, that dilutive blurring is not the same

as likelihood of confusion: Consumers are not buying a product based on a mistaken assumption that it has the characteristics indicated by the mark, but recognize there are two distinct uses of the mark. It is that latter parallel use which is targeted by dilution, avoiding the reduction in the mark's distinctiveness through the whittling away of its uniqueness in the consumer's mind. The Act defines "dilution by tarnishment" as "association arising from the similarity between a mark or trade name and a famous mark that harms the reputation of the famous mark." On these facts there is nothing to indicate a "harmful" association. Gym bags may not be exciting but they are not, generally speaking, reviled or held in ill-repute by the general public. As the only possible concern is "impairment of distinctiveness" of the famous mark, the best description of Mauer's claim is "dilution by blurring." **Answer B** is, therefore, incorrect and **Answer C** the best answer.

248.   **The best answer is B**. Every dilution case requires a famous mark (see Questions 242 and 245 above), so **Answer A** is necessary for Mauer to prevail. The Supreme Court in *Moseley v. V Secret Catalogue, Inc.*, 537 U.S. 418 (2003) interpreted the pre-amendment language of 15 U.S.C. § 1125(c)(1) to require a showing of *actual* dilution. Congress in the Trademark Dilution Revision Act of 2006 specifically changed that language to read "*likely* to cause dilution." Consequently, **Answer B** is now incorrect and **Answer C** is correct. Certain types of trademark use are excluded from dilution claims (including trademark fair use and parody (*see* Topic 16 — Defenses: Fair Use, Nominative Use, Parody/Free Speech) news reporting and non-commercial use). So **Answer D** is also a requirement in a dilution case (albeit that the defendant may carry the burden of proof). NOTE: The Trademark Revision Act also states that dilution can be found absent competition or economic injury thus further reinforcing that no actual harm need have occurred beyond the dilution (by blurring or tarnishment) itself. *See* 15 U.S.C. § 1125(c)(1), as amended

249.   **Mauer's chances of winning are good**. On the facts Mauer can make a solid claim that it has a famous mark. To determine whether a mark is famous the Trademark Revision Act of 2006 instructs courts to look at all relevant circumstances including the duration, extent and geographic reach of publicity; the amount, volume and geographic extent of sales; the actual public recognition of the mark; and whether the mark is registered. Mauer's case is strong on all factors. It has advertised and sold its Tough-Sac garbage bags nationwide for an extended period of time. Additionally, the mark is the subject of an incontestable federal registration and, most importantly, is widely recognized by the general consuming public. Regarding whether the mark is suffering dilution by blurring the Trademark Revision Act again indicates that all relevant factors should be considered but specifically indicates a court should assess the similarity between the marks, the inherent *or acquired* distinctiveness and degree of recognition of the famous mark, amount of use by others, the defendant's intent to create an association and proof of actual association. On these facts the strong similarity between the marks "Tough-Sac" and "Tough-Bag" and the high level of acquired distinctiveness and public recognition point strongly toward a *likelihood* of blurring —

which is all that is now required under the Trademark Revision Act. Finally, none of the exclusions (fair use/parody, news reporting or noncommercial use) appear applicable.

250. The Trademark Revision Act of 2006 retains the same basic approach to remedies. Remedies are generally limited to an injunction against continued use of the diluting mark ("Tough-Bag" in this case). *See* 15 U.S.C. § 1125(c)(1), as amended. Additional remedies (including damages and destruction of "diluting goods") are *only* available if the diluting mark was first used after the effective date of the Trademark Dilution Revision Act of 2006 (October 6, 2006) *and* the defendant is shown to have willfully intended to trade on the reputation of the famous mark or to harm (tarnish) its reputation.

251. The Trademark Dilution Revision Act of 2006 (as did the pre-amendment statute) requires that to be actionable the challenged use must occur "at any time *after the owner's mark has become famous.*" *See* 15 U.S.C. § 1125(c)(1), as amended. Consequently, timing must be considered in every dilution case. The question is whether the statutory phrase means that if the use commenced prior to a mark becoming famous it is "grand-fathered" and may continue or that once the mark has become famous any further continuing use can be enjoined. That question remains unresolved. One court has addressed the timing issue, but only in connection with an opposition brought by a junior user whose mark had now become famous against a registration by a senior local user. The court found that dilution only protected against subsequent-to-fame *adoptions,* not continuing use by a prior adopter. *See Enterprise Rent-a-Car Co. v. Advantage Rent-A-Car, Inc.,* 330 F.3d 1333 (Fed. Cir. 2003). That approach would mean that dilution only prevents *additional* whittling away by subsequent adopters.

252. **Very unlikely**. For the reasons discussed in Question 249, Mauer should have no trouble proving that the Tough-Sac mark is famous. Nor would there be any technical difficulty in proving a dilution by blurring *except* that WeHaveItAll's use of the mark refers to Maurer's actual garbage bags, not a different product. The trademark "fair use/ nominative use" exception from dilution claims is explicitly incorporated in 15 U.S.C. § 1125(c)(3), as amended, and will bar the claim. *See* Topic 16 — Defenses: Fair Use, Nominative Use Parody/Free Speech.

253. **The answer is D. Answers A, B** and **C** are all expressly enumerated in the defenses/ exclusions set out in 15 U.S.C. § 1125(c)(3), as amended. **Answer D** emphasizes the point that dilution law does *not* turn on whether consumers will be confused, but whether the third party use will blur (impair the distinctiveness) or tarnish (harm the reputation of) the famous mark. *See* 15 U.S.C. §§ 1125(c)(1) & (c)(2), as amended.

254. **The best answer is C**. The Question reveals the important relationship between dilution by tarnishment and the statutory exceptions. All of the Answers arguably involve some harm to the reputation of Ultra's "Glory" trademark. However, public policy consider- ations preclude the use of trademark dilution to prohibit all but one of the uses. Specifically, **Answer A** and **Answer B** both raise important free speech considerations and the statute expressly permits such uses of the mark despite the possibility that the

use will harm the reputation of the famous mark. *See* 15 U.S.C. § 1125(c)(3)(A)(ii), as amended. **Answer D** could similarly be considered to implicate free speech concerns, but as the use identifies the actual Ultra product it also likely constitutes trademark "fair/nominative use" (assuming there is no consumer confusion as to Ultra's sponsorship or affiliation of or with the retailer's — *see* Topic 16 — Defenses: Fair Use, Nominative Use, Parody/Free Speech). Consequently, whether or not the presence of the goods in a discount store will harm Ultra's desired image for its products, the remedy — if there is one — must be found outside trademark dilution law. *See* 15 U.S.C. § 1125(c)(3)(A), as amended. Although one might argue that the pornography shop is engaging in "parody," it would appear that its actual objective is to ride on the mark's reputation. Consequently, either a blurring or tarnishment dilution claim (depending on whether one focuses on the harm to distinctiveness or reputation) is likely to be sustained, making **Answer C** the best answer.

255. **The best answer is B.** Use as a trade name is not, standing alone as on these facts, is not use as a trademark (and would therefore not support an infringement claim). So both **Answer C** and **Answer D** are incorrect. The Trademark Dilution Revision Act of 2006 expressly authorizes a dilution claim not merely against third party trademark use, but also third party *trade name use* which is likely to cause blurring or tarnishment. **Answer A** is therefore incorrect and **Answer B** is the best answer. The logic of this expansion of trademark law is that even though third party trade name use does not involve information about a product's characteristic, it nonetheless creates another consumer association regarding the famous mark and thus can whittle away at a famous mark's distinctiveness or harm its reputation. *But see* Topic 1 — Justifications and Sources of Trademark Law (discussing the appropriate reach of trademark law based on its policy objectives).

256. **The best answer is D.** Trade dress can, of course, serve as a trademark provided it is distinctive and non-functional, so **Answer B** is incorrect. *See* Topic 5 — Distinctiveness: Non-word Marks, Colors and Trade Dress. The Trademark Dilution Revision Act of 2006 added a provision which specifically addressed trade dress dilution. It states that unregistered trade dress can be protected against dilution provided the claimant can prove that taken as a whole it is non-functional, famous and to the extent it incorporates other registered marks it is famous separate and apart from the fame of those registered marks. *See* 15 U.S.C. § 1125(c)(4), as amended. **Answer A** is clearly incorrect (trade dress can qualify for dilution protection). **Answer C** is correct in referencing the need for the trade dress to be considered as a whole, but omits the Revision Act's requirement that the trade dress be famous *apart from* the incorporated independently famous "Glory" mark (that mark cannot "carry along" the trade dress with its fame). **Answer D** includes both those requirements and the facts' statement that it is non-functional satisfies the third, making it the best answer.

257. **Use in commerce.** As with all federal statutory rights, the dilution right is limited by Congressional power to legislate under the commerce clause. *See* Topic 1 — Justifications and Sources of Trademark Law. The Trademark Dilution Revision Act of 2006

did eliminate the somewhat confusing requirement that the challenged use be a "commercial use in commerce," replacing it with the more traditional articulation "use of a mark or trade name in commerce." *See* 15 U.S.C. § 1125(c)(1), as amended. The "commercial use" language now appears as the exception/defense "any noncommercial use" found in 15 U.S.C. § 1125(c)(3)(C), as amended. Presumably it contemplates "free speech" uses not explicitly covered by the fair/nominative use and news reporting exceptions.

258. **The answer is A**. To bring an anticybersquatting action under Lanham Act § 43(d) (15 U.S.C. § 1125(d)) does not require the mark be famous as stated in **Answer B** (fame is required for a federal dilution action), merely that Algarve "own the mark" (**Answer A**). **Answer C** and **Answer D** set out the two additional core requirements of the action — bad faith intent to profit from the mark and registration, trafficking (transactions including sales, loans, licenses and other transfers for consideration) or use of a domain name. *See* Lanham Act § 43(d)(1)(A)(i) & (ii).

NOTE: Although not required, showing the "Ocotillo" mark was famous prior to Fred's registration of the domain name does affect the action. The statute expressly includes the additional right to prevent dilution of a famous mark caused by the registration. *See* Lanham Act § 43(d)(1)(A)(ii)(II).

NOTE: Anticybersquatting remedies apply to marks used in "domain names." Lanham Act § 45 (15 U.S.C. § 1127) defines a domain name as "an alphanumeric designation which is registered with or assigned by any domain name registrar, domain name registry, or other domain name registration authority as part of an electronic address on the Internet."

259. **No**. Lanham Act § 43(d)(1)(A) only requires that the action be brought by "the owner of a mark," not that the mark be registered. A federal registration does, of course, help prove that ownership.

260. **Yes**. The Anticybersquatting Consumer Protection Act added the anticybersquatting rights to the Lanham Act effective November 29, 1999. Section 3010 of that Act expressly states that it applies "to all domain names registered before, on or after the date of enactment of this Act" so it makes the rights applicable to all domain registrations whenever they were registered. However, the Act also states that the damage remedies are not applicable to "the registration, trafficking, or use of a domain name before that date." So although the date of Fred's registration is not relevant to his liability for cybersquatting, it will limit Algarve to equitable remedies if it was before November 29, 1999.

261. **The best answer is B**. Lanham Act §§ 43(d)(1)(A)(ii)(I) & (II) (15 U.S.C. §§ 1125(d)(1)(A)(ii)(I) & (II)) set out two tests which define the required nature of the domain name. Subsection (I) says that for marks which are distinctive at the time of registration of the domain name, the domain name must be "identical or confusingly similar to [the] mark." Subsection (II) addresses marks which were famous at the time of registration, stating that in such cases the domain name must be "identical or confusingly similar to or dilutive of [the] mark." Consequently, it is not sufficient that

the domain name merely contain the mark, so **Answer A** is too broadly stated (although probably not by much in most cases). The courts have held that the "confusingly similar" to standard in anticybersquatting actions is not the same as the "likely to cause confusion" standard for infringement, so **Answer C** is incorrect. *See Sporty's Farm L.L.C. v. Sportsman's Market, Inc.*, 202 F.3d 489 (2d Cir. 2000), *cert. denied*, 530 U.S. 1262 (2000); Question 262 below. Although the statute requires, as stated in **Answer D**, that the domain name have been registered after the mark became distinctive (necessary for ownership of the mark), that is not sufficient for liability. Therefore, although **Answer B** omits the test applicable to famous marks (which includes "dilutive of"), its reference to "identical or confusingly similar to" is the best answer.

NOTE: Presumably the reference to "dilutive" in Lanham Act § 43(d)(1)(A)(ii)(II) includes both dilution by "blurring" and dilution by "tarnishment" which are now distinct claims under the Trademark Revision Act of 2006. *See* Topic 14 — Dilution.

NOTE: Lanham Act § 43(d) expressly call out "a personal name which is protected as a mark" for protection against domain name cybersquatting. In addition to those rights (which are governed by the terms applicable to all forms of cybersquatting), the Anticybersquatting Consumer Protection Act provided in § 3002(b) (codified in Lanham Act § 47 (15 U.S.C. § 1129)) a special right against "any person who registers a domain name that consists of the name of another living person, or a name substantially and confusingly similar thereto, without that person's consent, with the specific intent to profit from such name by selling the domain name for financial profit to that person or any third party." That right allows persons whose names have been used to sue even if their name is not protected as a mark, but is only available regarding domain names registered on or after November 29, 1999 (the effective date of the Act).

262. **Algarve will very likely win.** Although the "identical or confusingly similar to the mark" standard isn't entirely clear, on these facts most courts will ignore the ".com" portion of the domain name as merely indicating the commercial registry and find the domain identical to the mark. (If the ".com" is not ignored the identical standard seems impossible to satisfy and, therefore, irrelevant, which would be contrary to the canons of statutory construction). In making the comparison, it is likely that the "sight, sound, meaning" and strength of the mark considerations which apply to "likelihood of confusion" will provide guidance are not relevant as the test is not "likely to cause confusion," but merely the relationship between the domain name and the mark. *See Sporty's Farm L.L.C. v. Sportsman's Market, Inc.*, 202 F.3d 489 (2d Cir. 2000), *cert. denied*, 530 U.S. 1262 (2000). Similarity of goods, channels and other market factors are not relevant as to whether or not a consumer is likely to view the mark and the domain name as "confusingly similar."

263. **The best answer is C.** Lanham Act § 43(d)(1)(A)(i) (15 U.S.C. § 1125(d)(1)(A)(i)) requires that the mark registrant (or its authorized licensee — others are not liable under Subsection (d)(1)(A)) have a "bad faith intent to profit from [the] mark . . ." making **Answer D** which explicitly tracks that language the best answer. **Answer B** refers to the part of the "nature of the domain name test" which applies only if the domain name

is not identical to the mark, while **Answer A** misstates that test, so neither is the "other core requirement." Finally, anticybersquatting "bad faith intent to profit from the mark" is more specific than "bad faith use of the mark," so **Answer C** is incorrect. *See* Topic 18 — Remedies.

264.   **It uses a "factors" analysis applied to the particular facts and circumstances**. In simple terms the plaintiff mark-owner must demonstrate that the defendant does not have a legitimate reason for incorporating the mark in the registered domain name. Lanham Act § 43(d)(1)(B) (15 U.S.C. § 1125(d)(1)(B)) sets out a non-exclusive list of considerations to aid in making that determination. The Section lists factors favoring the defendant because they offer legitimate reasons for use of the mark in the domain name, such as defendant having an interest in the mark (its *bona fide* use on different products), fair use (*see* Topic 16 — Defenses: Fair Use, Nominative Use Parody/Free Speech), noncommercial use — free speech (use in commentary on the brand or other matters). It also lists indicators of bad faith, including intent to divert consumers, the offer to sell the domain name to the owner or others without any legitimate use by defendant, a pattern of behavior indicative of bad faith (multiple domain registrations of domain names incorporating others' marks and/or related offers to sell) and providing false or misleading contact information in connection with the domain name registration.

265.   **The best Answer is A**. As on the facts Algarve owns rights to the "Ocotillo" mark and the domain name is likely to be found identical to the mark, the key issue is whether Algarve can show that Fred's registration involves a "bad faith intent to profit from the mark." Applying the factors set out in Lanham Act § 43(d)(1)(B) (15 U.S.C. § 1125(d)(1)(B)), none provide strong evidence of that intent. For example, there is no obvious intention to divert consumers, no offer to sell the domain name to Algarve (yet) and no indication the registration is part of a pattern of bad faith registrations. Regarding **Answer C**, Algarve may attack Fred's use as tarnishing or disparaging its mark (factor (V)) — which is clearly is. That effort will likely fail, however, as good faith "criticism sites" (whether or not providing accurate information) will be protected under nominative fair use and free speech defenses provided (as in this case) there is no likelihood of confusion as to source, sponsorship or affiliation. **Answer B** and **Answer C** are classic *bona fide* uses — the former using the mark in its normal primary rather than trademark meaning (for the cactus species) and the latter may involve use as a mark (the facts leave it unclear as to whether it is merely part of a trade name or also used as a mark) but the domain name clearly was selected in reference to Fred's non-competing business (on the facts Fred likely has independent rights in the mark for car repair services at least in his area of use). That leaves **Answer A**. Fred will point to his actual use of the site. However, the posting of his home photos does not explain how he came to select "Ocotillo" as the domain name. Further inquiry may show that Fred lives on Ocotillo Street, that is the name he has given his home or some other personal connection. Or it may show that he has merely posted the photographs as a cover for an eventual attempt to sell the mark to Algarve. In all events, **Answer A** is the best of the four answers on the facts given.

266.   **The best answer is D**. The Anticybersquatting Consumer Protection Act provided for injunctive relief under the same terms as for regular infringements (under Lanham Act § 34(a) (15 U.S.C. § 1116(a))), monetary damages under the same terms as for regular infringements (under Lanham Act § 34(b) (15 U.S.C. § 1117(a)). *See* Topic 18 — Remedies. It also expressly authorized the court to order forfeiture or cancellation or transfer of the domain name to the plaintiff mark-owner (Lanham Act § 43(d)(1)(C) (15 U.S.C. § 1125(d)(1)(C)) and, as an alternative to actual damages and profits an award of statutory damages of "not less than $1000 and not more than $100,000 per domain name as the court considers just" (Lanham Act § 35(d) (15 U.S.C. § 1117(d)). **Answer A** and **Answer B** both understate the available remedies, so are incorrect. **Answer C** lists the statutory damages as in addition to regular damages and profit awards, so overstates the available relief. **Answer D** states it correctly in the alternative, so is the best answer.

267.   **The best answer is A**. Section 3010 of the Anticybersquatting Consumer Protection Act makes damage remedies unavailable for violations based on registration, trafficking, or use of a domain name before its November 29, 1999 effective date. Fred's registration occurred before that date, so Algarve will be limited to equitable relief as stated in **Answer A**. **Answers B, C** and **D** all include monetary damages so are incorrect.

NOTE: Federal anticybersquatting rights are in addition to federal claims for infringement (likelihood of confusion) or dilution and state law claims of all kinds (infringement, dilution and unfair competition). Consequently, if the related requirements are meet monetary damages may be available against a cybersquatter under those causes of actions even for pre-effective date registrations. *See* Topic 18 — Remedies.

268.   **The best answer is C**. Lanham Act § 43(d)(2) (15 U.S.C. § 1125(d)(2)) authorizes civil *in rem* actions against the domain name (rather than the domain name's owner) provided that the owner of the mark is either (i) not able to obtain *in personam* jurisdiction over [a known defendant owner of the domain name] or (ii) through due diligence has not able to find [that owner defendant]. **Answer C** and **Answer D** reflect these two options; however on these facts the problem is not jurisdiction but identification making **Answer C** the best answer. **Answer A** is an alternative approach but involves a suit against the owner rather than an *in rem* action (and would require eventual discovery of the owner's name and personal jurisdiction before the suit could proceed on the merits), so it is incorrect. The ICANN Uniform Domain Name Dispute Resolution Policy (UDRP) is not judicial in nature, being triggered by the registration contract with the domain name registrar. So **Answer B** is also incorrect.

269.   **The best answer is D**. Lanham Act § 43(d)(2)(A)(ii)(II) (15 U.S.C. § 1125(d)(2)(A)(ii)(II)) requires that the plaintiff use due diligence to find the person who would have been served as the defendant, as stated in **Answer D**. That Section does go on to state that upon such a showing, service of process may be effected by "sending a notice of the alleged violation and intent to proceed" to the registrant "at the postal and email address provided by the registrant to the registrar" (**Answer B**)

and publishing notice of the action "as the court may direct promptly after filing of the action" (**Answer C**). *Id.* However, neither of those actions is sufficient to bring the suit if the predicate showing of due diligence to find the defendant has not been made (which arguably includes both sending the notice and post-filing publication and, perhaps, additional search efforts). **Answer A** is part of the problem in such *in rem* actions, but not the central issue, which is the inability to find the defendant.

270. **The best answer is B**. The federal courts have exclusive jurisdiction over the *in rem* anticybersquatting cause of action under the Lanham Act (28 U.S.C. §§ 1331 & 1138), so neither **Answer C** nor **Answer D** is correct. Lanham Act § 43(d)(2)(A) (15 U.S.C. § 1125(d)(2)(A)) provides that such *in rem* actions jurisdiction lies in the judicial district in which "the domain name registrar, domain name registry, or other domain name authority that registered or assigned the domain name is located," so **Answer B** is the best answer (despite its omission of the other two options). The location of the defendant (**Answer A**) is irrelevant in an *in rem* action which is brought against the domain name itself.

NOTE: The alternative basis for an *in rem* Lanham Act action is inability to gain personal jurisdiction over the domain name owner/registrant despite knowing who it is and how to find (and even serve) him. The basic problem usually is that the mere existence of the domain name in a local jurisdiction is not sufficient to meet the minimum contacts requirement for personal jurisdiction. The courts have, however, found that as the cybersquatting dispute is over the property (domain name), the location of that property (apparently considered the situs of the registrar) in the jurisdiction provides sufficient local interest to support *in rem* jurisdiction. *See Harrods Ltd. v. Sixty Internet Domain Names*, 302 F.3d 214 (4th Cir. 2002). There is some confusion regarding whether Lanham Act § 43(d)(2)(C) (15 U.S.C. § 1125(d)(2)(C)) which defines the *situs* of the domain name is intended to expand the possible jurisdictions in which the action may be brought.

271. **The best answer is A**. The courts have interpreted the *in rem* action as supporting claims for anticybersquatting, infringement and dilution based, *inter alia*, on the language of Lanham Act § 43(d)(2)(A)(i) (15 U.S.C. § 1125(d)(2)(A)(i)) which authorizes claims for violation of *any* rights of a [registered] mark, or protected under subsection (a) [unregistered marks] or (c) [the dilution cause of action]. The same requirements apply to the merits of each cause of action despite the *in rem* nature of the lawsuit. *See Harrods Ltd. v. Sixty Internet Domain Names*, 302 F.3d 214 (4th Cir. 2002). So **Answer A** is better than **Answer B** or **Answer C**. There is no need for the mark to be federally registered, so **Answer D** is incorrect.

NOTE: There is a reasonable argument that the "territorial nature" of trademark law does require the mark involved be protected under United States trademark law. *Cf. Barcelona.com v. Excelentisimo Ayuntamiento de Barcelona*, 330 F.3d 617 (4th Cir. 2003).

272. **The best answer is D**. Lanham Act § 43(d)(2)(D)(i) (15 U.S.C. § 1125(d)(2)(D)(i)) relief is expressly limited to "forfeiture or cancellation of the domain name or the transfer

of the domain name to the owner of the mark." Arguably that same Section involves a form of injunctive relief — orders to the domain name registrar to maintain the status quo and give the court control over the domain name — but that relief only applies during the pendency of the action to facilitate the ultimate order. So **Answer D** is better than **Answer C**. No monetary awards, including statutory damages are permitted, so neither **Answer A** nor **Answer B** is correct.

NOTE: Although the *in rem* action can include claims for infringement and dilution, the limitation on available relief makes it of limited value for those purposes. *See Barcelona.com v. Excelentisimo Ayuntamiento de Barcelona*, 330 F.3d 617 (4th Cir. 2003).

273. **The best answer is A**. Paragraph 4(a) of the UDRP requires the complainant not prove the domain name is identical or confusingly similar to the complainant's mark (**Answer B**), that the respondent has no legitimate interests in the domain name (**Answer C**) and that the domain name was registered and used in bad faith (**Answer D**). As with the Lanham Act anticybersquatting action it is not necessary to prove that the domain name is likely to cause consumer confusion in the "source identification" sense required for traditional infringement, so Pine need to prove **Answer A**.

274. **The best answer is C**. There will be little problem showing that the domain name is identical or confusingly similar to the mark (the ".com" is ignored), so **Answer A** will be easy to prove. The absence of any prior connection and the lack of implementation of the associated website both indicate that BigGuys' has no legitimate interest in the domain name (**Answer D**). Arguably those facts combined with the false contact information also support the contention that BigGuys' registration was in bad faith (perhaps indicating its intent to block Pine's registration or to ultimately sell the domain name to Pine for a profit; UDRP Para. 4(b)) (**Answer B**). The UDRP's additional express requirement of bad faith *use* of the domain name (**Answer C**) raises significant problems on these facts. When the respondent has taken action — such as offering to sell the domain name — that "use" triggers URDP Paragraph 4(b) which lists it as evidence of both bad faith registration and use. In this case, however, BigGuys has engaged in no affirmative use. At least one panel has found that merely sitting on the domain name may be sufficient "passive use" to satisfy the requirement when the registration itself appears to be in bad faith. These special difficulties make **Answer C** the best on these facts.

275. Lanham Act § 32(2)(d) (15 U.S.C. § 1114(2)(d)), added as part of the Anticybersquatting Consumer Protection Act of 1999, authorizes a suit for "reverse domain name hijacking" — including a claim that a UDRP proceeding resulting in cancellation or transfer of the plaintiff's domain name registration was erroneous under law (or stated in the affirmative that the plaintiff's registration of the domain name was lawful and, most particularly, did not constitute cybersquatting).

NOTE: Although the UDRP involves "mandatory" arbitration, UDRP Para 4(k) authorizes court proceedings even after the conclusion of the UDRP arbitration proceeding and expressly defers to the judicial outcome.

276. The action is brought under the Lanham Act so the court will apply federal trademark law (including the anticybersquatting provisions of Section 43(d) (15 U.S.C. § 1125(d)) rather than the UDRP.

Pine will argue that: (1) it owns the "Spruce" mark as evidenced by its federal registration and that the mark's validity is not challengeable on these facts in light of its incontestable status, (2) when the ".com" is ignored, the mark and the domain name are identical, and (3) under the Section 43(d) "factors" analysis BigGuys' failure to use the site eliminates any indication of bona fides despite its related clothing line and its offer to sell the mark for such a considerable amount indicates both BigGuys was aware of Pine's "Spruce" mark and a bad faith intent to profit (if not at the time of registration, at the time of "trafficking in" the domain name). BigGuys will respond that (1) its registration was made in connection with the launch of its clothing line, (2) at the time, and currently, it holds non-conflicting rights in the "spruce" mark based on its clothing line use, (3) the offer for sale occurred after the clothing line's seasonal launch made it less useful to BigGuys leading them to approach Pine in good faith as a potentially interested purchaser and (4) although the amount requested reflects a substantial absolute profit, it is not a considerable amount in the context of the parties' businesses and constitutes fair value of the website address.

On these facts I believe that although BigGuys' case is not without problems, it is the more convincing (especially as Pine carries the burden of showing bad faith intent to profit). Consequently, the court should order re-transfer of the domain name to BigGuys.

NOTE: The courts have held that even when parties from different countries are involved (as is likely in Internet situations), as the suit arises under the Lanham Act the relevant law for determining the parties' rights is United States (not foreign) trademark law. *See Barcelona.com v. Excelentisimo Ayuntamiento de Barcelona*, 330 F.3d 617 (4th Cir. 2003). Ignoring foreign law raises the distinct possibility of conflicting decisions by foreign courts, a situation that has in fact materialized. Those conflicts have hardly been satisfactorily. Practically, the outcome is currently driven by the fact that most core domain registrars and registries (.com, .org) are located in the United States and are therefore subject to United States court orders. As non-domestic registrars become more prevalent other solutions will be required.

NOTE: The *Barcelona* court also held that as the UDRP proceeding was essentially private contractual law making, it owed no deference to (and generally give no weight to) the arbitrators' decision and reviewed the matter de novo.

277. **The best answer is D**. The "Amber Ale" mark raises a host of distinctiveness problems. *See* Topic 3 — Basic Distinctiveness: The Spectrum of Distinctiveness; Word Marks Including Acronyms and Foreign Words. It might be argued that the phrase is generic for yellow-colored pale ales so **Answer A** could have been an issue. The most likely argument would have been between its classification as descriptive or suggestive. That classification determination would have resulted in the mark being treated either as inherently distinctive (suggestive) or requiring evidence of secondary meaning to prove distinctiveness (descriptive) making **Answer B** and **Answer C** relevant to the registration of the mark. Because on the facts the mark clearly has been used as a mark in (interstate) commerce, **Answer D** would not have been an issue.

      NOTE: The registration of descriptive marks, such as this one, raises a significant competitive concern — in this case the use of the descriptive terms "amber" and "ale" on other producers' beer products. Trademark law's resolution of that problem is the subject of the following Questions.

278. **The best answer is A**. Prosit's federal registration gives it constructive nationwide use of the mark and related geographic priority over *all* uses subsequent to the date of its registration, whether adopted in good faith or otherwise. *See* Topic 9 — Registration: Constructive Use and Intent to Use. Consequently, neither Smallbeers' lack of knowledge (**Answer B**) nor its limited geographic use (**Answer D**) will protect it from a finding of infringement (although they may affect the remedies, *see* Topic 18 — Remedies). Additionally, the incontestable status of the mark makes a claim of invalidity based on descriptiveness (**Answer C**) unavailing. *See* Topic 12 — Registration: Incontestability. However, the mark's descriptive nature is relevant to Smallbeers' argument that it is only using the word "amber" in its product marking to describe the actual color of its beer, making **Answer A** the best answer.

279. **The best answer is C**. The doctrine that permits use of another's mark merely to describe a characteristic of one's own product (in this case the color of Smallbeers' pale ale) is called "fair use," so **Answer C** is correct. Although "good faith" is implicated in "fair use" (more in the Questions below) that is not the name of the doctrine, so **Answer B** is incorrect. Nominative use refers to a species of "fair use" which permits third-party use of another's mark in reference the *mark owner's products*. That is not the case on these facts (Smallbeers is referring to its own product), so **Answer D** is incorrect (again, more below). **Answer A** has nothing to do with fair use, being a phrase the Supreme Court used to describe restaurant décor when discussing the functionality of trade dress (product packaging, product design and, perhaps, décor as a tertium quid — a third

kind of trade dress). *See* Topic 5 — Distinctiveness: Non-word Marks, Colors and Trade Dress.

NOTE: It is important to distinguish between trademark and copyright "fair use." Although they have the same name they involve different issues and have very different requirements. *See* Question 281 below.

280.   **It is about appropriate cost-benefit balance**. Trademark law permits the user of a descriptive term to obtain trademark protection upon a showing of secondary meaning. *See* Topic 4 — Distinctiveness: Inherently; Secondary Meaning; Never. However, although secondary meaning means that consumers might be confused by third party adoptions of the mark (they associate the presence of the mark with the mark owner's particular product's characteristics), the mark still retains its primary "descriptive" meaning. That means the mark can *also* legitimately provide accurate information regarding other products which have that characteristic or use. In this case, for example, because secondary meaning exists, consumers have made a trademark connection between the phrase "amber ale" and Prosit's particular pale ale product. They, therefore, will expect beer bearing that mark to have the same characteristics as Prosit's pale ale. However, Smallbeers' pale ale is also yellow colored and use of the word "amber" does accurately describe the product to consumers. The fair use doctrine is trademark law's effort to find a balance allowing both general informational uses of the phrase — as a mark uniquely distinguishing and identifying Prosit's product *and* to describe the color of Smallbeers' pale ale. *See Brother Records, Inc. v. Jardine*, 318 F.3d 900 (9th Cir. 2003).

NOTE: Although the fair use doctrine is firmly entrenched in trademark law the Lanham Act only references it in Section 33(b)(4) (15 U.S.C. § 1115(b)(4)) as a defense to incontestable marks: ". . . . [U]se . . .which is descriptive of and used fairly and in good faith only to describe the goods or services of such party . . . ." The Lanham Act is not interpreted, however, as a stand alone regime, but as a supplement to the trademark common law. Consequently, although the Act clarifies how common law doctrines interact with specific new provisions of the federal law (e.g., an incontestable registration), the lack of a general reference does not mean the doctrine is not otherwise generally applicable. *See* Topic 1 — Justifications and Sources of Trademark Law.

281.   **The best Answer is A.** *Trademark* "fair use" is very different than *copyright* "fair use." **Answer A** states one kind of use that supports copyright fair use — use of the material for criticism or commentary of the original work. Although "commentary" (particularly parody) is a trademark defense it is distinct from trademark fair use, which permits even commercial competitive use of a mark on another's product provided it is being used only in its descriptive sense. Consequently, it is irrelevant to Smallbeers' fair use defense that the mark is or is not being used to comment on Prosit or its product (or anything else). What does matter is that Smallbeers is using the mark to accurately describe Smallbeers' own product, so **Answer B** is clearly relevant, while **Answer A** is not. When a claimed descriptive use causes consumer confusion the courts may not recognize the defense (*see* Question 282 below), so **Answer C** is also relevant. Finally,

for the fair use defense to be necessary, Prosit must have valid trademark rights in the "Amber Ale" phrase. Specifically, the mark's incontestable status (**Answer D**) eliminates a descriptiveness validity challenge meaning the "fair use" doctrine is necessary to avoid infringement.

282. **The best answer is B**. Although consumer confusion is clearly relevant to the fair use defense its precise role remains unsettled. In *KP Permanent Makeup v. Lasting Impression I*, 125 S.Ct 542 (2004) the Supreme Court held that the fair use defense is not negated by the existence of *some* confusion and, in particular, the defendant is not obligated to show its use will not cause confusion. So **Answer C** and **Answer D** are both incorrect. The Court also indicated, however, that confusion did remain a relevant consideration but did not clarify at what point it became determinative. So **Answer A** is incorrect and **Answer B** accurately expresses the current state of the law.

NOTE: The Restatement (Third) of Unfair Competition, § 28 (1995) uses an objective test. Under that approach the "fair use" confusion question is not whether some particular consumers are likely to be, or even actually, confused, but whether the defendant's use would confuse the "reasonable" consumer under the circumstances. The Court's position in *KP Permanent Makeup* arguably goes further — that even some confusion by *reasonable* consumers may be permissible provided it is not substantial. In all events, either test indicates that the owner of a descriptive mark may be forced to live with fair "descriptive" uses even when they may cause some actual consumer confusion.

283. **The best answer is B.** The Lanham Act § 33(b)(4) (15 U.S.C. § 1115(b)(4) language requires that the mark be "used fairly *and in good faith* only to describe the goods or services." So the defendant's motivations — both regarding knowledge of the mark and intent to confuse — are clearly a relevant consideration and **Answer A** is incorrect. However, it is unclear how that evidence affects the outcome. Because the statute makes "good faith" a requirement it might mean that subjective intent to confuse is determinative — either its presence **Answer D** or, more likely, by its absence **Answer C**. However, that approach does not seem helpful to achieving the doctrine's purpose of reconciling consumer reliance on the mark as a mark with permitting accurate, non-confusing descriptive uses. Specifically, neither preventing uses involving clear malevolent intent which cause no confusion nor permitting good faith uses which actually confuses consumers produce the doctrine's intended results. Consequently, the better approach to the "good faith" requirement may be to treat it as important evidence of how a reasonable consumer will likely perceive the use (**Answer B**). On that basis evidence of "bad faith" — Smallbeers clearly knew of Prosit's mark and there is evidence that it intended to confuse — might shift the burden to Smallbeers to show it failed. (Evidence of lack of knowledge or pure heart seem somewhat less relevant — the fair use issue is effects not motivations.)

284. The fair use inquiry focuses on whether consumers are likely to perceive Smallbeers use of the words "amber ale" as descriptive of its beer or as a trademark indication of source. On these facts Smallbeers will likely argue two points. First, it does not use

the mark in its actual form "Amber Ale" but instead as part of the phrase "Smallbeers Amber Pale Ale." Consequently, consumers may not even make a connection to Prosit's mark. Second, even should consumers recognize the mark, the specific use of the two words "amber" and "ale" in "Smallbeers Amber Pale Ale" make it clear to a reasonable consumer that "amber" is modifying "pale ale" to indicate its color and "ale" is being used exclusively in its generic sense to refer to the beer genus (class) of pale ales.

Prosit will also make two arguments. The first will seek to rebut Smallbeers' interpretative points, pointing out that although the mark appears as part of a phrase, "Amber" and "Ale" are both emphasized by capitalization. Coupled with the demonstrated strong secondary meaning of the "Amber Ale" mark, it is likely that consumers will see those words as connected to the mark. Additionally, Prosit may reinforce its argument by emphasizing that the notoriety of its mark in beer circles makes it very likely that Smallbeers was aware of its mark. The absence of significant affirmative steps to avoid confusion (say marking the beer as "Smallbeers, an amber pale ale") in such circumstances is indicative of Smallbeers' bad faith, tipping the balance strongly against it. Prosit's second point involves possible confusion as to "sponsorship or affiliation." Prosit will argue that even if consumers see the word "Smallbeers" as indicating that this particular "Amber Ale" is not actually produced by Prosit, the presence of Prosit's mark will lead consumers to mistakenly assume that Prosit is in some way associated with its production — for example, having authorized Smallbeers or, perhaps, as an affiliate of Smallbeers. *See New Kids on the Block v. News Am. Publ'g Inc.*, 971 F.2d 302 (9th Cir. 1992) (raising the sponsorship issue in the nominative use context).

I think (but reasonable minds can differ) that Smallbeers has the better of the argument. Their interpretation of the particular phrase seems by far the more likely — consumers will see Smallbeers as the manufacturer and amber as an adjective describing the pale ale product. Having made that interpretation, consumers will no longer make any connection to the "Amber Ale" mark and consequently will neither see it as a mark nor assume Prosit is involved in any way, including as Smallbeer's licensor, sponsor or affiliate.

285. **The best answer is D**. The new phrase "Smallbeers Amber Ale" makes Smallbeer's Question 284 argument that consumers will see amber and ale as being use descriptively and generically much less probable. The latter part of the marking is now identical to the Prosit "Amber Ale" mark and very likely to call it to mind. So Smallbeers is unlikely to win the case (**Answer A**). Prosit will likely avoid Smallbeers' fair use defense, but not win on that basis, so **Answer C** is incorrect. The prominent presence of Smallbeers name/mark at the beginning of the marking makes confusion over Prosit's sponsorship/ affiliation more likely than confusion over whether the beer is actually produced by Prosit. Consequently **Answer D** is better than **Answer B** on these facts.

286. It could add an **explicit disclaimer** of any association or connection with Prosit or its product on the label to clarify to consumers that it is using the words "amber ale" descriptively. However, issues would remain regarding the effectiveness of the disclaimer. The first difficulty would be demonstrating that the disclaimer was sufficiently

conspicuous at time of purchase to overcome the prominence of the "Amber Ale" mark. And, even if that were demonstrated there may still be "post-sale" confusion issues where the person drinking (or seeing others drink) the beer may not see the disclaimer. *see* Topic 13 — Infringement: Likelihood of Confusion.

287. **The best answer is D**. The "Smooth Skin" mark is arguably descriptive of the hand cream product. Its incontestable status makes an invalidity attack unavailing, so the central defense will be fair use — PGS is using the words "fairly and in good faith only to describe its product." The **Answer A** slogan, "PGS's Argos cream gives you smooth skin," is clearly fair use. The words "smooth skin" are used only in their descriptive sense, identifying the results of the use of the separately marked "PGS Argos" hand cream product. The lack of capital letters in **Answer B** makes it unlikely that a reasonable consumer will see the words "smooth skin" in their Miracle trademark sense — the logical reading being descriptive. **Answer C** is more problematic. Capitalizing the two words makes them standout in the sentence and, therefore, likely to call the mark to mind. A logical interpretation is that Miracle's product is being produced or distributed by PGS, either raising confusion as to source or sponsorship/ affiliation issues. PGS could, however, argue that all the words in the sentence are capitalized and, therefore, consumers viewing the phrase as a whole will see the words as descriptive, much like **Answer B**. Although **Answer C** is a difficult case, **Answer D** is even worse and, therefore, the most likely to fail the fair use test. Not only are the words constituting the mark capitalized, but the verb has been eliminated. As a result a reasonable consumer are likely to believe that the words refer to the Smooth Skin mark and that PGS has been authorized by Miracle to make and distribute a product with the related characteristics.

288. **The best answer is D**. Personal name marks raise the same conflict as descriptive marks. In both cases trademark law permits them to serve as trademarks provided secondary meaning has been demonstrated. However, they retain its primary meaning — in this case Renaldo actually is George's last name (**Answer A**) — however, permitting use on that basis alone would generate consumer confusion. The fair use doctrine, similarly, resolves this conflict. Under that doctrine George can use his own name to accurately name (describe) himself as the producer (a form of descriptive use). However, that use cannot cause consumer confusion, either regarding his brother's products or that his brother has sponsored or endorsed his efforts. Consequently, George cannot use "Renaldo" as a trademark on his wines (**Answer B**) as that would lead customers to believe they came from his brother. So he can only use his name "as his family name" to identify himself as the producer — for example, "made by George Renaldo" (**Answer C**). Given his relationship to Fred, that probably is not sufficient. Instead a "fair use" would probably require he go the further step of explicitly disclaiming any endorsement, sponsorship or affiliation by or with his brother. **Answer D** — "clearly identify and distinguish himself from Fred" — is the best answer.

NOTE: All marks which depend on secondary meaning for their distinctiveness raise the "fair use" issue. The analysis is generally the same: clear use in their primary rather than trademark sense, including no implications of endorsement, sponsorship or affiliation.

NOTE: Some courts have further indicated that the fair use doctrine also applies to inherently distinctive marks which have primary meanings. So, for example, the words "movie buff" might be treated as an inherently distinctive suggestive mark when applied to a video rental store, but that would not prohibit others from using the phrase to describe a "motion picture enthusiast." A competitor would, therefore, be permitted to state that renting from their store will "turn you into a movie buff" or that its store "is for the true movie buff." In such situations, however, there arguably is no need for the doctrine as in most instances the use will be at most indirectly associated with the goods or services, meaning the case can be resolved directly by the absence of any likelihood of confusion. The key point may be, however, that fair use might permit the use *despite* the existence of some confusion. *See* Question 282 above, discussing the *KP Permanent* case.

289.   **The best answer is C.** On the facts, LowCost is not using the "Sweet Scent" mark to describe the characteristics, use or results of LowCost's products, so **Answer A** (fair use) is inapplicable. Because there is no evidence that WHYNOT's mark is famous and, in all events, LowCost is using WHYNOT's mark to refer to WHYNOT's related products, the question of dilution is not clearly raised (but see the second NOTE below), so **Answer D** is unlikely to be relevant. The choice between **Answer B** and **Answer C** turns on the fact that the lawsuit is in California and, therefore, in the 9th Circuit. That Circuit (and several others, but not all) have developed a related fair use "sub-doctrine" — *nominative use* — to assess infringement cases in which the alleged infringer uses the mark to identify the *mark owner's* related goods rather than to describe its own. Because LowCost is using WHYNOT's mark to identify WHYNOT's related product, in the 9th Circuit, **Answer C** (nominative use) is a better answer than **Answer B**.

NOTE: A common form of nominative use is in comparative advertising. Although the third party is clearly using the mark in its trade mark sense, it is equally clearly being used to identify the mark owner's particular product.

NOTE: The above dilution analysis reflects the doctrine's core requirements — particularly the need for WHYNOT to show that the Sweet Scent mark is famous. The specific incorporation of "dilution by tarnishment" as a cause of action in the Trademark Dilution Revision Act of 2006, however, raises an interesting interpretative question. Assuming the "Sweet Scent" mark had been famous, the use of a mark holder's own mark by another is "use of a mark" and that mark is technically "similar to the famous mark" — so there is a question of whether a price discounter's use in reference to the mark owner's products "harms the reputation of the famous mark."

290.   **It might be — in the 6th Circuit the best answer would be B.** Although the 9th Circuit nominative use doctrine has been adopted in some other Circuits, it has not been adopted by all. In particular, the 6th Circuit has expressly rejected the doctrine, applying

the traditional likelihood of confusion test to such cases. *See PACCAR Inc. v. TeleScan Technologies, L.L.C.*, 319 F.3d 243 (6th Cir. 2003). That is not to say, however, that the actual outcomes substantively differ. For obvious reasons the "confusion" issues in all "mark owner goods reference" cases do not involve consumers confusing third party goods with those of the mark owner. Instead they turn on sponsorship or affiliation confusion — an issue discussed above in connection with traditional fair use. Consequently, although the test technically differs among Circuits, the nominative use analysis in the Questions below provides good conceptual guidance.

291. **The answer is A**. The point of the nominative use defense (like the fair use defense) is that it permits use of even a *valid* trademark if the requirements are satisfied. So **Answer A** is incorrect. Answers **B, C** and **D** are the three requirements for successfully asserting the defense. *See The New Kids on the Block v. News America Publishing, Inc.*, 971 F.2d 302 (9th Cir. 1992).

292. **YES.** The use of the mark occurs only in the weekly advertisement phrase: "**Sweet Scent** perfumes as much as 80% off suggested retail." There is no other way to identify the particular WHYNOT particular in this situation than by using the "Sweet Scent" trademark. Nor can anything other than the entire mark be used to have the reference clearly identify the product in question. So both the need to use and quantity used (no more than necessary) requirements of the defense are met. Finally, the reference appears in LowCost's weekly advertisement and only indicates that the product is available from LowCost at a deep discount. Little, if anything, in that advertising usage infers either that WHYNOT, which usually sells its product at a premium price, has in any way endorsed or sponsored LowCost's activities or is otherwise affiliated with LowCost.

293. **YES, now there are endorsement, sponsorship or affiliation concerns.** By calling itself The Sweet Scent Emporium, LowCost has gone beyond merely identifying the WHYNOT product it is selling, but identified itself as "the" place to purchase the product. That additional connection may lead consumers to believe that LowCost is an authorized distributor or affiliate of WHYNOT, thus raising endorsement, sponsorship or affiliation concerns.

294. **From worst to best nominative use defense: C (worst), A, D, B (best).** All of the answers provide some nominative use cover and raise some degree of endorsement, sponsorship or affiliation concerns. **Answer C** is, however, the worst; it is a typical reference to an authorized dealer thus carrying strong indications of sponsorship or affiliation. **Answer A** is somewhat of an improvement; although it still raises the same authorized dealership concerns, the mark now clearly serves primarily as an adjective for "repairs" (although the initial capitals arguably make it look like an official title). **Answer D** eliminates the initial capitals and the rephrasing reduces the official title concern, although it does not eliminate the possibility that Jake has been certified as a service provider by the mark owner. **Answer B** most clearly indicates that the mark is being used simply to refer to the vehicle's which Jake's Automotive fixes.

295.   **The best answer is D** (but a close call). Flam might argue that he is using the phrase "Rock-Your-World" in its descriptive sense and therefore is entitled to the fair use defense. However, his use of bold letters to call out the phrase and his connection with the band will most likely lead consumers to identify the phrase as the trademark referring to the band. Consequently, no fair use defense and **Answer C** is incorrect. It is true that Flam was only a member, not "the band" (there were others) and, on the facts, he does not own the mark (undoubtedly for the same reason). However, it is not true that he can never use the mark, so **Answer B** is incorrect. Flam can legitimately use the mark to identify the band with which he was previously associated — a nominative use. It is also correct that there is no way to describe his membership in the particular band without using the mark (**Answer A**). However, there is a good argument that the specific *way* Flam has used the mark (bold, prominent lead-in) goes beyond merely identifying the band leaving the impression that the band is endorsing or sponsoring his tour. That conclusion is reinforced by the unexpectedly large crowds who may have been relying on that connection in the expectation the show would be similar to those of the original band. It's a close call, but in my view **Answer D** is better than **Answer A** on these facts. *See Brother Records, Inc. v. Jardine*, 318 F.3d 900 (9th Cir. 2003).

296.   **The best answer is C** (but it's a close call with **B**, despite judicial authority to the contrary). The problem with the trademark fair use defense (or its nominative use cousin) on these facts is that Gooddeals is not using the marks either to describe Gooddeals' products or to identify products made by the trademark holder. Rather Gooddeals is using the mark on its own goods. So **Answer A** provides no assistance. The existence of the Gooddeals' mark and the disclaimer supports an argument that there is no likelihood of consumer confusion (**Answer D**) at the time of purchase. However, there are significant post-sale confusion issues once the packaging is removed (the tags are likely not visible), so that is hardly a secure defense. *See Au-Tomotive Gold, Inc. v. Volkswagen of America, Inc.* 457 F.3d 1062 (9th Cir. 2006); Topic 13 — Infringement: Likelihood of Confusion. Gooddeals best defenses focus on the fact that consumer's are not buying its products because they come from the trademark owners, but to obtain and display the mark. That supports the **Answer B** "aesthetic functionality" defense (inability to use the mark causes non-reputational disadvantage — *see* Topic 6 — Functionality). However, at least one court has rejected that argument on the grounds that the product/mark was not being purchased for its intrinsic aesthetic merits (the design of the cap or tee-shirt), but because of the mark's reputation. *See Au-Tomotive Gold, Inc. v. Volkswagen of America, Inc.*, 457 F.3d 1062 (9th Cir. 2006). **Answer C** takes Gooddeals defense back to trademark policy basics — to violate a trademark owner's rights requires use of the mark as a mark. Gooddeals could argue that on these facts consumers (including those post-sale) will clearly understand that the mark is not being used as a trademark but as a distinct "product" to show affinity or support for the related sports team. Consequently, protecting the trademark owner takes the regime beyond its legitimate consumer information objectives. *See* Topic 1 — Justifications and Sources of Trademark Law.

297.   **The best answer is C. Answer A,** *trademark* fair use (in contrast to *copyright* fair use), is not an available defense as the magazine is not using the mark to describe its goods.

Answer B, nominative use, is out because the mark is not being used to identify Grandluxe's particular products. On these facts, however, the magazine can reasonably argue that it is not using the mark in its "trademark sense" (**Answer D**). However, although the use clearly does not identify and distinguish a product (not signaling source), it is still being used to invoke its trademark significance — specifically the brand values it connotes. It is, therefore, important to identify a specific reason that the used should be permitted. That justification is found in the First Amendment and freedom of speech — using the mark to express an idea, making **Answer C** the best answer. How to more precisely define when free speech interests are implicated is addressed in the Questions below.

298. **The best answer is D**. Fair use (**Answer A**) is of no help since the use does not describe the tee-shirt. Neither is nominative use (**Answer B**) as the use does not identify Grandluxe's particular products. The central defense is First Amendment free speech, so **Answer C** is correct. On these facts, however, the free speech inquiry can be guided by trademark law's *parody* defense (**Answer D**), which applies when the mark is used to poke fun at, criticize or (notwithstanding the poor fit with the definition of "parody") to comment on the related product, the mark's brand "values" or the mark owner. On these facts there is a good argument that is precisely what the critic is doing — criticizing the brand values of the "Oro" mark.

299. **Some courts say yes** (but that doesn't make it right). Some courts have applied traditional First Amendment doctrine when deciding trademark "parody" free speech cases, including "alternative means of expression." The argument is that trademark owners should not be required to surrender their "property" rights to free speech interests when alternative means of expression are available to make the point. *See Mutual of Omaha Ins. Co. v. Novak*, 836 F.2d 397 (8th Cir. 1987), *cert. denied*, 488 U.S. 933 (1988). There are, however, two counter-arguments which merit consideration. First, on the merits — in the trademark context viable alternatives are unlikely (or very unlikely) to exist making the inquiry of extremely limited value. Effectively commenting on the mark values requires use of the mark (so as to call it to mind), particularly in traditional parody such as the critic's tee-shirt. Stated another way, the trademark's special ability to quickly conjure up and convey the related *brand* "values" (versus the values themselves) makes alternatives ineffective substitutes (imagine the critic putting "Buyers of 'Oro' products are a bunch of freaks that should be stopped" on the shirt). *See International Olympic Committee v. San Francisco Arts & Athletics*, 780 F.2d 1319 (9th Cir. 1986) (Kozinski, J., dissenting). Second, trademark law's limited "source identification" objectives make it questionable that trademarks involve relevant property interests which make an alternative means inquiry necessary. As the critic's use falls outside of the regime's reach and, consequently, the rights granted by the regime, there is no conflict with Grandluxe's property — it simply have no ownership interest affected by that use. *See* Topic 1 — Justifications and Sources of Trademark Law.

300. Although courts have distinguished between commercial and non-commercial use in drawing the free speech line, the appropriate distinction is between uses of the mark

as a mark (to propose a transaction based on the mark's signal of source — commercial use) and uses which do not (uses of the mark not as a trademark — non-commercial use). The latter is a strong indicator that the use involves permissible commentary, while the former indicates possible trademark confusion concerns. *See Mattel, Inc. v. MCA Records, Inc.*, 296 F.3d 894 (9th Cir. 2002), *cert. denied*, 123 S. Ct. 993 (2003) (discussing the distinction in the context of a dilution claim, which specifically articulates the general First Amendment defense in terms of "noncommercial use of the mark" 15 U.S.C. § 1125(c)(3)(C), as amended).

NOTE: Although both implicate free speech concerns, the trademark parody approach to commercial versus non-commercial use is very different from copyright fair use. The latter inquiry counts commercial activity against the parodist as potentially harming the copyright incentive. In contrast, trademark law policy focuses (or should) primarily on the use's source signaling effects, making other commercial benefits from use of the mark less relevant, if relevant at all. *But see* the next Question.

301.   The parody inquiry focuses on social free speech interests in allowing criticism and commentary, so it should be irrelevant what medium the parodist has chosen. That said, the more traditional the medium for commentary, the more likely the use will be perceived as permissible commentary and the more likely the parody defense will be successful. The next Question explores that context issue in more detail.

        NOTE: The same "likely to perceive" argument applies to challenged uses which involve profits (like sales of the tee-shirts) as well. The less "commercial" (in the making money sense) the activity, the more likely it is that the commentary nature of the use will be apparent.

302.   **The best answer is A.** On the above facts Friends intended a parody using the "Muscle" trademark. The problem is that a substantial number of consumers didn't "get" the point and were confused by the advertisement. Although the parody failed for at least some consumers, standing alone that does not mean there is an infringement. **Answer B**, as do some courts, looks to the traditional factors analysis to determine if the parody has *sufficiently* failed to generate the likelihood of confusion necessary for infringement. *See Anheuser-Busch, Inc. v. Balducci Publications*, 28 F.3d 769 (8th Cir. 1994), *cert. denied*, 513 U.S. 1112 (1995). On these facts a factors analysis points toward infringement. That some consumers were confused is convincing evidence of likelihood of confusion, but not necessarily determinative. However, Friends is not only using the identical mark on the same product but by publishing the "advertisement" in off-roading magazines Friends increased the probability that consumers would believe it was real. *Id.* The strong likelihood (if not actual) confusion revealed by the factors analysis makes the parody defense highly problematic; however, it does not fully deal with Friend's intention to parody and the effects of an adverse ruling on chilling free speech. The appropriate balance is, perhaps, found by restating the failed parody analysis. Although traditional factors analysis helps *identify* sufficient failure, the critical issue is whether consumers will see the advertisement as commentary/criticism by a third party or as coming from the trademark owner itself — something akin to fair use's concepts of

endorsement, sponsorship or affiliation indicating confusion over the trademark owner's involvement — thus making the speech "deceptive." Consequently, the "rule" regarding failed parody might be helpfully stated as follows: Either the parodist expressly disclaims involvement by the trademark owner or bears the risk of failure (as perceived by the "reasonable" consumer") despite its good faith intent. *Id.* Under that approach the likelihood of confusion means Friends' parody defense fails (**Answer C**) despite its good faith intent (**Answer D**) and Outdoor wins, not merely because the confusion factors point to a failed parody (**Answer B**) but because Friends took the risk of failure by failing to disclaim Outdoor's involvement (**Answer A**).

303. **The best answer is C.** As the earlier Questions reveal, the courts struggle with various doctrinal articulations of the trademark free speech defense, including permissible commentary/parody (**Answer A**), non-commercial use (**Answer B**), and non-trademark use (**Answer D**). Many commentators point out that true to trademark law's objectives, all of those formulations of the trademark First Amendment inquiry turn on whether in the particular circumstances consumers are likely to be confused (**Answer C**). If so, there is an origin-of-the-speech/source signaling problem and possible infringement. If not, the use falls outside trademark law's concerns and is protected, regardless of whether the use is labeled permissible commentary, non-commercial use or non-trademark use.

NOTE: The "likelihood of confusion" approach clarifies (at least for me) a number of otherwise complex issues. For example, if commentary/parody describes the full reach of the defense then it is difficult to explain how the magazine story in Question 297 qualifies, as the mark is being used primarily to describe the "wealthy" rather than offering any (direct) commentary on the mark or its brand values. However, the broader reach of the confusion inquiry easily extends to such uses; in that context the mark is clearly being used to make a non-trademark relevant point by a third party. Similarly, it reflects the central theme driving the failed parody inquiry in Question 302: is the use in the advertisement likely to be improperly attributed to the mark owner. Finally, it provides an answer to the open issue regarding whether the copyright fair use distinction between *parody* (poking fun, criticizing the work/creator/owner) and *satire* (using the work to comment on something else) should apply in the trademark parody context. Copyright fair use protects the former, but perhaps not the second as a potential interference with the copyright incentive. In the trademark context copyright law's incentive-effects distinction has no particular relevance; for both parody and satire the issue is whether the use will cause consumer confusion.

304. **It makes allocating the burden problematic.** If trademark free speech is treated as an affirmative defense then the defendant bears both the burden of production and proof/persuasion, meaning the defendant must demonstrate that its use qualifies as exempt parody, non-commercial or non-trademark use. If, however, that burden consists merely of showing no likelihood of consumer confusion then it can be convincingly argued that although defendant may have a burden of production, it does not bear the burden of proof/persuasion. To come out otherwise would inappropriately shift plaintiff's obligation to demonstrate likelihood confusion as part of its primary infringement case

to making the defendant prove its absence. *Cf. KP Permanent Makeup v. Lasting Impression I*, 125 S. Ct. 542 (2004) (holding that a defendant claiming fair use has no obligation to show its use will not cause confusion).

305.   **The best answer is B** (the reasoning here is a bit complex so it's worth a careful read, as are the concluding NOTES). The group's use of the "NatureSafe" mark does not describe its service, so the fair use defense (**Answer D**) is irrelevant and, therefore, not a concern (although nominative use is an interesting question, as the group's use arguably refers to Ergo's related products). Nor on these facts is a traditional infringement claim likely to succeed. A factors analysis points away from a likelihood of confusion. Although the name of the organization incorporates Ergo's well-known mark, the more complex and negative grammatical structure of the group's use makes the marks look, sound and mean similarities slight. Although both uses involve "organics/ environmentalism" and are likely to appear in similar "channels" targeting the same consumers, the differences (indeed conflicts) between Ergo's product use and the organization's commentary services use makes "bridging the gap" unlikely — there is little likelihood that a "reasonable" consumer would contribute to the group thinking it was furthering Ergo's produce cause (to say nothing of thinking they were purchasing Ergo's product). So **Answer A** does not raise significant concerns.

The group's major problem is a claim for dilution, which specifically does not depend on a likelihood of confusion. On the facts Ergo has a famous mark and will prevail if it can show that uses such as the group's will "whittle away" (blur) the distinctiveness or "harm the reputation" or tarnish the "NatureSafe" mark. *See* Topic 14 — Dilution. Both seem reasonable arguments. The group's use not only creates two distinct impressions of the mark in consumers' minds, but its negative message is explicitly intended to undermine its positive connotations. *See Mattel, Inc. v. MCA Records, Inc.*, 296 F.3d 894 (9th Cir. 2002), *cert. denied*, 123 S. Ct. 993 (2003). As a result, the free speech defense becomes crucial. In this situation, the federal dilution statute states that defense in very specific terms: "noncommercial use." 15 U.S.C. § 1125(c)(3)(C). As a result the group must show that its use qualifies under that doctrine (**Answer B**) not merely the more general articulation of "permissible commentary" (**Answer C**) or "no likelihood of confusion." That means to prevail it must be prepared to discuss the distinction between "proposing a transaction" and "other uses" and, most particularly, showing that its use is "not *purely* commercial speech." *Id.*

NOTE: The point here is that although "likelihood of confusion" is a useful rule of thumb, in law the technical details matter. So it is important to understand not only the essence of the trademark free speech defense (no confusion), but to be prepared to discuss the specifics of the parody, non-commercial use and non-trademark use articulations as well.

NOTE: The same no likelihood of confusion, possible diluton, free-speech (parody/ commentary, non-commercial or non-trademark use) defense analysis applies to "gripe" websites (for example, those in the form "NatureSafeSucks.com.")

306. **The answer is C.** The mark accurately describes the related product — it is a "Zistro" television. Therefore, it can be argued that either nominative use (**Answer B**) permits Eric's use or, alternatively, his use will not cause a likelihood of consumer confusion (**Answer D**). However trademark law's "exhaustion" or "first sale" doctrine (**Answer C**) specifically addresses this particular circumstance, expressly permitting the resale of a "genuine" trademarked good under the trademark (a genuine good is one which was approved and either marked by or with the authorization and under the control of the trademark owner). The doctrine terminates the trademark owner's control over marked genuine goods upon their initial authorized distribution (directly or indirectly) into the marketplace; which is why the doctrine is called the "first sale" doctrine or, alternatively, "trademark exhaustion" (referring to the "using up" of the owner's right of control over the mark). In part, the first sale doctrine reflects the fact that the sale of genuine marked goods does not cause confusion because the consumer obtains precisely what the mark promises — a good having the signaled characteristics (albeit obviously used in this case). The additional policy justification is avoiding too much control by trademark owners over market transactions in their goods. The doctrine ensures trademark law's objectives are accomplished by permitting the mark owner to control initial affixation of the mark (either directly or indirectly) thus guaranteeing authenticity, but thereafter promotes market efficiency by allowing free circulation of the good.

As a consequence of the first sale doctrine's more specific application, "nominative" use generally refers to mark uses other than its affixation to the related product; for example Eric's advertisement on Craig's list which accurately identifies the item for sale as a "Zistro" television. Eric is not using the mark to describe his own goods, so "fair use" and **Answer A** is not relevant.

NOTE: Unlike copyright law's "first sale" doctrine which explicitly appears in the Copyright Act (17 U.S.C. § 109); the federal Lanham Act makes no reference to the doctrine which arises from and applies via common law.

307. **The best answer is C.** The goods involved are clearly genuine and Zistro has authorized their first sale to its retailers. However, the first sale doctrine, like much (but not all) of trademark law, reflects as its core concern avoiding consumer confusion. Consequently, although it applies to the resale of genuine unaltered "Zistro" products such as those involved in this case, it only does so if there is no likelihood of consumer confusion. So **Answer B** is better than **Answer A** and **Answer D** is incorrect. However, TVsForLess' use of the name "The Zistro Preferred Center" raises a substantial likelihood that consumers will believe that Zistro Corporation (the owner of the "Zistro" trademark") has endorsed, sponsored or authorized (stands behind) TVsForLess' sales.

That confusion (much like that arising in fair use cases, see Topic 16 — Defenses: Fair Use, Nominative Use, Parody/Free Speech) probably eliminates TVsForLess' ability to rely on the first sale doctrine notwithstanding that the goods are genuine, making **Answer C** the best answer on these facts.

308. **The best answer is B.** The first sale doctrine is again made relevant by the authenticity of the products being sold so **Answer D** is incorrect. As a result of the new store name and the disclaimers there is virtually no (never say "never" in the law) likelihood of purchaser confusion (including initial interest confusion). Additionally, post-sale confusion is not an issue on these facts. Those seeing the goods post-sale will correctly assume the product is a genuine "Zistro" television. *See* Topic 13 — Infringement: Likelihood of Confusion. Therefore, **Answer B** and **Answer C** raise a non-issue. On these facts **Answer A** — first sale doctrine permits the sales — is now the most likely outcome.

309. **The best answer is B.** Although the mere presence of genuine marked goods may lead some consumers to assume Zistro Corporation is involved the courts generally find that the first sale doctrine applies unless the seller has done "something more" to imply the mark owner's connection. The argument is that reasonable consumers understand genuine goods are sold by both affiliated and unaffiliated retailers and will not assume mark owner involvement without some additional indicator. Absent such an indicator (usually an affirmative action by the alleged infringer) no express disclaimer is required to claim first sale protection. *See Sebastian International, Inc. v. Longs Drug Stores Corporation*, 53 F.3d 1073 (9th Cir. 1995); *Matrix Essentials, Inc. v. Emporium Drug Mart, Inc.*, 998 F.2d 587 (5th Cir. 1993). The name of the TVsForLess store does not raise any concerns nor are there other uses of the mark or mark owner's name (such as in signs or advertisements) which might indicate Zistro Corporation's involvement. So **Answer C** and **Answer D** are incorrect. **Answer A** is correct, but **Answer B** is the better answer because it explicitly addresses why possible consumer confusion arising from the mere presence of the goods is ignored on these facts.

310. **The best answer is D.** Flashy Dan's has modified the goods prior to sale and there is no indication to the consumer that the change has been made. As a result the trademark signal no longer accurately signals the characteristics of the producer/mark owner's goods. Therefore, the central requirement of the first sale doctrine — that the consumer gets what the mark promises — is not satisfied. *See Nitro Leisure Products, L.L.C. v. Acushnet Co.*, 341 F.3d 1356 (Fed. Cir. 2003). The absence of the mark owner's consent is relevant to that failure, so **Answer C** is correct. However, **Answer D** more precisely identifies the specific problem with relying on the first sale doctrine — the resulting consumer confusion — so it is the best answer. **Answer A** is incorrect as the genuine nature of the underlying garment does not eliminate the confusion arising from Flashy Dan's *additions*. Similarly irrelevant is that the trademark owner originally affixed its trademark (**Answer B**) to the goods, as it did so *prior* to the modifications.

311. **No.** The objective of trademark law is to ensure the mark's presence accurately indicates the characteristics of the good so consumers can make efficient, informed purchase

decisions. Consequently, the crucial first sale concern is the consumer confusion about what the mark *means* given Flashy Dan's undisclosed modifications, not whether the consumer is getting less or more value than the mark promises.

NOTE: Market theory strongly supports avoiding substituting an independent decision about the quality of the "deal." Trademark law's "job" is not to assess whether a consumer is or should be happy with the goods carrying the mark, it is merely to ensure that the mark consistently conveys accurate information about the underlying good. In this case, for example, consumers may be "put off" by Flashy Dan's additions (despite the resulting higher market value) and mistakenly assume those additions reflect a general characteristic of all similarly marked goods.

312.   **The best answer is D**. The first sale concern is that modifications will cause consumer confusion regarding the mark. Neither the fact that consumers know that the seller is Flashy Dan's nor the addition of Flashy Dan's mark eliminates that possibility which arises from the presence of the manufacturer's mark, so neither **Answer A** nor **Answer B** is particularly helpful to a first sale defense. The notice and disclaimer in **Answer C** expressly clarifies to the purchaser that the mark does not accurately identify the genuine product's characteristics, explains what in particular is different and that the change was made independently by Flashy Dan's without the involvement of the trademark owner. The result is to eliminate the confusion caused by the modifications despite the presence of the mark. The solution's shortcoming is possible post-sale confusion. *See* Topic 13 — Infringement: Likelihood of Confusion. Although the original purchasers will clearly understand the modification's deviation from the mark signal subsequent purchasers or observers of the good in the market will not. **Answer D** addresses both pre-and post-sale confusion by affixing the notice and disclaimer directly to the product, making it the best answer. *See Champion Spark Plug Co. v. Sanders*, 331 U.S. 125 (1947). The action is not dispositive, however, as it might still be argued that Flashy Dan's changes are so substantial that "it would be a misnomer to call the article by its original name" despite the disclaimer — more in the Question 322 below. *Id.*

313.   **The best answer is C.** The crucial first sale issue is whether under the circumstances the use of the mark will likely mislead/confuse consumers. That concern is not raised when the product has not been modified (**Answer A**) — the consumer gets precisely what the mark indicates. On these facts, however, Little Bottles' repackaging arguably constitutes a modification of the original *product*; although the shampoo is the same, the external appearance and size of the package have changed. Similarly, although the trademark accurately describes the shampoo contents (**Answer B**) and Little Bottles' use is nominative (**Answer D**) — the label referring to the genuine product — the repackaging issue raises the argument that the overall "product" is not genuine. Consequently **Answer C** which incorporates the requirement that the shampoo be genuine and notice to the consumer that it has been modified (repackaged) is the best answer. *See Prestonettes, Inc. v. Coty*, 264 U.S. 359 (1924).

NOTE: If repackaging seems a very technical approach to product modification, it is worth bearing in mind that some state statutes treat repackaging as a sufficient reason to restrict and even prohibit product sales, the *Prestonettes* and *Champion* decisions notwithstanding. *See* Question 314.

314.   **The best answer is C** (but getting there is a bit complicated). The problem in this case is that Little Bottles' repackaging caused an *additional* modification in the product which is not disclosed. The application of the first sale doctrine to such situations is a bit murky (to me at least). Some judicial decisions, including one by the Supreme Court, seem only to require that consumers can connect the product defect to the disclosed modification (so they know whom to blame, the modifier or the mark) to trigger first sale protection. *See Prestonettes, Inc. v. Coty*, 264 U.S. 359 (1924) (if rebottling of perfume causes deterioration and public was adequately informed of who did the rebottling, then first sale applies when the public is likely to "connect the dots" — my words not the Court's); *Enesco Corp. v. Price/Costco Inc.*, 146 F.3d 1083 (9th Cir. 1998) (to same effect when notice is given that the product has been repackaged with regard to the possibility of resultant chipping of the product). Other decisions can be read as separately inquiring into whether consumers will recognize the defect as a defect as opposed to believing it is a normal characteristic of the marked product. *See Matrix Essentials, Inc. v. Emporium Drug Mart, Inc.*, 988 F.2d 587 (5th Cir. 1993). For my money, the two are inter-related: consumers discover the product "doesn't work" as well as they hoped and in determining whether the poor performance is caused by a defect or it simply reflects a bad product they consider what they have been told about independent modifications. If they make a causal connection between the modification and the performance, they recognize the product characteristic is not signaled by the mark and are not "confused." Ergo the first sale defense applies.

Applying that test to these facts: Because the shampoo fails to lather and clean as a result of the rebottling it is not enough to *win* on the first sale defense that Little Bottles gave notice of its repackaging. So, although that notice is relevant to the first sale inquiry, **Answer D** is incorrect as stated. Similarly, **Answer B**, failure to give notice of the change resulting from the rebottling, puts the first sale defense in jeopardy but standing alone it does not mean Little Bottles' *loses*. The defect is indeed latent on purchase and consumers will only discover the shampoo does not work upon use (**Answer A**). However, that the consumers only eventually discover the shampoo doesn't lather or clean does not destroy Little Bottles first sale defense. The crucial question is whether consumers' recognize that characteristic is a defect caused by the rebottling or simply assume it is characteristic of products bearing the mark. **Answer C** states that test and is the best answer.

315.   **The best answer is D**. The issues of required notice of independent modification and connection to potential defects to such modifications only arises if the fundamental predicate condition of the first sale defense has first been satisfied — that the goods involved started life as *genuine* goods. To be genuine the goods need to have met the trademark owner's quality standards required for them to bear the trademark. In this

case the goods were specifically rejected by the mark owner, so affixing the mark, even with disclosure of that rejection, misleadingly indicates the goods were at least initially genuine. *See El Greco Leather Prods. Co., Inc. v. Shoe world, Inc.*, 806 F.2d 392 (2d Cir. 1986). So **Answer D** is correct and **Answers A, B** and **C** are not.

316. **No.** The pizzas sold by Trescheap are genuine and the first sale doctrine is triggered by Parnelli's sale to its authorized dealers. These facts involve the "quality control" exception — the failure to adhere to the trademark owner's requirements which affect the quality of the goods. On the facts the failure to dispose of the pizzas adversely affects their taste. Consumers will note the poor taste but are likely to assume that is simply the way "Nona" pizzas taste, making the presence of the mark misleading. The confusion from this alteration (although not intentionally "made" by Trescheap) is enough to prevent reliance on the first sale defense.

317. **Maybe**, but probably yes. The crucial question is whether consumers will "connect" the poor taste to Trescheap's disclosure of its "modification" of Parnelli's storage standard. Given the strong relationship between length of storage and taste the relationship is likely to be made. The question, however, remains that at some point "notice of modification" is insufficient because the nature of the change makes it "a misnomer to call the article by its original name." *See Champion Spark Plug Co. v. Sanders*, 331 U.S. 125 (1947); Question 322 below. Arguably a "fresh" frozen pizza with freezer burn has been so fundamentally altered that it simply no longer should be called a "Nona" pizza.

318. **Yes.** The "quality control/modification" exceptions to the first sale doctrine are designed to prevent consumer confusion not give trademark owner's absolute control over resale of their products following the first authorized distribution. On these facts there is no substance to the claim that Trescheap's non-adherence to Parnelli's requirement had any effect on the products' characteristics. Consequently, Trescheap is now selling a genuine good under the related mark and the first sale doctrine protects its resales.

319. **This is a matter of public policy debate, but probably yes.** Assuming there is no contracting defect (incapacity, fraud, unconscionability) Parnelli's agreements with its distributors are enforceable under contract law unless it violates some public policy. The central issue in such commercial dealings, therefore, is whether trademark law's first sale doctrine should be treated as merely an inter parties default which is alterable by agreement or as an unwaivable policy. That issue remains hotly debated, but absent independent antitrust concerns a producer's distribution arrangements are generally upheld by the courts. On these facts, it is unlikely that Parnelli has any significant market power and its concerns about maintaining the integrity of its distribution chain to enhance its inter-brand position makes it highly likely it can enforce the no-sale provision; although if the only justification is an untrue freshness concern, there could be a problem.

320. **The best answer is D**. The products are genuine in the sense that they were originally approved and had the trademark applied by the trademark owner. However, Power

Mary's has modified the used goods and although they appear "like new" they are not in fact up to that standard. The trademark on the goods is, therefore, likely to lead consumers to mistakenly believe the cars possess (or reflect) the characteristics of a new product and associate those characteristics with the mark. As a result the central requirement of the first sale doctrine — that the consumer is getting what the mark promises — is not satisfied. So **Answer D** is the best answer. *See Nitro Leisure Products, L.L.C. v. Acushnet Co.*, 341 F.3d 1356 (Fed. Cir. 2003);. **Answer A** is incorrect as the doctrine does not permit modification of genuine goods when the result is to confuse consumers. **Answer B** is incorrect because the modifications are inconsistent with the trademark signal. Finally, there is nothing beyond the presence of the mark to indicate involvement of the trademark owner, so **Answer C** is not a relevant first sale concern on these facts. *See* Question 309 above.

321. **Add a notice of its modification**, including some indication on the cars themselves. Under *Champion Spark Plug Co. v. Sanders*, 331 U.S. 125 (1947) leaving the trademark on a repaired or reconditioned genuine product does not prohibit reliance on the first sale doctrine provided the consumer is given clear notice that a third party has independently performed repair and/or reconditioning. The further requirement that reasonable notice be attached in some fashion to the product is designed to ensure that no post-sale confusion arises from removal of notices on packaging or at the point of sale. *See* Question 312 above.

322. **The best answer is C.** The first sale doctrine does permit refurbishment (**Answer D**), including modifications (**Answer A**) provided consumers receive notice of the changes sufficient to avoid confusion between the product received and the characteristics properly associated with the mark. In this case the notice seems adequate as it very specifically explains that the parts substitution has occurred, so **Answer B** does not raise major concerns. However, modifications can go too far, so substantially changing the identity and quality of the good that it is no longer reasonable to "call it by its original name [mark], even though the words 'used' or 'repaired' were added." *Champion Spark Plug Co. v. Sanders*, 331 U.S. 125 (1947); *Bulova Watch Co. v. Allerton Co.*, 328 F.2d 20 (7th Cir. 1964). Although that determination obviously turns on the specific facts, there is a good argument that a car "reconditioned" with inferior parts (particularly engine or mechanical parts) has been so significantly altered in ways which are difficult for the consumer to appreciate, even with notice, that it is no longer reasonable to assume that allowing it to carry the original mark will not produce confusion. *Cf. Nitro Leisure Products, L.L.C. v. Acushnet Co.*, 341 F.3d 1356 (Fed. Cir. 2003) (Newman, J., dissenting) (repainting a damaged golf ball so alters and/or disguises the changed characteristics as to make the mark misleading even when it is clearly labeled as "used/refurbished"). **Answer C** is the best answer.

NOTE: In these cases the relevant consumers' level of expertise may be important to determining whether the modifications are sufficiently material to invoke the "changed identity and quality" exception to noticed modifications. For example, if Power Mary's only reconditioned very rare cars sold only to automotive experts, then a court might find there was no likelihood of confusion.

323. **Legally no, but practically perhaps yes.** As explained in the answer to Question 311 above, the first sale issue is not whether consumers ultimately receive a good or bad deal in an objective sense, but whether continued use of the trademark is likely to cause consumer confusion regarding the relationship between the actual characteristics and those properly conveyed by the presence of the mark. As a technical legal matter, therefore, it should make no difference if a product longer having the same "identity or quality" as genuine marked goods diminished or improved quality. However, as a practical matter if a court focuses on the consumer rather than the complaining trademark owner, it may be more likely to find differences resulting in "improvements" are not sufficient to have so *substantially* altered the good as to make the mark misleading. On the other side of this argument, it will be important to note that merely because the consumer appears to have received a windfall that is not necessarily the case. For example, it may be far more costly to operate, maintain or repair the higher quality good. Consequently, trademark law (and first sale) should focus on ensuring consumers are not confused and can make their own informed choices, not if they "got a good deal."

324. **The best answer is C.** On these facts it is hard to argue that any consumer confusion will arise. The owners of the cars are modifying their own goods via Power Mary, a third party clearly unaffiliated with the manufacturer, so will hardly be confused by Power Mary's delivery of the customized vehicle bearing the trademark. It might be argued that post-transaction confusion might arise on the owner's resale of the customized vehicle as a result of Power Mary's modifications, but it seems more appropriate to view that confusion as caused by the car owner's resale rather than Power Mary's activities. The best analysis, therefore, is that Power Mary's activities do not implicate confusion over the mark because Power Mary's isn't using it as a mark in commerce and the issue of infringement never arises. On that basis, **Answer C** is the best answer and **Answers A, B** and **D** are, like the first sale doctrine itself, inapplicable on the facts.

325. **The best answer is C.** The facts raise the complex issue of "gray goods" or "parallel" imports" — that is goods which are genuine in the sense that they have been approved and marked by the trademark owner, but somewhere other than the United States and then imported into the United States. The question is far from resolved. The leading case involved a Customs seizure and the prohibition on importation of goods bearing infringing marks under Lanham Act § 42 (15 U.S.C. § 1124), not infringement alone. The court focused on whether use of the mark on the "foreign" goods was likely to be misleading or confusing to United States consumers (consistent with trademark law's primary focus notwithstanding the difficult fit with the literal statutory language). That issue was resolved by determining whether the imported product differed materially from the local product. *See Lever Brothers Co. v. United States of America*, 877 F.2d 101 (D.C. Cir. 1989). Under that test, the only clearly helpful answer is **Answer C** which involves a difference between the products (albeit one which may not be material). **Answer B**, which states there is no difference, is of no help against the first sale defense. The "affiliate exception" raised by **Answer A** applies the first sale doctrine if imported

goods are put on the market by the trademark owner or by an affiliate posing problems for BigDeals. **Answer D** reflects the "trademarks are territorial" approach; in essence that application of a trademark to products outside the United States in no way implicates its United States rights (including their exhaustion). A purely territorial approach, however, formalistically ignores consumer confusion as the centerpiece of trademark law — if the products are the same from the same producer, there seems little harm to trademark law's objectives; precisely the position taken by the *Lever Brothers* court.

NOTE: The "converse" of the affiliate exception mentioned above is a legitimate basis for finding infringement. If two entirely independent producers sell the same product under the same mark, one domestically and the other in a foreign market, there is little likelihood of confusion *within* either market. If, however, the foreign producer begins importing its product into the United States there will be substantial consumer confusion over the "source" of the competing products. And, even if the products are identical, because they come from independent producers there is no guarantee that will continue to be the case. Consequently, the one producer/owner per trademark rule must be invoked and importation barred.

NOTE: International law leaves the question of transnational exhaustion to local law, meaning each country is free to make its own determination, which not surprisingly vary considerably. The current United States position (material difference) is outlined in the answer above.

326.   **The best answer is A**. Lanham Act §§ 34(a) and 35(a) (15. U.S.C. §§ 1116(a) and 1117(a)) set out the primary remedies available in a federal trademark infringement action. Section 34(a) provides for injunctions and Section 35(a) for "(1) defendant's profits, (2) any damages sustained by plaintiff and (3) the costs of the action" as well as awards of attorneys' fees. Not all of these remedies will granted in every case as injunctions, profits, damages and costs are subject to "principles of equity" and attorneys' fees are limited to "exceptional" cases. There are several additional remedies not listed in any of the above answers (for example, statutory damages for use of counterfeit marks (Lanham Act § 35(c) (15 U.S.C. § 1117(c)), destruction of counterfeit (and perhaps other) goods (Lanham Act § 36 (15 U.S.C. § 1118)) and related to correcting registration status — including cancellation, rectification of registrations or restoration of cancelled marks (Lanham Act § 37 (15 U.S.C. § 1119)). As none of the answers contain those "extra" considerations or remedies, **Answer A,** which tracks the basic Lanham Act remedies, is the best answer, because **Answers B, C** and **D** all omit one or more of them. The following questions explore the related details.

NOTE: State trademark infringement remedies generally follow the Lanham Act but can vary in important ways. The following Questions focus on the Lanham Act, but will point out any important differences.

NOTE: A federal lawsuit under the Lanham Act can be brought for either registered marks under Lanham Act § 32 (15 U.S.C. § 1114)) or for unregistered marks under Lanham Act § 43(a) (15 U.S.C. § 1125(a)). *See* Topic 13 — Infringement: Likelihood of Confusion.

327.   **The best answer is C**. Both Lanham Act §§ 34(a) and 35(a) (15. U.S.C. §§ 1116(a) and 1117(a)) explicitly apply to registered and unregistered marks, so **Answer A** is incorrect. Although the basic remedies (injunctions, damages, profits, attorneys' fees) apply to both there are some additional remedies (for example, regarding counterfeit marks) and specific exceptions (for example, the marking/notice requirement prohibiting damages without actual knowledge) which only apply to registered marks. So neither **Answer B** nor **Answer D** is correct, making **Answer C** the best answer.

328.   **The best answer is B**. Injunctions are the preferred remedy in trademark infringement cases. Lanham Act § 34(a) (15 U.S.C. § 1116(a)) does speak in terms of a court having "the power to grant injunctions" (in lieu of "shall") and the decision to do so is subject to "principles of equity." That means that the court must consider the traditional factors governing issuance of injunctions (especially after the Supreme Court decision in *eBay v. MercExchange*, 126 S. Ct. 1837, 164 L. Ed. 2d 641 (2006), which, although a patent case clearly indicated the Court's view that intellectual property injunctions should be

treated in the same way as other kinds of injunctions). In almost every traditional trademark infringement case those factors will dictate issuing an injunction directing discontinuation of the infringer's confusing use. Although a compulsory, royalty bearing license might rarely reflect an appropriate balancing of the equities between the parties, permitting defendant's continued use will almost always directly contradict trademark law's primary "public interest" objective of avoiding consumer confusion. Additionally, by permitting continued violation the mark owner risks harm to its reputation (and the content of its mark's information signal) as a result of having lost control over its mark. Neither problem is readily addressed by other remedies, including money damages — making a finding of irreparable harm/inadequacy of monetary damages very likely. Consequently, the basic "rule of thumb" is that a prevailing trademark owner is very likely (if not more) to obtain a permanent injunction at the conclusion of the case, as stated in **Answer B**. **Answer A** and **Answer C** are both too tentative. **Answer D** inaccurately requires a showing of "exceptional circumstances" (the test for an award of attorneys' fees, not an injunction).

329. **The best answer is D**. Although permanent injunctions will generally be issued, the "principles of equity" requirement as well as the statutory admonition that its purpose be "to prevent violation of [the plaintiff's trademark rights]" constrain the terms. Lanham Act § 34(a) (15 U.S.C. § 1116(a)). Two key considerations are that the injunction gives reasonable notice of what is prevented and that the prohibition goes no further than reasonably necessary to prevent the violation (confusion). **Answer A** is too vague and should be rejected on the first ground. **Answer B** is probably simultaneously too narrow and too broad. It is too narrow because it only covers use of the "Vanti" mark, not derivations which may also cause confusion (the same argument might be made regarding the related products issue; *see* Topic 13 — Infringement: Likelihood of Confusion). It is too broad because it prevents use in all geographic territories while lack of a federal registration limits No-Motors rights to its areas of use (including consumer associations and perhaps reasonable expansion; *see* Topic 8 — Use: Product/ Service and Geographic Reach (Footprint)). **Answer C** addresses the too narrow concern (although it remains subject to claims that it is too vague; the courts are split on this issue) but it does not resolve the geographic over-expansiveness problem. **Answer D** addresses both issues making it the best answer of the four choices — although reasonable arguments can be made that it suffers from vagueness as well as "related products" under-inclusiveness.

NOTE: Courts have held that injunctions can prohibit behavior beyond the technical reach of the plaintiff's trademark rights in order to create a buffer or safety zone. Although that restricts the defendant from otherwise legal activities and the courts repeatedly assert that injunctive relief is remedial not punitive, the extra prohibition is justified on the grounds that infringement having been found, the defendant must accept the consequences of needing to ensure it is fully abated and does not re-arise in the future. Additionally, although the action will be brought in a particular court, courts can (and do) issue injunctions with effect beyond their geographic jurisdiction as reasonably necessary to accomplish the remedial objective.

NOTE: Another common example of equitable mitigation involves use of marks which are based on secondary meaning (descriptive marks, geographic marks and personal names). In such circumstances the injunction may prohibit defendant's use "as a mark" but allow fair and good faith use in the primary sense; for example to describe the goods' characteristics, geographic origin or to identify a person with that name as their producer. Such permitted uses may include the requirement that an express disclaimer of any mark owner endorsement, sponsorship or affiliation. *See* Topic 16 — Defenses: Fair Use, Nominative Use, Parody/Free Speech.

330. **The best answer is C**. The argument for issuing a preliminary injunction (preventing use of the mark before a final determination of infringement) is that if the defendant's use is ultimately found infringing the public will have suffered confusion (**Answer A**) and the mark owner harm to its reputation and mark message for that entire intervening period of time. Conversely, if infringement is not found, then the defendant has been inappropriately required to incur the inefficiencies of changing the mark as well as prevented from engaging in robust competition (**Answer B**). Because the court must consider both public interests and find an appropriate balance on the facts, **Answer C** is the correct answer. The relative hardships suffered by the parties are relevant to making that determination, but do not dictate the outcome (additionally, that inquiry tends to focus more on the individual parties with only an indirect consideration of the public interest). Consequently, **Answer D** is not as good an answer.

331. **The best answer is C**. In trademark case the courts consider the traditional factors governing issuance of preliminary injunctions. Albeit articulated differently in the different circuits, they generally consist of: probable success on the merits (**Answer B**), irreparable harm (inadequacy of monetary damages), preservation of the status quo (**Answer A**), balance of the hardships (**Answer D**) and interests of third parties (in particular, the public). Although all are relevant considerations to ensure an appropriate balance between avoiding confusion and interfering with efficient competition many courts require a relatively high degree of certainty of probable (clear, substantial likelihood) success on the merits as stated in **Answer C**. *See Brookfield Communications, Inc. v. West Coast Entertainment Corp.*, 174 F.3d 1036 (9th Cir.) 1999); *Tom Doherty Assocs. v. Saban Entertainment*, 60 F.3d 27 (2d Cir. 1995).

If the plaintiff makes a strong but less certain showing (likelihood of success) then the other factors — most particularly the balancing of the hardships — play a much larger role in the determination particularly as issuing a preliminary injunction will require the defendant to either leave the market or change its mark, in effect giving plaintiff full relief prior to an actual determination on the merits. (As a practical matter if a preliminary injunction does issue most trademark cases settle as there is little point for a defendant to both change its mark and continue to fight for the right to use the abandoned mark).

332. Once the plaintiff shows a clear or substantial likelihood of success on the merits the remaining factors follow in somewhat bootstrap fashion from that showing. The court

normally will presume resulting irreparable harm in the form of consumer confusion and harm to the mark owner's good name and reputation will follow. Regarding balancing of the hardships, the issue is frequently dismissed by the observation that given the strength of plaintiff's case, the defendant has brought the resulting harms on itself. Finally, "maintaining the status quo" is interpreted to mean the market situation prior to defendant's contested and now very likely confusing/infringing use causing risk of serious public harm, not the parties' situation before the lawsuit was filed.

333.   **The best answer is A.** The answer depends the strength of Oscelot's case on the merits, which in turn depends on the likelihood of confusion. A factors analysis (*see* Topic 13 — Infringement: Likelihood of Confusion) produces the following strong argument for infringement on the facts: Although not identical the marks are extremely similar in sight, sound and meaning. The initial "K" and the plural in Stationers' "Kats" mark does little to differentiate it from Oscelot's "Cat" mark, particularly as "Cat" is arbitrary making it a strong mark. The products are identical (in fact the very products covered by Oscelot's registration) and, because the two companies are competitors, undoubtedly sold in the same distributional channels, advertising in the same media and target the same consumers. Finally, it is difficult to believe that as a competitor Stationers' was unaware of Oscelot's mark (which has been not only in use but registered for five years as reflected by its incontestable status) adding, if not bad faith as least suspicion to Stationers' legitimate objectives in adopting the mark. As a finding of infringement is almost certain, irreparable harm both to Oscelot and the public (confusion) will be presumed and a preliminary injunction is extremely likely, making **Answer A** the best answer.

334.   **The best answer (in my view) is B**. Preliminary injunctions, like all injunctions, are equitable in nature. That means that the related considerations of unclean hand and laches are relevant to the decision. *See Brookfield Communications, Inc. v. West Coast Entertainment Corp.*, 174 F.3d 1036 (9th Cir.) 1999). On these facts Oscelot has waited a long time after discovering what appears to be a relatively obvious infringement to act. It might be argued that the delay was designed as a "set up," allowing Stationers to become significantly invested in the "Kats" mark so as to cause maximum disruption. If Oscelot did not care enough to take immediate action (laches) or affirmatively intended a "surprise attack" (unclean hands), then the court must seriously consider whether despite Oscelot's probability of success there is any need or equity in urgently intervening rather than letting the litigation take its normal course. But in the world of litigation one year is not a tremendously long delay (the courts speak of laches as involving "a lengthy period of time") and, in all events, determination of reasons and motivations requires further examination into the specific facts. *Id.* Although on the given facts things look unpromising it is hard to be more definitive that "unlikely" at this point (**Answer B**). **Answer A** is too optimistic, while **Answer C** and **Answer D** jump to what are, at this point anyway, unjustified conclusions.

NOTE: The effect of laches in particular, but also unclean hands, is different regarding the grant of a permanent injunction following a finding of infringement. In such cases, consumer confusion tips the balance in favor of granting injunctive relief despite the delay or motivations of the plaintiff mark owner. It may, however, affect the terms of the injunction — for exampling leading the court to grant additional time for compliance or even the right to sell off remaining inventory under the old mark.

335. **The best answer is D**. Although taking quick action has avoided all actual harm (including consumer confusion) trademark infringement and the related remedies are triggered by the *likelihood* of consumer confusion; the point being to *avoid* harm before it arises. Both preliminary and permanent injunctions are entirely consistent with that objective, so even absent a showing of any actual harm either is available if the necessary possibility/probability of confusion is demonstrated (**Answer D**).

336. In addition to the normal concerns affecting the issuance of pre-final infringement determination injunctions there are now First Amendment free speech considerations which may further increase the reluctance of a court — in particular that the injunction constitutes a prior restraint.

337. **The best answer is B**. Lanham Act § 34(d)(1)(B) (15 U.S.C. § 1116(d)(1)(B)) defines a "counterfeit mark" as "a counterfeit of a mark that is registered on the principal register in the United States Patent and Trademark Office for such goods or services . . . and that is in use, whether or not the person against relief is sought knew such mark was so registered . . . ." Lanham Act § 45 (15 U.S.C. § 1127) defines "counterfeit" has "a spurious mark which is identical with, or substantially indistinguishable" from, a registered mark. Bean Blossom holds a federal registration on the "Scriz" mark for pens and other writing implements so it satisfies the registration requirements of Section 34(d)(1)(B). **Answer B** states the other requirement, showing that Duo's mark is "indistinguishable" (identical or substantially indistinguishable) — something which is easily done on these facts involving identical marks on virtually identical goods, making **Answer D** incorrect. The statutory definition neither requires "bad faith" or even knowledge of the federal registration, so **Answer A** and **Answer C** are also incorrect.

338. **The best answer is D**. Lanham Act § 34(d) (15 U.S.C. § 1116(d)), added in 1984, expressly does cover the seizure of counterfeit goods *and* related records. So **Answer B** is incorrect. The extraordinary pre-trial nature of the seizure action makes a central showing that without the seizure the plaintiff will suffer immediate and irreparable harm (**Answer D**). That harm may arise from the distribution of the goods in light of their particularly confusing nature (counterfeits) but more likely it involves the probability that the defendant will secret or destroy the evidence (goods and/or records) or disappear before any effective legal action can occur. Section 34(d) does sets out a number of additional requirements, including the posting of an appropriate bond(**Answer C**). However, mere posting of a bond is insufficient to obtain the order. Finally, because the order issues prior to a final determination of infringement **Answer A** is not correct (although the required showing the mark is "counterfeit" demonstrates a strong likelihood of infringement, it is not a final determination).

339. **No.** Lanham Act § 34(d) (15 U.S.C. § 1116(d)) expressly requires the mark be registered. However, the courts have issued seizure orders in claims involving unregistered marks under Lanham Act § 43(a) (15 U.S.C. § 1125) when merited by the circumstances, including satisfaction of the statutory procedural safeguards. *See Pepe, Ltd. v. Ocean View Factory Outlet Corp.*, 770 F. Supp 754 (D.P.R. 1991).

340. **The answer is C.** Lanham Act § 35(a) (15 U.S.C. § 1117(a)) specifically lists an accounting of defendant's profits (**Answer A**), damages suffered by the plaintiff (**Answer B**) and costs of suit (**Answer D**). Although the Section does provide for trebling of damages, it specifically states that such awards "shall constitute compensation and not a penalty." The courts have generally interpreted this to mean that the Lanham Act precludes awards of punitive damage awards (**Answer C**). *See* Restatement (Third) of Unfair Competition § 36, comment n (1995).

341. **No (bit of a trick question, sorry).** The language of Lanham Act § 35(a) (15 U.S.C. § 1117(a)) does mean that punitive damages are not (technically) available under a federal cause of action. However, they can be recovered under some state trademark and/or unfair competition laws. Consequently, if Orange (as many plaintiffs do) joins a state claim to its federal cause of action, punitive damages can be awarded. Additionally, as discussed in the following questions, despite the express statutory language the courts' implementation of the Lanham Act's trebling provision makes it arguable that there is a punitive element to such awards.

      NOTE: Although there is considerable overlap in the basic remedial approaches under federal and state trademark law because the federal statute does not preempt state law it is important to remember they can differ. The following Questions focus on the Lanham Act provisions as a way to illuminate the basics but will also note when remedial differences exist.

342. **The best answer is A.** The courts take a "tort" approach to determining damages for the harm suffered by the plaintiff — that is the defendant should compensate for all injuries caused to plaintiff by its infringement. Consequently, that inquiry focuses on causation (**Answer B**) and proof of the fact (**Answer C**) and amount of harm (**Answer D**). Unlike contract law, forseeability is not directly relevant (although innocent infringement may mitigate some portions of the monetary relief, particularly an accounting for defendant's profits, as discussed in the Questions below). **Answer A** is, therefore, the least relevant of the four answers (bad faith is used to infer confusion, not vice versa).

343. **The best answer is D.** The courts are something less than clear regarding the role of proof of actual confusion. It is certainly reasonable to argue, as some courts do, that without some evidence of actual confusion at best harm is only speculative (and thus should not be awarded) and at worst did not occur (the defendant's actions having been stopped before likely confusion matured into actual harm). Under that logic **Answer A** is better than **Answer B**. However, bad faith is sometimes used as a proxy for proof of harm — creating a presumption that defendant succeeded in its design — thus

relieving the plaintiff of the obligation of offering proof of actual confusion. *See George Basch Co., Inc. v. Blue Coral, Inc.*, 968 F.2d 1532 (2d Cir. 1992). So **Answer D** is a better answer than **Answer A** (always required). As there is no requirement of bad faith in order to collect monetary compensation for damages actually suffered by the infringement, **Answer C** is incorrect (bad faith is used to infer confusion, not vice versa).

344. Although the "plaintiff must prove both the fact and amount of damages," the courts recognize that "proof of actual damage is often difficult." *Lindy Pen Company, Inc v. Bic Pen Corporation*, 982 F.2d 14000 (9th Cir. 1993). Consistent with the Lanham Act § 35(a) (15 U.S.C. § 1117(a)) reference to "equitable principles," most courts hold plaintiff to the tort law requirement of reasonable certainty, not definitive proof of causation or an exact quantification of the harm. One mechanism for accomplishing this balance is burden shifting. For example, a court may require the plaintiff only show a reasonable basis to assume causation (say, actual confusion) and a credible basis for quantification of harm (say, its reduction in sales or profit margins during the infringement) and leave it to the defendant to prove that harm did not in fact materialize (for example, by showing other reasons for declines in plaintiff's sales or profits, such as market changes).

345. **The best answer is C**. The courts have allowed all four answers as measures of plaintiff's actual harm; however, an accounting of Duo's profits is the hardest to justify as compensation for actual harm suffered. Profits on Orange's sales lost to Duo (the 75% of Duo's sales Orange would have made) clearly constitute demonstrable harm to Orange, so **Answer A** is non-problematic. An infringement additionally can cause damage to the mark's brand message — in this case as a result Duo's candy's lower quality which consumers have mistaken for Orange's product. So **Answer D** is appropriate, although that harm will be very difficult to quantify in any meaningful way. As opposed to damages for that harm, Orange may seek to ameliorate the problem through corrective advertising (which may be complementary to an injunctive requirement that Duo undertake the same), so those costs (**Answer B**) may be properly awarded (generally the courts use 25% of defendant's own infringing advertising investment as a rule of thumb). Although courts sometimes use the defendant's profits as a proxy for plaintiff's actual harm, in many (if not most) cases such an accounting is more reflective of defendant's gain than plaintiff's actual loss. *See George Basch Co., Inc. v. Blue Coral, Inc.*, 968 F.2d 1532 (2d Cir. 1992). On these facts, for example, such an award would constitute double recovery if added to Orange's lost profits on the 75% of over-lapping sales and would represent a windfall regarding the other 25% of sales which Orange would not have made in any event — because, perhaps, Orange lacked the extra capacity, those sales fell outside Orange's actual geographic market (which may be more limited than its trademark rights under federal registration constructive use) or the sales were generated by Duo's special marketing efforts. Consequently, **Answer C** is the least appropriate as a measure of Orange's actual harm.

NOTE: Courts sometimes also award a reasonable royalty for use of the mark during the period of infringement as part of plaintiff's compensation for harm suffered. Such awards may appropriately reflect lost revenue from third party licensees (including actual and lost potential licensees targeted by a mark owner's licensing program) or from the unauthorized use of the mark by an ex-licensee. In situations where there is no established royalty rate, like this one, courts have expressed under-compensation concerns. That risk can lead courts to intentionally err on "the high side," shifting the risk (now of over-compensation) to the defendant who caused the uncertainty by its infringement.

346.   **The best answer is A.** The accounting-of-profits remedy is a matter of significant confusion in trademark law, with much variation among the Circuits. The following indicates how most courts approach the issue as well as the important exceptions.

Unlike compensatory damages (for actual harm suffered) or injunctive relief, most courts award an accounting of the defendant's profits only on a showing of the defendant's deliberate and willful infringement (**Answer A**). *See George Basch Co., Inc. v. Blue Coral, Inc.*, 968 F.2d 1532 (2d Cir. 1992). Knowledge of a federal registration may be probative of that bad faith but it is not a requirement, making **Answer D** incorrect. Nor is the existence of a federal registration (unlike a Lanham Act claim involving counterfeit marks) so **Answer C** is also incorrect. Finally, although some courts will award an accounting of defendant's profits without proof of bad faith based on proof of actual damages (presumably as rough compensation), those courts also use bad faith alone as an alternative basis for making the award (the Ninth Circuit is an example). Consequently, **Answer B** is not as frequently key to obtaining the award, making **Answer A** the best answer.

NOTE: A few courts, following the Supreme Court's decision in *Hamilton-Brown Shoe Co., v. Wolf Bros. & Co.*, 240 U.S. 251 (1916), award an accounting if the infringer is a competitor of the mark owner (presuming actual harm). Most courts, however, require a showing of bad faith/willfulness even by a competitor, based on the Supreme Court's subsequent decision in *Champion Spark Plug Co. v. Sanders*, 333 U.S. 125 (1947) which they interpret as requiring further assessment of relevant equitable considerations before making the award. *See George Basch Co., Inc. v. Blue Coral, Inc.*, 968 F.2d 1532 (2d Cir. 1992).

347.   **The best answer is B** (but the issue is a matter of substantial doctrinal uncertainty and very lively debate). The courts and commentators have advanced three theories — **Answer A** (ensuring fair compensation of the plaintiff), **Answer B** (preventing unjust enrichment) and **Answer C** (deterring continued and/or subsequent infringement by the defendant and others). Additionally, **Answer D,** which serves as the vehicle for accomplishing deterrence, may reflect the most candid articulation of what motivates many grants of the accounting remedy. If forced to chose, Lanham Act § 35(a) (15 U.S.C. § 1117(a)) offers some assistance. The Section's reference to "equitable principles" supports the ensuring fair compensation and preventing unjust enrichment rationales while the Section's express requirement that any upward adjustments of the profits remedy not reflect punishment argues against explicit punitive and perhaps even deterrence motivations when making the award. Consequently, **Answer A** and **Answer**

B are more consistent with the statutory language than **Answer C** and, most particularly, **Answer D**. For the reasons noted in the answer to Questions 345 and 346 immediately above, the ensuring fair compensation argument (**Answer A**) frequently does not reflect the facts, generally over-compensating the plaintiff. Additionally, the compensation motivation does not logically correspond to the requirement that an award rest on a predicate finding of defendant's willful infringement (the problems of proof leading to under-compensation apply regardless of intent). The bad faith requirement does, however, strongly correlate to the unjust enrichment — disgorgement of ill-gotten gains — justification. In addition, it is sometimes stated that under such circumstances (intent to deceive), the accounting/disgorgement remedy also vindicates the public harm from the deception. As a result **Answer B** is the best (or at least most coherent) rationale.

NOTE: The above should not be read as implying that actual awards are not articulated in terms of, or reflect, the other justifications; they are and do.

348. **The best answer is B**. Lanham Act § 35(a) (15 U.S.C. § 1117(a)) expressly requires Orange (the plaintiff mark owner) only prove Duo's (the defendant) sales. Duo must then prove any applicable reductions ("costs or deductions claimed") to its gross revenue, thus shifting the burden (and difficulty) of disproving economic gain to the infringer. **Answer B** states this rule, making it correct. **Answer A** ignores the burden shifting to defendant and is, therefore, incorrect. **Answer C** and **Answer D** misstate the nature of the accounting remedy *once granted*. Although some courts may require Orange prove it lost sales/profits (actual harm) to obtain an accounting; once an accounting is granted harm to the plaintiff becomes irrelevant. Instead the amount awarded is measured by *defendant's* sales and profits (whether as a "rough" proxy for harm to plaintiff or as an equitable or deterrent/punitive disgorgement).

349. **The best answer is some combination of B and D**. The confused state of trademark damages law again makes a precise answer impossible. Lanham Act § 35(a) (15 U.S.C. § 1117(a)) expressly authorizes an upward adjustment of a profits award by up to three times the actual profits found. But it also states that such an adjustment "shall constitute compensation and not a penalty." *Id.* As a result some courts find that an upward adjustment is only appropriate when required to ensure full compensation (**Answer B**) in light of the related quantification uncertainties (for example, the reputational harm from the inferior quality of Duo's candy). Most courts, however, base the upward adjustments on the defendant's willful infringement which strongly suggests a punitive (and deterrent) objective (**Answer D**). In all events, trebling is not automatic (unlike antitrust law) so **Answer A** is incorrect. Finally, Section 35(a) expressly makes "trebling" applicable to (only) defendant's profits, so **Answer C** is also incorrect.

NOTE: Although a court may increase damages awarded for actual harm proven by the plaintiff that increase is technically made under Section 35(a)'s general mandate that the court consider equitable principals not the specific statutory authorization which only refers to defendant's profits. As a result courts may apply different standards when considering increases in actual damage versus profit awards (generally, using uncertainty for increases in compensatory damages and bad faith for defendant's profits).

NOTE: The Section 35(a) "trebling" limitation does not arise in a state trademark or unfair competition action when the applicable state law authorizes punitive damages. In those cases, the normal punitive damage policy objectives and related tests (including Constitutional limitations) apply.

350. **The best Answer is B**. Lanham Act § 29 (15 U.S.C. § 1111) states that, although otherwise optional, if the owner of a federally registered mark fails to give notice of that registration in the prescribed manner (including in words or using the "R" in a circle) it may not collect profits or damages "unless the defendant had actual notice of the federal registration." As Nateast holds a federal registration for the "Star" mark its failure to give notice means that it can only collect those monetary damages from the date NewMed had actual notice of the registration (usually from the date of the demand letter and, in all events from the date of the lawsuit if properly plead). That limitation applies regardless of whether Nateast can prove it suffered actual harm or NewMed acted willfully. **Answer B** is, therefore, correct and **Answers A, C** and **D** are all incorrect.

NOTE: If the "Star" mark had not been registered then the notice requirements (obviously) and related limitations do not apply, even in a suit brought under Lanham Act § 43(a) (15 U.S.C. § 1125(a)) which provides a federal infringement cause of action for unregistered marks. The interesting question is whether regarding its federally registered "Star" mark Nateast may be able to claim profits and damages for any infringement *prior to* the issuance of its federal registration as well as after NewMed obtained actual knowledge.

NOTE: Suits on trademarks registered under state law are covered by the applicable state law, so the Lanham Act damage limitations for failure to give notice do not apply.

351. **The best answer is A**. Lanham Act § 35(b) (15 U.S.C. § 1117(b)) states that in cases involving the intentional and knowing use of a counterfeit mark a court must *automatically* award treble the profits or damages, whichever is greater, except in extenuating circumstances, as stated in **Answer A**. That mandatory trebling, which appears to be largely punitive/deterrent of intentional counterfeiting, does not depend on an equitable need to fully compensate Nateast, so **Answer B** is incorrect. Additionally, the courts have held that because the definition of a counterfeit mark (found in Lanham Act § 34(d)(1)(B)(i) (15 U.S.C. § 1116(d)(1)(B)(i))) expressly makes defendant's knowledge of the plaintiff's federal registration (which registration is required for counterfeit mark status) irrelevant, the notice provisions of Lanham Act § 29 (15 U.S.C. § 1111) do not apply. **Answer C** (which otherwise correctly states the effect of failure to give proper notice) and **Answer D** (which does not) are, therefore, not applicable on these facts.

NOTE: As the Section 35(b) requirement of the intentional and knowing use of a counterfeit mark makes "good faith" improbable, it is difficult to imagine what "extenuating circumstances" a court might find to avoid the otherwise mandatory trebling in such cases.

352. **The best answer is D** (but only as a technical matter). Actions involving counterfeit marks provide substantially greater remedies. In addition to treble damages (*see* Question 351 immediately above), Lanham Act § 35(b) (15 U.S.C. § 1117(b)) provides for a mandatory award of attorneys' fees (for intentional and knowing use of a counterfeit mark) — **Answer B**. That Section also authorizes the court, in its discretion, to award pre-judgment interest — **Answer C**. Lanham Act § 35(c) (15 U.S.C. § 1117(c)) gives the prevailing plaintiff the option in *any* action involving a counterfeit mark (willful or otherwise) to elect at any time prior to entry of final judgment by the trial court statutory damages instead of actual profits or damages — **Answer A.** (The amount of statutory damages varies considerably depending on willfulness and applies by type not number of actual goods — meaning in this case NewMed would only be liable for statutory damages for each class of infringing machine, not the actual number of infringing machines produced or sold). All of these amounts are payable to the defendant. Although counterfeiting is also a criminal offense (and a significant one, involving fines of up to $5 million and considerable possible jail time (up to ten years)) those awards do not inure to the trademark owner (except indirectly), so **Answer D** is the "best" answer to the question as stated.

353. **The best answer is C.** Lanham Act § 35(a) (15 U.S.C. § 1117(a)) expressly lists "costs of the action" as one element of plaintiff's monetary damages (apparently as a matter of right) and further provides that the court "in exceptional cases may award a reasonable attorney (sic) fee to the prevailing party." **Answer C** most closely parallels that statutory language (costs to prevailing plaintiffs — although the answer says "may," attorneys' fees to the winner in exceptional cases) making it a better answer than **Answers A, B or D.**

NOTE: Costs of the action include the actual court costs (fees) and perhaps other non-attorneys' fees litigation costs such as expert witness fees. The "exceptional cases" requirement for attorneys' fee awards has been interpreted to mean bad faith — for defendants willful infringement and for plaintiffs bringing actions without any reasonable basis merely to harass (abuse of process).

NOTE: As always, state law may differ regarding the parties entitled to costs or fees, what constitutes allowable costs or reasonableness of fees and the circumstances under which costs and fees may be awarded.

354. **The best answer is D.** Under the Trademark Revision Act of 2006 a prevailing plaintiff in a dilution action is entitled to an injunction (under and pursuant to the terms of Lanham Act § 34 (15 U.S.C. § 1116)). To obtain monetary damages (which awards are governed by the terms of Lanham Act § 35(a) (15 U.S.C. § 1117(a)) discussed above) the plaintiff must expressly show that the defendant "willfully intended to trade on the recognition of the famous mark" with regard to dilution by blurring or "willfully intended to harm the reputation of the famous mark" with regard to dilution by tarnishment. Lanham Act § 43(c)(5) (15 U.S.C. § 1125(c)(5)). The Act's damages provisions only apply to "uses in commerce" after the date of the Act (October 6, 2006).

355.   **The best answer is C.** Rights in trademarks last as long as the mark continues to uniquely identify and distinguish the owner's products or services. That means trademark rights have an indefinite duration rather than a fixed term (unlike patents and copyrights), so **Answer D** is incorrect. However, once their unique "source identification" ability disappears all rights terminate, including for registered and even incontestable marks, as stated in **Answer C**. That can happen for a number of reasons, including failure to use (**Answer B**), but standing alone failure to use is not sufficient to cause loss of trademark rights (for the reasons discussed further in the following questions). Failure to renew a federal registration on a timely basis (**Answer A**) results in loss of rights arising from the registration (which will lapse) but does not automatically terminate all rights in the mark. *See* Topic 10 — Registration: Process; Basic Requirements and Benefits.

356.   **The best answer is A.** In order to claim rights in the "PowerT" mark it must uniquely identify and distinguish Diesel's particular trucks. To do that the mark must be distinctive. "PowerT" likely started its trademark life as a suggestive, and thus inherently distinctive, mark. However, the public's subsequent adoption of PowerT as the generic term for the entire product class causes it to ceases being distinctive and, therefore, no longer protectable as a trademark (even with secondary meaning). This public appropriation of a mark is called "genericide." *See* Topic 3 — Basic Distinctiveness: The Spectrum of Distinctiveness; Word Marks Including Acronyms and Foreign Words. Lanham Act § 45 (15 U.S.C. § 1127) defines "abandonment" — in part — to include "any course of conduct of the owner, including acts of omission as well as commission, [which] causes the mark to become the generic name for the goods . . . ." Although that is one possible cause of genericide — the Lanham Act definition perhaps contemplating the owner's failure to prevent such public adoption — loss of trademark rights through genericide only require that transformation into the generic term has occurred, not that it arise from the owner's conduct. Consequently, **Answer B** is not as good as **Answer A**. Generic status is a permitted basis for challenging the validity of an incontestable mark in an infringement action under Lanham Act § 33(b) (15 U.S.C. § 1115(b)) (**Answer C**) and for canceling a registration despite the passage of five years under Lanham Act § 15 (15 U.S.C. § 1065) (**Answer D**). *See* Topic 12 — Registration: Incontestability. However, those outcomes are reflections of genericide causing loss of *all* rights in the mark, making **Answer A** the best answer.

357.   **The best answer is D**. Abandonment of a trademark requires both the owner's discontinuance of use and that the owner has no intent to resume such use. *See* Lanham Act § 45 (15 U.S.C. § 1127) (defining "abandonment" as when use "has been

309

discontinued with intent not to resume such use"). The burden is on the defendant (NuTrucks in this case) to prove abandonment (both non-use and absence of intent to resume use) by a preponderance of the evidence (although some courts call for clear and convincing evidence). **Answer D** is therefore correct and **Answer C** is not. Diesel has no affirmative obligation to prove its intention to recommence use (**Answer A**) or that it did not intend to abandon the mark (**Answer B**) — although the burden of production (but not proof) does shift to the mark owner once the defendant has made out a *prima facie* case of abandonment.

NOTE: Some courts draw an important distinction between the mark owner's "intent to abandon" and "no intent to resume use." Although the owner may subjectively intend/desire to maintain rights in the mark (therefore, having no intent to abandon), retaining rights requires the owner have an affirmative intent to resume use. Trademark policy, as reflected in the requirement of use to obtain rights, strongly supports this position. If mere subjective intent/desire to retain rights were sufficient, a trademark owner would be permitted to "warehouse" all its previously used marks indefinitely, thus barring beneficial market use by others. *See* Topic 7 — Acquiring Rights: Use.

358. **The presumption of abandonment arising from a three year period of non-use.** The Lanham Act § 45 (15 U.S.C. § 1127) definition of "abandonment" provides that "[n]onuse for 3 consecutive years shall be *prima facie* evidence of abandonment." On these facts NuTrucks can demonstrate Diesel has not used the "PowerT" mark on its dump trucks for a continuous period of three years. Consequently, it can rely on the presumption eliminating the (difficult) requirement that it also offer evidence that Diesel does not intent to resume use. Instead the presumption shifts the burden to Diesel of producing affirmative evidence of its intent to resume use.

NOTE: Although the *prima facie* case shifts the burden to plaintiff of producing evidence rebutting the presumption, the ultimate burden of proof remains with the defendant.

359. **From LEAST to MOST helpful: A, C, B, D.** NuTrucks will rely on the Lanham Act presumption (three consecutive years of non-use) shifting the burden to Diesel to produce evidence either of actual use during that period or of its intent to resume use. Registration and incontestability (**Answer A**) are of no help on that issue. Evidence of actual use during the relevant period is extremely helpful; however, that use must be "bona fide use of such mark made in the ordinary course of trade, and not made merely to reserve a right in [the] mark." Lanham Act § 45 (15 U.S.C. § 1127) (definition of "abandon-ment"); Topic 7 — Acquiring Rights: Use. **Answer C** involves use of the "PowerT" mark during the relevant three year period. However, even assuming that use is trademark use (which is questionable on the facts), the emblazoned tee-shirts clearly do not use the mark to signal-source of Diesel's dump trucks (or related goods). Additionally, because infrequent tee-shirt sales are not in the ordinary course of Diesel's truck business such use does not qualify under the statutory language as relevant use for abandonment purposes. *See Emergency One, Inc. v. AmericanEagle, Ltd.*, 228 F.3d 531 (4th Cir. 2000). Regarding intent to resume use, an affidavit from Diesel's President (**Answer B**) is helpful. However, courts are skeptical of such self-serving assertions

by the plaintiff and generally require some additional objective supporting evidence. The business plan calling for future adoption of the mark on a new dump truck strongly supports Diesel's asserted intent to resume use, making **Answer D** the most helpful answer.

360. **Timing of the planned resumption of use**. To avoid abandonment it is necessary that the plaintiff mark-owner show its "intent to resume *in the reasonably foreseeable future.*" *See Silverman v. CBS Inc.*, 870 F.2d 40 (2d Cir. 1989). The additional requirement is designed to ensure that the intent is more than an inchoate possibility which could lead to indefinite warehousing. Although liberally interpreted, exactly how soon is sufficiently soon to satisfy the requirement is uncertain. A helpful "rule of thumb" is that the more certain and definite the time of resumption, the less important the actual future date of resumption (within limits, obviously).

361. **The best answer is C**. On the facts, Diesel has legally abandoned the "PowerT" mark. The residual association demonstrated by Diesel does not constitute *use* of the mark, so **Answer A** is incorrect. The issue is how to deal with the possibility of consumer confusion arising from that continued association notwithstanding Diesel's lack of trademark rights. Prohibiting all use by NuTrucks would result in the very "warehousing" the abandonment doctrine seeks to avoid, so **Answer B** is an undesirable solution. Conversely, limiting NuTrucks' use of the "PowerT" mark to its dump trucks permits the use most likely to cause confusion. A possible compromise is to permit NuTrucks' use of the mark on its dump trucks but require that it mitigate consumer confusion by making appropriate disclaimers of any Diesel involvement as stated in **Answer C**.

NOTE: A court requiring disclaimer might require not merely advertising and point of sale disclaimers, but that NuTrucks use a combination mark such as "NuTrucks/ PowerT" which would avoid post-sale confusion as well ("is Diesel making PowerT dump trucks again?)

NOTE: If instead of stipulating to non-use and its lack of intent to resume Diesel had offered evidence of its actual use and/or intent to resume use in the foreseeable future, a court might then consider "residual association" as a further factor in deciding whether Diesel had abandoned the mark.

362. **The regulatory requirement raises the "excused" exception to abandonment**. A trademark owner can explain its nonuse by reference to facts which prevented continued use. Generally, external conditions (such as the regulatory requirements in this case) are accepted by the courts as evidence of non-abandonment and related issues of timely resumption are treated very generously. However, at some point continued nonuse eventually leads to abandonment. For example, the question will eventually arise whether Diesel's failure to resolve the regulatory issue and resume use of the mark amounts to "no intention to resume use in the reasonably foreseeable future."

363. **The best answer is C**. On these facts Slice has abandoned the "Glide" mark. Not only does its four years on nonuse raise the Lanham Act presumption, the facts affirmatively

state that it had no intention of resuming use of the mark in the foreseeable future or otherwise for an extended period of time, so **Answer A** is incorrect. Although abandonment is a defense regarding Slice's prior rights in the "Glide" mark (**Answer B**), abandonment of those rights does not mean that Burn wins on the facts as they stand today. Rather when a mark is abandoned it again becomes part of the public domain for adoption by anyone. Slice remained free (as did others) to adopt the mark for use on razors in any "open" geographic territories, which is what it did six months ago. Slice's new adoption does not, however, "relate back" to its prior rights which were abandoned, so **Answer D** is incorrect. Rather Slice now has rights in its new area of use — that is, the Southeastern United States plus areas of consumer association and, perhaps, reasonable expansion. *See* Topic 7 — Acquiring Rights: Use. As Burn's subsequent adoption and use is in a remote geographic area, it wins despite Slice's "new" rights in the mark as stated in **Answer C**.

NOTE: Slice's long period of prior national use may raise "residual reputation" issues which could require Burns use disclaimers of association despite the fact that Slice has no current trademark rights in that territory, as discussed in Question 361 above.

NOTE: Burn's good (or bad) faith in adopting the mark is not relevant to the abandonment analysis but it does affect is ability to use the mark in light of Slice's new adoption. Specifically, if Burn did not adopt in good faith, it may still be barred from use even in its Northwestern market territory. In all events, possible future "conflicts" makes considering obtaining a federal registration a good idea. *See* Topic 7 — Acquiring Rights: Use.

364. **The best answer is A.** Although Slice stopped using the "Glide" mark itself, use by Makem as a controlled licensee constitutes permissible derivative use sufficient to maintain Slice's rights against a claim of abandonment. *See* Topic 7 — Acquiring Rights: Use. **Answer A** is correct, and **Answer B** is not. Because on these facts, the mark has not been abandoned it is not returned to the public domain for adoption by others so neither **Answer C** nor **Answer D** is correct.

NOTE: Absent a federal registration (as in this case), nonuse in a particular geographic market might support a claim of *partial* abandonment — for example, in Burn's Northwest market. Because Makem has continued Slice's nationwide use, that issue does not arise and Burn's use of the mark anywhere will constitute infringement (the products being identical).

365. **The best answer is B.** Although license use can constitute derivative use by the mark owner, failure to adequately control licensee use (a so-called "naked" license) results in abandonment. If the mark owner does not ensure the mark reliably indicates the presence of the characteristics the consuming public expects, the mark ceases to uniquely identify and distinguish that product (or worse, is affirmatively deceptive), with a resulting loss of trademark rights. *See Dawn Donut Co. v. Hart's Food Stores, Inc.,* 267 F.2d 358 (2d Cir. 1959); Lanham Act § 45 (15 U.S.C. § 1127) (definition of "abandonment" Para. (2) — "course of conduct of the owner . . . causes the mark . . .

to lose its significance as a mark"). A crucial question in licensing situations, therefore, is whether the licensor mark-owner exercises sufficient supervision over the licensee's product bearing the mark. Express contractual provisions (**Answer A**) are evidence of that control and harmful to Burn's abandonment claim. They are not, however, dispositive. The critical issue is whether, in fact, the licensor mark-owner exercised quality control. So although **Answer C** does not include explicit contractual quality control requirements, the actual inspections are harmful to Burn's case. Finally, lack of inspection can be excused if the relationship between the parties is such that the licensor can reasonably rely on the licensee's performance, making **Answer D** problematic for Burns abandonment claim. Although **Answer B** imposes contractual quality standards and monitoring rights, the fact that no monitoring has taken place nor, alternatively, does any reasonable basis exist for Slice's reliance, makes it the most helpful to Burns and the best answer.

NOTE: Trademark licenses also must be examined for compliance with other laws. In particular the antitrust laws have provided fertile ground for challenge. Claims include monopolization (although the courts have held that owning a trademark does not by itself raise a presumption of market power nor does a "brand" constitute a relevant product market) and horizontal or vertical market restraints (with the former being sometimes problematic agreements among competitors — particularly if it involves market divisions, while the latter producer-distributor agreements generally raise few difficulties under the rule of reason analysis if sufficient interbrand competition exists). The trademark "misuse" doctrine generally involves attempts to leverage the licensing of a mark to gain other unrelated market advantage (for example, tying the trademark license to a requirement that the licensee purchase other products from the licensor). The doctrine's reach beyond conduct violating the antitrust laws is unresolved.

366. **From MOST to LEAST LIKELY valid assignments: C, D, B, A (although reasonable minds can differ).** Because the purpose of trademark law is to help customers identify the source of a particular good in the marketplace, trademark rights are commonly described as being *appurtenant to* (connected with) the trademark owner's business, and most particularly, the products and services which it produces. *See Hanover Star Milling Co. v. Metcalf*, 240 U.S. 403 (1916). Other transfers would permit assignee use of the mark in contexts which do not reliably signal the expected product characteristics, thus misleading consumers. That means that trademarks can *only* be assigned (by sale or otherwise) in connection "the goodwill of the business in which the mark is used, or with that part of the goodwill of the business connected with the use of and symbolized the mark." Lanham Act § 10(a)(1) (15 U.S.C. § 1060(a)(1)). Purported transfers absent that connection (called "assignments in gross") convey no rights in the mark.

Because the assignment in gross prohibition seeks to ensure the integrity of the mark signal post transfer, the crucial assignment issue is whether the "goodwill" (in terms of expected product characteristics) will be present in the goods produced by the assignee under the mark. **Answer C** is the "model" such assignment in which the mark is transferred with the previously associated business assets thus ensuring the mark signal remains clear and reliable (although there may be issues if there are post-transaction quality changes). It is not necessary, however, that the assignee purchases the mark owner's business assets, only that post-transaction the product remains substantially similar to that expected by consumers. On that basis **Answer D** is likely valid, carrying a very low risk of consumer confusion as the competitor's razors are very similar to those sold by Slice under the "Glide" mark. Although **Answer B** involves assignee sales of shaving razors there is no information on the vital issue of the razor's characteristics, rendering that transaction problematic. Finally, regarding **Answer A** the lower quality of the new goods associated with the mark post-transaction probably makes that assignment invalid. (Arguably even a substantial increase in post-assignment quality is problematic, as the mark still no longer accurately signals what consumers expect to receive.)

NOTE: Lanham Act § 10(a)(1) (15 U.S.C. § 1060(a)(1)) expressly prohibits the assignment on an intent-to-use registration prior to the filing of the necessary "use" affidavit making it "live," except to a successor in interest to the applicant's related ongoing business. Any attempted assignment voids the registration even if an actual use affidavit is subsequently filed. This stricter statutory "goodwill" requirement (ITU assignment only permitted to a actual business successor not merely ensuring post-assignment continuity of product characteristics whether or not assets are transferred) reflects a policy against creating a market in "future" trademarks under the ITU system (consistently with the requirement that registrants have a bona fide intent to use the mark themselves).

367. **The best answer is D**. On these facts, under the assignment in gross prohibition, Floorit acquired no rights in the "Glide" mark as a result of its purchase because the transfer bore no connection to the shaving razor business with which mark was used. **Answer A** is, therefore, incorrect. Floorit has never used the mark, so it cannot have acquired any rights in that fashion, making **Answer B** also incorrect. Exercising quality control is important to avoid abandonment in licensing situations, but has no effect on assignments in gross (neither saving nor destroying the rights in the mark), so **Answer C** is not correct. That leaves **Answer D** which properly reflects Floorit's lack of rights in the "Glide" mark either by purchase or use.

368. **The best answer is B**. Under the assignment in gross prohibition Floorit acquires no rights in the mark through its purchase from Slice, so **Answer A** is incorrect. However, Floorit has acquired rights in the "Glide" mark through its own use. Although those rights cannot "tack" on Slice's prior usage, it does predate use by the competitor. Applying the normal use-related priority rights that means Floorit can prevent adoptions posing a likelihood of confusion. On the facts, a competitor (thus selling in the same geographic market) has adopted the identical mark on the same product, so Floorit will prevail, making **Answer B** correct and **Answer C** (no need for quality control of Floorit's own use) and **Answer D** (true, but unnecessary given the use-based rights) incorrect.

369. **It is unclear.** It is unclear how the assignment in gross prohibition affects the assignor. It can be argued that the transaction being void the rights to the "Glide" mark remain

with Slice. However, as with most such transactions, Slice has stopped using the mark and the assignment itself seems to clearly indicate that it has no intention to "resume use in the reasonably foreseeable future" thus fulfilling the conditions for arguing an abandonment.

NOTE: In either event, Slice's use of the "Glide" mark was related to shaving razors so floor polishes fall outside its related goods product footprint. A lawsuit by Slice would not be a winner.

370.   **The best answer is B**. United States trademark rights, as all national trademark rights, are granted based on sovereign control over the related territory. As a general proposition, therefore, trademark rights only apply to activity within that sovereign's jurisdiction. However, the United States courts have held that provided certain conditions are satisfied United States trademark rights can be applied to prevent activities occurring outside the United States. In particular, such extraterritorial application is possible when: (1) the challenged conduct has a substantial effect on United States commerce, (2) the defendant is a United States citizen and (3) enforcement raises no conflict with rights established by, or actions of, other governments in their jurisdiction. *See Vanity Fair Mills, Inc. v. T. Eaton Co., Ltd.*, 234 F.2d 633 (2d Cir. 1956) interpreting *Steele v. Bulova Watch Co.*, 344 U.S. 280 (1952). That exception makes **Answer A** incorrect. On the given facts (so far) it is highly unlikely the *Vanity Fair* conditions are satisfied, so **Answer B** is better than **Answer C**. Finally, the court in *Vanity Fair* expressly rejected plaintiff's argument that the International Convention for the Protection of Industrial Property (Paris Union) was "self-executing" — specifically that it automatically protected trademark rights Union-wide under *United States law*. The court held that the Paris Convention actually reflects three propositions: (1) the basic principle that national trademark rights generally apply only within the nation's jurisdiction, (2) national rights should provide effective protection against unfair competition within that jurisdiction (including as articulated in the Convention) & (3) national rights should be made available on a non-discriminatory basis to both locals and foreigners. Consequently, the court found the availability of treaty rights is based on their incorporation *into the law of the relevant jurisdiction*; in this case Italy where the alleged violation is taking place, not the United States. That means Pressit's Paris Convention claims, if any, arise under its Italian legal rights, not its United States rights. Additionally, in such cases (as the *Vanity Fair* court concluded) a United States court is unlikely to have jurisdiction over the case, lacking as it does any United States nexus in law or fact. Thus, **Answer D** is incorrect. (The possibility exists that Italian courts may find the Paris Convention triggers rights under Italian law depending on their reading of Italy's implementing legislation. The Paris Convention "incorporation" issue is discussed regarding famous marks protection in Question 374 below and in its "part of United States law" form in Question 375 below.)

NOTE: The Second Circuit's "effects" factor noted in the above answer requires a "substantial effect on United States commerce." The Fifth and Ninth Circuits, however, only require "some effect" to satisfy the effects requirement, while the Fourth Circuit looks for a "significant effect."

371.   **The best answer is A** (although others do affect the outcome, it is the most significant; read on). The *Vanity Fair* factors listed in the answer to the previous Question could be interpreted as calling for a "totality of the circumstances" assessment. However, the opinion can be read as treating some factors as more important than others. Specifically, the court's statement that "we think the rationale . . . was so thoroughly based on the power of the United States to govern 'the conduct of *its own citizens* upon the high seas or even in foreign countries *when the rights of other nations or their nationals are not infringed* . . . .*" (emphasis in the original) appears to focus the inquiry first on the nationality of the defendant and then the potential interference with local trademark rights as concerns. *See Vanity Fair Mills, Inc. v. T. Eaton Co., Ltd.*, 234 F.2d 633 (2d Cir. 1956). It may, therefore, be that unless the defendant is a United States citizen (**Answer A**) the other factors are irrelevant and extraterritorial jurisdiction will not exist (perhaps, in part, to avoid practical enforcement difficulties). However, if the defendant is a United States citizen, the court *then* looks whether enforcement will adversely affect the rights of "other nations or their nationals" (**Answer C**) on grounds of comity (in *Vanity Fair* the court did not resolve the foreign trademark rights issue because the defendant was not a United States citizen). Finally, if there are no adverse effects the court will consider factors relevant to effects on United States commerce (**Answer D**) and the equities (**Answer B**) to determine the appropriateness of extraterritorial enforcement under the particular circumstances.

372.   **The best answer is D.** On the facts, Pressit cannot satisfy the *Vanity Fair* factors and, therefore, will not obtain traditional trademark infringement relief such as an injunction against all further sales by an infringer (**Answer B**). That does not mean, however, Pressit may not obtain some relief. A United States court will likely require even a foreign defendant acting exclusively outside the United States avoid actions which are likely to cause substantial consumer confusion in the United States when it can reasonably do so under the circumstances. *See Sterling Drug, Inc. v. Bayer AG*, 14 F.3d 733 (2d Cir. 1994) (holding reasonable injunctions properly balancing the respective interests of the foreign rights holder in publicizing their product against "significant trademark-impairing effects on American commerce" are permissible). On these facts a court would, therefore, likely favorably consider an injunction requiring at least any English version of Miracolo's internationally accessible web site clearly state that neither it nor its product is connected with Pressit. Consequently **Answer D** is better than **Answer A** on these facts. If Miracolo had sold its Echo olive oil in the United States then Pressit's United States trademark rights would support a United States court injunction against those sales. That is not the situation here and, in all events, such an injunction would involve domestic, not extraterritorial, application of Pressit's United States rights, so **Answer C** is incorrect. (In *Sterling Drug* the court noted that an injunction against foreign actions likely to cause adverse effects in the United States was "extraterritorial" as it applied United States law to the defendant's activities outside of the United States.)

373.   **The client should take immediate steps to obtain national trademark rights in any jurisdiction of concern.** Obtaining national rights generally involves seeking national

registrations. Unlike the United States, many jurisdictions have no requirement a mark actually be used (or even there be a bona fide intention to use) to obtain a registration, so generally there will be little impediment to immediately obtaining parallel international rights upon United States adoption of a mark. Some jurisdictions do, however, require non-residents prove they have previously acquired trademark rights in their "home" jurisdiction usually by registration (for which purposes a domestic registration on the Supplemental Register suffices — making obtaining foreign national rights in marks without the requisite secondary meaning possible). Additionally, supplemental national registrations filed with members of the Paris Union (most countries) within six months after an initial application in a Union country (including the United States) which met that original country's requirements will be given the same filing date and related priority as the initial Convention application.

United States accession to the Protocol Relating to the Madrid Agreement Concerning the International Registration of Marks has further simplified obtaining international rights. A Madrid Protocol application does not create international rights; however, it does significantly facilitate the mechanics of obtaining a related bundle of national registrations. It does so by "automatically" generating national applications in all Protocol jurisdictions identified for "extension" in the original application. Those derivative applications are then separately reviewed and granted by those nations under their local laws. The downside to a Madrid Protocol registration is that all national derivative rights depend from the original application, so if the original "international registration" fails so do all the others. However, in that event the registrant has three months thereafter to file with the "dependant" national offices converting the local "Madrid" registration into a national registration, which registration will both save the registration and maintain the original priority date.

374. **The best answer is C.** The Paris Convention protects famous marks which are well known "*in the country*" where confusion is likely against such confusion arising from use of the mark on "identical or similar goods" by another in that country. That protection applies even if the owner has no relevant local trademark rights in the jurisdiction. *See* Article 6*bis*. To obtain Paris Convention relief against Miracolo's use in Italy Pressit must, therefore, demonstrate its "Echo" mark is being used on identical or similar goods (which it is) *and* that Pressit's mark is well known *in Italy*. **Answer A** is, therefore, irrelevant and incorrect. **Answer B** raises the degree of fame issue; specifically whether relevant niche fame is sufficient to satisfy the requirement. The Paris Convention has been read as requiring national not merely niche fame making **Answer B** incorrect (a similar degree of fame issue has been resolved against niche renown for dilution purposes under the Lanham Act; *see* Topic 14 — Dilution). In contrast, the Trade-Related Aspects of Intellectual Property (TRIPS) accord expands on the Paris Union protection of famous marks, focusing the fame inquiry on the "relevant sector of the public" — that is likely consumers of the related product. *See* Article 16.2. Although **Answer D** (well known in Italy) would likely include **Answer C**, **Answer C** states the actual test (and inquiry) under TRIPS and is, therefore, the better answer (**Answer D** would satisfy the Paris Convention requirement, but the Answer refers expressly to TRIPS).

NOTE: As noted in Question 370 above, if Pressit is to rely on the famous mark doctrine to stop Miracolo's use of the "Echo" mark in Italy, it will likely need to bring that claim under Italian law in an Italian court as it is the rights under Italian law, not extraterritorial application of its United States rights and United States law, which will provide relief.

NOTE: TRIPS further expands protection of famous marks against "goods and services which are not similar to those for which a mark is registered" if such use would damage the interests of the owner of the famous mark — arguably, including the concept of "dilution" found under the Lanham Act. *See* Article 16.2; Topic 14 — Dilution.

375.   **The best answer is B**. It is not necessary to have a registered mark (anywhere, including the United States) to obtain rights under the Lanham Act, so **Answer A** is incorrect. *See* Topic 13 — Infringement: Likelihood of Confusion. Standing alone Pasta's prior Italian registration does not create any rights under the Lanham Act (via the Paris Convention or otherwise), so **Answer C** is incorrect. (Which is not to say that Pasta may not have rights under the Lanham Act via incorporation of the Convention; just that more than a prior foreign registration is required to trigger them (if they exist) — including a fairly complex "incorporation" argument which has yet to be fully tested in the trademark context and probably a showing of likelihood of confusion or fame (neither of which seems likely on these facts). *See Davidoff Extension S.A. v. Davidoff Int'l, Inc.*, 221 U.S.P.Q. 465 (S.D. Fla. 1983) (arguing, perhaps in dicta in light of evidence of the foreign mark owner plaintiff's actual use of its mark in the United States, that Lanham Act § 44(h) (15 U.S.C. § 1126(h)) incorporates the Paris Convention's "unfair competition" Article 10*bis* substantive protections which include "*confusion* by any means . . . with . . . the goods . . . of a competitor")). Nor, for similar reasons (and absent "fame") does Pasta's first use in Italy trigger any Lanham Act rights under TRIPS, so **Answer D** is incorrect. Finally, although there is an open debate regarding what constitutes sufficient "use in commerce" for purposes of obtaining use-based trademark rights under the Lanham Act (more to come in the Questions below) the courts all agree that some use in either interstate or foreign commerce is required under the federal Commerce Clause limitation on the reach of the Lanham Act. *See International Bancorp v. Societe des Bains de Mer et du Cercle des Etrangers a Monaco*, 329 F.3d 359 (4th Cir. 2003); *Buti v. Perosa, S.R.L.*, 139 F.3d 98 (2d Cir. 1998); *Person's Co., Ltd v. Christman*, 900 F.2d 1565 (Fed. Cir. 1990). On these facts no relevant use exists under any test — there is no indication of any United States contact with the mark anywhere in the world or even any effort by Pasta to develop such contacts. As a result Pasta is very unlikely to have any rights under the Lanham Act, making **Answer B** the best answer.

NOTE: This and the following Questions address what constitutes sufficient *non*-United States use to trigger United States trademark rights. If Pasta's Barrita products were marketed and sold in the United States it would have the same rights as any similarly situated United States trademark user, including applicable rights under the Lanham Act.

376. **The best answer is D**. Knowledge of foreign use can constitute a bad faith bar to adoption and use of a foreign mark in the United States, so **Answer A** is incorrect. However, the Federal Circuit has held the bad faith bar does not apply merely because the United States user had knowledge of the prior foreign use (perhaps in contrast to the test for bad faith arising from knowledge of a geographically remote *domestic* use). *See Person's Co., Ltd v. Christman*, 900 F.2d 1565 (Fed. Cir. 1990). So **Answer C** is incorrect. Rather the bad faith bar inquiry is triggered only if it can be shown that the United States adopter acted "solely to block the prior foreign user's planned expansion into the United States" — with it remaining unclear whether showing such intent is dispositive of bad faith standing alone. *Id.* That approach makes **Answer B** incorrect and **Answer D** the best answer.

NOTE: The court in *Person's* also noted a further bar to United States adoption arising from the Paris Convention and TRIPS protection of foreign marks having the requisite fame in the United States. That doctrine does not require knowledge. In all events it clearly does not apply on the stated facts as Pasta has neither the requisite niche, much less national, fame in the United States.

377. **The best answer is C**. Although there is debate on the point, the Circuits appear to be split on whether merely advertising to United States consumers in the United States is sufficient to trigger Lanham Act protection. In *Buti v. Perosa, S.R.L.*, 139 F.3d 98 (2d Cir. 1998) the Second Circuit (arguably) held that plaintiff's advertising of its restaurant services in the United States without actually rendering those services (or sales of products) "in commerce" did not give rise to rights under the Lanham Act. However, in *International Bancorp v. Societe des Bains de Mer et du Cercle des Etrangers a Monaco*, 329 F.3d 359 (4th Cir. 2003) the Fourth Circuit granted protection to a mark holder which had advertised its services (a casino) in the United States but only provided such services abroad. In doing so the court focused its analysis on three issues: (1) whether the claimant was engaged in commerce which could be regulated by Congress, (2) whether the use of the mark was sufficient under the Lanham Act definition of that phrase to trigger related rights and (3) that services rather than goods were involved, as the Lanham Act definition of use differs between the two. Regarding the first element the court held that United States citizens' purchases of services sold by "a subject of a foreign nation" — even when the purchases occur abroad — constitute "foreign trade" subject to federal Commerce Clause regulation and governed by the Lanham Act. Regarding elements (2) & (3), the key was the Lanham Act definition of the requisite "use in commerce" for services. For goods such use generally must involve affixation, whereas for services the mark only need be "used or displayed in the sale or advertising and the services are rendered in commerce." Lanham Act § 45 (15 U.S.C. § 1127) (definition of "use in commerce). Consequently, the court found that advertising of services using the mark in the United States coupled with purchases in foreign trade (as defined above) triggered Lanham Act protection for the service mark. However, the *Societe* decision (1) expressly distinguished *Buti*'s contrary holding (which was also a services case) based on its view that the plaintiff in that case had conceded that its services were not "part of trade between Italy and the United States" and

consequently not "in commerce" and (2) stated that the analysis would differ if goods (and trademarks rather than service marks) were involved in light of the different Lanham Act definition of the relevant "use in commerce."

Applied to the facts of the Question: Neither *Buti* nor *Societe* supports a clear win for Pasta, so **Answer A** is incorrect. Nor, however, do those decisions mandate that Pasta lose the case. For the "use" definitional reasons set out in *Societe*, Pasta will have a very hard time arguing that its case is stronger because it involves goods rather than services. But, provided it does not concede the commerce point Pasta can argue (albeit weakly) that as its pasta products are consumed in Italian restaurants by United States consumers asking for it by name, the connection with those services should bring its claim under the *Societe* rationale. Additionally Pasta can argue that its advertising has been sufficiently successful to permit its "Barrita" mark be protected as a famous mark under the Paris Convention (known nationally and the identical product) or TRIPS (within the relevant sector of the public). As a result the best answer among **Answer B** (a strong argument Pasta should win), **Answer C** (a weak argument it should win) and **Answer D** (certainly lose), is **Answer C**.

378. **They should take immediate steps to obtain national trademark rights under United States law.** If foreign trademark owners are either currently using or have the bona fide intent to use a mark in the United States they can file Lanham Act applications and obtain the same benefits as other registrants under the statute. They can also avail themselves of the Madrid Protocol if their country is a party. In addition, Lanham Act § 44 (15 U.S.C. § 1126) implements special treaty-based registration rights available to qualifying foreign mark owners. Specifically, a foreign mark owner whose country of origin is a party to a trademark treaty to which the United States is also a party (including the Paris Convention and TRIPS) or whose country offers reciprocal rights to United States citizens can obtain a United States Lanham Act registration for a mark which: (1) has already been registered in their country of origin or for which an application is filed within six months from the date of a related application for registration in their country of origin (with the same priority date) & (2) the applicant states it has a bona fide intention to use the mark in commerce. The resulting Section 44 registration will be on the Principal Register if the mark qualifies, otherwise on the Supplemental Register and unlike Madrid Protocol filings (which depend from the original filing) once issued the registration is an independent United States national right. *See* Lanham Act § 44(f) (15 U.S.C. § 1126(f)). Moreover, unlike domestic "bona fide intent to use" registrations, no subsequent proof of actual use is required to "perfect" the registration. However, the courts have held that a Section 44 registration is subject to United States trademark law, including abandonment and the related three consecutive year non-use presumption of Lanham Act § 45 (15 U.S.C. § 1127 (definition of abandonment).

379. **The best answer is B.** The primary claim on these facts is for "false advertising" — Best Juices' misrepresentation of the nature, characteristics, qualities or geographic origin of Beverages' goods, services or commercial activities in commercial advertising or promotion. That claim is authorized under Lanham Act § 43(a)(1)(B) (15 U.S.C. § 1125(a)(1)(B) (**Answer B**). Although Best Juices has used Beverages' "Nature's Own" trademark, because the advertisement refers to Beverages' product and raises no confusion concerns the use will be protected as a fair (nominative) use. *See* Topic 16 — Defenses: Fair Use, Nominative Use, Parody/Free Speech. Consequently, no action will lie under either Section 32 (15 U.S.C. § 1114) (**Answer D**) which provides relief for infringement of federally registered trademarks or Section 43(a)(1)(A) (15 U.S.C. § 1125(a)(1)(A) (**Answer A**), which provides relief for infringement of unregistered trademarks (and, therefore, would not be relevant in any event). Finally, Best Juice's use of Beverages' "Nature's Own" mark in reference to Beverage's own product does not trigger dilution concerns (either by blurring or tarnishment — the latter notwithstanding the advertisement's false statements about the actual product; as dilution by tarnishment focuses on "harm by association"). Consequently, no claim can be made under Section 43(c) (15 U.S.C. § 1125(c)) (**Answer C**). *See* Topic 14 — Dilution.

380. **The best answer is A.** Prior to the 1988 Trademark Revision Act false advertising claims were limited to misrepresentations concerning the advertiser's *own* goods, not those of competitors. *See Bernard Food Industries v. Dietene Co.*, 415 F.2d 1279 (7th Cir. 1969), *cert. denied*, 397 U.S. 912 (1970), *Samson Crane Co. v. Union National Sales Inc.*, 87 F. Supp. 218 (D. Mass 1949). So **Answer A** (the false claim does not concern the advertiser's goods — Best Juices' in this case) identifies the primary difficulty. False advertising is not a trademark infringement action. It turns on false claims rather than confusion as to source, so **Answer B** is incorrect. The statement does appear in an advertisement (as discussed further in the Questions below), and in any event that requirement is not unique to pre-1988 Trademark Revision Act law, so **Answer C** is incorrect. **Answer D** is particularly relevant to pre-1988 Trademark Revision Act law but does not affect the ability to bring a claim but the available remedies, so **Answer D** is incorrect (see the next Question).

NOTE: The logic for excluding false claims about a competitor's goods prior to 1988 was that those concerns gave rise to distinct non-trademark/non-passing off causes of action, in particular claims for trade libel or product disparagement.

381. **The best answer is D.** Even when a false claim was made regarding the advertiser's own goods the pre-1988 Trademark Revision Act Lanham Act precluded recovery if

the plaintiff (Beverages here) could not prove that it had suffered a resulting diversion of trade. Such a showing was extremely difficult when numerous producers of the genuine product (having the falsely advertised characteristic) existed as there was no way to be certain the plaintiff would have made the sale had the false claim not been made. The requirement practically limited relief to cases in which the plaintiff was the "sole producer" of genuine goods and, therefore, would was the only other possible seller. If, as stated in **Answer D,** Beverages was not such a sole producer it would have been very difficult to make the necessary showing of harm to its interests. As explained in the answer to Question 380 above, the pre-1988 Trademark Revision Act Lanham Act only made false statements about the advertiser's (defendant's) own goods actionable. **Answer A** incorrectly inverts that requirement — indicating that the claim must involve the plaintiff Beverages' not defendant's Best Juices' goods. As also explained in the answer to Question 380 above, confusion as to source is not an element of a false advertising claim and the statement does appear in an advertisement (which is a continuing requirement post-1988), so **Answer B** and **Answer C** are both incorrect.

NOTE: Lost or diverted sales were required for recovery under pre-1988 Revision Act law based on the argument that because Congress had included the cause of action in the Lanham Act, a trademark statute, Congress must have intended to addressing similar "passing off" concerns — that is a diversion of sales from a genuine producer to the false advertiser. *See American Washboard Co. v. Saginaw Manufacturing Co.*, 103 Fed. 281 (6th Cir. 1900).

382. **The best answer is A.** Because the Lanham Act rests on Congress' power to regulate interstate commerce that "nexus" has always been required — so **Answer A** does NOT reflect a post-1988 Revision Act change. *See* Topic 1 — Justifications and Sources of Trademark Law. The 1988 Revision Act did, however, explicitly permit actions for misrepresentations about *either* the advertiser's or another's product (**Answer B**), eliminated the requirement that the plaintiff must show actual diversion of sales to obtain a remedy (**Answer C**) and explicitly separated Section 43(a) (15 U.S.C. § 1125(a) into claims related to (1) false advertising (Section 43(a)(1)(B)) & (2) false designations of origin and infringement of unregistered trademarks (Section 43(a)(1)(A)) (**Answer D**).

383. **The best answer is A.** Standing to bring a suit under Lanham Act § 43(a) (15 U.S.C. § 1125(a)) is afforded to "any person who believes that he or she is or is likely to be damaged [by the false advertisement]." Although the statutory language would appear to include consumers the courts have consistently found that class does NOT have standing. So **Answer A** is the correct answer. *See Proctor & Gamble Co. v. Amway Corp.*, 242 F.3d 539 (5th Cir. 2001). In contrast, the courts have generously interpreted the language as it applies to commercial enterprises. Although proof of actual loss supports standing (**Answer B**), it is not required. It is sufficient that the plaintiff show it is "likely to be damaged" (**Answer C**), with many courts willing to find that likelihood (and standing) based on the mere fact that the plaintiff directly competes with the false advertiser (**Answer D**).

NOTE: Consumer remedies are found under common law fraud, contract breach of warranty and federal and state consumer protection statutes, including state "Baby FTC Acts" the majority of which provide private causes of action for unfair trade practices.

384. **The best answer is C.** It is not necessary a plaintiff prove it suffered actual economic harm caused by the defendant's misrepresentation to have standing (**Answer A**). Nor is such proof necessary to obtain injunctive relief (**Answer B**) and, thereby, "win" the case (**Answer D**). However, such proof is generally required to collect monetary damages (**Answer C**).

385. **The best answer is C.** Lanham Act § 43(a)(1)(B) (15 U.S.C. § 1125(a)(1)(B)) explicitly requires the challenged misrepresentation appear in "commercial advertising or promotion." The courts have been less than clear about what precisely that means, but a good rule of thumb is that it must involve general outreach to the market as contrasted to one-on-one discussions. *See First Health Group Corp. v. BCE Emergis Corp.*, 269 F.3d 800 (7th Cir. 2001). Applying that test, **Answer C** is the most "personal and direct." Each of **Answers A, B** and **D** involve more general publication to the marketplace.

386. **Arguably the posting does not involve commercial advertising or promotion.** The courts have generally found that actionable a false advertising claims must involve "commercial speech" by a market participant (competitor) seeking to influencing consumers to by the advertisers product (either by falsely lauding its own or by misdescribing those of others). Unless the very happy Bitty customer has some agency relationship to Bitty (thus allowing his acts to be attributed to Bitty) it is unlikely that his independent false posting constitutes "commercial advertising or promotion" by Bitty.

NOTE: First Amendment issues arise when a market participant's false statement is not clearly "commercial," for example an attack on a competitor's political stance on a social issue. In such instances even false speech may be protected. Moreover, even if the issue is relevant to market competition and perhaps "commercial speech" the court would then need to tackle the slippery question of the level of protection afforded such speech.

387. **The best answer is A.** A Lanham Act false advertising claim requires proof of three elements: (1) a false statement of fact about the advertiser's or another's goods, services or commercial activities, (2) actual deception or a tendency to deceive relevant consumers and (3) that the false statement is material — that is likely to influence consumer purchasing decisions. It is, sufficient, but not necessary to make out the first element (falsity) that the plaintiff prove that the challenged statement is literally false on its face. However, the element only requires proof that the defendant made a "false statement of fact" — which can be demonstrated by literal falsity *or* by showing that the statement conveys a false message to consumers based on the context in which it was made. So **Answer A** is not a *required* element of Candle's suit and is incorrect — it is **Answer B** which accurately states the falsity requirement. Even if Candle's

proves the statement is false statement of fact, it also has the burden of proving the remaining two elements — that the statement either has deceived or has a tendency to deceive relevant consumers (**Answer C**) and that the statement is likely to influence actual purchasing decisions (**Answer D**).

NOTE: As the following Questions discuss, Candles may be able to prove the latter two elements based on presumptions raised by certain kinds of false statements or proof of No-Drips' intent to deceive; but they remain elements of Candles' Lanham Act false advertising case.

388.   **The best answer is C** (but none of them is free of doubt). To be actionable a challenged statement must be a false statement of fact about the product. The key line-drawing issue is whether the assertion is *factual* or merely one of *opinion* (including puffery). That determination generally turns on whether the statement can be objectively demonstrated to be either true or false. Alternatively, and particularly in cases of puffery, the courts may elide the false statement of fact and reliance requirements and find that the challenged statement is so general, vague and boastful that is it unlikely to engender consumer reliance. *See Southland Sod Farms v. Stover Seed Co.*, 108 F.3d 1134 (9th Cir. 1997). Applying those tests to the above statements, **Answer A** and **Answer B** can clearly be proven false. The addition of the word "rarely" in **Answer C** and **Answer D** raises a subjective element and triggers the opinion defense. Both Answers would likely be found false statements of fact under the circumstances, however, the Question requires choosing the LEAST likely. The additional "Tests show" language in **Answer D** introduces a further factual claim making it more likely factual (and, importantly, to induce consumer reliance) than **Answer C**, making **Answer C** the "best" answer. *Cf. United Industries Corp. v. Clorox Co.*, 140 F.3d 1175 (8th Cir. 1998) ("tests prove" comparative advertising claims should be examined more critically; the plaintiff need only show the tests were insufficiently reliable to establish the fact for which they were cited in support to prevail on the falsity requirement).

NOTE: When by its nature a factual claim reasonably implies to consumers that substantiating testing has been performed (for example, the comparative claim "better than x" for an FDA-exempt nutritional supplement) and in fact it has not, a court may find the mere lack of testing carries the burden regarding falsity, even when no express claim of testing has been made and no additional evidence of its actually falsity is introduced by the plaintiff.

389.   **The best answer is D**. The defendant's lack of intent to make a false statement is not an absolute defense; if the statement was false, deceived or had a tendency to deceive consumers and influenced their purchasing decisions Lanham Act false advertising liability attaches. So **Answer D** is incorrect. Willfulness and intent do, however, affect both presumptions and remedy as indicated in the remaining Answers. Generally, intent to deceive raises a presumption that the consumer deception element has been satisfied, so **Answer A** is correct. Similarly, although the plaintiff must normally show causation to collect monetary damages, some courts will presume causation when defendant's

intent to deceive is shown, so both **Answer B** (the general rule absent intent) and **Answer C** (the "some courts" exception) are correct.

390. **The best answer is B**. Home-Fridge needs to demonstrate that the statement is false, so **Answer D** is not only desirable but necessary. However, the courts have created various classifications of "falsity" which affect the remainder of Home-Fridge's case and, therefore, keep **Answer D** from being the best answer. The best classification for plaintiffs is literally (or explicitly) false — or as sometimes stated, false on its face (**Answer C**). The primary benefit of that classification is courts will generally presume that literally false statements have a deceptive effect, thus relieving the plaintiff of proving that element of their case. On these facts, however, the classification does not apply. It is literally true that no restaurants use Home-Fridge refrigerators or freezers, so **Answer C** is not the best possible classification in this case.

All courts also agree that even a literally true statement (as well as ambiguous statements) can be "false" for false advertising purposes when they are misleading (deceptive) in the specific context, as stated in **Answer A**. *See American Home Products Corp. v. Johnson & Johnson*, 577 F.2d 160 (2d Cir. 1978). Home-Fridge has a good case for such a "misleading in context" classification based on the argument the statement implies that restaurants chose Pro-Fridge over Home-Fridge products as a matter of preference when in fact they do not. The problem with "misleading" falsity is that courts require proof that the false implication has in fact been conveyed to consumers (usually by survey evidence showing consumer perception) and is, therefore, likely to deceive. Many courts, however, have carved out an additional special class of contextually false ("misleading") claims — "false by necessary implication" — as stated in **Answer B**. As the name suggests the category covers situations where the misleading consumer inference is inevitable — that is a necessary implication — on the specific facts. In light of that necessary implication, such statements are treated as though they are literally false, even though technically true (or ambiguous) on their face. As a result they raise a presumption of deception rather than requiring supplemental proof that the false implication has been adopted by consumers. On these facts Home-Fridge can make a very good case for "false by necessary implication" classification — that consumers will draw the false implication of choice/preference by restaurants seems inevitable on these facts. So **Answer B** would be better than **Answer A**. *See Johnson & Johnson-Merck Consumer Pharm. Co. v. Smithkline Beecham Corp.*, 960 F.2d 294 (2d Cir.) (discussing the "misleading in context" and "false by necessary implication" doctrines and citing to the *Cuisinarts* case which is similar to these facts).

NOTE: Visual portions of advertisements are a fertile area for false by necessary implication analysis. For example, an orange being squeezed into an empty container of orange drink product which, in fact, contains no natural orange juice does not explicitly state the product is made from orange juice, but despite that ambiguity the conveyance of a false implication to consumers is inevitable.

391. **The best answer is D**. As discussed in the prior Question, the preferred classification was false by necessary implication — a category of misleading statement which is treated

as literally false. In such cases courts presume consumer deception. That presumption, however, is not conclusive but subject to rebuttal by the defendant (a highly problematic proposition — the better defense, being lack of materiality as discussed in the Questions below). So **Answer D** is correct and **Answer C** is not. **Answer A** and **Answer B** are incorrect on these facts, as proof of consumer deception is only required if the statement is found neither literally false nor false by necessary implication — a situation discussed in the next Question.

392. **The best answer is C.** When the statement is not classified as literally false or false by necessary implication there is no presumption of deception and plaintiff bears the burden of proving that element, normally by offering survey evidence showing public reaction to the statement. So **Answer A** is incorrect on these facts. The actual burden of proof, however, turns on the remedy being sought. If the plaintiff has requested only injunctive relief, then it need shown only a "tendency to deceive." However, to obtain monetary damages the plaintiff must present evidence of actual consumer deception (the increased burden reflects the need to show causation to obtain monetary damages and without actual deception the necessary causation cannot exist). Only **Answer C** recognizes that important nuance, correctly stating the "damages" burden of proof. Neither **Answer B** nor **Answer D** can be identified as correct or incorrect without knowing what remedy Home-Fridge has sought, so neither can be the best answer.

NOTE: Regarding the quantum of deception required, plaintiff only must show the misrepresentation deceived a "substantial portion of the relevant consuming public" (those to whom the advertisement was addressed). What constitutes "substantial" is uncertain, although it is considerably less than 50% (one court, for example, accepted likely deception of 25% of survey respondents).

393. **The best answer is A.** The third element of a Lanham Act false advertising case is "materiality" — that the misrepresentation must have a likely effect on consumer purchasing decisions; or, stated conversely, even a literally false statement is of no competitive concern if it is irrelevant to consumers. The courts have not clearly articulated the "materiality" test but, unsurprisingly, look at the likely effects of the misrepresentation on market competition leading to an inquiry into the nature of that competition and, in particular, the "inherent quality or characteristics" of the goods or services. **Answers B, C** and **D** all specifically address the relevance of the false Pro-Fridge statement to a residential purchaser decisions. **Answer B** indicates the statement is of no concern (no connection in consumers minds to their residential purchase from either Home-Fridge or Pro-Fridge) and, therefore, immaterial even though false. Conversely, **Answer C** (quality an inherent characteristic) and **Answer D** (raising consumer concerns about Home-Fridge's products) point toward materiality. Pro-Fridge might argue that **Answer A** indicates the advertisement had no effect on consumers. However, it does not directly address the relationship between the false statement and the purchaser decisions. There are many reasons Home-Fridge's business may not have declined *despite* the advertisements adverse effect. Or, it may be that the advertisement kept Home-Fridge from increasing sales. That ambiguity makes it the least relevant of the considerations.

394. **The best answer is D**. In *Dastar Corp. v. Twentieth Century Fox Film Corp.*, 539 U.S. 23 (2003), the Supreme Court held that "origin of goods" for purposes of Lanham Act § 43(a)(1)(A) (15 U.S.C. § 1125(a)(1)(A)) violations "refers to the producer of tangible goods that are offered for sale, and not to the author of any idea, concept or communication embodied in those goods." In developing that test, the Court specifically rejected the possibility that "origin" referred only to geographic source, making **Answer A** incorrect. Therefore, the crucial question in this "false designation of origin" case is whether the LowCost labeled products were actually manufactured by (or for) LowCost, not LowCost's failure to attribute their original design to Producers, making **Answer D** the most relevant to Producer's claim. As LowCost is the producer of the products it is selling under its label, it is the legal "origin" for Lanham Act purposes and has no liability for "false designation of origin." **Answer B** would have been very significant had the Court found "origin" meant "originator" of the concept. However, it explicitly rejected that position in favor of "producer" of the particular physical exemplar, thus eliminating any attribution requirement for "origin" purposes. According to the *Dastar* Court **Answer C** raises a distinct issue — whether LowCost's copying of Producers' designs violates Producers' copyright. In the copyright case the "useful article" doctrine will be very relevant; however, it has no relevance to a false origin claim.

NOTE: The Court's *Dastar* opinion also has significant consequences for false attribution claims. *See* Topic 22 — Right of Publicity, False Endorsement and Attribution.

395. **Yes**. On these facts Producers likely has a "reverse passing off" trademark infringement claim. In *Dastar* the Court indicated in dicta that "the [Sec. 43(a)] claim would undoubtedly be sustained if [defendant] had bought some of [plaintiff's goods] and merely repacked them as its own." *Dastar Corp. v. Twentieth Century Fox Film Corp.*, 539 U.S. 23 (2003). *See also* Topic 13 — Infringement: Likelihood of Confusion.

NOTE: If LowCost bought *and modified* original Producers' products then sold them under *Producers'* mark, LowCost might be liable for traditional infringement despite the first sale doctrine. *See* Topic 17 — Defenses: First Sale. Such modifications might also give rise to a false attribution claim. *See* Topic 22 — Right of Publicity, False Endorsement and Right of Attribution.

396. **Yes**. As indicated in the answer to Question 394 the "false origin" analysis does not preclude other intellectual property claims. In particular if the chair designs are copyrightable, Producers could sue for violation of those rights. Producers may even have an "attribution" claim under § 106A of the Copyright Act (17 U.S.C. § 106A(a)(1)(A)) if its products qualify as a "work of visual art" (albeit unlikely). Additionally, if the furniture designs are non-functional trade dress, Producers may have a traditional likelihood of confusion trademark infringement claim arising from likely confusion over source (in this case the fact that LowCost, not Producers, made the products points toward, not away from, liability).

397. **No.** Right of publicity is a creature of state statutory and common law. Although the Lanham Act has been extended (as discussed in the final Questions in this section) to cover false endorsement and false designation of origin (attribution) claims those are not, strictly speaking, right of publicity claims.

398. **The best answer is A.** The "right of publicity" involves the unauthorized commercial use of an individual's "persona" in ways which cause that person commercial harm. Under right of publicity statutes and common law that protected persona (the related property "res" in publicity claims) universally extends to a wide range of personal attributes, including the individual's name. The challenged use need not include the individual's likeness, so **Answer A** is incorrect. **Answers B, C** and **D** each reference a key element of a right of publicity claim.

399. **The best answer is C.** Right of publicity grew out of right of privacy doctrine and, consequently, the two retain a degree of overlap. In particular, privacy rights frequently include unauthorized "appropriation of name and likeness" which forms a frequent basis for right of publicity claims. However, generally speaking privacy is more concerned with intrusion and disclosure while right of publicity focuses the use's commercial effects — a fundamental difference reflected in the elements of the two claims. So **Answer A** and **Answer D** are both incorrect. Between **Answer B** and **Answer C**, although as stated in **Answer B** right of privacy did provide some of the conceptual underpinnings for the right of publicity, the better description of the current relationship between the doctrines is the intrusion/disclosure versus economic value misappropriation distinction in **Answer C**, making it the best answer.

NOTE: The right of publicity's emphasis on misappropriated economic value also clarifies it is not a plaintiff's "hurt feelings" or "pain and suffering" — which harm is more appropriately addressed in privacy or defamation — but lost commercial value which trigger the right.

400. **The best answer is D** (but it's an unsettled issue so read on). Right of publicity's focus on the commercial harm arising from misappropriation makes a central issue in such cases the existence of commercial value in the plaintiff's persona. Celebrity status is one way to demonstrate that value exists (**Answer D**). **Answer C** focuses on privacy intrusion concerns rather than right of publicity misappropriation of commercial value, and is incorrect. **Answer A** and **Answer B** raise the unresolved issue of whether non-celebrities are covered by the publicity right, creating an ambiguity regarding the right answer. The "no coverage" argument is that non-celebrity personas do not reflect the

relevant investment or the kind of exploitable commercial value protected by the right. *See Comedy III Productions, Inc. v. Gary Saderup, Inc.*, 21 P.3d 797 (2001), *cert. denied*, 534 U.S. 1078 (2002) (indicating that one of the requirements for publicity rights may be investment by the plaintiff in his persona — a form of incentive justification, much like copyright law); *Lerman v. Chuckleberry Publishing, Inc.*, 521 F. Supp. 228 (S.D.N.Y. 1981) (indicating that some actual exploitation of their persona by the plaintiff may be required). Consequently, non-celebrity misappropriation is more properly addressed by privacy, not right of publicity. The "coverage" argument is that although non-celebrities suffer less harm, commercial exploitation of their persona still involves unauthorized appropriation and related harm (the amount, for example, such use would bring if contracted for with an unknown actor). *See* Restatement (Third) of Unfair Competition, § 46 comments a & d (1995). If non-celebrities are covered then **Answer A** and **Answer B** are both incorrect and **Answer D** — that celebrity is an indicator of relevant harm — is the best answer. *Cf. Waits v. Frito-Lay*, 978 F.2d 1093 (9th Cir. 1992), *cert. denied*, 506 U.S. 1080 (1993) (amount of damage tied to fame and notoriety). If non-celebrities are *not* covered then both **Answer A** and **Answer B** are arguably correct, making the "best" answer a toss-up. Certainly reasonable minds can (and do) differ on the matter; full credit for seeing and understanding the issue and related arguments.

NOTE: Although right of publicity has been extended to "group personas" (for example a band) it does not apply to corporate entities.

401. **The best answer is A.** Right of publicity statutes frequently provide a list of protected persona attributes, commonly including name, likeness, signature and voice. However, the courts have recognized that the essential question in determining whether a misappropriation has occurred is whether looking at the context taken as a whole the reasonable consumer will connect the attribute to the plaintiff. *See Vanna White v. Samsung Electronics America, Inc.*, 971 F.2d 1395 (9th Cir. 1992), *cert. denied*, 508 U.S. 951 (1993). Under that approach, misappropriation occurs not just from use of the plaintiff's actual likeness, name or voice, but through use of strongly associated iconic emblems — for example, catch phrases ("Here's Johnny" for Johnny Carson), nicknames ("The Greatest" for Muhammad Ali) and even unique performance styles or mannerisms (Vanna White's turning of the letters on the game show answer board called to mind by a robot wearing a blond wig performing the same task). Applying that test to the facts, Tom has good misappropriation claims for **Answer B** (Tom's professional "Rocket Mann" nickname — particularly given the double "n"), **Answer C** (Tom's photo) and **Answer D** (his recognizable running shorts). The starting blocks with the "be like a rocket (small "r") out of the blocks" described in **Answer A** is highly problematic given the strong connection to Tom's nickname and activities but it is the weakest case among the four Answers.

402. **It depends on the applicable state law.** The states have taken different positions on "descendability." The majority position, both statutory and at common law, treats the right of publicity as a species of "property right" in the intangible persona and, therefore,

transferable on death. Some of those states have, however, limited the post-death right to a fixed term of years while a very few only allow post-death transfer if the individual actively exploited the rights during her lifetime. A small minority of jurisdictions protecting publicity rights view them as personal and automatically terminating when the person dies.

403.   **The best answer is B.** On the facts JenA can make out a basic right of publicity case. The comedy group has appropriated JenA's readily identifiable personal mannerism and style without her consent. Those mannerisms and her style constitute central elements of the commercial value of the new skits and their use without authorization deprives her of the related economic benefits. So neither **Answer C** nor **Answer D** is correct. **Answer A** raises the appropriate relationship between right of publicity claims and copyright law's protection of original expression fixed in a tangible medium. On the facts her performances, including her particular style, have been fixed through her special notation, triggering copyright protection. The comedy skits are very likely derivative works infringing those rights. The question, therefore, is whether JenA has *both* a copyright and a right of publicity claim, or if the former preempts the latter under Section 301(a) of the Copyright Act (17 U.S.C. § 301). The courts are split on the issue. The majority favor non-preemption on the grounds that an individual's persona is neither "authored" nor fixed (as distinct from any specific and perhaps copyrighted embodiment, like a particular photo) and, therefore, right of publicity protection is not equivalent to copyright protection. *See Toney v. L'Oreal USA, Inc.*, 406 F.3 905 (7th Cir. 2005). Under the majority view the comedy group's skits would simultaneously infringe JenA's copyright in the performances AND constitute a misappropriation of her persona. JenA faces greater difficulty with the argument that the group's skits are parodies of, and commentaries on, her, her style and her work and therefore immunized as First Amendment free speech (**Answer B**) against her right of publicity claim (as well as copyright infringement). That defense is recognized and taken very seriously by all courts in right of publicity cases. The courts' greater receptiveness to the First Amendment defense makes it the more serious concern, and **Answer B** better than **Answer A**.

404.   **The courts vary on their approach to the First Amendment defense — applying "balancing," "predominance" and "transformative" tests.** The "balancing" approach advocates case-by-case weighing of the free speech implications against the government interest in protecting the commercial value of an individual's persona (investment) under the particular circumstances. As almost all the (difficult) cases present both interests such balancing is virtually impossible without some reference standard. The "predominance" test offers such a standard by focusing the inquiry on whether the use primarily involves exploitation of the commercial value of the plaintiff's persona. If so, a violation exists despite any *additional* material (such as commentary). The "transformative" test finds the necessary standard in a modified application of copyright fair use doctrine (used to draw the infringement versus free speech distinction in that regime). That inquiry focuses on the first copyright fair use factor — "the purpose and character of the use" — specifically, whether the challenged use consists primarily of the persona

or if the persona merely serves as the foundation for commentary or expression. *See Comedy III Productions, Inc. v. Gary Saderup, Inc.*, 21 P.3d 797 (2001), *cert. denied*, 534 U.S. 1078 (2002) (alternatively articulating the test as whether the persona serves as one of the "raw materials" or is "the very sum and substance" of the challenged work). On these facts, a court would likely find under all three tests that the comedy group's work was parody/commentary on JenA, her works and performance art in general and, therefore, did not violate her right of publicity (or her copyrights).

405.   **The best answer is A**. The closer the connection between the use of JenA's persona and clearly protected speech (the skits in this case) the more likely the First Amendment defense will apply. *Cf. Rogers v. Grimaldi*, 875 F.2d 994 (2d Cir. 1989) (First Amendment protection of use of a celebrity name in a work's title requires the use not be "wholly unrelated" or "simply a disguised commercial advertisement for the sale of goods or services"). On that basis **Answer A** is the most problematic. There is no indication that the picture in the advertisement connects her in any way to the specific skits based on her work. Instead it merely calls attention to the comedy group, enhancing their efforts to sell their separate product. *See Vanna White v. Samsung Electronics America, Inc.*, 971 F.2d 1395 (9th Cir. 1992), *cert. denied*, 508 U.S. 951 (1993). In contrast, although not free from doubt, **Answers B, C** and **D** are closely connected to the performance of the particular skits and the related protected commentary. **Answer C** (the photo backdrop) and **Answer D** (the pre-show clips of JenA performing the works) are arguably part of the protected speech as they help call to mind the person and mannerisms being parodied. **Answer B**, while also closely related to the skits, may not even implicate the right of publicity in the first instance. Using JenA's name to accurately identify her as the source of the underlying work is merely factual reporting and, therefore, arguably does not involve appropriation of her persona at all.

406.   **The best answer is B**. Lanham Act § 43(a) (15 U.S.C. § 1125(a)) covers "false endorsements" under both its prohibition of use of a "word, term, name, symbol or device . . . which is likely to cause confusion . . . as to . . . sponsorship or approval of his or her goods, services or commercial activities . . . by another person," and as a "false designation of origin" leading to such a likelihood of confusion (I find the first cited language marginally more relevant in light of the test described below, but the "false designation of origin" language usefully distinguishes false endorsement claims from trademark infringement). A false endorsement claim requires: (1) the use be commercial (as contrasted with First Amendment protected speech, *see Rosa Parks v. LaFace Records*, 329 F.3d 437 (6th Cir. 2003)) (**Answer A**), (2) the plaintiff did not actually sponsor or endorse defendant's goods (**Answer D**) & (3) the public is likely to believe the plaintiff did sponsor or endorse defendant's goods (**Answer C**). It is not necessary that the defendant *expressly* state the plaintiff's sponsorship or endorsement of the goods or services (**Answer B**). It is sufficient that consumers are misled by the facts and circumstances into assuming that such an endorsement or sponsorship exists — a "false implied endorsement." *See Waits v. Frito-Lay*, 978 F.2d 1093 (9th Cir. 1992), *cert. denied*, 506 U.S. 1080 (1993); *Allen v. National Video, Inc.*, 610 F. Supp. 612 (S.D.N.Y. 1985). *Compare Oliveira v. Frito-Lay*, 43 U.S.P.Q.2d 1455 (S.D.N.Y. 1997)

(court skeptical that consumers will likely connect use of "Girl from Ipanema" sung by muppet Miss Piggy as an endorsement by Oliveira the original singer of the song, but denying a motion to dismiss).

NOTE: Tracking ordinary trademark infringement analysis, implied sponsorship or endorsement claims generally focus on the likelihood of confusion over the existence of sponsorship or endorsement. Actual confusion is a factor to be considered but is neither dispositive nor required.

NOTE: Beyond prohibiting false endorsement claims the Lanham Act also prohibits federal registration of marks which "falsely suggest a connection with persons, living or dead." *See* Topic 11 — Registration: Grounds for Refusal.

407. **Yes, but only slightly**. In impersonator cases (look alikes and sound alikes) it is also necessary to show that consumers would likely make the connection to the "real" person as well as likely be confused regarding his implied sponsorship or endorsement (either because consumers believed it was the actual person or assumed the imitation was done with the individual's approval). *See Waits v. Frito-Lay*, 978 F.2d 1093 (9th Cir. 1992), *cert. denied*, 506 U.S. 1080 (1993); *Allen v. National Video, Inc.*, 610 F. Supp. 612 (S.D.N.Y. 1985). Otherwise, the elements remain the same: the group's use must not involve protected free speech, no actual sponsorship or endorsement by JenA and likelihood of consumer confusion regarding her sponsorship or endorsement of the group.

408. **Probably not**. To prevail on a trademark infringement claim JenA would have to show that she had trademark rights in her likeness or the photo. Although the courts generally treat a person's personal attributes as a *quasi*-mark for false endorsement purposes applying a "likelihood of confusion" standard regarding their use to test for a related violation, they only very rarely find those attributes are actual trademarks. Applying trademark rules, JenA must show that she is using her likeness as a mark in connection with particular goods and services and, as with other marks which have an independent primary meaning, show secondary meaning. Those requirements can rarely be met. *See ETW Corp. v. Jireh Publishing, Inc.*, 332 F.3d 915 (6th Cir. 2003); Topic 4 — Distinctiveness: Inherently Distinctive; Secondary Meaning; Never.

NOTE: To clearly distinguish false endorsement claims from trademark infringement — confirming that the former violation can exist even without a valid trademark — some courts have articulated a distinct three part inquiry: (1) there must be an effect on interstate commerce (jurisdictional), (2) there must be a false designation of origin or a false description (3) of goods or services. As noted above, the key second element, however, generally focuses on the likelihood of confusion test driving trademark infringement with some courts explicitly employing the same "factors" analysis. *See Allen v. National Video, Inc.*, 610 F. Supp. 612 (S.D.N.Y. 1985); Topic 13 — Infringement: Likelihood of Confusion.

409. **The best answer is D** (but it's a close call). Of the four possibilities traditional trademark infringement (**Answer C**) is the most problematic as it raises the problem discussed

in previous Question proving that Nifty's name is being used as a trademark and has the requisite secondary meaning. A false endorsement (**Answer B**) claim has substantial potential as Nifty clearly did not endorse the film and it does not require he hold trademark rights in his name. The central debate will be whether consumers are likely to see the phrase "A Nifty Bampo Story" as implying his endorsement of the film or as merely a factual (albeit false) statement regarding the source of the story. A false advertising claim (**Answer A**) also has considerable merit given the movie is not a Nifty Bampo story and being literally false, deception will be presumed. The argument will center on whether the non-mystery nature of the film makes the false statement immaterial to consumer purchasing decisions given the "different genre" facts of the case. *See* Topic 21 — False Advertising and False Designations of Origin. A false "attribution" claim (**Answer D**) is, in effect, a trademark "passing off" claim under Lanham Act § 43(a) (15 U.S.C. § 1125(a)) which does not require trademark rights, proof of a likelihood of confusion or inquiry into materiality. When a seller (the movie company in this case) falsely represents their goods (the contained story, not the movie itself) as coming from another by express identification of the actual source (versus use of a mark) it constitutes "false designation of origin" not "infringement" and, as such is sufficiently deceptive to support a violation standing alone. *See King v. Innovation Books*, 976 F.2d 824 (2d Cir. 1992) ("no evidence of public confusion is required where . . . the attribution is false on its face"). Under that approach a false attribution/designation of origin claim would require no evidence beyond proof of the statement's falsity, making it the best among three reasonably promising alternatives.

410.   **The actual connection requires Nifty show the changes by Small Films so substantially distorted his work that naming him as its "source" was deceptive.** When the plaintiff was the actual source of a work the courts may still find passing off if, in light of changes made, the work can no longer be fairly attributed to the plaintiff without deceiving the public. *See Gilliam v. American Broadcasting Companies, Inc.*, 538 F.2d 14 (2d Cir. 1976); *King v. Innovation Books*, 976 F.2d 824 (2d Cir. 1992) (distinguishing between false on their face attributions and those involving altered works). Proving that claim, however, requires a very substantial modification to the "core" of the work.

411.   **The best answer is D** (but it's close). On the facts, Small Films' failure to credit Nifty is a "false designation of origin." However, in this situation Small Films is not passing off its goods as coming from Nifty when they do not (an affirmative false attribution claim). Consequently, regular passing off under Lanham Act § 43(a) (15 U.S.C. § 1125(a)) does not apply and **Answer B** is incorrect. However, the courts have held that Section 43(a) also reaches "reverse passing off" — palming off of another's goods as one's own — when there is "bodily appropriation" (meaning taking in whole, not merely offering generally similar goods — raising, of course, the problem of determining the reach of bodily appropriation; generally the courts view that as requiring taking *in toto*). *See Smith v. Montoro*, 648 F.2d 602 (9th Cir. 1981). If it were not for the Supreme Court's decision in *Dastar Corp. v. Twentieth Century Fox Film Corp.*, 123 S. Ct. 2041 (2003) the best answer under prior law would, therefore, have been that Nifty would win, with **Answer C** nudging out **Answer A** for greater specificity concerning why

and likelihood — Nifty would likely win on a false designation of origin — reverse passing off claim based on Small Films' "probable" bodily appropriation of his entire work (the issue being whether the screen play is enough to taint the movie). However, the Court in *Dastar* considerably muddied the reverse passing off waters by holding that "false designation of origin" means only that the defendant did not actually produce the good in question, not that it failed to attribute its genesis to its actual "author." *See* Topic 21 — False Advertising and False Designations of Origin. Because the Court did not address the issue directly, it is unclear how the *Dastar* holding affects reverse passing off actions and, most particularly, "under-attribution" false designation of origin cases. That leaves the proper choice between **Answer C** (Nifty likely to win a reverse passing off claim) and **Answer D** (Nifty likely to lose) unresolved. On one hand, in dicta the Court noted that a "bodily appropriation" of a physical good, repackaged and sold under another's name would be a violation. On the other, the logical application of the "manufacturer not author" *Dastar* test to creative (communicative) works (involving authorship, not tangible things) strongly favors Small Films. As the "producer" of the physical product in this case (the movie) it arguably has not falsely designated its origin by failing attribute the underlying "creative" screen play to Nifty. On balance **Answer D** (likely to lose) seems the best answer post-*Dastar*. That said, the Court was unclear in *Dastar* regarding how a valid copyright in the creative work (the Court stated the independent copyright infringement claim survives) or modifications of the creative work by the defendant might affect false designation/attribution rights, so we'll have to see how the case law develops.

NOTE: The question also exists as to how *Dastar* affects claims for false advertising based on under-attribution; specifically, does the lack of false designation of origin liability also mean such an omission is not "false" or "deceptive" for false advertising purposes?

PRACTICE FINAL EXAM: ANSWERS

412. **The best answer is D**. For "Miracle" to qualify as a trademark it must be used to signal source in the trademark sense — meaning that it identifies and distinguishes the hand cream made by Miracle Corporation in the marketplace. Although "Miracle" does identify the producer, because it does not appear on the product it is not signaling source to the consuming public. As on these facts it is not being used as a trademark, **Answer D** is correct and **Answer A** is incorrect. The name of a company — a trade name (**Answer C**) — can serve as a trademark; however, it must be used as a trademark which is not the case here. That "Miracle" may be arbitrary (**Answer B**) and therefore distinctive is relevant to determining if it can be protected as a trademark, but only if it is first being used as a trademark. *See* Topic 1 — Justifications and Sources Of Trademark Law.

413. **The best answer is B**. To qualify as a trademark "Sleek Skin" must be used to "signal source" in the trademark law sense — that is, identifying and distinguishing Miracle's hand cream in the marketplace. "Signaling source" means it consistently and reliably indicates the presence of the related product characteristics, not that it identify the particular producer — so **Answer A** is incorrect. The fact that "Sleek Skin" is not the producer's name neither disqualifies it from being, nor makes it a trademark. What matters is that it be used to signal source. **Answer B** correctly states *both* that the failure to identify Miracle as the producer is not fatal, but also that "Sleek Skin" *can* be, not that it *is* a trademark. Both **Answer C** and **Answer D** make the absence of the actual producer name issue dispositive (either for or against trademark status) and are, therefore, incorrect. *See* Topic 1 — Justifications and Sources of Trademark Law.

414. **The best answer is B**. Sleek Skin is being used on the product and, therefore, arguably as a trademark. However, in order to signal source in the trademark sense it must be "distinctive" — that is capable of uniquely and reliably identifying a particular product's characteristics. To do so, it need not be the producer's (or anyone's) trade name (**Answer C**) or federally registered (**Answer D**), so both of those answers are incorrect. On these facts there is a question about whether "Sleek Skin" is distinctive and, therefore, perhaps not able to signal source. **Answer B** more specifically describes that particular problem,

making it better than **Answer A**. *See* Topic 1 — Justifications and Sources of Trademark Law and Topic 3 — Basic Distinctiveness: The Spectrum of Distinctiveness Word Marks, Including Acronyms and Foreign Words.

415.   The *spectrum of distinctiveness* is used to classify marks with regard to their ability to signal source. Under that classification system "hand cream" is the name for the entire class of products, making it generic. Generic terms are never protectable as trademarks. They do not identify and distinguish a particular product in the class and, even if they came to do so (through secondary meaning), to allow one producer control over such "class labels" would put other competitors at a serious competitive disadvantage. *See* Topic 3 — Basic Distinctiveness: The Spectrum of Distinctiveness Word Marks, Including Acronyms and Foreign Words.

416.   **The best answer is C (but it's a very close call with B)**. The spectrum of distinctiveness (generic, descriptive, suggestive, arbitrary/fanciful) is used to classify marks with regard to their ability to signal source. For a hand cream used to moisturize dry skin the words "Sleek Skin" is neither *generic* (the name for the class of products — **Answer A**) nor *fanciful* (an invented term — **Answer D**) (or arbitrary — unrelated to the product in any way). Rather it is arguably *descriptive* (**Answer B**) or *suggestive* (**Answer C**). The test for making that determination is: applying the public interpretation (dictionary definition) does the mark describe the ingredients, characteristics, use or outcome of the product or is a leap of imagination is required to make the connection (courts also consider the need or actual use of the mark to describe competing products). The argument in this case will center on whether "Sleek Skin" describes the outcome of the product's use or merely suggests that outcome (as distinguished, for example, from the phrase "moist skin" or even "smooth skin"). For my money, the linguistic connotations point toward the suggestive classification leading me to pick **Answer C** over **Answer B**. Reasonable minds can (and in cases do) differ; the important point here is to see and understand the issue. *See* Topic 3 — Basic Distinctiveness: The Spectrum of Distinctiveness Word Marks, Including Acronyms and Foreign Words.

417.   **Suggestive marks are inherently distinctive (requiring no additional showing of distinctiveness) while a descriptive mark is not.** The spectrum of distinctiveness contains an important division regarding the distinctiveness of marks. Marks classified as suggestive, arbitrary or fanciful are treated as inherently distinctive — that is deemed able to identify and distinguish the related product without any further showing. Descriptive marks are capable of being distinctive, but are not treated as such without a further showing. Generic marks are never distinctive and can never serve as trademarks. *See* Topic 4 — Distinctiveness: Inherently Distinctive; Secondary Meaning; Never.

418.   **The best answer is D**. In order to claim a descriptive mark as a trademark the claimant must demonstrate that it has taken on trademark significance to the consumer public. That showing of *secondary meaning* involves proof (usually by means of consumer surveys) that consumers do not see the term merely as describing a product ingredient,

characteristic, use or outcome (the term's primary meaning), but it has taken on special significance as identifying and distinguishing the *specific* characteristics of the claimant's *particular* product. Although **Answer C** is correct, **Answer D** more precisely identifies what is required to meet that requirement, making **Answer D** the better answer. *See* Topic 4 — Distinctiveness: Inherently Distinctive; Secondary Meaning; Never. The "Sleek Skin" mark is not arbitrary on these facts — it is connected to the product's use and outcomes, so **Answer A** is incorrect. The "fair use" doctrine permits non-trademark competitive use of a descriptive mark with demonstrated secondary meaning, not the right to claim such a mark as a trademark, so **Answer B** is incorrect.

419. **The best answer is C**. An arbitrary mark is one which has a pre-existing independent meaning but no connection to the related product. "Pica" (**Answer C**) is such a word. It has an independent meaning (as a type size) with no connection to the product. "Azzat" (**Answer A**) is an invented word, so it would be classified as fanciful rather than arbitrary. "Aloe" (**Answer B**) is a real word, however, it is arguably connected to a moisturizing cream as a possible ingredient (if the product does not contain aloe it may be deceptive or deceptively misdescriptive, but it is nonetheless not arbitrary). "601" (**Answer D**) raises the special issue of how the spectrum of distinctiveness classification system applies to *non-word marks*. Although 601 has a pre-existing independent meaning unconnected to the product, thus arguably making it arbitrary, the question remains whether consumers will see it as a number rather than a trademark. To classify it as arbitrary and, therefore, inherently distinctive would fail to consider that source signaling concern. As a general proposition, therefore, non-word marks require further distinctiveness analysis. In the case of numbers (and colors as well as personal names — which also may be seen by consumers in that pre-existing role rather than as trademarks), the courts require a showing of secondary meaning. *See* Topic 5 — Distinctiveness: Non-Word Marks Colors and Trade Dress.

420. **The best answer is C**. Obtaining trademark rights in even an inherently distinctive mark requires use. That use must be *"bona fide"* — used in the ordinary course of trade in the market, not mere token use for the purpose of obtaining trademark rights. Putting the mark on the cream jars (**Answer B**) evidences Miracle's adoption and intent to use the mark as a trademark, but is not actual market use sufficient to obtain trademark rights. Similarly, despite the large quantity involved, Miracle's internal shipment of labeled jars from its plant to its warehouse (**Answer D**) is not market use involving offers to consumers. The market sale transaction to the retailer (**Answer C**), albeit small, is *bona fide* use in the ordinary course of trade, generating rights in the trademark. Although a federal registration (**Answer A**), among other things, is prima facie evidence of Miracle's valid rights in the mark, it is not necessary to obtain trademark rights. *See* Topic 7 — Acquiring Rights: Use.

421. **The best answer is D**. Merely having valid rights in the mark is insufficient; the alleged infringer's activities must fall within the product and geographic scope of Astro's trademark rights — which are measured by the "likelihood of consumer confusion" on the facts. Absent a federal registration, Astro's rights in the "Kart" mark arise from,

and are limited by, its use. That means Astro has rights only in the geographic market in which it is selling its camping equipment plus any additional territories where consumer associations between the mark and Astro's products may cause confusion (and, perhaps, a zone of natural expansion). On these facts, which involve marking and sales only in the Eastern United States, there is nothing to indicate that there is any consumer awareness in (or likely expansion into) in Arizona. Although Duo's *product* is clearly within Astro's rights (it is the same product and, therefore, likely to cause confusion), because Duo is *selling* outside the geographic scope of Astro's rights it will win the lawsuit. That makes **Answer D** correct and **Answers A, B** and **C** incorrect. *See* Topic 7 — Acquiring Rights: Use.

422.   **The best answer is B.** Geographic trademark rights in "Kart" follow the "first use plus consumer associations" geographic scope rule. That means the owner of the rights in Nebraska will be the first to use or the first to develop consumer associations in the state. Either **Answer A** or **Answer B** is, therefore, correct. However, as **Answer B** will always flow from **Answer A**, but is not dependent upon actual use and can occur earlier, it is (arguably) the best answer. Neither being the literal first adopter of the mark "somewhere" nor being the geographically closest first adopter is sufficient to create trademark rights in Nebraska, so both **Answer C** and **Answer D** are incorrect. *See* Topic 7 — Acquiring Rights: Use.

423.   **The best answer is A.** Merely having valid rights in the mark is insufficient; the alleged infringer's activities must fall within the product and geographic scope of those rights — so **Answer C** is not sufficient. Here the products are identical, so the issue is geographic scope of Gern's trademark rights. Gern obtained rights in Iowa (and other territories where it can show consumer associations leading to likelihood of confusion and, perhaps, a zone of natural expansion) starting with its use in 1995. On these facts, those rights most likely do not include Oregon. Gern's federal registration in 1998 gave it constructive use from the date it filed its application and priority in all "open" geographic markets on that date (territories in which there was no conflicting use at that time). Twofer's Oregon adoption was in good faith and started in 1997, before Gern's federal registration. As a result it did not violate Gern's use-based rights in the mark at that time. Because Twofer's Oregon use came before Gern's registration-based priority was triggered by filing its application, Twofer's Oregon used-based rights are "grandfathered" in as a good faith prior user despite Gern's subsequent federal registration (Oregon was not an "open" geographic territory at the time Gern filed its application). **Answer B** correctly indicates that Twofer escapes liability because it is not selling in Iowa. However, that is only important because Twofer's Oregon use pre-dates Gern's federal registration which would have given it nationwide rights in the mark. Consequently, **Answer A** is a better answer than **Answer B**. For the same reason Gern's federal registration is unavailing, making **Answer D** incorrect. *See* Topic 9 — Registration: Constructive Use and Intent to Use.

424.   **The best answer is D.** On these facts Twofer's use in Oregon commenced *after* Gern's federal registration and its related priority in all "open" territories after the date Gern

filed its application. That makes Gern the senior user (constructively) and the winner of the infringement suit by virtue of its federal registration (the identical mark and products making consumer confusion likely). So **Answer D** is correct and **Answer A** and **Answer B** are not. Gern's used-based rights do not extend to Oregon, so **Answer C** is incorrect. *See* Topic 9 — Registration: Constructive Use and Intent to Use.

425. **The answer is B**. Federal registration provides a presumption of validity (**Answer A**), the possibility of incontestability (**Answer C**) and constructive use in all "open" territories (**Answer D**). It is not necessary for a mark to be registered to obtain protection against dilution, either under state or federal law, so **Answer B** identifies something which does not depend on or arise from a federal registration. *See* Topic 10 — Registration: Process Basic Requirements and Benefits, and Topic 14 — Dilution.

426. **The prohibition on federal registration of disparaging marks**. If a substantial composite of Native Americans (the target group) views the mark as slighting, deprecating, degrading, or affecting or injuring them by unjust comparison, they can bring an opposition to Scuzt's registration. *See* Topic 11 — Registration: Grounds for Refusal.

427. **The best answer is A**. The Lanham Act categorically prohibits the registration of a deceptive mark (including, as in this case, one which misdescribes the product, consumers are likely to believe that misdescription and that mistaken belief is likely to influence their purchase decision). Marks found to be deceptively misdescriptive (satisfying only the first two but not the third requirement listed above) or descriptive (accurately describing an ingredient, characteristic, use or effects of the product) are also barred from registration. However, either of those latter two kinds of marks can be federally registered upon a showing of secondary meaning. **Answer A** is therefore the most likely to bar registration both on the facts and because Scuzt may overcome the prohibition regarding **Answer B** and **Answer C**. **Answer D** is incorrect, as all three classifications can be a bar to federal registration. *See* Topic 11 — Registration: Grounds for Refusal.

428. **The best answer is D**. The Lanham Act draws an important distinction between deceptively misdescriptive marks and *geographically* deceptively misdescriptive marks. The former, which do not affect purchase decisions, can be registered if secondary meaning is shown. The latter, which are assessed using the same three requirements as *deceptive* marks including mistaken belief affecting consumer purchase decisions, can never be registered. On these facts the mark is geographically deceptively misdescriptive not deceptively misdescriptive, as the geographic source misdescription affects consumers' purchase decisions. **Answer A** is incorrect and so is **Answer C** (which additionally inaccurately describes such marks as never registerable). **Answer D** correctly identifies the absolute prohibition on geographically deceptively misdescriptive marks, which cannot be registered despite a showing of secondary meaning, making **Answer B** incorrect. *See* Topic 11 — Registration: Grounds for Refusal.

429.   **The best answer is A.** The Lanham Act (the federal trademark statute) does not preempt but rather "supplements" state trademark law (both statutory and common law), so **Answer C** is incorrect. The Lanham Act permits a federal claim on either registered or unregistered marks provided it is used "in commerce." That is a very low barrier measured by the reach of the Commerce Clause on which federal trademark legislation rests (versus patent and copyright laws genesis in the Intellectual Property Clause; *see* Topic 1 —Justifications and Sources of Trademark Law). On these facts that requirement is easily satisfied by Mona's nationwide sales. So **Answer B** (limiting federal lawsuits to registered marks) and **Answer D** (which states the federal copyright law, not trademark law, requirement of registration prior to bringing suit) are both incorrect. Consequently, Mona can bring either or both state and federal trademark claims against Ersalts as stated in **Answer A** (both claims are usually brought to take advantage of differing remedies). *See* Topic 1 — Justifications and Sources of Trademark Law and Topic 13 — Infringement: Likelihood of Confusion.

430.   **The best answer is C.** To prevail in a trademark infringement lawsuit Mona must prove Ersalts' use of the "Tramwell" mark is likely to cause consumer confusion. That showing requires proving *both* that Ersalts' product and geographic activities fall within Mona's trademark rights, which determinations are based on finding a likelihood of confusion. So **Answer C** is better than either **Answer A** or **Answer B** standing alone. Although the defendant's bad faith can be evidence of likelihood of confusion, infringement does not depend on the defendant's motivations only the likely effect on consumers whom trademark law seeks to protect. So if consumer confusion is likely Ersalts' good or bad faith is irrelevant, making **Answer D** incorrect. *See* Topic 13 — Infringement: Likelihood of Confusion.

431.   **The best answer is A.** The courts use a "factors" analysis to determine likelihood of confusion. Although the specific factors vary by jurisdiction, in the absence of a strong showing of actual confusion, they generally reflect inquiry into the relationship between the marks (similarity, strength), the connection between the products (in terms of function/use — related goods; channels of advertising and sale) and the nature of the purchase transaction (likely to rely heavily on the mark). On these facts, the marks being identical (**Answer C**) is highly relevant, strongly favoring Mona's position. **Answer B** addresses whether consumers are likely to "bridge the gap" between gloves and home furnishings — that is make a source signaling connection despite differences in function/ use of the products. Although in this case that seems highly unlikely, the issue itself is very relevant (it is likely to be at the core of Ersalts' defense). Ersalts will also argue that the infrequent nature of furniture purchases (**Answer D**) means that consumers are unlikely rely heavily on the trademark signal thereby avoiding confusion. Mona may argue that the presence of both products in large department stores (**Answer A**) means they are marketed and sold in similar channels targeting the same consumers. However, that argument generally does not carry much (if any) weight, as such stores advertise and sell such a wide variety of products that the presence of both products in those channels does not demonstrate relevant distribution channel overlap. Therefore, although

it is (minimally) relevant, **Answer A** is the least relevant answer on these facts. *See* Topic 13 — Infringement: Likelihood of Confusion.

432.   To win its trademark infringement lawsuit Pazzo must show that it (1) has valid rights in the trademark ("Danziano") and (2) that Secondo's use is likely to cause consumer confusion.

To have valid rights in the mark it must be (a) distinctive and (b) been used by Pazzo as a trademark. The facts state that Danziano is an invented word, so it is best categorized as "fanciful." It will, therefore, be treated as inherently distinctive; not requiring any showing of secondary meaning to qualify as a mark. The facts also indicate *bona fide* use in the ordinary course of trade by Pazzo by virtue of its extensive market sales of products bearing the mark (that use is also "in commerce" satisfying the Lanham Act jurisdictional requirement). The geographic scope of Pazzo's rights should be broken down into two distinct time periods. From the time it started use until its application for a federal registration three years ago, it had use-based rights in Illinois, Indiana, Michigan and Ohio (its area of actual use) plus any additional areas in which it can show consumer associations between the mark and its products likely to cause confusion. *See* Topic 7 — Acquiring Rights: Use. From three years ago until today, federal registration constructive use extended it rights to all "open" geographic areas at the time it filed its application. *See* Topic 9 — Registration: Constructive Use and Intent to Use. The product scope of Pazzo's rights extends to the product itself (pasta sauces) and any sufficiently "related" goods as give rise to a likelihood of consumer confusion. *See* Topic 7 — Acquiring Rights: Use.

Turning to Secondo's use, the first issue concerns likelihood of confusion based on overlap with the geographic scope of Pazzo's rights. On the facts, Secondo's use prior to Pazzo's federal registration is only problematic in Ohio (assuming there are no consumer associations in Pennsylvania). Post-registration, Pazzo's constructive use national rights raise problems for Secondo's expansion into New York and New Jersey (its Pennsylvania pre-filing use and related rights being grandfathered and valid despite Pazzo's subsequent registration). Regarding the possible pre-filing infringement in Ohio and post-filing infringement in Ohio, New York and New Jersey it is necessary to perform a "factors" analysis of the two products involved to determine whether consumer confusion is likely. *See* Topic 13 — Infringement: Likelihood of Confusion. There is no evidence of actual confusion or bad faith on the facts, so the inquiry will focus on the similarity of the marks and the relatedness of the goods and their distribution channels. The two marks are identical, favoring Pazzo. The two products — sauces and pre-grated cheese are not; however, the related (complementary) nature of their use, the strong likelihood they are distributed in overlapping channels to the same target consumers and the relatively strong consumer reliance on trademarks in such purchases (taste cannot be determined by inspection) also all favor Pazzo. This strong likelihood of consumer confusion in the problematic geographies (Ohio, New York and New Jersey) means that Pazzo will likely prevail — despite the absence of Secondo's lack of intent to infringe; avoiding consumer confusion, not willfulness, driving trademark law. In granting relief, however, a court may permit Secondo to continue its use in New York and New Jersey until Pazzo is ready to expand into those territories (*see* Topic 9 — Registration: Constructive Use and Intent to Use).

433. The change affects the distinctiveness determination. Foreign words (at least those in current use in a "live" language) are generally first translated and then tested for distinctiveness. In this case, that means Pazzo's mark is likely to be classified as descriptive — tomatoes being the key ingredient in its pasta sauces. That classification requires Pazzo show evidence of secondary meaning in order to claim trademark rights. Pre-registration, if there was no secondary meaning prior to Secondo's use in Ohio, there is no infringement because despite the overlapping geographic territory and strong relatedness of the products Pazzo simply had no valid trademark rights at that time. Post-registration, Pazzo's federal registration is *prima facie* evidence of its valid rights in the "Pomodoro" mark. But that does not prevent Secondo from challenging Pazzo's rights on descriptiveness grounds as the mark has only been registered four years and is, therefore, not incontestable. So if Pazzo cannot show supporting secondary meaning, its registration will be cancelled and along with it constructive use-based trademark rights in New York and New Jersey. *See* Topic 3 — Basic Distinctiveness: The Spectrum of Distinctiveness Word Marks, Including Acronyms; Topic 4 — Distinctiveness: Inherently; Secondary Meaning; Never; and Foreign Words; and Topic 12 — Registration: Incontestability.

434. **The best answer is D**. A federally registered mark can be challenged as descriptive at any time prior to its becoming incontestable, so mere federal registration (**Answer A**) does not make the descriptiveness problem disappear. A federally registered mark (not an unregistered mark) becomes incontestable provided it remains registered and continuously used for five after registration (plus no adverse proceeding is pending or adverse decision has been made regarding the owner's rights) and the necessary filing is made under Section 15 of the Lanham Act. Incontestability makes the federal registration presumption of validity conclusive; however, even an incontestable mark can be challenged on the specific grounds listed in the Lanham Act (Sections 14, 15 and 33(b)). Consequently, **Answer C** is not accurate. Those grounds do not include descriptiveness (the issue in this case), making **Answer D** correct. **Answer B** is correct; the *registration* cannot be cancelled on descriptiveness grounds after five years. However, merely avoiding cancellation of its registration does not afford Pazzo the conclusive presumption despite possible descriptiveness (registration only provides *prima facie* evidence of validity); that only comes from the incontestability of the mark. *See* Topic 12 — Registration: Incontestability.

435. **Yes, there is a potential deceptiveness issue**. Pazzo still has an incontestable mark; however, incontestable marks can be challenged on the grounds that they are deceptive. The relevant test is whether the mark misdescribes the product, a consumer is likely to believe that misdescription and that mistaken belief will affect the purchase decision. Those requirements are likely to be met on these facts thus providing a basis for

Secondo's challenging the validity Pazzo's trademark despite its incontestable status. *See* Topic 12 — Registration: Incontestability.

The full consequences of a successful challenge by Secondo's are unclear. Although the Lanham Act prohibits *registration* of deceptive marks, it does not expressly prevent *use* of deceptive (or other federally unregisterable) marks. Consequently, Secondo may have the registration cancelled and with it Pazzo's constructive use rights in New York and New Jersey. It would not escape infringement in Ohio where Pazzo's rights are based on prior use unless a court found that its deceptive (not descriptive) mark is invalid under common law. *See* Topic 11 — Registration: Grounds for Refusal.

436. **The best answer is D**. The Question involves a service mark — that is, a mark used on services rather than goods. Service marks are treated (almost) identically to trademarks, so the distinctiveness classification rules are the same. The basic rule for acronyms and misspellings is that classification follows likely consumer perception. If consumers treat such a mark as equivalent to the underlying or correctly spelled word(s), then the mark classification follows that meaning. In this case consumers will readily seen the "creative" misspelling and make the connection to the word "quick." So the "fanciful" misspelling will be ignored, making **Answer A** and **Answer B** incorrect. The word "quick" most likely will be treated as descriptive of the internet services, describing a key characteristic and requiring no imagination to make the connection. So **Answer D** is better than **Answer C**. *See* Topic 3 — Basic Distinctiveness: The Spectrum of Distinctiveness Word Marks, Including Acronyms and Foreign Words.

437. **The best answer is D**. The "Aworthy Approved" label is not used to identify Aworthy's services (its evaluations) or products (its magazine), but those third party products which meet its evaluation standards. That makes it a certification mark (**Answer C**) rather than a trademark (**Answer A**) or service mark (**Answer B**). It is not a collective mark. Although one might argue there is a "group" of approved cars, the manufacturers do not belong to any organization so their use of the label is not indicating either membership or the products of group members. The "Aworthy" name alone may be a service mark (identifying the evaluation service) and/or a trademark (on the magazine). *See* Topic 2 — Service Marks, Certification Marks and Collective Marks.

438. **The best answer is A**. The "Aworthy Approved" label is a certification mark. Such marks must be made available to all products which meet the applicable requirements (as set by the mark owner) without discrimination (**Answer A**). Such marks cannot be used on the owner's own products, so **Answer B** is not only incorrect but would cause loss of certification mark status. No organization (collective) exists so there are no dues (**Answer C**); in fact, charging for the right to use may indicate either a violation of the "all qualifiers" requirement or availability to non-qualified producers on payment of a fee — both of which would cause loss of certification mark rights. Finally, there is no requirement that the qualifying producers actually use a certification mark to maintain its status, so **Answer D** is incorrect. *See* Topic 2 — Service Marks, Certification Marks and Collective Marks.

439. **Yes.** There are virtually no ontological (nature of the mark) limits on what may qualify as a trademark — including words, phrases, drawings, graphics, composites, sounds and smells. *See* Topic 5 — Distinctiveness: Non-Word Marks Colors and Trade Dress.

440. **The best answer is D (although B and C are good second choices).** Smells can serve as trademarks, so **Answer A** is incorrect. A fundamental problem with using smell as a trademark in this situation is that the bottles will generally be closed thus prohibiting the smell "mark" from communicating with consumers in the marketplace (**Answer B**). That difficulty might be overcome by adding the smell to the packaging, for example by scenting the box or adding an identifying label noting its presence in the perfume. But even if that problem is overcome Scents faces the problem that the smell of a perfume is part of the product and, consequently, consumers may not treat it as a mark. That issue has led the Supreme Court to hold that product design (which seems an apt description of the smell in this case) is never inherently distinctive (**Answer C**). Thus Scents would have to show secondary meaning prior to obtaining trademark rights. That "part of the product" analysis, however, also raises the more serious functionality concern (**Answer D**); which would prohibit a trademark claim even with demonstrated secondary meaning. The smell of a perfume is essential to its use or purpose (and may affect its cost or quality). Even were a court willing to consider alternatives (questionable as a matter of law), permitting capture of a particular smell in the cologne/perfume business would very seriously and adversely affect competition on the product merits. Better, therefore, to deny trademark protection and channel the formula that produces the smell into patent law. *See* Topic 5 — Distinctiveness: Non-Word Marks Colors and Trade Dress and Topic 6 — Functionality.

441. **The best answer is B**. The drawing avoids the functionality problem, but raises the issue of how it should be classified for distinctiveness purposes. The difficulty arises from applying the spectrum of distinctiveness to non-word marks. As the flower in the drawing is "common" it will likely be identified by consumers and, therefore, should arguably be classified in the same way as the word-name for that flower. As that flower's essence forms the primary ingredient in the product, the likely classification will be descriptive, meaning Scents will be required to show secondary meaning before claiming the drawing as a trademark. Although **Answer A** and **Answer C** are both correct, **Answer B** is more specific and, therefore, the best answer. Regardless of the outcome, distinctiveness classification will be an issue on these facts, so **Answer D** is incorrect. *See* Topic 5 — Distinctiveness: Non-Word Marks Colors and Trade Dress.

442. The basic functionality test requires examination of whether the claimed mark is essential to the use or purpose of the article or affects its cost or quality. It will, therefore, be important to determine how the new shape affects the usefulness of the wine glasses — for example, does it make it easier to hold, better balanced or the like. Consideration must also be given to whether the shape makes the glasses cheaper to make (less material, easier production process) or to ship or store. Finally, the Supreme Court appears to have stated that once a product design feature is determined to be functional then no consideration of alternatives is appropriate. However, the issue remains somewhat

confused in subsequent application by the lower courts, with some continuing to view alternatives as at least a factor to be considered. Consequently, at least a debate over the relevance and, perhaps, the effect of available alternative competitive designs is likely. *See* Topic 6 — Functionality.

443. **Aesthetic functionality**. Although the shape of the glass may not be relevant to its performance, cost or quality, it may be sufficiently aesthetically appealing to the consuming public to place Glassware's competitors at a "significant non-reputation-related disadvantage." Or, alternatively stated, does the shape "serve a significant non-trademark function?" If so, then the shape cannot be protected as a trademark. In determining aesthetical functionality the issue of alternative designs plays a larger role. So Glassware's ability to show that other designs exist may preclude a finding of aesthetic functionality and permit it to claim its particular shape as a trademark. *See* Topic 6 — Functionality.

444. The existence of a *utility* patent (not a design patent) on a product feature strongly indicates that the feature is functional and, therefore, cannot serve as a trademark. The Supreme Court has, however, indicated (but did not hold; specifically reserving the issue of whether patenting prohibits a trademark claim) that where a feature is only incidental to the patent a claimant might be able to prove it is not functional and protectable as a trademark. *See* Topic 6 — Functionality.

445. **No, on protecting the shape as a trademark, perhaps yes on obtaining unfair competition relief**. The strong policy against permitting trademark law from interfering with competition on the product merits prevents functional elements of product design from ever serving as a trademark. However, strong consumer associations may provide a basis for requiring competitors adopting a functional feature to include appropriate disclaimers of Glassware's involvement to avoid possible consumer confusion. *See* Topic 6 — Functionality.

446. **The best answer is C**. Product packaging (a form of trade dress) can be protected as a trademark, so **Answer D** is incorrect. Additionally, protectability of product packaging is approached differently than product design. The Supreme Court has held that although product design is never inherently distinctive (thus requiring a showing of secondary meaning, as well as non-functionality), product packaging can (but need not) be. So **Answer C** is correct and **Answer A** and **Answer B** are incorrect *See* Topic 5 — Distinctiveness: Non-Word Marks Colors and Trade Dress.

447. **The best answer is A**. Product packaging (trade dress) can be protected as a trademark, so **Answer D** is incorrect. The issue is whether Pharma's package is "inherently distinctive" and, therefore, automatically protectable rather than requiring a showing of secondary meaning (**Answer B**). Determining whether trade dress is inherently distinctive raises the difficult issue of how to classify non-word marks. Some courts apply the spectrum of distinctiveness, with limited analytical success in instances where there is no equivalent word such as this one. Others inquire as to whether the package

is "unique or unexpected" under the circumstances. Under a "spectrum" analysis one could argue that Pharma's packaging is fanciful (invented) or perhaps more accurately arbitrary (the colors exist, but bear no relationship to the product) and, therefore, inherently distinctive as stated in **Answer C**. Although a reasonable approach, that analysis fails to consider the essential distinctiveness issue — consumer perception given what is happening in the marketplace. In particular, if gradated colors in pharmaceutical packaging are common, consumers may fail to even notice Pharma's particular implementation. On the other hand if such packaging is uncommon, it will likely stand out. Applying that alternative "unique or unexpected" approach, the facts indicate that Pharma's packaging should qualify as inherently distinctive (**Answer A**). Although **Answer A** and **Answer C** are both arguably correct, **Answer A** reflects a better analysis on these facts. As in either case the packaging is inherently distinctive there is no need for Pharma to show secondary meaning, making **Answer B** incorrect. *See* Topic 5 — Distinctiveness: Non-Word Marks Colors and Trade Dress.

448.   **Lack of use; file an intent to use application.** Even if a mark is sufficiently distinctive to qualify as a trademark, no rights can be obtained until the mark is actually used. Pharma's difficulty is that while it is preparing to ramp-up its launch of the new package during the next six months someone else might gain priority in some or all geographic markets by being the first to actually use the trade dress. The Lanham Act addresses this problem by permitting a limited-term (6 months, with extensions up to 3 years in appropriate cases) "reservation" based on an intent-to-use (ITU) registration. Pharma will need to affirm that it has a *bona fide*/good faith intent to use (including perhaps offering some corroborating evidence). It will also ultimately have to "perfect" its registration in the product packaging by filing timely proof of its actual use. Upon such filing Pharma's priority in the mark will relate back to the date of its ITU application, giving it rights over even subsequent good faith adopters during the six month ramp-up period to launch. *See* Topic 9 — Registration: Constructive Use and Intent to Use.

449.   **The best answer is A**. Although "Quik-Tix" involves an arguably fanciful misspelling, under the misspellings and acronym rules for determining distinctiveness it will be assessed based on the likely consumer perception of the mark: "quick tickets." Given the nature of Events' service the mark will be classified as descriptive, making distinctiveness an issue (**Answer A**). Events has clearly used the mark so non-use (**Answer B**) is not an issue. Registration is not required to obtain service mark rights, so **Answer C** is incorrect. Incontestability is a benefit accruing to mark owners not an impediment to obtaining rights, so **Answer D** is also incorrect. *See* Topic 3 — Basic Distinctiveness: The Spectrum of Distinctiveness Word Marks, Including Acronyms and Foreign Words.

450.   **The fair use defense**. Although valid rights in a descriptive mark (such as "Quik-Tix") can be obtained through a showing of secondary meaning, trademark law mitigates the competitive costs of granting those rights by permitting others, including competitors, to use the mark in its descriptive (non-trademark) sense (fair use). Global will argue

that it is engaging in such fair use in its phrase "Your provider of quick tickets." *See* Topic 16 — Defenses: Fair Use, Nominative Use Parody/Free Speech.

451. **The best answer is D.** The fair use test turns on the likelihood that consumers will/will not make the trademark connection — that is, see the use as in a trademark or merely descriptive sense. "Quick Tickets" (**Answer A**) is merely the "correct spelling" version of the "Quik-Tix" mark, so it is the most problematic, particularly as both words are capitalized. "Global's Quick Tickets" (**Answer B**) and "Quick Tickets from Global" (**Answer C**) improve the situation by clarifying that Global is the source. However, the correct spelling connection coupled with the initial capitals still may call the Event's trademark to mind and, arguably raise questions of its sponsorship, endorsement or affiliation with Global's offering. "Quick tickets from Global" (**Answer D**) most clearly uses the words in their descriptive sense — being both a coherent grammatical phrase using them as adjective and noun as well as dispensing with the problematic initial capitals. *See* Topic 16 — Defenses: Fair Use, Nominative Use Parody/Free Speech.

452. **The best answer is C.** On the facts CompD has purchased genuine products to which Arial, the mark owner, has affixed its "eFriends" mark. The first sale doctrine (**Answer C**) permits the resale of such products because the presence of the mark will not mislead or confuse consumers. Fair use (**Answer B**) permits the use of a mark in its non-trademark sense (descriptively) so it is not relevant on these facts. Nominative use (**Answer A**) is a species of fair use which permits use of a mark to identify the related product. Although that is arguably what is occurring here, the first sale doctrine is more apt as CompD has not generated a new "referential" mark use; it resells products previously marked by Arial, the mark owner. These defenses apply equally to registered and incontestable marks, so **Answer D** is incorrect. *See* Topic 17 — Defenses: First Sale.

453. **The best answer is A (although in some jurisdictions it would be B).** The issue on these facts is CompD's use of the mark in its advertising to refer to Arial's product, not the sale of products bearing the mark. On these facts, therefore, the better defense is nominative/fair use, not first sale (**Answer C**). The nominative use species of the fair use defense is, however, only recognized in some jurisdictions. Where it is available **Answer A** is the best answer while where it is not **Answer B** would be. These defenses apply equally to registered and incontestable marks, so **Answer D** is incorrect. *See* Topic 17 — Defenses: First Sale.

454. **Endorsement, sponsorship, affiliation.** This "extra" use of the mark to identify a particular portion of the store raises concerns that consumers might believe that Arial has endorsed, sponsored or is in some other way affiliated with CompD's sales of its products and, therefore, stands behind those sales. The issue is resolved by use of express disclaimers that Arial is in no way involved with CompD's activities — which might be placed on the "eFriends Center" sign, in the center itself and/or at the cashier. *See* Topic 17 — Defenses: First Sale.

455. **The best answer is D.** Modification puts the first sale defense in jeopardy because the mark no longer reliably signals the presence of the genuine product characteristics. So **Answer A** is incorrect. The defense can, however, be salvaged despite the modification if notice is given regarding who made the modification (other than the mark owner), its nature and in the circumstances consumers will connect any differences in the product characteristics from those signaled by the mark to the modification. **Answer B** is better than **Answer C**. The problem is that although CompD gave the necessary notice of modification at the point of sale, the notice is not available post-sale (it is not attached to the product). Consequently, although initial purchasers can connect the modified characteristics to CompD's changes, those obtaining or seeing the product in the after market will not have the necessary notice and may, therefore, mistakenly assume those characteristics are those of the genuine "eFriends" product. *See* Topic 17 — Defenses: First Sale.

456. **The best answer is D.** Under the Lanham Act a prevailing plaintiff is entitled, upon proof and subject to principles of equity, to injunctive and damage relief. That includes injunctions ordering cessation of use (as well as perhaps corrective advertising and other rectifying actions), damages suffered as a result of the infringement and costs (but attorneys' fees only in exceptional cases) plus, in appropriate circumstances, an accounting of the defendant's profits. Only **Answer D** reflects the full range of remedies, making it better than **Answers A, B** or **C**. *See* Topic 18 — Remedies.

457. **The best answer is B.** Although injunctions are "routinely" issued to successful plaintiffs in trademark infringement cases, the courts must still apply the regular equitable tests. These include adequacy of monetary relief/irreparable injury (**Answer D**), relative burdens on the parties (affected by defendant's bad faith — **Answer C**) and the public interest (implied in **Answer A**'s reference to likely consumer confusion). However, none of those considerations is enough standing alone; the injunction will or will not issue based on the overall evaluation as stated in **Answer B**. (It is not necessary that Bredwell show actual future confusion will result from continued use (or actual harm); a trademark injunction is granted if necessary to avoid *likely* consumer confusion. *See* Topic 18 — Remedies.

458. **Likelihood of success on the merits.** Obtaining preliminary injunctive relief turns, as with permanent injunctions, on equitable considerations. However, because a preliminary injunction is frequently equivalent to "winning" in a trademark case (the defendant must start using a new mark or cease business), the courts generally require a particularly high showing that the plaintiff is likely ultimately to succeed on the merits. If that showing is made the other equitable factors generally follow along. If not, then very careful consideration will be given to irreparable harm, relative burdens and public interest. *See* Topic 18 — Remedies.

459. **The best answer is C.** Lost profit damages in trademark cases follow traditional tort principles, requiring the plaintiff to prove *both* the fact of (causation) and amount of its damages (foreseeability is not required, although innocent infringement may mitigate

damages somewhat). The courts recognize, however, that proof with certainty is very difficult and will generally accept a reasonable basis/credible showing on both issues as stated in **Answer C**. **Answer A** omits any showing of the amount of harm, so it is incorrect. Although some courts require a showing of some actual confusion, arguing that without it no damages could have occurred, **Answer B** makes it mandatory in all jurisdictions (and cases) which is incorrect. Additionally, it fails to acknowledge the relaxed standard regarding proof of amount. Finally, although defendant's bad faith may be accepted as evidence of causation, it is not required, so **Answer D** is incorrect. *See* Topic 18 — Remedies.

460.   **Yes, but . . .** The availability of the "accounting" remedy (disgorgement of defendant's profits) is relatively confused doctrinally. Most courts require defendant's "bad faith" (willfulness) to make the award, so merely proving its right to lost profit damages will not be sufficient. If Bredwell does obtain an accounting, it must only prove the amount of Gudnuf's sales with the burden shifting to Gudnuf to prove "all elements of cost or deduction." Additionally, double damages cannot be awarded, so Bredwell will only receive a "net" award relating to actual sales lost to Gudnuf — presumably the greater of its or Gudnuf's profits on such sales. *See* Topic 18 — Remedies.

461.   Uncertain, but **C** and **D** are the best possibilities, with the slight nod going to **D** in practice. Lanham Act enhancement of damages (up to three times actual damages) is discretionary with the court, so **Answer A** is incorrect (although treble damages are virtually automatic, as are attorneys' fees, for counterfeiting). Although most courts will enhance damages in willful infringement cases, they can (and do) vary the amount of the increase, so **Answer B** is incorrect. The courts are split (and inconsistent) regarding **Answer C** and **Answer D**. Most, however, (in fact if not explanation) seem to track **Answer D** (based on a showing of willfulness) despite the express Lanham Act admonition that such enhanced is to be compensation not a penalty, making **Answer D** marginally more consistent with actual practice. (Punitive damages may be separately available under state law). *See* Topic 18 — Remedies.

462.   **The best answer is C.** Lanham Act remedies (including damage awards) apply to both registered and unregistered marks, including the basic right to enhanced (treble) damages, so **Answer A** and **Answer D** are incorrect (although to trigger counterfeiting "automatic" treble damages requires a registered mark). The Act does, however, require that owners of registered marks give notice of registration (in words or the circle with the "R" inside) or their damages will be limited to those occurring only if and after the defendant has actual notice of the registration. So **Answer C** is correct and **Answer B** is not. *See* Topic 18 — Remedies.

463.   **The best answer is D, but B is close.** Attorneys' fees are available to the prevailing party, plaintiff or defendant, under the Lanham Act but *only* in "exceptional cases" (as opposed to costs of the suit which automatically go to a prevailing plaintiff). That means either willfulness by defendants or bad faith-abusive litigation by plaintiffs. Consequently, **Answer A** and **Answer C** are incorrect. **Answer B** arguably implies the

requisite bad faith on Gudnuf's part — necessary to trigger the accounting. However, in some courts the accounting may rest on "inadequacy of compensation" grounds so **Answer B** is not as good as **Answer D** which clearly states Bredwell's bad faith in bringing the lawsuit. *See* Topic 18 — Remedies.

464.   **Likelihood of confusion; which is expressly not required in a dilution action.** Although the marks are identical and Superior's federal registration eliminates all geographic market concerns, there is a substantial question of whether Duper's home décor knickknacks are likely to cause consumer confusion. Superior's "Star" mark product scope derives from its use on high-end jewelry making it problematic that consumers will bridge the gap to tacky home knickknacks. *See* Topic 13 — Infringement: Likelihood of Confusion. A dilution action expressly does not require a likelihood of confusion, so that issue ceases to be a concern. *See* Topic 14 — Dilution.

465.   **The best answer (post-Trademark Dilution Revision Act of 2006) is B.** Prior to the Revision Act there was considerable confusion over whether "niche" fame (**Answer A**) was sufficient to satisfy the requirement that the mark must be "famous" to bring a dilution claim, so **Answer C** *would have been* the best answer. The Revision Act, however, resolved the issue in favor of requiring *national* fame as stated in **Answer B**. **Answer D** raises a subsidiary issue; specifically, the Second Circuit limitation that the famous mark also be inherently distinctive rather than merely having acquired (secondary meaning) distinctiveness. The Revision Act also resolved that issue in favor of permitting dilution claims in either case. *See* Topic 14 — Dilution.

466.   **The best answer is D.** The Supreme Court had indicated that, perhaps, dilution only existed in its "blurring" incarnation (that is, the whittling away of the mark's distinctiveness by parallel albeit non-confusing use) and that "tarnishment" (harmful associations) was not a relevant category. That view would support **Answer B** over **Answer C**. Some judicial opinions also indicated that other kinds of dilution might exist, giving some support to **Answer A**. The Trademark Revision Act of 2006 specifically lists *both, but only*, dilution by blurring and dilution by tarnishment as federal dilution causes of action. On these facts it can be argued that Duper's use both whittles away the distinctiveness of the "Star" mark *and* harms its reputation, making **Answer D** the best answer (also indicating that the Supreme Court was on to something when it couldn't find any justification for a separate category of "dilution by tarnishment" — dilution affects distinctiveness, whether that whittling away is harmful to reputation or innocuous isn't relevant). *See* Topic 14 — Dilution.

467.   **No.** The Supreme Court read the pre-Trademark Revision Act of 2006 Lanham Act dilution provision as requiring proof of actual dilution setting off a lively debate over how that might actually be demonstrated. The Revision Act, however, expressly changes the requirement to a "likelihood of dilution" thus resolving the problem, leaving lawyers to think creatively (and by analogy to confusion perhaps) to proving a likelihood of dilution by circumstantial implication. *See* Topic 14 — Dilution.

468. **Probably not**. The Trademark Revision Act of 2006 lists fair use, news reporting/ commentary and noncommercial use (including activities protected under the First Amendment such as parody and other commentary on brand values) as available defenses. On these facts, none of those exceptions are applicable. Duper's use is as a mark on its products to identify them in the marketplace (proposing a transaction, so commercial trademark use), the mark is not descriptive or otherwise amenable to a "fair use" claim and there is no reasonable argument that Duper's use was intended as commentary of any kind. *See* Topic 14 — Dilution.

469. **The best answer is A**. Unlike likelihood of confusion infringement, successful federal dilution plaintiffs generally only receive an injunction stopping the diluting use of the mark as stated in **Answer A**. To obtain monetary relief (which is otherwise governed by the same Lanham Act provision applicable to regular infringement suits — **Answer D**, not **Answer B** or **Answer C**) requires a showing of Duper's intention to trade on the reputation of the famous "Star" mark or to harm its reputation. Duper's evidence that it was unaware of Superior's "Star" mark eliminates that possibility, so unlike a regular infringement suit, no monetary relief will be awarded. **Answer A** is correct and **Answer D** is not. *See* Topic 14 — Dilution.

470. **Only anticybersquatting** and, perhaps, not even that. On the facts Heter's "Honey Bee" mark is not being used by the domain name registrant as a trademark on its goods so a traditional *likelihood of confusion* infringement suit will not lie. *See* Topic 13 — Infringement: Likelihood of Confusion. As there are no competing, related goods or any goods or services offered on the website, even an *initial interest confusion* infringement claim is not available. *See* Topic 13 — Infringement: Likelihood of Confusion. As the "Honey Bee" mark is only famous in Heter's product niche, it does not have the requisite general fame now required to support a dilution action. *See* Topic 14 — Dilution. It is possible, however, that the registrant's minimal use indicates that the domain name was registered with "bad faith intent to profit from the mark." Although the facts are hardly dispositive on the point, they at least offer a basis for making the anticybersquatting claim. *See* Topic 15 — Anticybersquatting.

471. **The best answer is B** (although reasonable minds can differ). **Answer D** is incorrect as anticybersquatting relief does not require a federally registered trademark. The "bad faith intent to profit" determination is based on a statutorily based "factors" analysis which looks at possible legitimate justifications for the registration versus indicia that the registrant was motivated by profits from resale of the domain name to the mark owner or others. **Answers A, B** and **C** all offer some support to Heter's bad faith assertion. **Answer A** involves a proposed transfer to Heter. Although a transfer in order to settle the suit is arguably a benefit, it is not the kind of "profit anticipation" contemplated by the anticybersquatting right — obtaining net gain from the registration on sale. Additionally, it can be explained as the rational response of a defendant with no ulterior motives (in contrast, perhaps to an offer to sell Heter the mark when sued, but even then hardly conclusive of cybersquatting motivation). **Answer C** is also potentially indicates bad faith, but can be explained as clerical error; particularly as the

answer implies only the address, not the other contact information is incorrect. **Answer B** coupled with registrant's lack of use other than the picture of a honey bee, the capital "B" (not the traditional spelling) provides good (albeit refutable) evidence of bad faith; indicating that the registrant has no legitimate purpose for the registration other than a connection to Heter's mark. I, therefore, think it is the best of the four answers. *See* Topic 15 — Anticybersquatting.

472.   **Technically yes, practically no**. To support an anticybersquatting claim the challenged domain name must be identical or confusingly similar to the mark (or dilutive of, in the case of famous marks). That means that Heter will either have to convince the court to ignore the ".com" and the lack of a space and find the mark and domain name identical (as courts frequently do) or, alternatively, that the domain name is confusingly similar (a very likely outcome). Although those arguments must be made, the issue is unlikely to raise any significant barriers to Heter's success on the merits. *See* Topic 15 — Anticybersquatting.

473.   **The best answer is C**. The Lanham Act provides for *in rem* actions against the domain name (seeking only its forfeiture, cancellation or transfer, not other remedies) when either personal jurisdiction cannot be obtained over a known registrant or the registrant-owner cannot be found after duly diligence inquiry. On these facts, the latter (**Answer C**) is applicable while the former (**Answer D**) is not. **Answer B** is one of the two statutory requirements for showing due diligence (the other being publishing notice as directed by the court promptly after filing the *in rem* action). Although those actions are the means for proving due diligence and effecting service of process, the actual basis for the *in rem* action is stated in **Answer C**. The mere registration of a domain name has generally been insufficient "contracts" to find personal jurisdiction over the registrant and, in all events, the defendant is unknown, so long arm jurisdiction is unavailing. So **Answer A** is incorrect. *See* Topic 15 — Anticybersquatting.

474.   **The best answer is C.** Trademark rights remain valid until the mark ceases to identify and distinguish the mark owner's goods (an indefinite term). That loss of rights can occur for a variety of reasons including genericide, naked licensing (failure to control licensee quality), assignments in gross (transfer without related goodwill) and, as applicable to this case, the cessation of use with no intent to resume (the latter being referred to as "abandonment"). The Lanham Act definition of abandonment contains a presumption that a mark has been abandoned (and all trademark rights terminated) after a period of three years on non-use. On these facts that had occurred before "one year ago" (on the facts three years of non-use expired two years ago) so CityWear's rights are presumptively invalid (**Answer C**). That is true because abandonment overcomes the presumption of validity of CityWear's existing federal registration (**Answer B**) and the incontestable status of the mark (**Answer A**). CityWear can, however, rebut the presumption of abandonment, so **Answer D** is incorrect. *See* Topic 19 — Duration of Rights Abandonment And Loss of Rights.

475.   **LensCo has the better case, but not by much**. The first issue in a trademark infringement lawsuit is whether CityWear (the plaintiff) has valid trademark rights.

CityWear was, and currently, is using the word "Striders" as a trademark — that is to identify and distinguish its particular products. LensCo will argue that the word "striders" applied to walking shoes is descriptive and, therefore, only distinctive upon a showing of secondary meaning. CityWear will respond that it can show secondary meaning from long use, but, in all events, the incontestable status of its registered mark prevents LensCo's challenge on descriptiveness grounds. LensCo will reply that abandonment overcomes CityWear's claim of incontestability, not only permitting the descriptiveness challenge, but putting validity of the mark in serious question. As discussed in the answer to the immediately preceding Question, there is no evidence of any actual use by CityWear during the three year period (and for another year plus after that) triggering the statutory presumption of abandonment. As on these facts (long term nonuse coupled with evidence of further interest in the mark) it is highly unlikely CityWear can show any bona fide intent to resume use within a reasonable time, it will lose on abandonment.

The abandonment finding means CityWear cannot claim rights in the "Striders" mark from its prior use and registration (which will be cancelled). Consequently, CityWear's case will turn on the rights arising from its more recent use. Incontestability having disappeared with abandonment, the distinctiveness issue will need to be addressed; in particular, whether "striders" is descriptive (and requires secondary meaning which is unlikely after only 10 months of use) or suggestive (and inherently distinctive, thus requiring no showing of secondary meaning). Applying the "dictionary definition; ingredient, characteristic, use, outcome; leap of imagination; need/use by competitors" factors test, there are good arguments both ways. In my view they very marginally favor CityWear (descriptive of either the purpose or outcome of using the product and no leap of imagination required to determine the product involves shoes).

Even assuming the mark is distinctive, CityWear still needs to demonstrate a violation of its trademark rights. There is no evidence the "Striders" mark is "famous" so no dilution claim will lie. That means CityWear will need to show a likelihood of consumer confusion. On the facts LensCo cannot argue a fair use, free speech or other defense (it is clearly using the mark as a mark to propose a commercial transaction). Consequently, the question will be whether CityWear can proof LensCo's use falls within the geographic and product scope of its post-abandonment rights. The geographic scope of CityWear's new rights are exclusively use-based (the old registration being subject to cancellation and there being no indication of a subsequent federal registration). Consequently, CityWear's rights will be limited to its actual California market, any additional territory in which consumer associations exist between the "Strider" mark and its products which may cause confusion plus, perhaps, a zone of reasonable expansion. Additional facts will be required to make a final determination; however, based on those provided CityWear's long-term exclusive focus on the California market makes it unlikely that there are any, much less, significant, relevant consumer connections in LensCo's Southeastern market.

The product scope issue will turn on the likelihood of confusion "factors" analysis. The marks are identical and there is no indication of either actual confusion or LensCo's bad faith, so the focus will be on whether consumers are likely to "bridge the gap" between CityWear's walking shoes and LensCo's sunglasses based on market-use factors (overlapping channels of distribution/advertising, targeting the same consumers, proximity or relatedness of the goods, and the nature of the purchase decision). More specific facts will be required to reach a final determination; however, some preliminary conclusions can be drawn from the existing information. CityWear will argue that consumers will make a connection between walking shoes and vacation sunglasses as they frequently purchase and/or wear one with the other. It will also argue that purchasers of cheap pair of sunglasses, an impulse purchase, are very likely to rely significantly on a recognizable trademark. LensCo will reply that CityWear's high-end products and channels do not overlap in any meaningful way with LensCo's throw-away vacation sunglasses, so consumers are unlikely to either see or purchase them together. Additionally, LensCo will argue that the purchase of disposable vacation sunglasses is driven by "try-them-on" individual inspection, rather than reliance on the mark.

Combining the product scope uncertainties with the very problematic geographic concerns, the preliminary assessment must give the (slight) advantage to LensCo.

476. **The best answer is C.** If Risso wins under the Paris Convention or TRIPS treaty provisions it will not be based on its United States trademark rights but on a determination that Spanish trademark law incorporates those treaties' provisions. Additionally, on these facts a United States court is very unlikely to find it has jurisdiction over the case as it lacks any United States nexus. So **Answer B** is incorrect. United States courts will enforce United States trademark rights extraterritorially in limited circumstances, so **Answer D** is incorrect. Extraterritorial application turns on a finding that: (1) the challenged conduct has a substantial effect on United States commerce, (2) the defendant is a United States citizen and (3) enforcement raises no conflict with rights established by, or actions of, other governments in their jurisdiction. The fact that Dos is using the mark on the same product (**Answer A**) is relevant and helpful to Risso's case as it supports a possible effect on United States commerce. The difficulty is that Risso is likely to lose the case for extraterritorial application of its United States rights. Not only is there no evidence of any actual effect on United States commerce (United States consumers are unlikely to be aware of Dos or its product), but neither Dos nor its owners or managers are United States citizen *and* enforcement will interfere with Dos' rights in the mark under Spanish trademark law. Thus **Answer C** is the best answer. *See* Topic 20 — Extraterritorial Application and Trademark Treaties.

477. **The best answer is B.** Standing to bring a false advertising claim under Lanham Act § 43(a)(1)(B) (15 U.S.C. § 1125(a)(1)(B)) requires the plaintiff "believe that he or she is or is likely to be damaged by the [false advertisement]" as stated in **Answer B**. Being a competitor makes that damage likely (and may even be presumed by some courts) but is not enough to always provide standing, so **Answer A** is not as good an answer as **Answer B**. Although Manzana must show the advertisement is false to prevail on its claim, falsity is not relevant to standing so **Answer C** is incorrect. **Answer D** relates

to the fact that consumers do not have standing to bring Lanham Act false advertising claims. It, however, states the exclusion incorrectly (backwards — by stating Manzana must be a consumer to have standing), so it is incorrect. *See* Topic 21 — False Advertising and False Designations of Origin.

478. **The best answer is D**. To be liable for Lanham Act false advertising the defendant must have made a false statement of fact regarding either the defendant's or another's product, service or commercial activity. That generally means a statement which can be objectively confirmed to be either true or false — such as the "twice as fast" claim in this case. Subjective quality statements — like the one lauding Mega's "exceptional" functionality — are more likely to be treated as mere opinion or puffery and, therefore, not actionable (in part because consumers don't treat them as fact and in part because they therefore are unlikely to rely on or be misled by them). Consequently, Manzana will have to first demonstrate the "exceptional functionality" claim involves "fact" rather than merely a subjective opinion as stated in **Answer D**. It is not clear that either the "twice as fast" claim will be found literally false as stated in **Answer A** (it is literally true that *some* tests do show that to be the case) or that the "exceptional functionality" claim — if factual at all — is true as stated in **Answer B** (the Mega system isn't any more functional the standard system in its class, so it is not exceptional at least in that regard), so neither of those answers provides a definitive distinction between the claims. Moreover, it is the factual nature of the former and subjective nature of the latter which make the former more likely false and the latter more likely true (as a matter of opinion). **Answer C** refers to the original requirement that the false statement of fact be about the advertiser's own product which was eliminated under the 1988 Trademark Revision Act (thus permitting claims regarding all misrepresentations). However, not only is the limitation no longer relevant but **Answer C** misstates the now defunct requirement, so it is incorrect on all counts. *See* Topic 21 — False Advertising and False Designation Of Origin.

479. **A Lanham Act false advertising claimant (with standing) must prove four elements to make its case**.

First, it must show that the challenged statement was made in "commercial advertising or promotion." That generally requires the statement go beyond one-off, personal statements to involve a more "public" dissemination. In addition the statement must be commercial speech by a competitor seeking to influence relevant consumer purchasing decisions, thus minimizing First Amendment concerns that the false advertising claim is impairing free speech interests and public debate. The fact that the challenged statement appears on Personal Electronics' product web page likely satisfies the first requirement and there are no indications that the advertisement involves anything more than straight-forward marketing attempting to induce consumers to purchase the Mega OS.

Second, the challenged statement must involve a false statement of fact. The "twice as fast" statement can be objectively demonstrated to be either true or false and, consequently, is likely to be viewed by consumers as fact rather than opinion. Although Personal Electronics will argue the statement is literally true (tests have shown that Mega is twice as fast as Zeno) it is misleading when put in context of all the test results. Manzana will argue that in light of the full range of tests the statement is false by necessary implication (a form of literal falsehood) as consumers will inevitably infer that the tests showed Mega was *always* twice as fast as Zeno.

Third, the challenged statement must be deceptive (if consumers have not been deceived, then there is no competitive harm). If the statement is found false by necessary implication the court will likely presume consumer deception. If the statement is found to be merely misleading then, unless Manzana can show Personal Electronics' affirmatively intended to deceive consumers, Manzana will need to offer survey evidence showing the misleading implication was in fact perceived by and deceived a substantial number of relevant consumers (likely more than 25%). Importantly, if Manzana is only seeking injunctive relief its evidence on deception need only demonstrate a "tendency to deceive." If, however, Manzana is seeking monetary damages it will require evidence of actual consumer deception (and thus possible actual harm to its financial interests).

Fourth, the statement must be material — that is likely to affect consumer purchasing decisions (if it is irrelevant to consumers there is no competitive harm). That inquiry will focus on the relationship between the statement and the relevant competition. In this case, the Mega OS's speed is an inherent quality or characteristics of the product and a core part of the related competition for consumers, so the statement will likely be found material.

Regarding remedy, in order to collect monetary damages Manzana must not only prove actual deception but that it suffered economic harm caused by the misrepresentation. It will, therefore, have to present evidence of its lost sales unless the court is willing, as some are, to infer causation based on a showing that Personal Electronics' affirmatively intended to deceive consumers.

Outcome on the merits: A court likely will find the statement appeared in qualifying commercial advertising or promotion, was factual (rather than mere opinion) and false by necessary implication in light of the other undisclosed test results. It will, therefore, presume deception. Even if it does not, Personal Electronics' failure to disclose its other test results supports a finding of intent to deceive and the presumption of deception on that basis. Unless Manzana can prove it suffered actual harm from the statement or convinces the court to presume causation from Personal Electronics' intent to deceive, Manzana will only obtain injunctive relief. *See* Topic 21 — False Advertising and False Designation Of Origin.

480. **The best answer is A**. The use of an Allison look-alike, voice and style impersonator without Allison's consent supports both right of publicity misappropriation (**Answer C**) and false endorsement (**Answer B**) claims. The trademark infringement claim (**Answer D**) would track the false endorsement argument, claiming likelihood of

confusion as to sponsorship or affiliation (or designation of origin) but would further require Allison show she holds trademark rights in her likeness and voice, which seems highly unlikely on these facts. Although trademark infringement is, therefore, a very weak claim, the false designation of origin/reverse passing off doctrine (**Answer A**) has no apparent application to these circumstances whatsoever. Silver is not passing off Allison's singing or acting services as its own, but affirmatively seeking to connect its own clearly identified services to her "star power" in order to assist in their sale. As that claim is even less likely to be successful than a trademark infringement claim **Answer A** the best answer. *See* Topic 22 — Right of Publicity, False Endorsement And Attribution.

481. **The best answer is D**. The right of publicity protects against unauthorized appropriation of the persona of another which causes that person commercial harm. Intrusion into the individual's private affairs is not an element of the claim so **Answer D** is irrelevant. Commercial use (**Answer A**) is relevant both because the challenged use must not implicate free speech interests (such as parody or commentary on Allison, her style or even fame or stars generally) and must cause Allison commercial harm. The right of publicity also requires appropriation of protected personal attributes (**Answer B**) (in this case the look-alike and voice/style qualify). Finally, Allison must show that she has relevant commercial interests in her persona which have been harmed by the use (**Answer C**) (likely shown by the nature of the use and her celebrity). *See* Topic 22 — Right of Publicity, False Endorsement And Attribution.

482. **The best answer is C**. The two claims overlap considerably with right of publicity violations frequently implicating false endorsement concerns and vice versa. The two causes of action, however, address different concerns which are reflected in their varying elements. Publicity is a commercial offshoot of privacy and protects against misappropriation harm to the individual whose persona is used whether or not there is associated consumer deception or confusion. In contrast, false endorsement tracks the consumer deception/confusion concerns of trademark law (although it does not require a valid trademark). That key difference between the claims is articulated in **Answer C**. Both claims do involve an individual's persona (making **Answer A** incorrect), albeit for different reasons. Right of publicity involves use of an individual's persona without consent while false endorsement focuses on whether the use of an individual's persona generates deception/confusion regarding his endorsement or sponsorship of the defendant's product or service. Both doctrines are limited by free speech First Amendment doctrine — permitting use of an individual's persona for parody and other commentary — so **Answer B** is incorrect. Finally, for there to be either a right of publicity *mis*appropriation or a *false* endorsement, the individual must not have given consent to the use, so **Answer D** is incorrect. *See* Topic 22 — Right of Publicity, False Endorsement And Attribution.

483. **The best answer is A**. All of the listed actions arise under Lanham Act Section 43(a) (15 U.S.C. Sec. 1125(a)). These particular facts specifically involve false "under-attribution" or reverse passing off — that is QuickTurn passing off Quimpet's candy

bars as its own. Because QuickTurn is taking physical Quimpet products (not creative or communicative materials) and repackaging and reselling them in unmodified form, the *Dastar* "origin" doctrine (false designation of origin claims are limited to misidentification of the producer of the physical good, not a failure to attribute the actual author) is (probably) avoided. So **Answer A** is the best answer. False advertising (**Answer D**) is a possible second choice as a false under-attribution also arguably misrepresents the nature, characteristics or quality of QuickTurn's product. However, making that case is more difficult than the false under-attribution claim because it requires showing the omission is a false or misleading statement in the particular context, that it caused consumer deception and was material to consumer purchasing decisions. *See* Topic 21 — False Advertising and False Designation Of Origin. False endorsement (**Answer B**) requires QuickTurn either expressly or impliedly indicated that Quimpet was endorsing or sponsoring QuickTurn's own product; a problem which does not arise on under-attribution (failure to identify) facts such as these. For similar reasons trademark infringement (**Answer C**) does not apply on the facts — it would arise if QuickTurn had been selling its own candy bars under Quimpet's "Delight" trademark. *See* Topic 22 — Right of Publicity, False Endorsement And Attribution.

484. **The best answer is D** (but even that is problematic). The *Dastar* origin "doctrine" now applies, meaning that QuickTurn will argue that it has not falsely designated the origin of its "Just as Good" candy bars under the "origin means producer not author" distinction drawn by the Supreme Court in that case. The fact that QuickTurn produces the "Just as Good" candy bar avoids false attribution liability as *Dastar* affirmatively does not require it attribute the source of the incorporated "ideas" (recipe and production methods) to Quimpet. (Under *Dastar* QuickTurn does, however, remain independently liable for violating other rights (trade secret, copyright, patent) Quimpet may hold in the recipes and production methods.) For the reasons set out in the answer to the previous Question, neither **Answer B** nor **Answer C** is applicable to the facts (Quimpet's name or mark have been omitted not used to confuse consumers). **Answer D** remains viable but problematic as *Dastar* also casts a shadow over false advertising under-attribution claims — the Court having left it unclear whether the "producer versus authorship" rationale also means that failure to identify the source is not an actionable misrepresentation regarding nature, characteristics or quality of the QuickTurn produced "Just as Good" product. *See* Topic 22 — Right of Publicity, False Endorsement And Attribution.

485. **False designation of origin over-attribution claims do not require valid trademark rights.** Although both trademark infringement and over-attribution claims involve passing-off of QuickTurn's goods as Quimpet's, on these facts QuickTurn is using Quimpet's *company name* not its "Delight" *trademark*. Unless Quimpet can show that it holds valid, relevant trademark rights in its company name it cannot bring a trademark infringement lawsuit. In contrast, an over-attribution false designation of origin claim does not turn on likelihood of consumer confusion arising from use of a valid mark but from having designated a specific false source of the goods — in this case arguably attributing them to Quimpet. In such cases, courts may find a violation based on the false attribution alone, whether or not trademark rights exist and without further inquiry

into the likelihood of consumer confusion. On these facts there is a question about whether "Quimpet-style" is, in fact, a false attribution of origin but it is still the better claim if Quimpet does not hold valid trademark rights in its company name. *See* Topic 22 — Right of Publicity, False Endorsement And Attribution.

INDEX

INDEX

NOTE: The sub-heading "Application Examples" identifies questions involving "overall" application of related doctrine, covering a variety of relevant issues.

TOPIC   **QUESTION**

Domain Names

See Anticybersquatting

Exhaustion of Rights

See First Sale Doctrine

Extraterritorial Enforcement

Treaties

US Rights

Fair Use Doctrine